THE GROWTH OF ENGLISH SOCIETY

ALSO BY E. LIPSON

★

THE ECONOMIC HISTORY OF ENGLAND
VOL. I. THE MIDDLE AGES.   Twelfth Edition
VOLS. II & III. THE AGE OF MERCANTILISM. Sixth Edition

EUROPE IN THE XIXTH CENTURY*
1815-1914
Eleventh Edition

EUROPE 1914-1939*
Eighth Edition

*These two also in one volume, *Europe in the
Nineteenth and Twentieth Centuries*

★

ADAM AND CHARLES BLACK: LONDON

THE GROWTH
OF
ENGLISH SOCIETY

A Short Economic History

BY

E. LIPSON

FOURTH EDITION

In the sweat of thy face
shalt thou eat bread.
THE BOOK OF GENESIS

ADAM & CHARLES BLACK
LONDON

FIRST PUBLISHED 1949

SECOND EDITION 1951 · THIRD EDITION 1959

FOURTH EDITION 1959

REPRINTED 1964

A. AND C. BLACK LTD
4, 5 AND 6 SOHO SQUARE LONDON W. 1

MADE IN GREAT BRITAIN
PRINTED BY ROBERT MACLEHOSE AND CO. LTD
THE UNIVERSITY PRESS, GLASGOW

To
J. D. NEWTH

PREFACE

I have sought in this volume to present—in a form designed for students and general readers —the fruits of forty years' study of English Economic History.

Part II ('The Age of Mercantilism') embodies the substance of the Lowell Lectures delivered in the United States. Part III ('The Age of Machinery') is based on the lectures given when I taught the subject at Oxford. Throughout I have drawn freely on my other writings.

E. LIPSON

NOTE TO FOURTH EDITION

In the present edition I have reviewed briefly the salient features of the post-war economic situation.

E.L.

FOREWORD

This book is not a history of the rulers of England, nor of her system of government and political parties, nor of her social habits. It is intended to give an account of the economic life of the English people. It is concerned with the men who drove the plough, extracted the minerals, wrought at the furnace and the forge, wove at the loom, and distributed their products over the whole face of the globe. It is designed to show how in our island home man has fulfilled the Scriptural injunction to earn his bread by the sweat of his brow. Upon the broad back of the toiling masses was built through the ages, stone by stone, the edifice of all that England has meant to a world in whose affairs she has taken no mean part. If she may lay claim to be the modern birthplace of free institutions which have protected and cherished the liberty of the individual; the heart of a far-flung empire which has carried English concepts of justice into the remotest places of the earth; the source of humanitarian movements which have sought to express the nobler instincts of mankind; the abode of culture in which the arts and sciences have blended to make an impressive contribution—a large portion of the credit belongs to 'the common man,' whose exertions wrung from the soil something more than the barest necessaries of existence. It was these sustained exertions that fashioned an environment in which an ever-widening circle of the community was enabled to live what in Ancient Greece was called 'the good life.'

From the rude forefathers of the English hamlets, situated in an island on the remote fringe of the Roman Empire, there was to spring a nation whose standard of life even for the masses would one day embrace amenities and luxuries unknown to the Caesars. The economic history of the English people takes as its theme a great adventure in the field of economic enterprise. It tells of the struggle to wrest from nature the secrets by which her forces could be employed in the service of man on land, on sea and in the air: it tells of merchant pioneers entrusting their frail barks on perilous seas in the discovery of new lands with which to carry on commercial intercourse: it tells of inspired inventors seeking to economize in the use of human labour and to afford leisure for the cultivation of pursuits other than the purely economic.

CONTENTS

CONTENTS

PART I
THE MIDDLE AGES

Chapter One

THE CORPORATE SOCIETY

I. THE VILLAGE COMMUNITY

When in the fifth century various groups of adventurers, Saxons, Angles and Jutes, set sail from their homeland on the Continent of Europe in order to invade the island in which they were destined to found a great nation, Britain had already attained a considerable degree of civilization. She was governed by officials and planted with settlers, who pursued the Roman way of life and reproduced its characteristic traits. Roads were constructed, the most permanent fruit of the military occupation; improved methods of tillage were introduced; mineral wealth was exploited; and the resources of the country were developed. None the less Britain always remained the outpost of the Empire, valuable only for her strategic position and for her corn tribute as the granary of the north. She was the last province to be acquired and the first to be abandoned; and alien influences failed to take abiding root as in Gaul or Spain. Side by side with the large private estates (villas) of the Roman pattern, Celtic life flowed on in all its primitive aspects. This thin veneer of an exotic culture in Britain did not survive the disruption of society that followed the recall of the legions. The English Conquest lasted a hundred and fifty years. Step by step the Welsh were thrust backwards, though their grasp of the soil was tenacious and the conflict was stubborn. The struggle was accompanied by the sack of towns and the destruction of country estates. All our evidence points to the conclusion that English society was not built upon the fabric of Roman civilization. The Saxon Conquest was not the substitution of Teutonic chieftains for Roman overlords; it was the displacement of one nation by another. The native population in the main was not absorbed; it was either exterminated or driven westward. The English

I

language, law and religion, and the names of English villages, seem decisive proof that the bulk of the people was not of Celtic but of Teutonic blood. Moreover air-photography has shown the breach of continuity between the Romano-British and English agrarian systems: the ancient fields were rectangular areas while the mediaeval fields were comprised of long narrow strips.

In their new home the tribes which migrated from the northern coast of Europe settled down in free village communities, composed of peasant proprietors who owned the land they occupied. Here and there a local chieftain established a personal ascendancy which elevated him into a territorial magnate, with his followers clustered around his estate in a village to which they gave the name of their leader. Here and there, more especially in the west, the villas of Roman Britain survived with the native inhabitants in a condition of subjection to their alien lord. Nevertheless in general the great mass of the nation consisted of independent peasants tilling their own land. Thus the foundations of English society rested at the outset upon freedom, and for nearly a thousand years the path of evolution led from freedom to servitude. The process by which a race of free cultivators became gradually transformed into one of dependent serfs gives a unique interest to the Anglo-Saxon epoch; and it runs like a thread throughout the mediaeval half of English history.

A vital factor in the movement that converted England into a land of manorial communities and servile tillers of the soil was the burden of taxation. In particular the imposition of Danegeld, levied originally as a tribute to buy off the Danes and afterwards retained as a permanent land-tax, was attended by important social consequences. Its incidence was extremely heavy, for it sometimes approached one-third of the annual value of the land. Inability to pay the tax constrained the small landowners to borrow from their wealthy neighbours, who were afforded a hold over the impecunious villagers. In this way the solvency of the peasants was imperilled, and with its loss went their best title to the rights of freemen. Economic influences operated in the same direction. The Church and other large proprietors with land to spare settled it with tenants, over whom at a stroke they could establish a 'lordship.' In other cases the manorializing process was at work in the village itself. The devastations of the Northmen who raided these shores, the recurrence of bad harvests, the harshness of the criminal code, would easily suffice to ruin the peasants and enable rich proprietors to tighten their grasp upon land which once lay in the absolute ownership of the villagers.

The momentous revolution which disrupted the economic basis of Early English society, and covered the face of the country with servile communities, was powerfully reinforced by the growth of the feudal system defined as the social and political domination of a military and land-owning aristocracy. The weakness of the central government forced men in an age of general insecurity to 'commend' themselves to a lord and become his clients in return for a promise of protection. The lordless man who had no patron to befriend him was depicted in Anglo-Saxon poetry as a social outcast. 'He who experiences it knows what a cruel companion anxiety is to one who has no kind guardians.' In theory commendation need only be a purely personal bond without implicating the land. Still what was really essential in those troubled days was security of tenure; men required protection not so much for themselves as for the title to their property in case a violent neighbour wrested their land from them. But when a freeholder relied on a lord to safeguard his tenure, feudal doctrine regarded the title to his land as dependent upon the will of his lord who was now held to be the true owner. At the same time the growth of private or seigniorial courts, either as a result of royal grants or by usurpation, brought large sections of the community under the judicial authority of a lord and made possible the degradation of great masses of the freemen. If a suitor attended a private court instead of a national court his legal status gradually deteriorated; often the mediaeval serf occupied, as a dependent tenant, land held by his forebears as freehold until they had been deprived of the national warranty.

Yet another factor in the growth of the manorial system was the rise of a military aristocracy. The Anglo-Saxon militia or fyrd, consisting of peasant cultivators, was unable to cope with the perpetual raids of the Northmen. A professional force with leisure to fight and with the resources for providing equipment grew indispensable. English society came to be transformed by the permeation of feudal conceptions. A threefold social division began to emerge in the warriors who fought, the clergy who prayed and the peasants who toiled. The ceorls, the peasant class, lost their former standing and sank to the bottom of the new social hierarchy. They were no longer called upon to fight save on rare occasions; and once the warrior was differentiated from the husbandman, the claim of the latter to be a full freeman inevitably lapsed.

The various influences which in an haphazard and piecemeal fashion were remoulding English rural society during the early centuries of its growth were brought to a head by the Norman Conquest. The Saxon lords were supplanted by an alien aristocracy and only retained an inconsiderable portion of their lands. The Normans were thus afforded an opportunity to put into practice continental ideas with which they had long been familiar. The door was opened to foreign influences on an unprecedented scale, and the changes effected in the structure of society were far-reaching. For the unarmed cultivators of the soil the Conquest spelt disaster. The mailed hand of the Norman lord pressed heavily upon the English peasantry and forced them down into servitude. The numerous class of freeholders which existed on the eve of the invasion disappeared altogether in many parts: they were degraded into villeinage and the sign of their altered condition lay in the exaction of week-work. The position of the bulk of the villagers, the class of villeins, still further deteriorated. They were deprived of their personal status as freemen; they were excluded from the national courts since small private courts sprang up all over England; and the obligations attached to their tenure became more onerous in the shape of heavier labour services and legal restrictions on their movements. The encroachments of the Normans upon the liberties of the English people were attended by one redeeming feature. The household slaves were settled on the land and eventually were absorbed into the ordinary villein stock. With their disappearance slavery in England became a thing of the past.

The free village communities of Early England were now transformed into manorial communities, although some lordless villages escaped the general servitude especially in the eastern counties where Danish immigrants had settled. Henceforth for several hundreds of years the typical English village was a manor, that is, an estate owned by a lord and occupied by a population of dependent cultivators. The lord with his retinue of servants and officials was the core of the manorial system. He was the legal proprietor of the whole estate but retained only a portion of it in his own hands. This was the home farm or demesne: it usually consisted of strips interspersed among those of the tenants whose primary obligation was the duty of cultivating it. At first landowners were accustomed to travel from one estate to another consuming the produce of their demesnes; not until the practice died out did they establish themselves in permanent residences and erect the stately mansions which adorn the countryside to our day. Even the king made journeys for the same purpose, and it explains why Magna Carta enjoined that the courts of justice should remain in a fixed place. The demesne, however, was something more than a mere farm providing food for the lord's table and clothing for his household. It contained a hall or court where the lord or his steward directed the administration of the estate. The hall constituted an economic centre around which were grouped in varying degrees of subjection the peasantry whose

5

affairs it rigidly controlled and regulated. The manor was organized on capitalist lines, and the relation between the lord and the tenants was essentially one of capital and labour.

Among the various strata of the manorial population the villeins ranked first in number and economic importance. The villein took his name from the vill, like the burgess from the borough and the citizen from the city. He was the typical villager of the middle ages, and without his services the work of the manor could not have been carried on. His holding was a virgate or yardland which normally comprised thirty acres: it was not a compact farm but a bundle of strips dispersed among the other tenements. The holdings were hereditary and mostly descended to the eldest son upon payment of a heriot which was usually the best animal. Besides his strips of cultivated land every tenant enjoyed rights of pasture upon the commons or 'waste' land, and he also possessed a homestead surrounded by a farmyard. The villein was thus far from being a landless labourer; and the general diffusion throughout the country of a numerous class of small but relatively well-to-do peasants gave stability to the manorial system of which they formed the indispensable foundation. His position involved corresponding obligations in an age in which every right proceeded from the perform-ance of a duty. His main service was to work on the lord's demesne for two or three days a week—though not neces-sarily for the whole day—ploughing with his own oxen, carrying produce to the market or elsewhere, together with all the other daily incidents of farming. In addition to this week-work, extra services or boon-works were exacted at harvest-time. Finally he made numerous contributions to the lord in money and in kind. He was not required to perform all his duties in person provided he sent a substitute who might be one of his own labourers.

Villeinage was both a tenure and a status. As a servile tenure it had three outstanding features. First it was precarious. Tenants had no legal security and were liable to summary

ejection at the lord's discretion. Usually they had little reason
to apprehend the loss of their farm, since they were the basis
of feudal society and by their work and rents the higher ranks
of the social structure were maintained. The value of a
manorial estate depended, indeed, upon the number of
tenants and the extent of their services and payments rather
than upon the fertility of the soil. The second feature was
the uncertainty of the services attached to the tenure. In
the famous words of Bracton, a thirteenth-century jurist, the
tenant in villeinage 'ought not to know in the evening what
he will have to do on the morrow.' Here again economic
reality did not correspond to the definitions of feudal common
law. Manorial practice had hardened into custom which
generally enjoyed an authority scarcely less binding than
law, and very little was left to arbitrary caprice. The third
feature of base tenure furnished the real economic test whether
a tenure was free or unfree. The latter was held on condition
of labour service on the lord's farm and the former by the
payment of a money rent.

The tenant in villeinage was commonly, though not necessarily, a villein in status. He was personally unfree and subject
to a lord. He was bound to the soil, and a fugitive could be
reclaimed and punished unless he paid a fine to live away from
the manor. He could be taxed 'high and low.' Without the
lord's licence he could sell neither ox nor horse, nor educate
his son at school, nor apprentice him to a free handicraft,
nor place him in the Church. His daughter, and sometimes
also his son, could not marry without the payment of a fine
known as merchet or 'service of blood-ransom,' and regarded
as the most assured test of servile status. Notwithstanding
these restraints on his personal liberty the English serf was
not a slave, the chattel of his owner, devoid of all rights and
property. He was free against everyone but his lord. Criminal
law recognized no distinction between serf and freeman.
The serf could bring a criminal action against the freeman,
and in his turn could be prosecuted by any other serf or freeman. In civil law he could sue in all cases other than those

7

affecting his villein tenement (which in the eyes of feudal common law belonged to the lord), and if deprived of his 'wainage' or implements of husbandry he could sue even his lord. Again the fact that the lord's exactions as a rule were based on custom implied a recognition that the villein had a right to his belongings. The serf's position in the state also diverged widely from that of a slave. He shared in the obligations imposed upon men of free status, he sat on juries, he possessed arms, he paid taxes.

The cottage tenants, recruited from the younger sons of villeins and from household slaves settled on the soil, occupied a lower place in the manorial hierarchy. Their legal condition was stamped by the traits of villeinage—its precarious tenure, its compulsion to labour services, and its dependent status—but in their economic situation the poor and struggling cottagers presented a wide contrast to the relatively substantial farmers of the villein class. Their usual holdings contained five acres, and their obligations were proportionately less because they worked for the lord only one day a week. Despite their social inferiority to the other villagers, they fulfilled an important function in the manorial economy. They served the purpose of a labour reserve which could be utilized at harvest-time and other seasons; hence they could satisfy the fluctuating demands for additional labour which in later days were met by a more or less floating population. The cottagers are significant for yet another reason. To eke out the resources provided by their scanty acres, they worked for hire upon the lord's demesne or upon the holdings of the wealthier villeins. Thus they foreshadowed the rise of a wage-earning class which was destined to supersede villeinage and establish itself as the foundation of modern rural society.

The tenants in villeinage formed an indispensable element in the structure of the manor. The free tenants, who enjoyed a unique and privileged position, in a sense stood outside the manor to which they were attached mainly by the slight services owed to the lord in recognition of his authority over them—though they were equally concerned with the other villagers in the communal system of agriculture. Their land was protected in the king's court and in personal status they were free men. The freeholds lacked the uniformity of size preserved in unfree tenements by the practice of indivisible inheritance and by the restraints imposed on alienation. Their services were frequently nominal and in any case did not include the servile burden of week-work on the lord's demesne, the distinguishing mark of base tenure. Apart from boon-works at harvest-time their obligations took the shape of a pecuniary rent. Although the Norman Conquest depressed many of the free tenants into villeinage, their numbers eventually increased with the creation of new holdings carved out of the demesne or the waste land. In this way provision was made for a growing population without interfering with the existing manorial tenements. The class of free tenants was also recruited from tenants in villeinage who had managed to commute their labour services for the payment of rent in money.

The various groups of tenants comprising the manorial community were knit together not only by their common interests in agrarian affairs but also by their common subjection to the lord of the manor. The latter's authority was exercised through an administrative staff consisting of a steward, bailiff, reeve and other officials, to whom different duties were assigned. These servants of the demesne linked up the estates belonging to the lord in different parts of the country; while within the manor they were the brain of the community, regulating all the manifold economic activities of mediaeval rural life.

The manor has been described in its classical, that is, complete form: but in all stages of economic society we must expect to find numerous variations from the orthodox pattern. The normal manor, in which the lord's demesne was cultivated by the labour services of unfree tenants, appears to be typical of the midlands and the south, more particularly on the estates of the Church and other great landowners.

In the border counties, on the other hand, a more variegated pattern is discernible. In the lordless villages a free peasantry continued to survive; on some estates money rents preponderated over labour dues; and everywhere there existed small non-manorial properties worked by the owner with the aid of his family and some hired labour. The fortuitous growth of the manorial system would naturally produce a variety of deviations from the classical form; notwithstanding it remains true to say that the manor was the dominant type of mediaeval rural organization.

We have sketched one side of the older rural society—the structure of the manor and the economic rights and obligations of the various classes included within it. The other side was the system of agriculture which prevailed in England throughout the middle ages and even persisted to the early decades of the nineteenth century. This was the open field system, which took its name from the fact that at certain periods the arable fields were thrown open to the trespass of man and beast. In a modern farm the land devoted to tillage is enclosed all the year round by permanent or 'live' hedges. In open field husbandry the soil under crop was protected against trespassing between seed-time and harvest, while the corn was growing, by temporary enclosures rudely constructed year by year at the sowing of the seed. Once the harvest was reaped and the corn gathered into the barn, the fences were removed and the fields then lay open; the village cattle could therefore stray in and graze upon the stubble.

Two forms of open field husbandry must be distinguished —extensive and intensive. Extensive cultivation meant that annually fresh ground was broken up by the plough, and after the raising of the crop it was abandoned for other soil. Under intensive cultivation the same land was retained for arable purposes. The former practice was adapted to a primitive stage where nomadic tribes were able to wander at will over a wide area. In process of time, however, men came inevitably to acquire more fixed habits, and the roving instinct was then superseded by a feeling of attachment to their homestead. Moreover the growth of population and the gradual restriction of territory owing to the encroachment of neighbouring tribes would stimulate the transition to settled agriculture, especially when it was learnt by experience that the more advanced system of tillage improved the quality of the crops. There are grounds for thinking that the change over had already taken place among the Saxons before their invasion of Britain. The adoption of intensive culture involved new methods of laying out the land. The arable soil of the village was now held in permanent occupation but it needed periods of rest to recuperate its fertility. Accordingly it was cut up into large tracts which were cultivated in turn. This gave rise to the two-field and three-field systems. In the two-field system the whole arable area was arranged in two fields, of which each in turn was tilled one year and lay fallow the next. The field under cultivation was either sown entirely with wheat, or one-half of it was sown in autumn with winter crops (wheat or rye) and the other half in the early part of the year with spring crops (barley or oats). The field that lay fallow was ploughed twice over at the beginning of the summer. In the three-field system the land was divided into three fields, of which two were cultivated every year (one with winter crops and the other with spring crops), while the third lay fallow and was ploughed twice. The merit of the three years' rotation of crops, which ultimately became widespread, was that it produced more crops for the same amount of ploughing; though it was claimed for the two-course rotation that it yielded crops of better quality.

The most striking feature of English agriculture down to the last century was the method by which land was distributed among the village community. A modern farm is a compact holding separated by hawthorn hedges from neighbouring holdings. Not so the farms of an older England. They were composed of small strips strewn in every direction over the open fields and lying intermingled among other tenements. The whole arable land of the village was carved into a multitude of strips, which were intended to represent the measure of a day's ploughing—that is, the customary acre. This practice of splitting up a farm into tiny plots and dispersing them among the numberless plots of other owners gave the open fields a chequered appearance, and turned them into a mosaic of patches and maze of proprietary claims. The genesis of intermixed ownership, which is not extinct in various parts of the world at the present day, is lost in the mists of antiquity. It is probable that the distribution of land in scattered strips was designed in its origin to secure equality. Arable land is not uniform either in soil or position, and one area differs much from another in fertility and advantage of situation: hence in parcelling out the territory among the members of the village community it was necessary to allot it piecemeal and avoid compact properties. The strip system, though it proved inconvenient, had its roots in the primitive instincts and deep-rooted concepts of mediaeval rural life —the equality of the shareholders in the common fields; and this accounts for the tenacity with which it persisted for many centuries. Intermixed ownership was devised in the interests of the community as a whole: it sacrificed the individual but its original purpose was to promote equity in the allocation of each man's property. Everyone was given a share alike of soil that was good and bad, and soil that was near and far. In England even to-day relics of a pre-historic system still survive in parishes devoid of hedges, where the land lies in open fields divided into parallel strips; and the holders—as in the Isle of Axholme in Lincolnshire —resist proposals for a redistribution which would give each one his full acreage in a single piece, for fear of receiving some poorer land. At Laxton in Nottinghamshire nearly a thousand acres, held by thirty tenants, are split up into more than twelve hundred separate plots.

The intermixture of strips was due to the presence of a strong element of communalism in the mediaeval village, in which the principle of private ownership was recognized yet free enterprise was obstructed. The communal aspect of rural life was reflected also in the system of co-operative farming in place of separate cultivation. All the leading operations of agriculture seem to have been carried on in common. While individual ploughing and reaping were not unknown, especially on the newer holdings carved from the waste, the more usual practice would be for the tenants in the open fields to associate together in a general partnership, ploughing and reaping every strip as its turn came round. The produce of the strips went to the individual owners, for rural life was only communal in one direction. There was co-operation for purposes of production, but there was no sharing-out of the produce among those who had taken part in the work.

The defects of the open field system made it an easy target for attack by those who favoured individualist farming. Less produce was raised: time was wasted in moving about from one strip to another: a greater number of horses were required: drainage of land, cross-ploughing and proper supervision became more difficult: the absence of hedges deprived the cattle of shade and shelter: disease was rampant among them, and improvement in the breed was impossible: charges of trespass gave rise to quarrels. Above all under a system of intermixed ownership 'no man can truly be master of his own' free to manage his property as he wished. He was bound by the general will and his liberty of action was controlled by his neighbours. The common fields were subject to a uniform course of husbandry: each was ploughed and sown alike whatever the nature of the soil. Agricultural operations were decided by the village community as a whole—the rotation of crops, the regulation of ploughing, sowing and reaping, the allotment of meadows, the treatment of the waste, the rules for fencing and removal of hedges. The open field farmer, tied hand and foot by the compulsory character of mediaeval husbandry, enjoyed little opportunity to try experiments or exercise special

13

skill; he was constrained to work in accordance with time-honoured practices however obsolete—though improvements were by no means unknown.

Nevertheless the open field system was not devoid of merits. It served to prevent excessive negligence, since a definite standard of tillage could be maintained where every peasant worked under the eyes of his neighbours and was subjected to the unremitting supervision of the manorial officials. Further village life was much exposed to the disturbances of war, and when the tiller of the soil was summoned from the plough his land was cared for by those who remained at home. Still more important the system of dispersed ownership gave the labourer an opportunity to occupy a few acres of land and attain some measure of economic independence; while every cottager could strive to improve his position adding strip to strip as thrift enlarged his scanty resources. The day was at hand when in the interests of economic efficiency the open fields would begin to vanish from the countryside; when that day dawned the labourer was divorced from ownership of the soil, land accumulated in the hands of the few, and the rural population was driven into the towns.

To complete the picture of English agriculture in the middle ages, other sides of agrarian life must be briefly surveyed. The produce of meadow, waste and wood was no less indispensable to the husbandman than the produce of the tillage: without them he must be (said an old writer) 'a buyer, a borrower or a beggar.' Meat was needed for food, wool for clothing, peat and turf for fuel, timber for building and repairing houses and for construction of hedges. Accordingly a mediaeval farm comprised not only a bundle of scattered strips in the arable but also 'rights of common.' The meadows, like the ploughed lands, were divided into strips which were annually re-allotted among the tenants in the open fields—even to this day lots are drawn for the strips in the meadows of Yarnton by the Thames near Oxford. In addition villagers had the use of the large stretches of uncultivated land or waste. The waste was not partitioned into strips and there was no individual ownership, yet the principle of equality was at work here as in other directions. The use of the waste was 'stinted,' that is, the number of cattle allowed to each holding was fixed as well as their kind; but frequently the privilege was extended to those who were not strip-holders. Another right of common was over woods and forests, which in mediaeval England covered a very extensive area.

Human society is never completely static. Every social system contains within itself the seeds of its own decay: it is always dissolving and reforming in an infinite sequence. Sometimes the process of change is so gradual and imperceptible that it creates a delusive appearance of absolute immobility. At other times it is enormously accelerated by catastrophic influences which sweep over mankind with the force of a tornado. The break-up of the manor exhibited both sets of tendencies, the slow disintegration of the old order and the sudden impact of an overwhelming calamity. The net result is writ large over the face of modern England. Villeinage as a tenure and virtually as a status became extinct before the end of the middle ages—several centuries before it disappeared in many European countries; and the original freedom of English villages was regained after an eclipse which for some of them had darkened their horizon for close upon a thousand years.

The essence of the manorial system lay in the intimate connexion established between the lord's demesne and the community of unfree tenants; and the fundamental purpose of serfdom was to provide labour for the home farm. Accordingly the forces which dissolved the fabric of manorialism were the commutation of services and the alienation of the demesne. In the one case the lord released his tenants from their customary obligations and exacted money wherewith to hire free labourers. In the other case he ceased to be a farmer engaged in the direct exploitation of the land, and developed into a landlord who leased his estate and lived on the income accruing from rents. In both cases alike, whether he employed hired labour or abandoned farming altogether, the lord had no further need for compulsory labour; and a natural economy, where services were rendered in kind, was superseded by a money economy in which a cash nexus supplied the basis of all economic relationships.

The commutation of forced labour for payments in money began at an early date. Servile work was often inefficiently performed, and its abolition gave the lord a freer hand in the management of his estate while it also enabled him to dispense with a crowd of officials. The tenant had still more to gain by emancipation from the daily routine of the home farm. He could concentrate on his own holding and raise produce for an urban market, which furnished him with the means of paying his rent in money. In the long run the peasantry alone profited by the change. The amount of the commuted payment—provided it was permanent—was fixed once and for all. When in later centuries the purchasing power of money diminished, the copyhold tenants were protected from a rise in rents corresponding to the new price level—in our own day these rents often mustered only a few pence. The obligations demanded from a tenant in villeinage need not be commuted all at the same time, for there were varying degrees of commutation. Moreover the arrangement was often temporary—a manor might alternate between money and services as it best suited the lord's interests. This irregular sale of 'works' makes it difficult to determine the real extent to which free labour had displaced servile labour before the middle of the fourteenth century. The uncertainty is heightened by the fact that the labour dues of villeins were assessed in the manorial account rolls in terms of money from motives of convenience, even when no money-equivalent was actually paid. Thus on a Cambridgeshire manor in the thirteenth century the 'works' exacted from the tenants were valued

16

in money, but their permanent commutation did not take place until two centuries later.

In the middle of the fourteenth century England was struck by the Black Death: it proved to be an economic catastrophe of supreme importance. The great pestilence which ravaged the kingdom for fourteen months (1348–9) is believed to have swept away one-third, perhaps one-half, of the population. The figures of the chronicler are to be accepted with caution, yet the court rolls of manors and the diocesan institution books yield irrefragable testimony that the mortality was overwhelming. The villeins who survived the calamity seized the opportunity afforded by the general prostration and social disorder to demand their release from forced labour. There were now stronger motives than ever to induce them to commute their services. Hitherto their position, when contrasted with the wage-earning class of rural labourers, had been in many respects enviable. They owned as a rule a substantial holding, their tenure was secure in practice, their duties were determined by custom. But the Black Death caused an unprecedented rise in wages, which were sometimes doubled; and the prosperity of the hired labourers aroused the discontent of the villeins. They became less compliant and submissive: they longed to win their freedom and to share in the golden opportunities enjoyed by the emancipated workers. The new appreciation of the value of labour suddenly laid bare the economic and social degradation of servitude. The manorial yoke grew increasingly irksome for another reason. The lord claimed the services of one man for one holding, and hitherto the burden had been shared among the members of the house-hold, while sometimes a virgate supported more than one household. When the plague carried off a considerable part of the population, the surviving tenants found their obliga-tions excessive not from any coercion or increased pressure on the part of the lord but because the burden now fell entirely upon their own shoulders, since their households were sadly reduced. As a consequence the villeins showed themselves determined to shake off the shackles of bondage, and eventually they broke out in open rebellion in the Peasants' Revolt of 1381 which was the first great struggle between capital and labour.

The emancipation of the English villeins was not achieved without a struggle. The very circumstances which gave to economic freedom a fresh significance enhanced in the eyes of the lords the value of the old servitude. With the increased cost of hired labour the commutation of services ceased to be profitable. None the less at the moment the lords, despite their reluctance to accept money in lieu of labour rents, were powerless against forces that brooked no opposition. The villeins owing to their depleted numbers held a weapon in their hands which rendered their masters impotent and accelerated the end of villeinage in England. This was desertion *en masse* from the manor. 'They run suddenly away out of their own country to strange places unknown to their masters.' The practice of migration became general, and there is abundant evidence to show how widespread was the dispersion of the rural population over the countryside. Tenants relinquished their heritage in order to seek their fortunes further afield in the confidence that they controlled the labour market; while the lords made the utmost concessions from dread of losing their tenants altogether. Confronted with ruin, their harvests rotting on the ground, their land bare of inhabitants—for sometimes not a single tenant survived on the manor—the lords were constrained to comply with the demands of the villeins. Their feverish rivalry for tenants left the latter masters of the situation and placed them in a position to dictate their own terms.

The immediate effects of the pestilence were indisputably violent though on some manors, especially those belonging to the Church, a rapid return was made to the *status quo* of 1348. Thus upon the estates of the see of Winchester in the south-west of England there are no signs of chaos and no abrupt changes. It must be remembered that in normal times only a portion of the services owed by the tenants was actually demanded, and therefore the lord had a reservoir of labour to draw upon in times of stress. This surplus of ordinary years, which was temporarily commuted because it was not needed, served to cover the deficiencies caused by the pestilence; and so in some cases there was no ruin of the countryside nor collapse of the manorial organization. Ecclesiastical bodies, however, enjoyed a corporate experience denied to private landowners, and their more systematic methods of estate management were calculated to hold in check the forces of disintegration. On secular manors, less highly organized, a temporary dislocation might easily develop into a permanent disruption of the manorial economy. Accordingly, in estimating the place of the Black Death in the historical evolution of the English peasantry from servitude to freedom, we must avoid either exaggerating or minimizing its importance. On the one hand, the transition from a natural economy to a money economy was not due to a sudden and devastating revolution compelling the immediate replacement of labour services by money rents, for the latter were widely prevalent before the great pestilence. On the other hand, stress should not be laid upon the transient nature of the visitation. Its enduring influence is reflected in the remarkable increase of free labour within a period of thirty years. Without the plague the disintegration of the manor as a result of normal forces—the increasing use of money for economic purposes, the demand of the lord for a more flexible instrument than the inelastic and cumbrous dues, the accumulation of capital in the hands of servile tenants, the growth of urban markets—must assuredly have been a more irregular and infinitely slower process. Doubtless on many manors the pendulum swung back again and the lord reasserted his impaired authority over his tenants; yet sooner or later the traditional structure of rural society must have succumbed to the reluctance of the rustic population to suffer the compulsion to forced labour. The Black Death left behind it a legacy of bitterness and unrest, which continued to disturb village life until in the course of the next hundred years the old manorial order had completely dissolved and bondage in England became almost extinct.

When the payment of money superseded the exaction of personal service the lord could no longer cultivate his demesne with compulsory labour. An obvious expedient was to employ the pecuniary compensation received from the tenants in hiring free labourers—the nucleus of a rural wage-earning class was constituted by cottagers and by villeins who had secured emancipation through manumission or residence away from the manor—but the sharp rise in wages made this impracticable. The government then tried legal compulsion. The Ordinance of Labourers (1349) and the Statute of Labourers (1351), which represented the first serious effort on the part of the state to regulate the labour conditions of the country as a whole, sought to keep wages at the old level. Their failure forced the lord of the manor to alienate the demesne to tenants; he ceased to be a farmer and became a squire living on his rents. At first he provided seed-corn and stock as well as the land—a practice known as 'stock-and-land' lease, which developed into the modern system by which the landlord furnishes only the land and buildings and the tenant the stock and capital. On the monastic estates the monks continued to farm their own demesnes on an extensive scale down to the dissolution of the monasteries. Elsewhere the cultivation of the soil passed out of the hands of its owners, and the way was prepared for the formation of a numerous and widely-spread class of small peasant proprietors and tenant farmers—the nation's pride, the yeomen of England.

The abolition of villeinage as a tenure was followed by its abolition as a status. When the compulsion to forced labour lapsed, the villein came to be merged into the freeman. Commutation by destroying the economic foundations of villeinage revealed itself a powerful lever in the enfranchisement of the English peasantry. The distinctive marks of bondage were obliterated as a result of a gradual revolution which turned labour dues into money rents. Again the flight of the villeins dispersed a large part of the manorial population and so led to a substantial decrease in the number of bondmen; while the dissolution of the manor relaxed the lord's grasp on his subjects, and caused the memory of their original servitude to die out once its primary purpose had vanished. However personal serfdom survived the decay of economic serfdom, and was not destroyed either by the Black Death or the Peasants' Revolt. It lasted throughout the fifteenth and sixteenth centuries; and though the mass of the customary tenants obtained emancipation there still existed thousands of bondmen under the Tudors. They were no longer liable to enforced labour yet they could be taxed arbitrarily at the lord's will. The bondmen were often, in fact, men of substantial position who were too wealthy to be allowed manumission and could be heavily mulcted. Personal serfdom thus lived on solely as an instrument of extortion. It had lost all economic significance when it ceased to be the keystone of mediaeval husbandry. Henceforth English rural society no longer rested upon unfree tenure and unfree status but upon free contract between landlord and tenant and between employer and employed.

Chapter Two

THE CORPORATE SOCIETY

II. The Town Community

The towns were the birthplace of the middle class. In them the inhabitants, drawn from different localities and engaged in a variety of pursuits, were knit together by a feeling of common interests and fused into a corporate body whose solidarity was strengthened by the fortified walls which encircled and protected them. Here the citizens acquired their training in self-government and communal activities; here they carried on the fight for municipal freedom against the territorial lords who claimed authority over them. Here were laid the foundations of England's greatness as an industrial and commercial country. Here was fostered domestic architecture; and here the popular drama sprang into being. Nevertheless, while many towns flourished, the wealth of Early England lay in her fields not in her workshops, and the great mass of the nation followed the plough. The typical figures of mediaeval society were the knight and the husbandman rather than the trader and the artisan. Indeed the sharp cleavage between town and country, one of the striking features of modern economic life, did not exist in the middle ages when the urban community never completely shed its rural characteristics. In the economy of the burghers the broad acres that stretched beyond their walls were no less a part of their heritage than the restricted area where stood their houses and shops. The persistence of the agricultural element is shown by repeated injunctions against stray cattle wandering about the streets in the metropolis and elsewhere; even the offices of cowherd, hogherd and herdsman were numbered among municipal institutions as late as the sixteenth century.

The Saxons regarded towns, in the words of the Roman historian Tacitus, 'as the defences of slavery and the graves

22

of freedom;' and they preferred to live in the midst of their open fields. The cities of Roman Britain, at least thirty in number, were abandoned and when not actually destroyed by fire they were left bare of inhabitants—a fate which London and Canterbury may not have escaped; and it has remained for modern investigators to bring to light the very sites of leading municipalities. Yet the cessation of town life in England was only temporary. The insecurity of their position as conquerors and later the Danish incursions induced the English to seek the safety that fortresses alone could afford in troubled days. Sometimes they turned to the old urban seats (like Colchester) whose ruins furnished materials for the restoration of the walls. Other settlements owed their importance to the natural advantages of their situation. The place where a river could be forded was of considerable value; and Oxford, as the name indicates, grew where cattle-drovers could easily cross the stream. Bristol, again, traced its prosperity to its harbour which made it the greatest seaport of the west. A third group came into existence by the side of monasteries and castles, to whose needs the townsfolk ministered. A notable example in Domesday Book of the way in which towns rose up at the gates of monastic houses is Bury St. Edmunds. It contained 'bakers, alebrewers, tailors, washerwomen, shoemakers, robemakers, cooks, porters; and all these daily wait upon the saint and the abbot and the brethren.'

The growth of town life was stimulated by foreign influences. In particular the Danes who settled in England recognized the significance of boroughs both as centres of trade and as fortresses to keep in subjection a hostile population. The lesson of the Danish invasion was not lost upon King Alfred and his successors, and the reconquest of the Danelaw was accompanied by a line of strongholds around which the nascent town could slowly develop. The coming of the Normans was a landmark in the history of English municipalities, although the immediate effect was the ruthless destruction of houses to make room for the feudal castle.

23

The strength of the central government gave the urban communities internal peace; and if it prevented them from gaining the degree of independence attained by the great cities of the German and Italian leagues, it saved them from a tumultuous and precarious existence. It afforded opportunities for unostentatious advance in which without fear of their powerful neighbours they could build up their economic resources. Moreover municipal progress was promoted by the closer relations with the Continent which now ensued, since they fostered commercial intercourse and stimulated the influx of merchants and artisans from abroad.

The economic development of the boroughs after the Norman Conquest was closely intertwined with their efforts to achieve self-government in their local affairs. The control which feudal law enabled the mediaeval landowner to exercise over all who dwelt on his estate entitled him to interfere in their concerns and to benefit by their industry. At the same time they were constrained to acknowledge the political authority of the sheriff as the representative of the Crown. No town could hope to win prosperity or a thriving trade so long as it lay in the power of an alien ruler to play the part of local tyrant and impose his own will upon his subjects. Accordingly immunity from external interference whether of lord or sheriff, and the concentration of power within their own hands, constituted the goal which the townsfolk kept steadily before their eyes. Yet only gradually did the boroughs accomplish their emancipation. The struggle was spread over many centuries and fills a notable chapter in the history of English freedom.

The feudal claims were as old as the town itself, for at first the townsfolk were manorial tenants burdened with agricultural services and other obligations. Subsequently the burgesses were allowed to commute their rural duties for a rent when the lord learnt to appreciate the importance of trade as a source of profit. At Bury St. Edmunds the cellarer of the abbey used to go through the town collecting the money payments; but all the old women came out, says the chronicler, and brandished their distaffs in his face cursing him and his men; and so the abbot accepted a composite sum. Manchester did not entirely shake off the manorial yoke until the middle of the nineteenth century; a hundred years earlier its inhabitants were still taking their corn and malt to the lord's mill and their bread to the lord's oven. The monopoly of milling flour was a particularly valuable source of revenue: the Dee Mills of Chester even passed into a proverb on extravagance—'If thou hadst the rent of Dee Mills thou wouldst spend it.'

The extent to which the towns secured their freedom from feudal control was determined more by circumstances than by their own sense of corporate consciousness. There were three classes of towns—those situated on the royal demesne, those owned by secular lords, and those belonging to the Church. The greater number and generally the more important boroughs were held directly of the king, who showed himself an easy master content to let them manage their own business provided they paid their dues regularly into the Exchequer. The towns on the baronial estates were able to profit by the lord's penuriousness and to wring privileges from his necessities. In marked contrast those connected with bishoprics or monastic houses were disadvantageously placed. Here the controversy persisted throughout the centuries, and it proved almost impossible to wrest concessions from corporate bodies which clung tenaciously to their privileges. There is ample evidence to show how complete was the grasp of the Church over the towns on its domains. It chose the mayor or bailiffs, administered justice, levied market tolls, exacted agricultural services at harvest-time, and even denied the burgesses the right to sell or bequeath their land. The Church did not invariably assume an unyielding attitude, and sometimes it was induced to concede the status of a free borough. Yet it was rare to find abbots who pursued an enlightened policy; the more progressive among them were cramped in their

25

efforts by the narrow conservatism of those over whom they ruled. When Abbot Sampson granted a charter to Bury St. Edmunds, his action evoked a storm of criticism and he was told: 'That man, Abbot Ording, who lies there, would not have done such a thing for five hundred marks of silver.' Even when a charter was extorted from the fears or pecuniary needs of a monastery its terms were far from generous.

The reluctance of the ecclesiastical authorities to tolerate the slightest infringement of their liberties is vividly illustrated in the narrative of the mediaeval chronicler. 'Herbert the dean built a wind-mill upon Haberdon. The abbot, when he heard of this, was so wroth that he would hardly eat or speak a single word. On the morrow, after mass, he bade the sacristan send his carpenters thither without delay and overturn everything.' The dean thereupon came before the abbot and protested that he was within his legal rights, but the abbot answered angrily: 'I will never eat bread until that building be overturned. You are an old man, and you ought to know that neither the king nor his justiciar may change anything or build anything within the jurisdiction of the monastery without the leave of the abbot and the house. Nor is this without harm to my mills as you pretend, for the burghers go to your mill and grind their corn at their pleasure, while I cannot lawfully hinder them since they are free men.' This occurred at Bury St. Edmunds early in the thirteenth century, and a parallel incident is recorded in the middle of the fifteenth century at St. Albans. A tenant of the monastery erected a horse-mill and commenced to grind his own barley. The abbot ordered his officers to confiscate the millstones. When they arrived the offender was away but his wife met them 'after woman's fashion with execrations and curses, and gathering together all her frail and chattering sex' she forcibly recovered possession of her mill. Her triumph was short-lived and the abbot had the last word, compelling the refractory tenant to sue for pardon on his knees and refusing him permission even to grind oats.

26

'My friend,' he replied to his entreaty, 'every one knows that if you give a man an inch he takes a yard. Go home and mend your ways.'

From generation to generation the burgesses conducted the struggle for municipal freedom, and the long conflict was marked by extreme violence and bitterness. At Dunstable the inhabitants prepared to abandon their homes; undaunted by the threat of excommunication they resolved 'to descend into hell together' rather than submit to the arbitrary exactions of the monastery. There were frequent risings of the towns against ecclesiastical domination, especially in times of civil commotion. Thus in 1327, when the country was torn by dissensions which culminated in the deposition of Edward II, a great riot broke out at Bury St. Edmunds, the monastery was forcibly entered and the abbot and his monks were carried off to prison. None the less the Church almost invariably gained the upper hand. The towns with their relatively feeble resources were powerless in the face of influential corporations which were fortified by experience and backed by material wealth, spiritual forces and royal favour. The men of St. Albans made repeated bids for independence before they finally relapsed into complete dependence upon the abbey. When Queen Eleanor visited the monastery (1274) the townsmen accompanied by a great multitude of women, 'whose attack was formidable since it is difficult to restrain successfully the anger of woman,' forced their way in; and the Queen censured the abbot for keeping the people away from her. Even the stubborn resistance of Bury St. Edmunds, which was protracted for three centuries, ended in utter submission to the sacristan 'lord of the town,' whose sanction it sought to frame by-laws. Nor did the Reformation always bring freedom to English monastic towns. At Peterborough the dean and chapter succeeded to the jurisdiction of the monastery, and down to the nineteenth century exercised the right to appoint the city magistrates.

Apart from the claims of their feudal lords, lay and

27

ecclesiastical, other difficulties confronted the towns in their endeavour to achieve independence and self-government. The sheriff, who was the political representative of the Crown and local head of the county administration, enjoyed abundant opportunities for meddling with the concerns of the borough communities. As judge he tried cases that lay outside the competence of the municipal courts; as military leader he raised armed levies among the townsmen; as revenue-officer he gathered in the royal dues. He thus had unnumbered occasions for the misdeeds with which he was charged—miscarriage of justice, exactions of money and other acts of oppression. The sheriff was the best-hated man in the shire, and his unpopularity is reflected in the legends of Robin Hood. The desire to exclude him from their walls furnished the great incentive that first stimulated in the townsmen a longing for freedom; and the growing feeling of corporate identity became the mainspring of their municipal development. Hence they sought to purchase from the king a charter conferring upon them various franchises or privileges. Foremost among them was the right to farm the revenues of the borough, that is, to replace the royal officers in the collection of the royal dues for which they paid annually a fixed composition to the Exchequer. Another franchise was the holding of their own court coupled with immunity from external courts that lay outside their jurisdiction. The borough court grew into something more than a judicial tribunal, for it formed the kernel of the town administration. The third franchise was the election of their magistrates—the bailiffs and later the mayor. A frequent clause in borough charters bestowed freedom on a fugitive villein who resided safely for a year and a day within the walls of the town. The most valuable economic concession was the grant of a gild merchant, in which the corporate consciousness of the nascent borough was crystallized into a specifically mercantile institution charged with full control over all buying and selling in the municipal area. The place of this institution in the growth of a communal society is indicated in the following paragraphs.

When town life began to develop in England it was natural that the rural elements—who usually comprised the nucleus of the embryonic municipal bodies in the capacity of artisans and traders—should enter into the same relationship with each other as they and their forebears had been accustomed in an agrarian environment. The instinct of the mediaeval Englishman was to act in concert with his fellows in his undertakings, and its strength was fortified by the conditions under which the early towns grew up. Exclusive franchises were conferred upon the boroughs, and for its grant of concessions the Crown exacted a price: it was therefore inevitable that the townsmen should seek to confine participation in their privileged position to those who were willing to bear their share of the fiscal burdens. The corporate functions of the urban community found a vehicle in the historic gilds—the gilds merchant and craft gilds; and the latter governed trade and industry just as the village courts directed the affairs of the rural community.

No feature of Early English society has attracted greater attention than the gilds: none perhaps has been more consistently idealized. To this day there frequently survives, as the symbol and relic of an age that has passed away, the outer shell of a gildhall once the focus of the trading and industrial activities of the urban community; London possesses its livery companies, the lineal descendants of the craft gilds; and numerous towns adhere to antiquated procedures and practices which were formerly a living reality. Over the face of modern England are imprinted many such vestiges of the old order, and they carry us back to the time when economic life was organized on a corporate basis and men worked in the closest association with their fellows.

The gilds flourished in an environment so completely different from our own that only by an effort of the imagination can we visualize its peculiar character. They were the product of a 'town economy' as distinguished from the modern 'national economy.' In this stage of social evolution the town rather than the state constituted the mainspring of the economic system, whose course of development was moulded and shaped by municipal policy. A rigid commercial monopoly isolated every urban community from its neighbours and sought to set up impenetrable barriers. Each town strove to become an exclusive and self-dependent unit equipped with active powers of aggression and defence; and the restrictions laid upon the 'foreign' competition of strangers whether within or without the gates and the right of reprisals were all economic weapons in the municipal armoury. At the present day we may still find traces of an insular spirit—once an outstanding feature of social conditions in England—in those parts of the country where anyone who was not born in the locality is considered a 'foreigner,' even though he has resided there for many years. The isolation and independence of English mediaeval towns exerted influence in the jealous exclusion of non-freemen from a participation in their mercantile privileges, in the claim to exercise full economic control over their own affairs, and in the intermunicipal relations of the boroughs with one another.

The mercantile privileges of a town were usually vested in a body known as the gild merchant, into whose hands fell the monopoly of urban trade during the twelfth and thirteenth centuries. It was established in England after the Norman Conquest and became a widespread institution, although it is not found in all towns, for example, in London and Norwich. The gild merchant was not identical with the borough community because its primary function was the maintenance of a commercial monopoly—whereas the municipality was responsible for the farm of the borough and for the administration of police and justice. Moreover there was a well-defined distinction between gildship and burgess-ship: not all gildsmen were burgesses and not all burgesses were gildsmen. The qualification for the gild franchise was the payment of 'scot and lot,' that is, membership dues and common charges. The qualification for the borough franchise was residence, ownership of a burgage (urban) tenement or other source of annual income, and the performance of civic duties. The gildsman possessed status as a trader, but was debarred from any share in the political life of the community unless he was also a burgess: the burgess enjoyed civic rights, but was debarred from trade unless he was also a gildsman. Finally the gild and the municipal body had (though not invariably) each its separate organization—one had an alderman and a gild court, the other had bailiffs or a mayor and a borough court. In reality however the line of demarcation tended to grow indistinct since the composition of the two corporations would more or less coincide, and eventually they merged.

The fundamental purpose of the gild merchant was the control of trade; in particular its members claimed the exclusive right to buy and sell within the borough, retail or wholesale, on market days and at all other times without payment of toll. The restrictive practices of the gild brethren were limited in certain directions, for they were conscious that to shut out all merchant strangers from their midst would tend to their own hurt. Hence non-gildsmen were allowed to buy and sell wholesale provided they paid toll, dealt only with gildsmen, and did not purchase certain enumerated commodities such as grain, wool, unfulled cloth and untanned leather, which the town reserved for its own use. Apparently the rule against retail trading did not apply to country folk bringing their produce to the urban market nor to the sale of provisions by non-gildsmen: but in general the unenfranchised trader dwelling within the borough was forbidden to sell retail or to keep open shop. In addition a gildsman might not enter into partnership with a non-gildsman, nor travel in the country with merchant strangers showing them where to buy merchandise; and craftsmen

31

were not allowed to teach their trade or 'mistery' to rural dwellers.

An important privilege possessed by the members of the gild merchant was the right of 'lot,' which entitled them to share in the commercial transactions of a fellow-gildsman. If any gildsman made a purchase anywhere, it was open to other gildsmen to claim a portion of it at the price at which the commodity had been bought, though they were usually required to be present at the original sale. The rule was intended to foster equality of opportunity and prevent the monopoly of the trade falling into the hands of the few. 'The men of greatest credit and wealth into whose hands the best bargains were most like to come did not respect their own private gains and were willing that the younger people should be partakers with them.' When this was said in the sixteenth century the practice had already decayed owing to the increasing tendency to individualism which marked the later middle ages. The communal aspect of the gild merchant was further exhibited in the system of collective trading. The authorities were accustomed to make wholesale purchases of commodities which were then distributed among the gildsmen at retail prices. These joint purchases, known as 'common bargains,' were intended to promote equal chances for trade among the brotherhood, to provide funds for public objects, and to put merchant strangers at a disadvantage by preventing competition among the prospective buyers.

Other functions served by the gild merchant illustrate the fraternalism inherent in the gild concept. The gildsman who fell ill was given bread, wine and cooked food, and was visited by men of standing; if he were in prison in any place in England the officers of the gild were enjoined to go at the cost of the fraternity and procure his deliverance; if he fell into poverty he received pecuniary aid. The brethren were expected to live in peace and amity with each other and to settle their disputes by arbitration; and if one gildsman struck another he lost his gildship. Lastly the member of a

gild merchant possessed a recognized status; he was backed
by the resources of his society and supported by its recommendations when he travelled to another borough. The
merchant who was at variance with the authorities of a
town could turn to the rulers of his own city, who would
take active steps to defend his interests or avenge his wrongs.
Nowadays the individual seeks redress for his injuries in a
court of law; in a ruder age he found the means of protection
in fraternal union with his fellow-gildsmen. It was the
peculiar feature of town life in the middle ages that an
Englishman's privileges and burdens were borne by him
not as the citizen of a nation but as the member of an urban
community, and that their nature and extent depended
mainly upon the elastic terms of a royal charter or municipal
treaty.

The exclusive monopoly which a mediaeval town sought
to exercise in the sphere of trade was curtailed by the right
conferred on many chartered boroughs to carry their
merchandise all over England free from toll. No mercantile
concession was valued more highly than that which released
traders from local customs barriers; and sometimes it was
extended to ecclesiastical bodies and tenants on royal
estates when they purchased wares for their own use. The
exemption of qualified persons from the payment of tolls
was a normal practice, and even in the seventeenth century
it still remained valid. Thus it warns us not to minimize
unduly the degree of internal free trade shared by merchants
and others in the middle ages; and it shows that the claims
of the gild merchant, when put to the test of law and
economic usage, undergo an appreciable shrinkage. The
multiplication of grants of immunity broke down the
protective system of the English towns, and enabled the great
mass of the traders throughout the country to assert freedom
of traffic.

The close corporation which was established by the trading
community of every borough enjoyed extensive privileges
but it was also burdened with corresponding obligations. In

c

particular its members were held responsible for debts contracted by any of their fellowship in the way of trade. Most boroughs were granted or usurped the right to distrain on the fellow-burgesses of defaulting debtors. The procedure ordinarily adopted was for the authorities of the town where the creditor belonged to approach the debtor's municipality with a request for the payment of the debt; if justice were not done, they proceeded after repeated warnings to seize the goods of any trader of the offending community who passed through the town. This practice, termed 'withernam,' hampered commercial intercourse. Accordingly some towns treated the discharge of a debt due to a stranger as a communal liability, recovering payment from the debtor; others punished the recalcitrant debtor by expulsion or imprisonment, or by 'closing his house with bolts and forbidding him ingress.' It also became the custom to procure a royal charter giving protection from wrongful distraint. Towards the close of the thirteenth century Parliament forbade the system of intermunicipal reprisals, but in some parts of the country it had not died out two hundred years later. The system of intermunicipal reprisals, analogous to international reprisals, draws our attention to a marked characteristic of English mediaeval towns. Each borough presented to its neighbours the same impenetrable front which modern nations exhibit towards one another. The burghal communities advanced claims or made threats of reprisals after the fashion of independent city states armed with powers of coercion and aggression. They carried on their mutual relations just as they conducted their dealings with foreign towns; and with native and foreign cities alike they concluded treaties in order to settle controversies or to accord reciprocal privileges.

An important aspect of town administration was the stringent control of the market on the behalf of the consumer. The mediaeval burghers were not convinced that man's self-love is God's providence, or that the economic interests of the individual and of society necessarily coincide, and they imposed restrictions designed to curb the greed and fraud of unscrupulous dealers. To regulate the weight of bread and the price of ale according to the cost of grain, a sliding scale was instituted known as the assize of bread and ale. To establish a uniform standard of weights and measures in place of an infinite variety of local practices Parliament poured out a stream of legislation. To prevent a 'corner' in trade incessant attempts were made to extirpate the kindred abuses of engrossing, forestalling and regrating. Engrossers purchased produce while it was still in the fields; forestallers bought up goods or victuals on their way to the market; regraters obtained commodities in the market itself at advantage for resale at higher prices. These offences violated current conceptions of commercial morality—to the mediaeval mind it was intolerable that middlemen should manipulate supplies with the object of forcing up prices. The provision dealers were particularly unpopular. It was the common belief that millers stole flour, that bakers gave false weight, that brewers adulterated the ale. A mediaeval riddle asked: 'What is the boldest thing in the world?' The answer was: 'A miller's shirt, for it clasps a thief by the throat daily.' A familiar figure was the fraudulent ale-wife whose traditional punishment was the 'cucking-stool.'

> 'Of cans I kept no true measure,
> My cups I sold at my pleasure.'

Offending bakers were sometimes drawn upon hurdles through the streets with the defective loaf hanging round their necks; and the seller of unsound wine was compelled to drink a draught of the wine which he sold, while the remainder was then poured over his head—a poetic form of justice. The municipal authorities tended to be lax in their enforcement of the law, and in one city the commons rose and threw loaves at the mayor's head because he connived at breaches of the assizes.

In the light of what has been said it is evident that the mediaeval town formed a complete whole, a self-dependent unit, in which the general control of economic life was subordinated to the will of a privileged body. The aims of municipal policy were avowedly inspired by jealous exclusiveness. The burgesses or gildsmen—who bore the financial burdens by which their franchises were sustained —showed the utmost determination to assert their claims over all who stood outside their circle. It was immaterial whether the stranger within their gates was native-born or an alien from beyond the sea. He was in either case subjected to disabilities natural to a condition of society in which burghal development had outstripped national development. Yet if we condemn the narrow range of vision which placed the municipality before the state and the burgher before the Englishman, we may recognize certain compensating features. The struggle for freedom bred within the townsmen a spirit of monopoly, but it also generated an eager active existence in which citizenship was charged with real responsibilities and duties. The citizen of our own day, who is scarcely conscious of his status, may look with wonder upon his mediaeval forebears who were required to fill municipal offices, serve on juries, keep watch and ward (police), suppress riots and disorder, answer the call to arms in defence of the town, maintain and repair the walls, pave the streets in front of their houses, make bridges and highways, and perform other public works. Among the burgesses there seems to have been a genuine sense of solidarity, a co-opera-tion of social and economic forces for the common welfare, which made the old English borough a school of political training and discipline. It paved the way for the time when the municipality would be merged into the state and the burgesses into the nation.

Hitherto we have been concerned with the town as a centre of trade: we must now view it as a seat of industry. This phase in its development was marked by the rise of the craft gild, which may be defined as a group of producers associated together in the pursuit of a common calling.

Membership was compulsory on every skilled worker engaged in a particular industry within the same town, and it gave him in the eyes of the world both status and prestige. The profound importance of the craft gilds in the economic life of the English people merits close attention, but their significance does not lie in the historical aspect alone. In spite of the lapse of centuries they still afford an inspiration to the modern age. The problems that they handled may differ widely from our own, which are more complex and involve larger issues: yet in the effort to provide fair remuneration for the worker, and to reconcile the conflicting claims of producer and consumer, there were evolved fundamental principles of industrial regulation to which we may one day again return.

The craft gild comprised three classes of members—the masters, the journeymen and the apprentices. It was usually necessary to pass through all the three grades of membership: the apprentice became a journeyman, the journeyman rose to the position of a master. The most instructive feature of the craft gild was the institution of apprenticeship, which embodied an ideal binding on all alike who work with hand or brain—the ideal of technical training and sound craftsmanship. It appears in London early in the thirteenth century and rapidly spread through every town in England. We can readily grasp the reasons for its universality. It constituted a discipline by which the craftsman was initiated into the secrets of his craft, and was taught the standards of good workmanship. In addition its generally obligatory character protected the qualified artisan against unskilled competitors, while eventually it developed in the hands of exclusive gilds into an instrument of monopoly. Apprenticeship was a contractual relation involving reciprocal duties on the part of master and apprentice alike. In the 'indenture' or agreement the master, who sometimes received a premium, undertook to provide bed and board and technical instruction; sometimes also a small salary; sometimes even his schooling and a knowledge of languages. If he neglected his

37

duties the apprentice was at liberty to withdraw from his service. The master was expected to supervise the conduct of the apprentice, to regulate his apparel, and assume responsibility for his 'good demeaning and bearing.' To enforce his authority he was allowed to chastise an offender who proved refractory. The apprentice, as his share of the covenant, had to show obedience, self-control and fidelity to his master's service; he was forbidden to frequent taverns or gaming-houses 'whereby he doth waste and embezzle his master's goods.' He must not, says an old author, 'lie forth of his master's doors, he must not occupy any stock of his own, nor marry without his master's licence, and he must do all servile offices about the house.' The management of unruly youths was far from being an easy task, and riots were common especially among London apprentices. Readers of Scott's *The Fortunes of Nigel* will recall the description given in the opening chapter of the eagerness with which they caught up their weapons and rushed into the affray.[1] A favourite theme in literature is the contrast in the fortunes of the industrious and the idle apprentice—the one marrying his master's daughter and riding in his coach as lord mayor of London, the other ending a dissipated career on the gallows at Tyburn. The two types were depicted by Hogarth in his satirical drawings of London life in the eighteenth century.

Nowadays apprenticeship, where it has survived, is simply a system of technical training. Far different was the institution in its original conception when it was above all a system of social training. It was intended to fashion not only good craftsmen but good citizens, inspired with loyalty to their city and ready to give willing service on its behalf when summoned to the field or the council chamber. In mediaeval times the status of citizenship, as was mentioned above, involved real responsibilities; and apprenticeship served as a period of initiation in the public duties which awaited the

---

[1] 'Up then rose the 'prentices all,
Living in London, both proper & tall.'

future burgher. The unique relations existing between master and apprentice have no parallel in modern industrial society, where a cash nexus constitutes the normal bond between employer and employed. The master stood in place of the parent to the apprentice who lived in his house, sat at his board, and associated with him in the workshop and the home on terms of personal intimacy. Apprenticeship became an integral element in the constitution of the craft gild because in no other way was it possible to ensure continuity of tradition—by which alone the reputation of the gild for honourable dealing and sound workmanship could be carried on from generation to generation—or to raise up (as one gild expressed it) 'honest and virtuous masters to succeed us in this worshipful fellowship for the maintenance of the feats of merchandise.'

The length of apprenticeship varied. At first there was apparently no fixed period but in London it lasted from an early date for seven years. The custom of London gradually spread until in the famous Statute of Apprentices (1563) it became the law of the land. Shorter or longer terms were also common—there is an instance on record of sixteen years. In practice the duration would depend mainly upon the requirements of the occupation and the amount of time needed to secure thorough training. Regulations were also laid down as to the age at which apprentices might be taken. Occasionally they were as young as eleven, though children of 'tender' years were considered unsuitable for most occupations. Alternatively it was insisted that apprentices should not be less than a certain age upon the expiry of their term. 'Until a man grow unto the age of twenty-four years' he was not 'grown unto the full knowledge of the art that he professeth.' The number of apprentices which a master might employ became in the later middle ages a burning controversy. Sometimes, on behalf of the apprentices themselves, it was laid down that a master should take only as many as he could teach and support. Sometimes journeymen sought to impose restrictions in order to increase their own chances of employment. In the main the decisive factor was the interests of the masters, yet they were divided in their views. The more enterprising desired to push their trade and become large employers of labour. The rest were reluctant to admit potential rivals into a share of their monopoly. Moreover it was the aim of the craft gilds to prevent the growth of industrial capitalism among their members. The underlying principle of the gild regime was order rather than progress, stability rather than expansion; and the rule which limited the number of apprentices was the counterpart of the rule which limited competition in other directions. Whatever the play of motives, it is certain that a determined effort was made to keep down the number of trained and skilled artisans. As a consequence the craft gilds in later centuries tended to become exclusive bodies arrogating a monopoly which they sought to retain in the hands of a privileged group. However in remoter centuries these problems seemed far distant. Drawn from the same social status, united by a sense of common interests, masters and men in the early days of industrial development could work side by side in willing co-operation undivided by the antagonism of capital and labour.

After completing his term of training the apprentice was free to seek employment in the capacity of a hired workman or journeyman, although he was expected to give a year's service to his master for wages. Every journeyman looked forward to the day when he would cease to be a wage-earner and take his place among the masters of the gild as a fully qualified craftsman, sharing in the corporate life of the town, bearing its burdens and participating in its privileges. Sometimes he was required to furnish a 'master-piece,' or submit to a test of his competence, before he was allowed to set up on his own. A few years necessarily elapsed ere he was in a position to claim entry into the inner circle of the gild; and the interval afforded a breathing-space in which he could accumulate sufficient capital to start a workshop. The amount of capital naturally varied with the nature of the occupation. As a rule fixed capital in the shape of machinery and buildings played a subordinate part in mediaeval industry, which rested on the basis of craftsmanship. Tools and technical skill were the resources upon which in general a master was content to rely to gain a livelihood. Circulating capital would be needed to buy materials and pay wages, but the material might be supplied by the customer. The fact that masters were thus recruited from the ranks of the labouring class meant that no impassable gulf separated them from their workmen. We need not idealize early industrial society to recognize that employers and men were on the same social and economic plane and shared a common fellowship as brethren of the same gild.

The primary function of the craft gild was to establish rigid control over industry. It enveloped the life of the mediaeval craftsman in a network of technical regulations which did not suffer the minutest details to escape scrutiny; yet it also embraced within its scope the religious, artistic and economic activities of urban society. In short its ordinances embodied a complete social system in which a man's occupation determined the colour and texture of his way of life.

Nothing is more remarkable in these gild enactments than the rules which set forth the duties and responsibilities of the brethren. They demonstrate clearly—and herein lies their perennial value—that the gildsmen cherished high standards by which their conduct, while often selfish, must in practice have been deeply influenced. In the best days of the gild its professions of good faith were not a mere cloak concealing a blind attachment to its own narrow interests. They represented a genuine anxiety to uphold the ideals of sound craftsmanship in order to safeguard the consumer against defective commodities and the producer against cheap labour. In mediaeval times industry was conceived in the light of a public service carried on 'for the common profit' of the community; and the ordinances of the gilds repeatedly insisted that dishonest wares brought discredit upon the industry. Accordingly the gilds sought to exclude from their membership all who sullied their reputation by bad workmanship, which damaged their name in the eyes of the public upon whose favour the craftsmen were dependent for their market. It was a widespread usage for an aggrieved customer to seek redress from the gild authorities, who exacted recompense from the offender; in one instance the gild itself shouldered responsibility for incompetent work. To ensure obedience to the by-laws, a systematic inspection of the workshops was instituted for the purpose of supervising the quality of the goods turned out by members of the craft. Further the artisan was bidden to pursue his calling not in upper rooms or cellars but 'in sight of the people'—a practice which still persists in oriental countries.

An important function of the craft gilds, which they shared with the municipality and subsequently with the state, was the regulation of wages and prices. In fixing the remuneration of the hired workman the gild officers 'conscientiously set his salary betwixt his master and him' after they had tested his capabilities. He was then required to bind himself for a long period of engagement, usually twelve months or even three or four years. The gilds also determined prices by enacting what the master craftsman should take for his work. We naturally hear most about this function when it was abused; and Parliament intervened to forbid 'unreasonable ordinances' detrimental to the community. The gildsman who set the brethren at defiance was roughly handled. The dyers at Coventry undertook to work only at certain rates; and when some of their fellows refused to be bound by the agreement, the gild hired Welshmen and Irishmen to waylay and kill them. This drastic treatment of 'blacklegs' represented the mediaeval substitute for picketing.

Religious obligations, especially the maintenance of lights upon the altar of the patron saint, figured prominently. The *fraternity* (the gild in its devotional aspect) developed into a craft gild when it merged with the *mistery* (the gild in its secular aspect). Yet sometimes the distinction between the two sides of the gild was preserved and each was then organized on a separate footing. Closely connected with the religious duties of the craft gild was the annual exhibition of a pageant as part of its contribution to the social life of the community. In the history of the mediaeval stage the gilds fill a significant chapter. During the later middle ages the drama was undergoing a transformation, and while still remaining primarily a vehicle for moral edification it was rapidly emancipating itself from ecclesiastical control. The mystery play (which is occasionally revived at the present day) attained its highest point of development with the institution of the great 'cycles,' in which Biblical incidents were portrayed in a succession of pageants representing the Creation of the World, Adam and Eve, Noah's Ark, David and Goliath, etc. There was no theatre and the pageants were exhibited in different parts of the city on movable stages, which were drawn by horses from one quarter to another. The repetition of the play—it might be performed a dozen times—enabled more people to be spectators. Sometimes the pageants were shown before the houses of those who paid most for the privilege, and the owners erected stands at their doors for which they made a charge. The municipal authorities devoted careful attention to minute details, insisting that the crafts should provide 'good players well arrayed and openly speaking.' A striking feature of the pageants was the love of music, which was a marked characteristic of the English people in the middle ages: in the accounts of the Bristol bakers the payments to minstrels were a substantial item. This intimate association of the craft gilds with the popular drama that was springing up in England illustrates how closely interwoven was the social life of the members of the gild community with their economic pursuits.

Among the agencies by which distress was relieved in mediaeval times the craft gilds occupy a foremost place. As friendly societies they contributed to the support of their

poorer members, while the institution of almshouses anticipated one of the features of modern charity. Throughout
the gild ordinances runs the conviction that those who had
served their fellow-men and had been 'of good rule' should
be cared for in their hour of need. The gilds also formed one
of the chief sources of education in the middle ages, for they
founded and maintained many free grammar schools.
Some famous schools are still supported by the London
livery companies, which thus carry on an honourable tradition. One gild, that of Corpus Christi, Cambridge, perpetuated its memory by founding the college that bears its name.
In this way the voluntary efforts of artisans helped to kindle
the lamp of knowledge. Another purpose of the craft gild
was to determine all disputes between its members, and no
craftsman was allowed to take legal action against a brother
gildsman without leave of the fellowship. The prohibition
helped to strengthen the feeling of solidarity among the
gild brethren; and the same end was served by the principle
that none should seek an unfair advantage. It was strictly
forbidden to entice a servant away from his master or a
customer from a dealer, or to offer more rent to gain
possession of a shop 'over the tenant's head.' If a master had
several journeymen he could be required to 'deliver' one to a
master who had none. A craftsman was expected to find
whatever work he could for a fellow-member who needed it.
The modern 'labour exchange' was foreshadowed in the
injunction that unemployed labourers should assemble with
tools in their hands at fixed hours and places where they
could be hired. These various ordinances afford a valuable
insight into the working of the mediaeval mind: they reflect
the spirit of mutual aid which sought to establish as nearly
as possible a condition of complete equality. Although the
craft gilds were close bodies which claimed a monopoly of
industry and put outsiders under grave disabilities, yet
within their own ranks a democratic principle reproduced
the forces which were at work in the village community and
the gild merchant.

The craft gilds have a long history, which goes back to the twelfth century. At first they were founded by royal charters, and their demand for autonomy drove them into collision with the municipal authorities whose jurisdiction they set at defiance. Subsequently they abandoned their pretensions to independence: they grew amenable to civic control and became strictly subservient to the rulers of the town, who enjoyed a discretionary power to elect gild officials, amend gild laws, punish bad workmanship, regulate wages and fix prices. With the increasing specialization of industry which brought about the general disappearance of the gild merchant in the fourteenth century, the craft gilds multiplied fast. All human institutions, however, are subject to the law of growth and decay; and the course of events demonstrated that the craft gilds were not immune from a universal tendency.

The efficient working of the gild society depended on the harmonious relations between the different grades engaged in production; and this was rendered possible by the fact that among the gildsmen there were no permanent classes of employers and employees, the one rigidly divided from the other by wealth and social status. The craft gild worked well so long as there was no extreme antagonism between capital and labour to mar their friendly co-operation; but under the stress of new economic forces such idyllic conditions could not be maintained. The root of the trouble was that the journeymen found their prospects of independence and economic advancement materially impaired owing to the growth of population and the gradual evolution of a capitalist structure of industry. There began to emerge a 'working class' comprising not only (as hitherto) the unorganized and unskilled labourers outside the craft gilds, but also their more favoured fellows—the skilled artisans— who were recognized members of the gilds. When the journeymen saw themselves sinking into the position of hired workers shut out from the ranks of the employing class, it was inevitable that they should form separate

45

organizations. These associations, known as yeomen or journeymen gilds, were the first combinations of wage-earners in revolt against their employers; and they foreshadowed the trade union movement of a later day. They appear in London at the opening of the fourteenth century, and became a widespread institution in the fifteenth century.

The gilds where harmony once had reigned, when there was no clash of interests between masters and men, now became the scene of contention and strife. The controversies centred largely over the conditions of employment. The employers alleged that the journeymen extorted excessive rates of remuneration—especially after the Black Death, when the rise in the cost of living produced a demand for higher wages. There were also disputes over hours of labour caused in some cases by attempts to extend the working day which was commonly twelve hours. Another source of friction lay in the jealousy with which the masters of the fifteenth and sixteenth centuries—like Ibsen's 'master builder'—strove to limit the field of competition and exclude potential rivals, for instance, by extorting a promise from apprentices that they would not set up as masters, or by exacting heavy fees for admission to the freedom of the city without which in former times no one could legally carry on his business. On the other side the masters levelled charges that the journeymen were unruly, difficult to control and reluctant to show due respect for their authority; that they absented themselves without leave or left their service without reasonable notice; that they indulged in drinking and became unfit for their work. From these mutual recriminations one clear fact emerges: the expansion of industry had disturbed the internal relations of the craft gild, whose equilibrium depended upon a genuine identity of interests among the different elements of which it was composed.

To defend their economic affairs and exert pressure upon the employers, the yeomen gilds had recourse to strikes: there are even examples of 'sympathetic strikes' in the fourteenth century. The masters also made common cause and rallied to each other's support in the struggle with refractory journeymen. In one place the bitterness grew so intense that the masters made an assault upon their journeymen 'with pole-axes, baslards and iron-pointed poles.' Authority sided with the masters. London from the outset pursued a policy of repression, forbidding 'servant workmen' to hold any meetings prejudicial to the trade under penalty of imprisonment. Other municipal bodies sought to crush the yeomen gilds, and their strenuous efforts to check associations among the hired workers were seconded by the government. A law of 1548 anticipated the combination acts of the eighteenth century by making it illegal for workmen to form unions in order to improve the conditions of labour. This persistent hostility partially accounts for the failure of the journeymen to establish a stable and permanent organization. A more important reason is that, while it was becoming increasingly difficult for wage-earners to achieve independence and mastership, yet it was not beyond the capacity of the more enterprising; and so the leaders of the movement were always falling away. The yeomen gilds survived though their character underwent a complete transformation. Instead of being independent societies formed in defiance of the employers and proscribed by the municipality, they were assigned a definite if strictly subordinate place in the livery company, and they fulfilled only administrative functions. The explanation of this striking change was that with the growth of industry the journeyman ceased (as hitherto) to be an unmarried man often residing in his employer's house, but settled down as a householder and lived apart. He became converted into a 'small master,' who differed from the master craftsman of the gild system because he no longer had contact with the consumer; instead he worked for the large master who furnished the raw material and disposed of the finished product. The transitional stage in which the

47

journeymen struggled to secure a safe economic footing was now at an end.

Within the craft gild itself disintegrating influences were at work undermining the gild structure and weakening the solidarity of the gild brethren. The growth of an oligarchy, due ultimately to differences of economic status, was facilitated by the reluctance of members to attend meetings of the assembly or to take office. The gild pageantry, the outward symbol of the social life of the fraternity, was discontinued because members would not support its charges. As the loyalty of the gild brethren to their obligations waned, their desire grew to exploit the privileges conferred upon them by their monopoly of trade. In their hands lay the control of industry, and the temptation was always present to abuse their trust. The regulations of the craft gild became oppressive when its members, ignoring the purposes for which the gilds were founded, utilized their position to advance their own interests and disregarded those of the community. Only members could set up on their own as master craftsmen and shopkeepers, and they endeavoured to exclude outsiders from their ranks by making the admission fees prohibitive. The outcry against the abuses of the craft gilds eventually found a response in two parliamentary enactments—one (1437) strengthening the authority of the civic magistrates; and the other (1504) requiring craft ordinances to be submitted for approval to the judges.

The gradual break-up of the old gild society was not due to the degeneracy of the gild regime, which was a symptom rather than a fundamental cause; it was the inevitable product of economic forces. The craft gilds belonged to a stage of industrial evolution where the master craftsman was an independent producer owning the raw material as well as the instruments of production, and selling the finished product direct to the consumer. Thus the essence of the gild system, as this stage may be termed, was the combination of handicraft and trading functions in the same hands. So long as the market was limited, the gild system answered to the needs of the time: when the market widened the mercantile functions passed to a special class of traders, while the master craftsmen confined to the purely manual functions lost their economic independence. As a consequence production and distribution were separated; and the gild system was supplanted by the domestic system where a class of employers acting as middlemen thrust itself between the artificer and the consumer, reducing the former to the status of a wage-earner. A new kind of industrial association marked the transition from the gild system to the domestic system. This was the livery company which differed from the craft gild in the emergence of two distinct classes—consisting of capitalists who wore the 'livery,' and small masters or yeomanry restricted to the manual parts of their occupation.

In forming an estimate of the craft gilds both praise and criticism must take into account the economic environment under which they flourished and the prevailing concepts of morality so widely different from the classical postulates of modern economics. For the purpose of a local market they were admirably designed to achieve their object, the limited production of a well-wrought article. The institution of apprenticeship provided opportunities for a thorough system of technical training, and the inspection of workshops promoted a high standard of craftsmanship. In addition the regulation of wages afforded a measure of protection against arbitrary oppression; the maxim of a just price, fair alike to seller and buyer, made economics a branch of ethics; the insistence upon the avoidance of deceit in business conduct created a social conscience. The chief criticism levelled against the craft gilds is that their rigid and uncompromising harshness fostered a spirit of jealous monopoly. Admittedly the efforts made in later days to confine membership to a narrow clique furnish a warning of the temptations to which all privileged bodies are prone. Yet in the early stages the gilds can scarcely be blamed for excluding from their

D

privileges those who were reluctant to share their charges. Moreover the discretionary power vested in the town authorities could be used to safeguard the community, and there are notable examples on record of its exercise.

'The old order changes.' For good or evil a new era was unfolding in which a corporate society organized on a gild basis slowly yielded place to an individualist society organized on a capitalist basis.

Chapter Three

THE CORPORATE SOCIETY

III. INDUSTRY AND COMMERCE

Industry

It is generally assumed that throughout the middle ages England remained economically in a backwater. This view is contradicted by authentic evidence of industrial proficiency, which warns us not to under-estimate the advance made at an early period by English craftsmanship. Already in the eleventh century its technical achievements had won it a considerable reputation in foreign countries. The chaplain of William the Conqueror praised the skill displayed by the women in working cloths of gold, and the distinction attained by the men in all manner of crafts. On this account, he added, the most expert German artificers were accustomed to reside in this country. The great number of craft gilds established in London and the provincial towns bears eloquent testimony to the diversified character of the manual arts in mediaeval England; while the remarkable expansion of the woollen manufacture and its conduct on a capitalist basis were in the nature of an industrial revolution. The advent of a progressive manufacturing class is reflected especially in the growing wealth of the towns, in the erection of gildhalls, gates and market crosses, as well as in paved streets. An emperor of the Byzantine empire, who visited these shores in the year 1400, commented upon the flourishing state of London in vivid terms: 'In populousness and power, in riches and luxury, London—the metropolis of the isle—may claim a pre-eminence over all the cities of the west.' He observed of the country as a whole: 'The land is overspread with towns and villages; though destitute of wines and not abounding in fruit trees, it is fertile in wheat and barley, in honey and wool; and much cloth is manufactured

51

by the inhabitants.' A Venetian at the end of the fifteenth century wrote in a similar strain: 'In one single street named the Strand leading to St. Paul's there are fifty-two gold-smiths' shops so rich and full of silver vessels, great and small, that in all the shops in Milan, Rome, Venice and Florence put together I do not think there would be found so many of the magnificence that are to be seen in London.' A sumptuary statute of the fifteenth century (1463) testifies to the luxury of the age in its complaint that men and women 'wear excessive and inordinate array.' Everywhere a class of rich burghers came into existence, who began to store up plate and tapestry in their houses and entertain kings at their table for their guests. Their standing was also evinced in a display of public spirit such as marked the best days of the Roman Empire, in the foundation of hospitals and schools, the repair of roads and bridges, the bequest of legacies to be employed in loans to young men embarking on their career. Fine churches built by wealthy clothiers still cover the countryside, though the industrial prosperity of which they were once the tangible sign has long passed away to other centres.

Among the industries of England the making of cloth—'the worthiest and richest commodity of this kingdom'—occupied in former ages a unique position: for seven hundred years it was pre-eminently the staple manufacture of the realm. It was described by Parliament in the fifteenth century 'as the greatest occupation and living of the poor commons of this land;' and writers vied with each other in the eulogy bestowed upon a 'pillar of the state.' The woollen industry had many claims to the exceptional prestige which it enjoyed. Firstly, the raw material which it consumed was raised at home. Secondly, it was the most widespread of English manufactures—every town, village and hamlet was associated with the weaving of cloth as a household occupation, so that in its progress were bound up the interests of the whole community. Thirdly, it was brought under national control before any other branch of industry, and it became the favourite child of the legislature hedged round by an elaborate code which survived down to the nineteenth century. Fourthly, its history is an epitome of the different phases of English industrial development, for it passed through all the various stages of evolution—the gild system where the worker owned the instruments of production and the raw material; the domestic system where he owned the instruments but not the material; and the factory system where he owned neither. It is especially noteworthy that capitalism existed in the woollen industry four centuries before the introduction of machinery. Finally, the social influence exerted by the textile arts is displayed in the enrichment of the English language by words and phrases connected in their origin with the making of cloth. No industry has left more traces in literature and on popular speech. Such phrases as 'to spin a yarn,' 'weavers of long tales,' 'the thread of a discourse,' 'a web of sophistry,' 'unravelling a mystery,' 'tangled skein,' betray at once their source. Shakespeare employed frequent metaphors from spinning and weaving—'The web of our life is of a mingled yarn, good and ill together;' 'Life is a shuttle;' 'Their thread of life is spun;' 'Ill weav'd ambition, how much art thou shrunk!' We still speak of 'fine-drawn' theories, and 'home-spun' youths; and life may still be described as a 'web' of which the 'thread' is cut short by the fates with their abhorred shears. There are several proverbial expressions, for instance—'Weave in faith and God will find thread.' Many personal names betoken the original occupation of some ancestor—Dyer, Fuller, Taylor, Tucker, Walker, Weaver and Webster. Local nomenclature has preserved names like 'Rack-Closes,' 'East-Stretch,' 'Tucking-Mill Field,' which refer to fulling and tentering cloth. And the close identification of women with the spinning industry is reflected in the use of the word 'spinster' to denote an unmarried woman.

The arts of spinning and weaving rank among the most

53

primitive of the industrial arts. Roman Britain is credited with an 'imperial weaving manufactory' at Winchester for the needs of the emperors—the wool, according to a geographer of antiquity, being spun until it was 'comparable to a spider's web.' In Anglo-Saxon times Edward the Elder 'sette his sonnes to scole, and his daughters he sette to woll werke, takyng example of Charlys the Conquestour.' It is even possible that textiles were being sent to the Continent as early as the eighth century. However the authentic history of the English woollen industry properly begins after the Norman Conquest. Its rapid progress was marked by the establishment of weavers' gilds; by the subjection of the cloth manufacture to state control so as to ensure a uniform standard of length, breadth, weight and goodness; and by the export of large quantities of the finer fabrics, of which one variety made in Stamford had gained a European reputation since it was found worth while in Italy to imitate it. To foster the infant industry a protectionist policy began to take shape as early as the thirteenth century, when the Oxford Parliament laid an embargo on the export of wool and ordered that 'the wool of the country should be worked up in England and not be sold to foreigners, and that everyone should use woollen cloth made within the country.' Those who longed to wear the more delicate fabrics woven on the looms of Flanders were bidden not to 'seek over-precious garments.'

A more judicious method of stimulating the native cloth manufacture was adopted in the next century. It was the fulfilment of a design which had been cherished for two generations, namely, to induce foreign craftsmen to settle over here and impart their technical knowledge to English artisans. The project was finally put into operation in the reign of Edward III in order to arrest a serious decline which was very noticeable in the towns, though the industry was spreading in the rural districts. Political and economic unrest in Flanders facilitated the emigration of cloth-workers who came over the sea with their belongings to ply their mistery within the realm. A law enacted in 1337 promised that 'all the cloth-workers of strange lands shall be in the king's protection,' with liberty to dwell where they pleased and to enjoy franchises (privileges) 'as many as may suffice them.' The experiment was attended with complete success. The presence of foreign 'captains of industry' in this country co-operated with other factors—the policy of protectionism and the natural forces of recovery and expansion —to bring about an industrial revival which extended even to districts where no alien settlement is recorded. Aided by these combined influences the English cloth-makers, in the glowing words of an old writer, grew so 'perfect in this mistery that it is the glory of our traffic and maintenance of our poor, many hundred thousands depending wholly on the same, chief pillar to our prince's revenue, the life of our merchant, the living of our clothier.' Measures were also taken to protect the native manufacture from foreign competition and to ensure an adequate supply of raw material: the same statute which promised lavish favours to alien settlers prohibited the import of cloth and the export of wool. These elements of protectionism were only fitfully maintained throughout the middle ages; but they mark nevertheless the definite adoption of an industrial protective policy which gradually crystallized into the famous mercantile system.

The expansion of the English woollen industry is one of the most striking economic phenomena of the later middle ages. In the second half of the fourteenth century the production of broadcloth for sale was trebled, and the quantity shipped abroad was multiplied ninefold. Another proof of progress was the substitution of manufactures for raw materials in the export trade. The quantity of wool sent out of the kingdom in the fifteenth century was only one-third, and in the sixteenth century only one-sixth, of its amount in the reign of Edward III. Nor was this shrinkage due to any curtailment of the area devoted to the growth of wool. On the contrary it was not less conspicuous at the time of the great agrarian movement which covered England with sheep-farms in place of corn-fields: but the wool now went to meet the ever-increasing demands of the home market. Despite the set-backs caused by the Wars of the Roses and international complications there is unmistakable proof of the increase of prosperity in the fifteenth century, and this must have greatly enlarged the domestic consumption of cloth; while the sharp recovery in its export in the latter part of the century was followed by an uninterrupted advance under the Tudors. The evidence of statistics affords convincing testimony to the trend of a revolution which was converting England into an industrial country, whose staple export was no longer raw materials but manufactured commodities.

The second great landmark in the history of the English cloth industry was the influx of aliens in the sixteenth century. Persecution in the Netherlands occasioned a large exodus of the most skilful section of the population; and England benefited (as she did in the seventeenth century when French Huguenots settled here) by a valuable addition to her economic assets. The Dutch and Walloon immigrants established a new branch of the woollen manufacture, the making of the finer fabrics known as the 'new drapery,' which included bays, says and other 'outlandish com-modities.' An old English rhyme ran:

> 'Hops, Reformation, Bays, and Beer
> Came into England all in a year.'

Some interesting letters have been preserved written by the newcomers to their kinsfolk at home. One entreats his father and mother to migrate to England without delay. 'I and my brother will supply you with what you require here as weaver, for there is a great trade doing. When you come to Norwich you shall have gold.' Another writes to his wife to sell what she has and to come over. 'There is good trade in bays, and I will look after a house as quickly as I can to get into business, for then it will be easy to make money. I will get ready the gear for making bays against your coming. Bring all your and your daughter's clothing, for people go well clad here. I let you know that we are merry and happy with each other. It is very dear to hear the word of God peacefully.' In spite of the advantages arising from the presence of aliens, friction often ensued on account of the jealousy of the native weavers, whose dislike of innovations and blind attachment to their own narrow interests proved an obstacle to the progress of the new manufacture. None the less in course of time the refugees were absorbed into the mass of the population; and the national resources were broadened and strengthened by the incorporation of a fresh element in the industrial system. To the strangers within her gates England owes an immeasurable debt of gratitude.

We must now glance at other branches of mediaeval economy. Of the extractive industries the chief was agriculture which gave England the most highly-prized of her raw materials, namely wool. This commodity occupied the place in national estimation now held by coal; and as one of the staple articles of export it can best be treated in the section on foreign trade. The other extractive industries were the fisheries—the herring was a main article of diet in the middle ages—and the mining of tin, lead, iron and coal.

The tin-mining industry enjoys a special interest because of its legendary associations. Cornish tin was a renowned product of Ancient Britain, though the attempt to identify the Cassiterides of antiquity with a part of Britain lacks convincing evidence. It is believed that the tin trade of Cornwall was considerable in pre-historic times, yet no vestiges of Phœnician traders have come to light. It apparently revived in Roman Britain but the veil of obscurity is not lifted until the twelfth century. At this period much of the tin used in Europe came from Devon; in the next century Cornwall supplanted its neighbour as the principal tin-producing area. The peculiar feature of the tin-mining industry was the organization of the miners in two corporations, the stannaries of Cornwall and the stannaries of Devon, each with its own laws and courts. They furnish the classic example of the 'free mining' system. The privilege claimed by the tinners, as confirmed in the charter of King John, consisted in 'digging tin and turfs for smelting it at all times freely and peaceably and without hindrance from any man everywhere in moors and in the fees of bishops, abbots and counts just as by ancient usage they have been wont to do.' Other groups of 'free miners,' exercising the right to discover and work a mine, existed in the lead mines of Derbyshire, the Mendip Hills (Somerset) and Alston (Cumberland): lead-mining largely owed its importance to the fact that silver was refined from the lead. Similar privileges were exercised by those engaged in digging for iron ore and coal in the Forest of Dean; here iron deposits had been worked by the Romans, and over a thousand years later 'prime and best' iron was still made from the cinders which they had discarded before the iron was entirely extracted. The use of coal, like iron, was known in Roman Britain but the real beginnings of its history date from the thirteenth century when references become frequent. Its export was viewed with jealous eyes, and in the middle ages it was sometimes even prohibited.

Turning from the extractive to the manufacturing industries, we are confronted with evidence of the most varied craftsmanship. Even a bare enumeration of the craft gilds to be found in any large urban centre would be impressive in its demonstration of the range of the industrial arts in Early England. Cloth-making enjoyed an undisputed pre-eminence, yet the metal workers achieved renown for the high quality of their wares. The tribute paid to the proficiency of English artificers at the time of the Norman Conquest shows that a long tradition lay behind the skill which continued to extort the admiration of foreigners four hundred years later. It is therefore not surprising that metal wares were finding a market abroad; and, together with the big shipments of cloth, they serve to indicate that English mediaeval industries were not restricted to a local or even national market but were supplying the needs of an ever-widening international market. The scope of one industry, however, was necessarily confined to domestic needs. This was the building industry which often required a great number of operatives. It is significant that masons' gild ordinances have come to light in London alone, and we may infer that the gild regime did not strike deep root among the masons because they were mostly wage-earners. The shipowners too were large employers of labour. In the fifteenth century William Canynges the younger of Bristol, according to a contemporary, had eight hundred men engaged in his ships while his workmen (carpenters, masons, etc.) numbered one hundred.

It is becoming abundantly clear that the traditional picture of mediaeval industry, as organized almost exclusively on the basis of small independent producers working with one or two assistants, does not correspond to the economic realities of the later middle ages. The rise of capitalism in the woollen industry will be described in the next chapter. When building and shipping are also taken into account, it is manifest that these three industries covered too wide a sphere to be treated as exceptions to the general rule; nor do they stand alone in the evidence they furnish of the infiltration of capitalism. The structure of the wool trade, as will be seen later, was essentially capitalist in type. Coal-mines, tin-mines, lead-mines and iron-works, despite the presence of groups of 'free miners,' disclose all the elements of a capitalist undertaking with an owner, foremen and hired workers. We may fairly conclude that outside the ranks of the gild craftsmen—whose independent status was itself slowly succumbing to economic pressure—there existed an indefinite number of wage-earners working under the direction of employers in enterprises conducted on capitalist lines. This early rise of capitalism links the mediaeval industrial system with the modern through the continuity of the forces common to both.

Commerce

In the middle ages the greater part of the internal trade of the country was carried on at fairs and markets—the former were held once a year and lasted a week though sometimes much longer; the latter were held once a week and lasted a single day. For several centuries, especially the twelfth, thirteenth and fourteenth, they were the chief centres of traffic; and some of the English fairs rivalled in fame those existing on the Continent. At a time when the stream of commerce was fitful and scanty these periodical gatherings afforded opportunities, which the towns were not yet in a position to provide, for the purchase and sale of products brought from a distance.

The fair started as a religious rather than as a commercial institution, since it originated in the assemblies which congregated around notable shrines on the feast days of saints. The concourse of strangers from remote parts assured merchants of the presence of buyers in an age when the population was dispersed. In addition the ostensible purpose for which the assemblies were held threw over the trader the cloak of religion, and ensured a degree of security which induced him the more willingly to brave the risks inseparable from his calling. The market cross became the emblem of the peace of commercial intercourse, although in a rude age men were stubborn to learn to respect the person of the trader and bandits molested travellers resorting to the mart or even invaded the mart itself. A fifteenth-century chief justice, Fortescue, in his famous panegyric of the English character boasted that 'there were more men hanged in England in a year for robbery and manslaughter than there be hanged in France for such manner of crime in seven years. There is no man hanged in Scotland in seven years together for robbery. But the Englishman is of another courage.' A further factor which promoted the development of markets and fairs was the legal insistence upon the presence of witnesses at all transactions in order to avoid traffic in stolen goods. The concentration of trade in recognized centres was also encouraged by the state because it facilitated the collection of tolls. Lastly, in contrast with the towns which were reluctant to extend their privileges to outsiders, full freedom was accorded indifferently at fairs and markets to native and alien, to burgess and stranger; and it was this policy of free trade and the open door which attracted merchants and afforded scope for the unrestricted play of economic forces. Owing to these various influences England was covered with a network of periodical marts, among which several enjoyed an international repute. The fair of St. Giles at Winchester is mentioned in *Piers Plowman*. Bartholomew fair, established in London, acquired importance as the chief cloth fair. Most renowned of all was Stourbridge fair near Cambridge: as late as the eighteenth century Defoe claimed that it was 'not only the greatest in the whole nation but in the world.'

We are fortunately not without materials for an attempt to reconstruct a picture of the life of a mediaeval fair. According to the classical doctrine a fair could only be set up in virtue of a royal grant or by prescription 'from a time whereof there is no memory.' It was often in the hands of private individuals, though the most frequent recipient of the privilege was the Church. While the fair lasted the owner was given the custody of the town where it was held, and he administered municipal affairs in place of the governing body which for the time being was superseded. Thus at York the bailiffs of the archbishop came upon the bridge, and there the rulers of the city delivered up their staves as the symbol of their authority; during the interregnum the former kept the peace, collected tolls and took all other profits 'as the city bailiffs do at other times.' The fair was opened by proclamation, which commenced with an injunction to 'keep the peace' of the king. It laid down that 'true' weights and measures must be used; that all food must be 'good and wholesome for man's body;' that the Sabbath day must not be broken by buying and selling nor by 'sitting, tippling or drinking in any tavern.' Finally it gave the exhortation: 'Therefore now at noon begin in God's name and the king's, and God send every man good luck and this fair good continuance.' At sunset the fair came to an end, and the marshal rode through its midst ordering every trader forthwith to shut his stall. The fair stood in the open fields, and booths and stalls were set up in rows to form streets. Dealers in the same commodities were commonly grouped together, an arrangement which favoured the convenience of the buyers and promoted competition among the sellers. The localization of trade is perpetuated to this day in the names of streets such as Bread Street, Milk Street,[1] Fish Street and Honey Lane. A twelfth-century description of London relates how 'sellers of all sorts of wares are all set apart by themselves in their several places.' In his *Survey of London* Stow has left us a valuable account of the different quarters of the city each associated with some mistery or trade—the mercers and haberdashers with their shops on London Bridge, the goldsmiths in West Cheap, the drapers in Candlewick Street, the butchers in East Cheap.

Of the eager active life of the fair we may learn something from the vivid glimpses of the London markets in the ballad *London Lykpenny*:

'Then to the Chepe I began me drawne,
Where mutch people I saw for to stande;
One ofred me velvet, sylke and lawne,
An other he taketh me by the hande,
"Here is Parys thred, the fynest in the land;"
I never was used to such thyngs indede,
And wantyng mony I myght not spede.
Then went I forth by London stone,
Throughout all Canwyke streete;
Drapers mutch cloth me offred anone . . .
Then I hyed me into Est-Chepe;

[1] Boston in New England has a Milk Street.

One cryes rybbes of befe, and many a pye;
Pewter pottes they clattered on a heape;
There was harpe, fyfe, and mynstrelsye ...
The taverner took mee by the sleve,
"Sir," sayth he, "wyll you our wyne assay?" '

The fairs were the channels by which native produce was distributed all over the realm. Here were bought the best grades of wool from Shropshire and Leominster and the Cotswolds, textiles of innumerable varieties, tin from Cornwall, salt from the Worcestershire springs, lead from the Derbyshire mines, iron from the Sussex forges. Here also forgathered the alien traders who flocked to these shores from many parts of Europe—merchants from Venice and Genoa with costly spices from the east and silks and velvets and 'things of complacence,' the Flemings with linen cloth, the Spaniards with iron, the Norwegians with tar, the Gascons with wine, and the Teutons with furs and amber. The deeper significance of the fair lies in the fact that it was both a cosmopolitan gathering and the common hearth of the nation; and association with men from distant places must have broadened the horizon and stimulated a keen interest in the world that lay beyond. To provide expeditious justice a special tribunal was set up—the piepowder court or court of the dusty feet so called from the attendance of way-faring merchants; and the law which it administered was not the common law of the land but the law merchant, a body of legal usages and doctrines binding on merchants throughout Europe in their mercantile relations.

England's oversea commerce was at first largely in the hands of alien merchants, who came not to reside permanently but to act as intermediaries between this country and the rest of the world. Their history, however, is the record of one long ceaseless struggle with the authorities of English towns. The burgesses did not seek to exclude their competitors, for Englishmen were not ready to absorb the whole of the carrying trade upon which depended the exchange of native produce for imported commodities. Yet they endeavoured to restrict them to wholesale dealings with enfranchised traders, and to prevent direct contact with consumers. In other words, their purpose was to monopolize the internal trade while leaving only a portion of the carrying trade to strangers. For centuries English commercial life was disturbed by unceasing strife over the rival claims of burgesses and aliens. The former laid down strict regulations that no foreign merchant might stay in England more than forty days or sell by retail, and that he must reside with an English host who was to witness all his business transactions. Such a policy could not be stringently enforced since it conflicted with the views of the king and the nobility. As landowners they were anxious to treat with continental dealers and save the profits of the middleman; moreover strangers paid higher customs duties and made loans to the state. Nevertheless the favour traditionally shown to aliens by the government in the teeth of the vested interests of a powerful and turbulent burgher class must have had behind it some larger concept of their important place in the national economy.

The system of compulsory 'hosting' survived intermittently into the sixteenth century: even Queen Elizabeth granted a patent empowering a London citizen to appoint hosts. It shows the persistence of the jealous hostility which sometimes flared up in riots and disturbances that were often engineered by native competitors. At the time of the Peasants' Revolt many Flemings, observes a chronicler, 'lost their heads and namely they that could not say Bread and Cheese but Brod and Case.' In addition to the Flemings other groups of foreign traders were the Gascons who brought wine, the Hansards and the Italians. The Hansards or Easterlings belonged to the Hanseatic League, a potent mercantile association of north German cities. Down to the reign of Elizabeth they enjoyed preferential tariffs, which in the case of cloth were lower than those paid by English exporters; they had the right to sell by retail and to reside where they pleased and for any length of time. Their establishment in London was called the Steelyard, and they also settled in provincial centres. The Italians obtained a large share of the wool trade and advanced considerable sums of money to the king. Venice, the greatest commercial city of the middle ages, sent every year a fleet of merchant vessels known as the 'Flanders Galleys' of which part visited Flanders and part England.

The presence of alien merchants drawn from different countries of Europe indicates how diverse were the channels of England's oversea commerce. The mediaeval trade routes ran in four directions. One led to Calais. Another connected this country with the Netherlands (Flanders, Holland, etc.) whose markets served a vast hinterland stretching to the shores of the Mediterranean. The third provided the link with northern Europe (Scandinavia and Prussia) and reached as far as Iceland. The fourth was the direct sea passage to southern Europe (Gascony and Italy).

The commodities which were handled in foreign traffic covered an extensive range. The main import was wine furnished by Gascony; other French imports included woad for dyeing, salt and stone. The Netherlands sent herrings, linen cloth and 'Flanders tiles,' while Spain supplied wool, oil, leather and iron. The Hansards brought corn, ship-building materials (timber, pitch and tar), wax, furs and iron; the men of Genoa came with silk, cotton, cloths of gold and pepper; and the great galleys of Venice and Florence were 'well ladened with things of complacence'—costly spices from the east, sweet wines and extravagant 'trifles.' The principal exports were wool and cloth: both were shipped abroad throughout the middle ages, but as the former declined the latter rose in quantity. Other exports comprised corn—in former days England was famed as a corn granary—tin, coal, pewter, various metal wares (daggers, basins, plates, buckles), leather goods (shoes, bottles, bellows), meat, cheese, butter, honey, herrings and salmon. A list of twentieth-century exports would be widely different, yet in both lists the most prominent would be textiles. There was also a re-export trade, that is, foreign goods were imported and then re-exported abroad.

One staple article of the export trade, cloth, was noticed above. The other, wool, held pride of place among the commodities produced in mediaeval England. The 'goddess of merchants,' as the poet Gower called it, furnished the main source of customs-revenue; and the esteem in which it was held is reflected in the Woolsack 'the seat of our wise learned judges.' Reputed the best in Europe it was said to surpass all other wools in 'the exceeding fineness of the fleece.' Dryden wrote:

> 'Though Jason's Fleece was fam'd of old,
> The British wool is growing gold;
> No mines can more of wealth supply:
> It keeps the peasant from the cold,
> And takes for kings the Tyrian dye.'

Pre-eminent among the pioneers of wool-growing were the Cistercians who devoted a year's produce to ransom Richard I from captivity. English wool varied greatly in quality: no less than fifty-one grades are enumerated in a fifteenth-century record. Notwithstanding a heavy customs duty (aliens paid a third and denizens a quarter of the value), large quantities were sent abroad until the later fourteenth century when a decline set in. The counterpart of the falling off in the export of the raw material was the growth in the export of the manufactured article. The seal was put on this transformation in the early seventeenth century by an embargo on the transhipment of wool which lasted for two hundred years.

The mechanism of the wool trade passed through various stages, which indicate that the commercial system of the middle ages already reproduced in essentials the complex features of an advanced economy. In the first stage the producer dealt directly with the foreign buyer. The Italian merchants were accustomed to buy up the whole clip of a monastic house and to make contracts for a term of years. The next stage developed when the producer came into contact with a native middleman (stapler) acting as the agent of the foreign buyer. The third stage was reached when another middleman (woolman) emerged as the agent of the producer—the grower selling his clip to the woolman who resold it to the exporter. Business was conducted by all parties to the transaction on a credit basis. The correspondence of a fifteenth-century firm of merchant exporters (the Celys) contains a letter from a woolman who had contracted to supply wool at a stipulated price but found he had 'misjudged the market.' 'Sir, I made a bargain with you at that season, the which I would I had slept the whiles.' He was unable to buy at the anticipated price, and the growers —'they that were wont to leave in my hand most part of their money'—were demanding cash. He asks for payment in advance 'or else I am hotly shamed.' After the wool had been purchased, it was taken from the interior to the coast on pack horses; then it was put on board different vessels as a measure of security and transhipped to the Continent. The proceeds were brought back to England in the form of goods, gold and silver, or bills of exchange drawn upon a merchant importer in London.

The whole structure of the oversea trade in wool came to rest upon the famous institution known as the staple. The history of the English staple is largely the history of England's commerce in the later middle ages. The staple was a continuous mart at which commodities were bought and sold, just as the fair was a periodical mart. Its underlying principle was to regulate the stream of traffic and force it into channels approved by the state. It facilitated both the collection of the customs-revenue and the enforcement of a suitable standard of quality; while it served a political purpose as an instrument of diplomacy since it was eagerly sought after by foreign governments. At first the staple was voluntary: it was the recognized centre of distribution where English produce was exposed for sale, but merchants remained free to frequent any port they chose. It became compulsory early in the fourteenth century, though its location was repeatedly changed—it was even moved to England on several occasions —until finally it was fixed at Calais after the latter came into English hands. The commercial significance of Calais as the chief seat of the export trade in wool for two hundred years was enhanced by the establishment of a mint; at one period by far the larger portion of English silver money was issued from the Calais mint; moreover the garrison of the town was paid out of the customs duties. The merchants in whose hands the control of the staple was placed were known as the Merchant Staplers. They formed an organized and privileged society under the rule of their own mayor and council, and they were armed with official sanction and powers of coercion.

English merchants had a greater share in the beginnings of English commerce than is generally supposed, for the carrying trade was not completely dominated by aliens. A saga of the twelfth century contains a speech made by King Sverri of Norway: 'We desire to thank the Englishmen who have come here bringing wheat and honey, flour and cloth.' Towards the end of the thirteenth century native merchants were responsible for one-third of the export trade in wool and in the next century their proportion rose to three-quarters. They also drew into their grasp the main part of the export trade in cloth. In addition the navigation policy was designed to develop the maritime resources of the country. The act of 1381, in order 'to increase the navy of England which is now greatly diminished,' laid down that 'the king's liege people' must employ only 'ships of the king's liegance;' though its purpose was virtually frustrated in the following year by a proviso that such ships must be available when they were required.

The extension of the market abroad was revealed in the increasing trend towards specialization in mercantile affairs. At first the term 'merchant' was loosely used, for originally it was applied to all who dealt in trade. The wider definition included the master craftsman who was not only an artisan but also a trader, because he bought the raw material and sold the finished product. This explains why as a rule he was freely admitted into the membership of the gild merchant. Then the interpretation of the word began to narrow. The 'pure' merchant 'adventuring beyond the seas' was differentiated, firstly, from the manufacturer. Secondly, he became distinct from those engaged in domestic trade, who formed their own companies such as the Goldsmiths, Mercers, Grocers, Drapers, Vintners, Haberdashers. Thirdly, he ceased to be a carrier of goods; for the shipper who owned the freights which he carried eventually developed into a shipowner, whose function was to carry freights for others. Further the merchant exporter might confine himself mainly to a single commodity—wool or cloth; or to a single market—Calais or Antwerp. In the later middle ages one can appropriately speak of 'business houses,' in which foreign trade involved regular connexions abroad based on commercial agents and factors, credit transactions, bills of exchange, and contracts made with producers at home—in short, the paraphernalia of modern mercantile life.

Among the different groups of English merchants that carried native wares to foreign countries the most prominent were the Merchant Adventurers who rose to great economic importance. The corporation already functioned in the thirteenth century, and it was fortified by royal charters which set the public seal on its claims and pretensions. It was ruled by a governor and a council, and the seat of government was located on the Continent. At the end of the sixteenth century its members counted several thousands. They were drawn from the whole realm but the merchants of provincial towns were organized as separate bodies though affiliated to the London company. The Merchant Adventurers constituted a regulated company, that is, membership was open to all who paid its admission fees and acquiesced in its control. Within its sphere of influence a regulated company had a complete monopoly of trade backed by the authority of the English state. The sphere of the Merchant Adventurers was the Netherlands, the principal market for English cloth; and two treaties concluded by Henry VII (the Magnus Intercursus and the Malus Intercursus) confirmed the privileged position which they enjoyed there. The enemies of the company were the 'interlopers' who were outside the fellowship but 'intermeddled' with its trade, basing their right to defy its monopoly on the traditional 'Englishman's liberty.' The system of chartered companies —two existed in the middle ages, namely the Merchant Adventurers and the Merchant Staplers, but subsequently they numbered a dozen—was recommended by certain advantages. It gave to merchants a recognized status as the members of a powerful corporation. At the same time it compelled them to submit to the discipline imposed upon peasant, artisan and trader alike, in which the individual was consciously subordinated to the interests of the community as interpreted by the majority. It also afforded the government an instrument by which it could direct oversea trade into the appropriate channels and ensure the payment of customs duties. Its great drawback was that it curtailed competition and checked enterprise; but it is difficult to determine how far the restrictions on individual initiative were detrimental to commerce in its early phases.

The expansion of English trade is reflected in the writings of contemporaries. A national policy was gradually formulated, and in substance it foreshadowed the mercantilist doctrines which moulded English economic thought down to the nineteenth century. The author of the *Libelle of Englyshe Polycye*[1] advanced the bold claim that England should control the commerce of the world. His thesis was that her command of the Straits of Dover, 'the wall of England,' enabled her to dominate the trade routes of

[1] Fifteenth century.

western Europe. The Emperor Sigismund upon his visit here had exhorted Henry V to guard Dover and Calais 'as your tweyne eyne to keep the narowe see.' The importance of the Straits lay in the fact that Flanders with her great cosmopolitan ports was the staple of all 'the nations of Christendom,' whose trade 'must needs pass by our English coast.' This placed them in our power; and since 'the wool of England sustaineth the commons' of Flanders, we were also in a position to ruin Flemish manufactures. Thus the whole world must necessarily seek our friendship and good will. Yet England was neglecting her opportunities by allowing the navy to fall into decay; and for the ship represented on English coins our enemies in derision were bidding us 'set a sheep.'

The *Libelle* devoted special attention to our commercial relations with the great Italian cities. It praised the Genoese because they brought us useful commodities—cloths of gold, silk, cotton, gold, wood, oil and pepper. But the trade of Venice and Florence was bitterly condemned; it was considered an intolerable evil that we should exchange our valuable commodities for extravagant trifles.

'The great galleys of Venice and Florence
Be well ladened with things of complacence,
All spicery and of grocer's ware,
With sweet wines, all manner of chaffare [merchandise],
Apes and japes [buffooneries] and marmusettes [monkeys]
    tailed,
Nifles [nicknacks], trifles that little have availed,
And things with which they fetely [cleverly] blear our eye,
With things not enduring that we buy.
For much of this chaffare that is wastable
Might be forborne for [as] dear and deceivable . . .
Thus these galleys, for this liking ware
And eating ware, bear hence our best chaffare,
Cloth, wool and tin . . .'

The *Libelle* insisted that the carrying trade should be in

English hands, and it sought to restrict the duration of foreign merchants to a period of forty days.

> 'And that they might be put to certain
> To go to host as we there with them do.'

The contention that England was in a position to exercise supremacy over all other countries was the motif of another work entitled *On England's Commercial Policy*; yet here it was based not on the ground of our strategic situation but on our industrial resources. No nation was able to dispense with English commodities, wool and cloth, and this gave us a hold by which 'we might rule and govern all Christian kings.' It counselled further that we should sell our wares dear. The authors of both poems were in fact essentially mercantilist in their standpoint. They shared the view that foreign countries by obtaining our goods enriched themselves at our expense: it was reserved for a later age to recognize that in a fair exchange both parties to a contract may equally benefit. They were anxious therefore that England should not part too easily with her products by exchanging them for mere trifles or by selling them too cheaply. It is transparent that the policy of 'economic penetration' as an instrument of political power was well understood five hundred years ago.

While the fifteenth century remained wedded to the traditional principles of economic statecraft, new horizons were dawning; and with the close of the middle ages a process of enlightenment set in. The native wool supply or the location of the staple abroad ceased to be counters in a game of diplomacy which sacrificed economic realities to dreams of conquest. English sovereigns ceased to be preoccupied with sterile schemes of territorial aggrandizement on the Continent of Europe. The glamour of the Orient and the call of a new world in the west were now beginning to cast their spell upon the minds of Englishmen and to enlarge their vision. Voyages of discovery revealed to the nation its true element, the sea; and its true destiny, the expansion of the English people.

PART II
THE AGE OF MERCANTILISM

Chapter Four

THE GROWTH OF INDIVIDUALISM

I. INDUSTRY AND COMMERCE

Industry

The oft-quoted expression, 'The end of the middle ages,' must not be interpreted to imply that there was an abrupt ending either to their characteristic institutions or to their basic economic concepts. These were carried on into the age of mercantilism to provide, in a different setting and with ever-diminishing vitality, the framework of an ordered society—until in the course of centuries by insensible degrees the old order was completely merged in the new. In this section we shall endeavour to describe the long drawn-out conflict between the corporate structure of society with its rural courts, urban gilds and oversea trading companies, and the dissolving influences of individualism with its insistence on free enterprise untrammelled by external control.

When the invention of printing and the discovery of America combined with the Renaissance and the Reformation to usher in the modern era, the traditional fabric of mediaeval economy continued to persist. To the naked eye England still seemed to be a land whose economic life was organized on a communal basis. Her agriculture was regulated by the village courts and her industry by the craft gilds; moreover the principle of association was extended to new branches of foreign commerce, so that Bacon even concluded that 'trading in companies is most agreeable to the English nature.' Actually the corporate system had been undermined by the subtle infiltration of the spirit of individualism, whose progress was for a long period so unobtrusive that it has largely escaped attention.

Individualism as a force in English society is almost as

75

old as the corporate system itself. Yet for centuries it remained the weaker force, and it sought to express itself inside the communal shell and not apart from it. In the village it manifested itself in the husbandman who added acre to acre in the open fields, or carved a holding out of the waste land, or accumulated a stock of corn for sale in the urban market, or purchased his emancipation from labour services. The notion that mediaeval rural economy was unprogressive is a travesty of the actual conditions which prevailed. The increasing mobility of real property gave rise to a land market in which holdings or fractions of holdings exchanged hands freely: an incipient capitalism was shattering the primitive equality of the original share-holders in the common fields: the customary system of tillage, in response to the growing demand for wool and corn, began to break down with the spread of piecemeal enclosures and profit-making husbandry. There are, indeed, abundant signs that a more vigorous peasantry was springing up under the spur of a restless individualism. In the towns the spirit of initiative was revealed in the enterprise of those who outstripped their fellows in the race, who raised themselves to wealth and honour, who developed the woollen manu-facture, who opened up markets abroad, all the while retaining their status as members of the urban gilds. Alike in agriculture, industry and trade there were spirited pioneers of a brave new world and opportunities for the penetration of a capitalist mentality.

However the great transformation of the traditional economic structure was brought about when individualism was no longer content to play a subordinate part, and strove to free itself from the tangled network of communal regulations. In agriculture the conflict came to a head between those who wished to retain, and those who aspired to destroy, the historic field systems. As the result of an immense acceleration of pasture-farming, the open fields with their intricate pattern of proprietary rights and customary routine were swept away in a torrent of commercialism. Even when their survival preserved in an attenuated form the control of the village community, the latter was only a vestige of the powers once enjoyed by the agrarian courts. In the boroughs the craft gilds, whose regime was consecrated to the principle of stability, vainly endeavoured to discourage the growth of capitalism among their members by limiting the number of apprentices and prohibiting excess of competition. When opportunity came knocking at the door the more enterprising gild brethren, ambitious to pass their rivals in the race and become large employers of labour, were able to set authority at defiance by moving to outlying districts where the writ of the craft gilds did not run. Thus in agriculture and industry an insurgent individualism was in revolt against the cramping restrictions of a communal society. Alone in foreign commerce the corporate system persisted in its old strength and actually extended its province in new directions, owing to the unique circumstances in which oversea trade was carried on, though the independent traders were growing in numbers and self-assertion.

The sphere of industry furnishes the most signal example of individualism emancipating itself from the restraints of an environment hide-bound by custom. It is doubtless true that seventeenth and eighteenth-century England counted numerous small producers wedded to the antiquated methods inherited from their forebears. None the less it was not the small producer who, before the middle ages had run their course, converted England into an industrial country of which the staple export was no longer raw materials but manufactured goods. It was not the small producer whose highly specialized fabrics displaced the products of Flanders, once a workshop of the mediaeval world, and found a market in every known quarter of the globe. It was not the small producer who transformed English towns from squalid and sparsely inhabited villages into prosperous urban communities with fine gildhalls, hospitals, market crosses and 'bar gates,' or whose piety adorned the countryside with the magnificent churches which excite our admiration. These changes were wrought by the 'adventuring' spirit of the 'captains of industry'—such as the fifteenth-century Tame of Fairford, who as a sheep-master raised his own material and as a manufacturer worked it up into cloth.

The advent of the large producer, in the premier industry of the country, dates as far back as the fourteenth century; and by the end of the middle ages the great body of workers engaged in cloth-making depended upon the discretion and foresight of a capitalist class. Even a factory system emerges into the light of day in the sixteenth century. John Winchcombe of Newbury—pronounced by Fuller, the church historian, to be 'the most considerable clothier (without fancy and fiction) England ever beheld'—gathered weavers, spinners and carders under one roof.

> 'Within one room being large and long
> There stood two hundred looms full strong.'

William Stumpe took over Osney Abbey and Malmesbury Abbey, where (wrote the antiquarian Leland) 'every corner of the vast houses of office that belonged to the abbey be full of looms.' Tuckar of Burford, who 'daily employs five hundred of the king's subjects,' sought to gain possession of Abingdon Abbey. Other great industrialists whose names have come down to us include Humphrey Chetham of Manchester, Peter Blundell founder of the Free Grammar School at Tiverton, the Springs of Lavenham and Thomas Dolman of Newbury.[1] Indeed innumerable indications testify that the capitalist spirit, as evinced in the conception and execution of speculative undertakings, is older than the 'Industrial Revolution.' In addition to the 'captains of industry' just mentioned, there were far-sighted merchants such as Sir Edward Osborne who played a leading part in establishing trade with the Levant, and financiers

---

[1] When Dolman gave up cloth-making, the weavers lamented:
'Lord, have mercy upon us, miserable sinners,
Thomas Dolman has built a new house and turned away all his spinners.'

such as Sir Thomas Gresham who negotiated public loans and manipulated the monetary exchanges.

In the seventeenth century many notable men rose into prominence—among them Sir Edwin Sandys a principal member of the Virginia Company, Sir Josiah Child the chairman of the East India Company, and Sir Ambrose Crowley the famous ironmaster. One example of capitalist enterprise in the reign of William III discloses a type which is often viewed as the creation of modern finance. This was Alderman Sir Joseph Herne—a financier through whom the English government subsidized its allies in the war against France, an army contractor, a company promoter, a merchant and a shipowner. Ambitious men pushed themselves up from the ranks, carved out a career, and acquired a controlling interest in capitalist concerns. The history of a peasant family in Northumbria furnishes an illustration. The founder, James Cole, lived in the reign of Elizabeth: he was a blacksmith who developed into a tradesman selling fish and grindstones. His son, Thomas, extended his operations by laying out his money at interest and he bequeathed much of his wealth to his nephew, Ralph, a grandson of James. Ralph migrated to Newcastle, invested his money in collieries, and became one of the chief coal-owners on the Tyne. The careers of the 'captains of industry' and merchant princes, whose names are here recorded, reveal the heights which men of commanding ability could scale either by their natural gifts or by their seizure of opportunities; while the immense fortunes which they raised compel us to revise our impressions of the prospects afforded in former ages.[1] The rank and file of the business world did not win the glittering prizes that are reserved for the chosen few, though upon their shoulders was reared the broad structure of industry and commerce. The important role of the shopkeeper—the indispensable link in the chain which connects the producer with the final consumer—still

---

[1] Sir Ambrose Crowley the ironmaster, who died in 1713, left a fortune of £200,000. In modern values he was a millionaire.

awaits its historian, but the autobiography of William Stout (1665-1752) allows us to follow step by step the course of one successful shopkeeper in a provincial town. It indicates how diligence and thrift enabled retailers to build up a substantial competence, and to pass into the higher grade of wholesale dealers and sometimes of merchants 'adventuring' abroad.

Abundant evidence is now available to prove that mercantilist England possessed a complex society, which functioned in an increasing measure under business leadership and bore many of the hall-marks of a capitalist system. The entrepreneur had emerged as the outstanding figure; and his activities were writ large over the whole field of economic endeavour, alike in the staple industries of the realm (cloth, coal and iron), in oversea trade and in the domain of public policy. His influence gradually permeated every branch of the national economy. The mediaeval fabric was profoundly modified in order to create scope for his enterprise: the chartered boroughs were forced to surrender their monopolistic claims so that he might draw upon cheaper supplies of labour in rural areas: the official regulation of industry was discredited by the steady advance of *laissez-faire* principles. The entrepreneur was the powerful dissolvent of a communal regime which had been organized on the basis of craft gilds and agrarian courts: he was equally the architect of the new England that rose upon the ruins of the old order. For good or evil it was the forces of individualism which marked out the path of progress, and won for this country the distinctive status which it enjoyed long before the nineteenth century. When the steam engine was harnessed to industry and transport it found an environment prepared for its reception—above all, a class of entrepreneurs accustomed to large-scale production, the handling of labour, the utilization of credit instruments, the dependence on imported materials and the requirements of distant and varied markets. The 'Industrial Revolution' came first to England principally because she already had a rich and diversified economic life, and—more than any other nation —had developed her industrial, commercial and banking institutions on lines which facilitated an extensive outlay on machinery and buildings.

The rise of individualism and the advent of capitalism cannot be explained alone in terms of self-interest, although the acquisitive instinct has been in all ages a potent influence in shaping economic conduct. Moreover the existence of capitalism before the Reformation forbids us to regard the capitalist spirit as the product of Puritanism. The explanation must be sought primarily in the impersonal and imponderable forces which govern the affairs of men. Three main factors have contributed to the evolution of a capitalist society— the extent of the market, the division of labour, and the nature of the processes. In the first place, where the market is local, it may be supplied by independent bodies of craftsmen. In the second place, where the division of labour is small, co-operation may be possible between the various groups of artisans without bringing them under unified direction. In the third place, where the processes require only a negligible amount of fixed capital in the form of appliances, it may be provided by the workers themselves. In the light of these factors we can best account for the development of industry on capitalist lines. An expanding market and a corres- ponding advance in production called for an intricate organization, while it also made the investment of capital a profitable venture; the division of labour—especially in the textile manufacture—seemed to necessitate a closer cohesion of its interdependent branches; and in other occupations the capital expenditure increased as the processes grew more difficult, for instance, in coal-mining and glass-making. The decisive influence was the first. In the face of the rising demand at home and abroad, it was found impracticable to maintain a procedure under which the market was supplied by small producers working on their own. Hence it was inevitable for the older industrial system, based on the co-operation of independent craftsmen, to be superseded by the entre-preneur as the master builder of the new economic order, in which the control of industry was transferred to employers of labour who stood outside the ranks of the manual workers.

Let us glance first at the home market. The myth that in former centuries England was a land of self-sufficing communities—where each locality, isolated from its neigh-bours, subsisted on its own produce—dies hard. Even in the middle ages there existed a national demand for the specialized wares of particular districts distributed through-out the realm by the fairs, and the cultivators of the soil found the means to purchase them by raising a surplus of corn for sale in the towns. If the oft-repeated generalizations as to the local range of the mediaeval market are misleading, still less are they applicable at a later period. In the Jacobean age London drew its supplies of broadcloth from the west country, worsted cloth from East Anglia, kersies from Yorkshire, coal from Newcastle, cheese from Cheshire, butter from Suffolk, wheat from the home counties; and the metropolis was unique only in the size, not in the nature, of its requirements. Native produce was not limited to a national market: it furnished also the needs of an inter-national market. It included wool, England's golden fleece; cloth of which it was said in later days that almost half of Europe wore England's 'livery;' and a miscellany of other articles. The growth of the international market constituted one of the epoch-making developments which gave a distinctive character to the age of mercantilism. After the discovery of America and of a fresh sea route to India, the products of this country ceased to be confined to 'a very small part of the earth'—Europe and Asia Minor: henceforth they found their way to the hemisphere in the west and to the empire of the Mogul in the east. Two new worlds, as Adam Smith justly said, were rendered accessible to the industry of Europe. The consequences made them-selves felt both in respect of the volume of production and the increased trend towards industrial specialization. Near the end of the seventeenth century it was calculated that the annual contribution to the national wealth made by the colonial and Indian branches of commerce was no less than three times that accruing from the European branch.

In opening up an unlimited field of enterprise, the extension of the market abroad was at once a challenge and a stimulus to the skill and ingenuity of the entrepreneur. Intercourse with India gave a marked impulse to the art of navigation, since distant voyages necessitated the building of 'goodly ships of such burthen as never were formerly used in merchandise.' This benefited the shipbuilding and carrying trades, while in addition woollen goods were exported in exchange for silks. Further the industry of calico-printing was exploited here by 'some of Britain's unnatural children, whom we call drapers,' who 'set all their arts to work to mimic the more ingenious Indians.' The prospect that the upstart cotton manufacture might displace the old-established woollen manufacture provoked acute dissensions, which have repeatedly recurred down to the present day whenever a vested interest is menaced by new improvements in industry or transport. 'I question not,' said one writer, 'but we shall have cotton cloth and knaves to make it a fashion and fools enough to wear it.' The fashion soon spread and—

> 'Our Ladies all were set a gadding,
> After these Toys they ran a madding
> And like gay Peacocks proudly strut it,
> When in our Streets along they foot it.'

The American colonies—another 'main branch' of England's wealth, described by the customs officials after the Restoration as 'his majesty's Indies'—absorbed a wide sweep of commodities, and they fulfilled the anticipations that the New World would 'create a new commerce.' At their first foundation they needed cattle and foodstuffs, arms and ammunition: subsequently their growing population took from England textiles, iron wares, shoes, hats, horses, household furniture and provisions such as flour, beer, cheese and butter. While the plantations opened up a fresh demand for the products of the parent state, they also developed into fresh sources of supply. On the eve of the War of Independence they accounted for as much as one-third of the oversea trade of the mother country. Apart from the beneficial reaction upon English industry and shipping, the obstacles to trade in Europe served (as in our own times) to accentuate the importance of the colonial market. Indeed England may be said to have called in the New World to offset the tariffs of the Old. In America trade followed the flag: in India, as also in Africa, the flag followed trade.

We may observe, at this point, that the discovery of America exerted a profound influence on England not only by extending the range of her markets but also in the sphere of monetary prices. The influx of precious metals from the New World served to promote the growth of a class of entrepreneurs, partly because it made the national wealth more liquid, and partly because the rise in prices swelled profits and so encouraged investments in industrial and commercial enterprises. In the middle of Elizabeth's reign men spoke of 'the great store and plenty of treasure which is walking in these parts of the world, far more in these our days than ever our forefathers have seen in times past.' Notwithstanding Spain's persistent efforts to keep intact the treasure which she drew from the Peruvian mines, it was drained away by the Dutch War of Independence, the English privateering expeditions and an adverse balance of trade. The precious metals in consequence were distributed over Europe. A large portion reached these shores. 'How many millions we have taken from the Spaniard,' exclaimed an Elizabethan writer, 'is a thing notorious.' The circulation of American silver produced an abrupt rise in the general level of prices, which caused an economic revolution in the sixteenth century and foreshadowed a political revolution in the seventeenth century. Owing to the fall in the value of money, rents rose sharply but rates of wages did not keep pace with prices.

The trend towards an individualist society was powerfully re-inforced by the institution of a more flexible system of industrial finance. Five significant developments facilitated the accumulation and employment of capital, and so created the requisite conditions for the growth of free enterprise. The first was the increase of wealth derived from the gains of those who produced raw materials and those who traded in them. The second was the influx of foreign investments which were attracted to this country at a much earlier date than historians have hitherto recognized: in the early seventeenth century Dutch capitalists financed English merchants as well as schemes of land drainage, and after the Restoration they provided money for the rebuilding of London. The third was the universal use of credit which enabled the fabric of industry and commerce to rest upon an infinitely wider foundation. It is a common misconception about the older economy that the credit system was almost non-existent. It is evident that if every transaction had to take place on a cash basis, the economic mechanism would have operated only in a very contracted field. The remarkable extent to which credit facilities prevailed in the middle ages is evinced both by the wool trade and by the abundance of mercantile debts relating to all kinds of business matters. The importance of credit grew enormously in the age of mercantilism. It was officially stated in the seventeenth century that a great part of English trade was conducted on a credit basis—one merchant in the reign of James I owed £20,000 and another in the reign of Anne £70,000. The instrument of credit transactions was the bill of exchange, whose usefulness is reflected in the measures taken to invest it with legal sanction and a negotiable character.

The fourth development was the advent of the modern

banking system. The money-lender was a familiar figure in English mediaeval society—we meet with the first known Christian usurer in the twelfth century[1]—but presumably as a rule he loaned his own capital. The practice of deposit banking started when he began to make advances with money entrusted to him by others who received remuneration in the form of interest. Among those who conducted financial operations the goldsmiths emerged as the most prominent by the middle of the seventeenth century. They grew accustomed to take custody of 'any man's money' and pay it out at his direction. Roger North relates how his brother, an eminent merchant in the Levant trade, 'hath come home in great amazement at his own greatness; for the banking goldsmiths came to him upon the Exchange with low obeisances, "hoping for the honour"—"should be proud to serve him," and the like; and all for nothing but to have the keeping of his cash. This pressing made him the more averse to that practice; and, when his acquaintance asked him where he kept his cash, he said: "At home; where should he keep it?" They wondered at him as one that did not know his own interest.' The goldsmiths used their deposits to make loans to merchants and needy landowners and above all to the government. Owing to the influx of American silver, the sovereign was no longer able to 'live of his own;' and the expedients adopted by the Early Stuarts to supply the deficiencies of their income involved them in a constitutional struggle with Parliament. After the Restoration the king relied habitually upon the goldsmiths for advances in anticipation of the revenue; but when the 'stop of the Exchequer' (December 1671) suspended the payments due to the government bankers, the breach of faith had its nemesis in a high rate of interest. Obviously a system under which the government raised mortgages on the revenue from

---

[1] The high rates of interest in the middle ages were due to the mistake of condemning all interest instead of excessive interest. Where the taking of any interest at all was a crime the lender required a substantial inducement to face the risk. Bishop Grosseteste (1253) asserted that Jewish lenders treated borrowers more fairly.

private bankers at ruinous rates could not continue indefinitely. The Revolution of 1688 by making England a participant in the continental struggle against France forced Parliament to face the real situation, and the solution was found in the creation of a national funded (that is, long-term) debt, on the basis of which was erected the Bank of England in 1694 to serve as a public agency for government borrowings. The Bank enjoyed the monopoly of joint-stock banking down to the nineteenth century, yet private banks still persisted. While in the metropolis the goldsmith developed into a banker, in the provinces merchants, manufacturers and shopkeepers turned bankers: thus Lloyd was an ironmaster and Barclay a linen draper. At the middle of the eighteenth century country banks mustered barely a dozen though at the close they had mounted to nearly four hundred.

The banks promoted the growth of industry and commerce in two ways. They created another form of credit instrument through the issue of bank notes, which for large payments became current in lieu of specie. Notes were issued by the Bank of England and by the country banks; the private banks in London discontinued the practice and cheques took their place. The various kinds of paper credit —bills of exchange and bank notes—enlarged the currency and broadened the basis of the credit structure: consequently they served in the nature of new resources and thereby quickened trade and manufactures. The other notable service rendered by the banks was the advance of loans which provided the entrepreneur with the means to extend the range of his operations and embark upon fresh enterprises. The use of borrowed capital on a considerable scale was made possible by the abandonment of the mediaeval attitude towards the 'damnable sin' of usury. The legal toleration of interest, which was fixed at 10 per cent. in the sixteenth century and at 5 per cent. early in the eighteenth century, marked a revolutionary change in public opinion; and it gave a clear indication of the decay of the traditional ethics under the insistent pressure of an expanding economic system.[1]

The fifth development in the sphere of finance was the employment of a joint-stock. Industry was financed not only by independent entrepreneurs utilizing their own or borrowed capital but also by joint-stock companies and partnerships. From the sixteenth century onwards these institutions furnished an important source of capital, since they enabled a concern whose nature or size demanded large sums to derive support from a circle of investors. Undertakings in which the entrepreneurs were responsible both for the circulating capital (materials and wages) and fixed capital (buildings and plant) might necessitate an outlay beyond the resources of individuals. The beginnings of joint-stock companies are connected with enterprises of this kind, for instance, the copper industry, coal-mining, the iron industry, glass-making, etc. Hence the modern methods of financing industry were being widely practised as early as the seventeenth century; and as a corollary two vital features of the present industrial system were already known in former ages. The first was the diffusion of the ownership of capital consequent upon the system of joint-stocks and (in the case of the domestic industries) the workers' property in their instruments of production—spinning and weaving appliances, cutlery tools and the like. The second was the separation of the ownership of capital and the functions of management—a divorce which occurs in joint-stock companies when the capitalist who invests money in a business ceases to be identical with the entrepreneur who is entrusted with the conduct of the business. The growth of joint-stock companies gave rise during the seventeenth century to a phenomenon similar to that which we are apt to consider peculiar to modern times—namely, 'that new mistery we call stock-jobbing.' One of the most memorable episodes in the history of the stock market was the South Sea Bubble

[1] The usury laws, to which legal exceptions were made at different times were not finally repealed until 1854.

88

(1720) which affords a parallel to the crash on the American stock exchange in 1929. The national excitement found vent in an outburst of frantic speculation. Men hastened to borrow money to buy shares, and women sold their jewels. On January 30, 1720, £100 stock in the South Sea Company could be bought for £129: on June 24, 1720, the price reached £1050. The Bubble was soon pricked; shares fell even more rapidly than they had mounted; and those who had bought beyond their means were ruined.

Industrial capitalists were drawn mainly from merchants engaged in handling raw materials or finished products, as well as from craftsmen who had risen from the ranks. Not all were of purely native origin. Alien entrepreneurs introduced numerous 'useful trades' and helped to build up the industrial supremacy of England. The successive waves of foreign settlers both 'captains of industry' and craftsmen —Flemings in the fourteenth, Dutch and Walloons in the sixteenth, French Huguenots in the seventeenth, and others who came in later centuries—are therefore notable landmarks in English history. Many of them were exiled from their own land through religious persecution which, like racial persecution in the twentieth century, enriched the state where they found an asylum; and they were welcomed by the government not only as refugees but as invaluable assets. Their immigration takes status as one of the major influences in England's economic development. Every branch of economy was stimulated by the inestimable services which they rendered. They introduced the 'new draperies' in the woollen industry, revived the decaying fortunes of the silk industry, started the making of fine linen, established the copper and brass industries, practically created the glass-making industry, promoted the growth of the steel and cutlery trades, developed the manufacture of china and paper and cordage, provided the engineering skill to drain the Fens and make harbours, and improved the art of dyeing. Their technical skill and expert knowledge of the industrial arts enabled this country to wrest from its rivals the secrets of important industries and become a workshop of the world; while the national fibre was greatly strengthened by the infusion of new blood.

The counterpart of mobility of capital is mobility of labour. We need to revise our notions of the immobility of the older English society: the practice of internal migration was a common phenomenon in early times. The stability of agrarian life was often apparent rather than real, and its conservatism was impotent to prevent massive changes. In the fourteenth century, after the Black Death, the discontent of the peasantry with the burdens of villeinage spurred on their ambition for better things, and the flight of serfs from the manor dispersed a considerable portion of the rural stock. In the next century industry began to prove more attractive than husbandry. It offered a wider scope to men of initiative and enterprise, who craved for new opportunities to achieve wealth and status. Although in some districts peasant families have clung to one locality for hundreds of years, we have learnt from manorial rolls and Tudor subsidy rolls that in other districts the inhabitants shifted from generation to generation—clear evidence of the mobile state of the countryside. Another factor was the expansion of the woollen manufacture, which caused a reverse trend from the corporate boroughs to the 'townlets.' Artisans flocked into the country influenced by the easy access to water mills, the cheapness of provisions, and the desire to escape the financial oppression and industrial supervision of the craft gilds. Mobility also became a marked feature of the iron and coal industries. The former was situated where supplies of timber and water-power were available; the latter was dependent upon the location of the coal measures. They drew their workmen from every part of the kingdom, and agents were sent out to seek them. The migratory movement was not confined to the lower ranges of the industrial hierarchy, for manufacturers and merchants alike recruited their apprentices from a wide area. Nor was it confined to the natives of England. Irishmen helped to build and work the furnaces and forges at Furness, and hundreds of them crossed over to render assistance at harvest-time; while Scotsmen came southwards to man the keels at Newcastle.

The position of labour in the new economic order, which by easy stages dissolved the fabric of mediaeval society, attests the early growth of capitalism. The structure of industry was being reconstituted on lines which were incompatible with the survival of the master craftsman in an independent capacity.

We can best account for the rise of a wage-earning class if we bear in mind that the criterion of the wage system is not the ownership of the instruments of production but the ownership of the raw material. So long as the craftsman owned the material on which he was engaged (as in the gild stage) he was independent: he could dispose freely of the finished product: he worked for a price not for a wage. When, however, the craftsman worked on material provided by a capitalist (as in the domestic stage) he had no right of property in the goods which he made: he sold not the fruits of his labour but the labour itself. Thus the advent of capitalism, in the sense in which the term is here defined, implies a phase in industrial evolution where an employer hires labour to work up the material supplied by him. The work might still be performed in the home, but the contrast between the domestic worker owning the instruments of production and the factory worker has a social rather than an economic significance. It follows that Engels's famous assertion—'the proletariat was called into existence by the introduction of machinery'—betrayed ignorance of the fact that a wage-earning class possessing no resources but its technical skill and a few tools existed in England for several centuries prior to the factory age.

The process of evolution was already far advanced towards the close of the middle ages when the tide of industrial capitalism began to submerge the defences erected by the craft gilds, and the skilled artisan was reduced to dependence upon an employer. The oldest and most widespread of English manufactures—the woollen industry—was conducted on a capitalist basis, and by the sixteenth century the majority of textile workers were wage-earners. The entrepreneur or clothier supplied the carders, combers and spinners with their wool, the weavers with their yarn, the fullers and dyers with their cloth. At every stage of production he owned the material, directed the processes, and disposed of the finished product. Even the most rapid survey of the industrial scene in the age of mercantilism discloses numerous other manufactures, besides the woollen, which were managed on capitalist lines.

In the cotton industry, as is indicated by the career of Humphrey Chetham one of the architects of Manchester's greatness, prominent makers carried on substantial operations early in the seventeenth century. In the silk industry 'workmasters' or silkmen were the employers of the silk weavers, and here the modern factory system had its beginnings early in the eighteenth century—Thomas Lombe was to silk what Richard Arkwright half a century later was to cotton. Capital for the development of a native linen industry was provided by joint-stock companies. In the hosiery industry frame-work knitters often worked on an employer's material and sometimes on an employer's frame. Nor was the capitalist system limited to the textile industries. Coal-mining was essentially a capitalist undertaking in which not only the hewers but the transport workers were wage-earners. Inasmuch as it was impossible to forecast the expenditure involved owing to the costly hazards of water and fire, it was peculiarly a field for capitalist speculation, and it presents the most striking examples of the sinking of capital in industrial ventures. In tin-mining the appearance of the capitalist producer was revealed already in the fourteenth century, when 'Abraham the Tinner' had in his employment over three hundred workers; and similar to other industries there were early complaints of the exploitation of labour. In the iron industry every stage of the extractive and manufacturing processes was, with a few exceptions, organized on a capitalist footing. The furnace and the forge were capitalist enterprises in which the raw material and fuel were owned and the product marketed by an entrepreneur, while capital was also invested in extracting the mineral as well as in the conversion of the metal into finished products. The copper and brass industries furnish the earliest instances of the formation of joint-stock companies to run a business which demanded buildings and expensive plant. The glass industry involved the disbursement of large sums for furnaces. The building industry together with the manufacture of paper, soap, salt and a variety of other commodities, conformed to the character of a capitalist business.

All these concurrent indications of the prevalence of capitalism in English industry—prior to the introduction of machinery—justify the conclusion that a capitalist society was no new creation when the great inventions inaugurated its second phase, that of power-driven machinery. Side by side with the small independent producer, working under his own roof on his own materials and with his own tools, there already ranged the large producer of the modern pattern. Long before the advent of the factory age the capitalist employer had become the pivotal figure in industry, whose organization was controlled and dominated by him.

The effects of the changed status of the workers, now transformed into a wage-earning class, were momentous. The strained relations, which at once developed between employers and employed, provoked an acute conflict of capital and labour protracted over many centuries. The fundamental divergence of interests was manifested in chronic disputes over wages. The employer treats wages primarily as the price paid for a commodity, while to the workman they are the means of subsistence; and this clash of concepts produces the bitter fruit of industrial strife.

The argument which passed for current coin in the nine-teenth century was familiar in former epochs: 'Cheapness of labour, and consequently the cheapness of goods, is the only means to increase their consumption either at home or abroad,' and so stimulate the demand for labour. More-over it is significant to observe that, as in later ages, the cause of industrial unrest was not low wages alone but also unemployment, for insecurity with its unsettling reaction on the standard of life is more demoralizing than poverty. Even in normal times, apart from commercial crises, irregularity of work was a recognized trait of the industrial order at least from the sixteenth century. It was due partly to the ebb and flow of trade and partly to technical difficulties —the intermittent supply of yarn in the woollen industry, the deficiency of water-power in the iron industry, the seasonal demand for fuel in the coal industry. In short there existed a working class often poorly remunerated, exposed to the hazards of unemployment, already largely divorced from the soil, and frequently working away from the home. It is therefore not surprising to find that Dean Tucker in the first half of the eighteenth century considered that the relations of master and man 'approach much nearer to that of a planter and slave in our American colonies than might be expected in such a country as England.' The employer is 'tempted by his situation to be overbearing' and to believe that he 'has a right to squeeze [his workfolk] whenever he can.' The men are equally tempted 'to get as much wages and to do as little for it as they possibly can,' and to look upon their employer as 'their common enemy.' His observations serve as a further reminder that the realities of economic life anterior to the 'Industrial Revolution' did not correspond to the idyllic picture which is apt to be drawn. Disraeli's description in *Sybil* of two nations warring with each other within the confines of a single state was true not only of his own age but of an older England.

The tangible sign of the cleavage between capital and

94

labour, and of the friction engendered by it, was the growth of trade unionism which preceded the introduction of machinery. Indeed trade unionism was so far from being the outcome of machinery that the invention and adoption of machines were, partly at any rate, inspired by the hope of liberating employers from their dependence upon labour. As early as the fourteenth century there were formed associations of wage-earners, but it was the collapse of the benevolent autocracy which did much to stimulate the self-assertion of the working class and to awaken the latent instinct of self-preservation. The workers were driven by the abandonment of the industrial code, instituted by the state with some measure of regard for their interests and protection, to depend upon their own efforts. Manifestations of trade union activity are to be found in the manufactures of wool, cotton, silk, linen, iron and leather, among others; and they register the degree to which capitalism had permeated English industries. During the eighteenth century repeated laws were enacted against associations of working-men in various occupations, and the combinations laws of 1799 and 1800 were only the climax of a series of measures dating back to the opening decades of the century. They were, however, powerless to repress a widespread trade union movement which persisted throughout the eighteenth century and bequeathed its traditions to later generations.

An analysis of the industrial structure reveals the extent to which the entrepreneur had assumed direction of the economic mechanism. At every stage of production and marketing we have evidence that men endowed with organizing abilities were finding a wider field for the exercise of their talents than lay within the four walls of their town.

Observe, first, that there had already developed an elaborate machinery for the distribution of raw materials. The kingdom was treated as a single economic unit upon which any locality could draw for the satisfaction of its

95

own special requirements. Thus the numerous industries which consumed large quantities of coal were able to obtain their fuel even when they were situated remote from the coal mines, and the wool merchants linked up the manufacturing districts with distant sources of supply. Moreover the importation of cotton, silk, flax, Spanish wool and Swedish iron, shows that manufacturers of cotton in Lancashire, Cheshire, Derbyshire and Dorset, manufacturers of silk in London, Derby, Coventry, Norwich and Macclesfield, manufacturers of linen in a dozen English counties, manufacturers of 'Spanish cloth' in the west country, and Sheffield cutlers famed in the days of Chaucer for their knives, were not precluded from utilizing materials produced in Europe and Asia on the one hand and in the New World on the other.

Observe, next, the scale of production. It is usual to associate the capitalist system with great undertakings. Small-scale production does not afford scope for the faculty of organization which is displayed in co-ordinating the various technical processes, in combining division of labour with supervision from a common centre, and in seeking out new markets both to provide raw materials and to absorb the manufactured articles. There is ample evidence of large-scale production in the seventeenth and eighteenth centuries. In the woollen and worsted industries makers of cloth were engaged in a substantial way of business—it was not unknown for clothiers to employ 1,000 workfolk, although not everyone on the clothier's books worked for him alone: in the silk industry master throwers kept 500 to 700 operatives and even 1,500: makers of sail cloth hired 5,000 or 6,000 persons: a salt-maker had 1,000 workers: a manufacturer of small metal wares ('toys') 600: a lace-maker and a calico-printer 200 or 300: a hat-maker and a glass-maker 100 apiece. These examples could be multiplied, but they are sufficient to refute the assertion that 'the class of capitalist employers was as yet but in its infancy.' Large undertakings constituted, in fact, a recognized feature of the extractive and manufacturing industries in earlier centuries, and they are an unmistakable proof of the functioning of the entrepreneur.

The size of the business unit might yield opportunities for the emergence of integrated concerns—this discloses an aspect of capitalism which is often looked upon as new. Thus in the iron industry it was normal for the owner of the furnace and forge to control part, at any rate, of the sources of his raw materials (iron ore, wood and coal), and he even extended his activities to the metal trades and worked up the iron into finished goods. The seventeenth-century establishment of Sir Ambrose Crowley presents a notable instance of an integrated business: it carried on all operations from the production of bar iron to the making of iron wares. In the copper industry there existed companies which owned copper mines, smelting works, rolling mills, manufacturing shops, together with ships for the transportation of materials. In the woollen industry the west country clothier concentrated in his hands every process of cloth-making from the time the wool was carded and spun until it was woven, fulled and 'finished'—a clothier might possess the flock from which he obtained his supply of raw material, and he might be a merchant exporter. In the coal industry the coal-fitters, who became the link between the sellers of coal and the shippers, sometimes owned the ships; and the hostmen who were the sole coal merchants at Newcastle sometimes owned the mines.

In certain respects the most striking manifestation of an entrepreneur regime is the creation of cartels, for the attempt to set up a controlled market presupposes an advanced phase in industrial evolution. Cartels can be traced back far beyond nineteenth-century capitalism. A cartel in the English coal industry came into being at the close of the middle ages and survived intermittently into the last century. It was a highly-organized type of trade association which exhibited all the principal devices of a controlled market and a rigid monopoly: it restricted membership, fixed prices, limited output, assigned each member a percentage of the output, and exacted contributions to a 'pool' to penalize those who exceeded their allotted quota and to subsidize those who fell short of it. At the distributing end of the coal trade the London market was exploited by combinations in every grade of middlemen through whose hands the commodity passed. Nor did the difficulties of communication, on which historians are apt to lay undue stress, daunt the London coal merchants; they instituted a system of intelligence by which they knew whether supplies at Newcastle were plentiful or scarce, and whether a coal fleet was at sea or held back by contrary winds; and they used their knowledge to 'rig' the market with a view to manipulating prices.

The prevalence of 'rings'—which entered into price agreements and regulated the supply of goods placed on the market in order to eliminate competition—was a feature of other industries besides coal, for example, iron and copper. Those who traded in provisions furnish parallel instances of tacit or overt understandings. Even the device of the 'boycott' is found among a 'ring' of London butter merchants, which at the end of the seventeenth century practically monopolized the butter trade with Suffolk by the threat to boycott local warehouse-keepers and carriers who acted for those outside the 'ring.' Another method of suppressing competition, familiar to alien importers in the early seventeenth century, was doubtless not unknown among native manufacturers: this consisted of 'dumping' wares on the market at low prices and of 'cornering' supplies of the raw material. These noteworthy examples of what is generally considered a modern practice—the tendency to make combinations and 'rings' among producers and distributors —serve to show that the fertile genius of the entrepreneur had already impressed its stamp upon a society which was fast assuming many of the traits usually identified with the most highly-developed form of a complex capitalist organization.

A seventeenth-century illustration of capitalist enterprise in the sphere of industry is the remarkable establishment erected in the north of England by the greatest ironmaster of the age, Sir Ambrose Crowley. It was conducted on a large scale since several hundred men were employed, but its signal feature was the autocracy which ruled it. Crowley created a 'model village' which anticipated Robert Owen's experiment at New Lanark. His iron works still retained some of their characteristic features in the early nineteenth century; and if they were known to Owen they may prove to be an unsuspected source from which the father of English socialism derived inspiration. Crowley laid down a code for the welfare of the workmen, made provision for the poor and sick through a contributory insurance scheme, instituted a school for the children—the schoolmaster was enjoined not to dismiss his scholars or absent himself 'upon any account of races, cock-fightings, rope-dancers or stage players'—and set up a body of arbitrators on which the workmen were represented. He displayed marked consideration for the self-respect of his workmen, instructing the 'surveyor' to 'have a great regard to what the workmen say and especially in hearing their allegations and reasons where they are rational.' Thus Crowley foreshadowed the leading principles of social reform in the nineteenth century together with the idea of devolution of control in industry. We have no reason to suppose that the Crowley regime, however exceptional it might have been, was in every respect unique: the survival of records is so purely a matter of chance that we must be careful not to draw misleading inferences from the paucity of evidence. We certainly get glimpses of other industrial establishments which drew labour from remote parts of the country, built houses, made loans to the workmen, and provided schools for their children.

The influence of the entrepreneur is evinced, not only in the intricate pattern of the production and marketing organizations of which he was the pivot, but in the variety and range of his industrial pursuits. 'The sort of men we call Undertakers,'[1] it was said near the end of the seventeenth century, 'are very instrumental in the public by advancing manufactures.' The introduction of a new branch of industry is generally a speculative undertaking which attracts those who are prepared to risk their capital in the hope of substantial returns. It was, therefore, owing to the exertions and sacrifices of the entrepreneurs that England was enabled to develop fresh industrial arts and attain a position of supremacy in world trade.

In enumerating the improvements which were discovered or adopted after the middle ages, one thing needs saying at the outset—namely, that they are not to be conceived as the manifestation of a newly-born spirit of capitalism created by the forces which the Reformation set in motion. The theory that industrial capitalism commences after the Reformation is disproved by the evidence given above. With this caution in mind let us take a bird's-eye view of the economic progress which England had achieved prior to the 'Industrial Revolution.' We have already alluded to the establishment of the 'new draperies' in the woollen industry during the second half of the sixteenth century. The same era witnessed the beginnings of machine-wrought hosiery, which resulted from the invention of the knitting-frame by William Lee in 1589; and the history of the cotton industry can now be carried back beyond the coming of the Armada. Silk, a mediaeval industry, grew into 'one of the most considerable branches of the manufactures of this kingdom' as a consequence of a revival in the seventeenth century; and in the next century even the linen industry was fairly widely distributed.

Outside the group of textiles a vital place in the national economy came to be occupied by coal and iron. Originally wood was not only the fuel for household consumption and manufactures of every kind but also the material

[1] In the seventeenth century the word 'undertaker' was used in the present sense of 'entrepreneur.' We still speak of an 'undertaking.'

for buildings, ships, carts, looms and tools. The growth of population and the expansion of industry (especially iron works) put an excessive strain upon native timber resources. The 'general destruction' of 'goodly trees' aroused national anxiety. 'No wood,' the warning was uttered, 'no kingdom.' The lament of the poet Drayton evinces that the ruthless exploitation of natural resources is an old phenomenon:

'These iron times breed none that mind posterity . . .
Jove's Oak, the warlike Ash, vein'd Elm, the softer Beech,
Short Hazel, Maple plain, light Aspe, the bending Wych,
Tough Holly, and smoother Birch, must altogether burn:
What should the builder serve, supplies the forger's turn;
When under public good, base private gain takes hold,
And we poor woeful Woods to ruin lastly sold.
This utter'd they with grief . . .'

Hence arose the need for extracting the subterranean mineral fuel in order to provide 'new fire' for the domestic hearth and for industrial requirements. The need was met principally by the rapid opening of the northern coal-beds. Newcastle was enthusiastically acclaimed:

'England's a perfect World! has Indies too!
Correct your Maps: Newcastle is Peru.'

The importance of the coal industry in the nineteenth and twentieth centuries is universally recognized. Its prominence in earlier ages has been obscured by focussing attention upon the use of coal for smelting iron ore and neglecting its relation to other fields of economic activities. In mercantilist England coal had grown into general usage as the indispensable fuel of the householder, and it was extensively consumed in a great variety of industries. Confined in mediaeval times mainly to workers in metal (smiths) and lime-burners, it came to be widely adopted. A French traveller in 1738 termed coal 'one of the greatest sources of English wealth and plenty' and 'the soul of English manufactures.' It was also employed in making iron wares though it was not suitable, on account of the sulphur in it, for smelting iron ore. In this way coal-mining was closely linked with the industrial progress of the country. Its historical significance is reflected further in the contribution which it made to the evolution of a capitalist society, and in the influence exerted on public policy (especially as regards price regulation) in the interests of the consumer. In addition the transport of coal along the coast or to the Continent was an immense stimulus to shipping, since it accounted for a large proportion of the mercantile marine and nourished a 'nursery for seamen;' its conveyance from the pits to the river-side led to the invention of 'railways' in the sixteenth century; and the drainage of water in the mines gave birth to the steam engine in the seventeenth century.

The economic importance of coal in the age of mercantilism was matched by the great advance in the metal industries. The extensive use of metals for both industrial and domestic purposes was revealed in a notable expansion of iron goods, though the home production of raw iron was hampered by a shortage of fuel. 'No particular manufacture can be named,' asserted Defoe, 'which has increased like this of the hardware;' and Burke described Birmingham as 'the toy-shop of Europe' because of its variety of small wares. A native industry of copper and brass was established in the sixteenth century as a result of the discovery of calamine. Other industries which were started or developed in the sixteenth and seventeenth centuries included alum, breweries, brick-making, glass, paper, salt, saltpetre, soap and sugar-refineries. Shipbuilding was stimulated by commercial intercourse with the Continent, the American plantations and India, as well as by the coasting trade in coal and other commodities; and the growth of a merchant navy laid the basis for an empire which rested on sea power. All these changes were far advanced prior to the introduction of machinery.

Thus England in the age of mercantilism was a busy hive of industry, in which specialization was pursued in a marked degree to serve a wide range of markets with varying tastes and fashions. Her mature status is evinced in the testimony of a correspondent who wrote in 1672: 'The English through all the world are counted the most ingenious in all manner of manufactures as cloth, serge, woollen stockings, silk stockings, both woven and knitted, all sort of leather, scarlet cloth, gloves, watches, knives, etc.' Long before the 'Industrial Revolution' the reputation of her wares had made England a workshop of the world.

The manifold developments which have been briefly sketched bear witness to the fertile activities of the entrepreneur. They were born of the restless spirit of the age—but inasmuch as the motive spring of human progress is intellectual curiosity, they had their counterpart in the foundation of the Royal Society. This body in its beginnings had close associations with the economic movements of the day. It set itself the task of gathering descriptions of mines and ores, iron-making, salt-making, cloth-making, paper-making and many other industrial arts. In these scientific inquiries into the actual workings of the economic mechanism was mirrored an England that had grown conscious of a boundless horizon and an illimitable field of new discoveries. Voltaire paid tribute to her technical contributions, when he pronounced that 'they entitle the age to be called the age of the English as well as that of Louis XIV.'

We have sought to indicate the salient features of the structure of industry which existed before the age of machinery. Perhaps the most prevalent misconception about its nature is the idealized picture often presented of the domestic system. It has been depicted almost in the light of a golden age where the artisan was his own master working as he pleased at his loom or bench, and where no rift between capital and labour marred as yet the social harmony. The current impression of the 'Industrial Revolution' owes much to the fact that its antecedents are viewed through rosy-tinted glasses. In reality the notion that English society passed from an age of gold to an age of iron is a poetical illusion. Admittedly the domestic system had one outstanding merit—the wide dispersion of the manufacturing community which contrasted favourably with the concentration in towns produced by the factory system. Spinning in particular was essentially a 'cottage' industry. The spinners were scattered over the whole countryside and the wool was conveyed by carriers or 'packmen' to depots established in the villages. The work was often carried on in the open air in streets and lanes; and even in the nineteenth century girls were to be found in the Highlands of Scotland herding on the hill-side busily spinning with the distaff. Nevertheless the domestic system was attended by many drawbacks which outweighed its merits.

First: there was no harmonious grouping of the industrial forces since employers and employees were separated by the barrier of wealth and status, and their relations were embittered by chronic disputes over wages. The domestic artisan might seem to enjoy greater social independence than the factory operative in the arrangement of his working day, though an independence which was purchased with twelve hours' labour a day was more nominal than real. Yet he was as economically dependent as the factory operative—despite the advantage that he might own all the instruments of production—for both alike were wage-earners.[1] Second: the embezzlement of the raw material was a frequent practice, and it was the principal defect in the eyes of the employer. Third: the long hours of labour worked under the early factory system were no novelty but a legacy of the domestic system when twelve hours constituted a normal working day. One writer (1700) remarked that 'no country but Great Britain can boast that after twelve hours' hard work its natives will in the evening go to football, stool-ball,

[1] Under the domestic system the weavers were not restricted to the service of one master; they might take work from several clothiers at once.

cricket, prison-base, wrestling, cudgel-playing, or some such vehement exercise for their recreations.' The state regulated the hours of labour in the reign of Elizabeth; and it instituted a monthly holiday during the Civil War—every second Tuesday in the month was to be a day of 'recreation and relaxation' for scholars, apprentices and other servants, and shops and warehouses were to be shut. Saturday evening was a closed time for spinning. A legend tells of a woman who appeared after her death to a fellow-culprit, displaying her burning hand with the words:

> 'See what I in Hell have won
> Because on Saturday I spun.'

Fourth: the factory system inherited another evil tradition, namely, that of infant slavery. The exploitation of child labour was no new practice but an integral feature of industrial life which met with general approval. The example of Germany—where 'every child, though but seven or eight years old, is put to work and is enabled thereby to get his own livelihood'—was held up to England. There, it was said, 'a man that has most children lives best whereas here he that has most is poorest. There the children enrich the father but here beggar him.' The eldest son of Crompton, the inventor of the mule, relates that 'soon after I was able to walk I was employed in the cotton manufacture;' and children assisted in making stockings as early as the age of four. In so far as the relations of parents and children were softened by feelings of natural affection, the evils of child labour might be mitigated. But one who was brought up under the domestic system declared that children 'were set to work as soon as they could crawl, and their parents were the hardest of taskmasters.' Fifth: the domestic worker, broadly speaking, was assured of less continuous employment than the modern factory operative, while the condition of an unemployed artisan was in some respects more unfavourable in former centuries. The mobility of labour was necessarily less in an age when migration was hindered by settlement laws[1] and the privileges of the corporate boroughs, and when the taking up of a new occupation was made difficult by the insistence on apprenticeship or some form of training which served to distinguish the 'legal' from the 'illegal' workman. Sixth: the connexion between agriculture and industry has been unduly stressed. The development of a proletarian class —that is, a class divorced from the soil, possessing no property, and living entirely upon wages—had made a considerable headway prior to the advent of the factory system. The opportunities for rural employment, available for men who were out of work, were not so frequent as is usually represented; all the indications are that the typical artisan was a landless artisan restricted solely to manufacturing. In any event men engaged in a sedentary occupation were unlikely to exhibit the physical qualities needed for farming operations—a fact overlooked by those who lay emphasis upon the combination of rural and industrial pursuits. Seventh: the invention of machinery did not destroy craftsmanship in the textile industries, where the monotonous routine of the work done by hand was already mechanical in character even before the adoption of mechanical devices.

This review of the economic conditions which prevailed under the domestic system applies more particularly to the west country—once the principal seat of England's greatest industry—as well as to East Anglia. In these areas capitalism had gained a footing from the earliest times, and there existed a highly-developed capitalist organization. In the north country (where nineteenth-century capitalism achieved its most signal triumphs) the traditional structure of society maintained its ground more successfully. The 'domestic manufacturers' or working clothiers of Yorkshire, the counterpart of the yeomanry in agriculture, were themselves manual craftsmen; and they enlisted the unstinted praise of contemporaries because of the friendly relations which subsisted

---

[1] Under the old poor law it was difficult to acquire the legal right to settle in any parish other than that of birth.

between masters and men, combined with equality of opportunity—the chance afforded to the workers of rising in the world.

It is the fashion to speak as though all industrial processes before the great inventions were performed in the homes of the artisans. Actually this was far from being the case since the domestic system was not universal. Apart from the extractive industries—agriculture and the mining of coal, iron, copper, tin, lead and alum—where the labourers naturally worked away from their dwellings, there were numerous occupations in which the operatives were concentrated under an employer's roof: in the woollen industry at the finishing processes, in the silk industry at the mills for throwing, in the linen industry at the factory for cambrics and lawns, in the iron industry at the furnace and forge, in the glass industry with its glass-houses, in the copper and brass industries with their smelting and battery works, in brewing, in brick-making, in building, in calico-printing, in net-making, in paper-making, in the pottery manufacture, in rope-making, in salt-making, in shipbuilding, in soap-boiling, in sugar-refining, in the tailoring industry, and in tapestry-making. This comprehensive list, which in the aggregate embraced the greater part of the working population (when the extractive industries are included), furnishes decisive proof that the 'Industrial Revolution' introduced no new form of industrial organization. In addition we occasionally find large establishments in other occupations which were normally conducted on a domestic basis—in the spinning and weaving branches of the woollen, silk and linen industries or in the production of metal wares. In all instances where the labour was done at the master's 'works' the operations would be carried on under the immediate inspection of the entrepreneur; and the general conditions in respect of discipline and regularity would not be essentially different from those of a modern factory—except that the dependence on water-power would result in spells of enforced idleness, which might be compared with the present-day practice of 'short-time' working in periods of slack trade.

The foregoing account may serve to dispel the common impression that England almost down to the nineteenth century was a country of peasant cultivators, where there was little industry and less trade and at most a network of independent artisans whose chief interests are represented as agricultural. The industrial community, according to the prevalent notion, was composed of small producers—handicraftsmen who worked under their own roof on their own materials and with their own tools, assisted by their families or a hired journeyman and apprentices, dividing their time between their cottage workshops and their farms, and supplying the neighbourhood with rude and unspecialized wares. A sprinkling of capitalists lurked obscurely in the background but they were not considered an integral, and much less an important, element in the older structure. In short the conventional view depicted a primitive economy, an immature industry, functioning for a local market. In the light of a fuller knowledge we can now present a more correct picture of what England was like before the nineteenth century. Owing to the revolutionary changes brought about by the growth of free enterprise, English industrial society in the age of mercantilism wore a widely different aspect from that generally portrayed. The key to its character must be sought not in the sphere of small producers but in the crucial position occupied by the entrepreneur. The latter found scope for his organizing ability in the enlarged scale of production based on a division of labour which was often minute. He found scope for his speculative instincts in sinking capital (whether his own, or borrowed, or provided by partners) in new industrial arts. He found scope for his technical insight in lowering the costs of production through an improved technique—the early utilization of coal, the erection of blast furnaces, and the adoption of innumerable mechanical devices. We shall find fresh evidence of his creative powers in the domain of foreign commerce.

Commerce

Although the fairs still occupied a considerable place in the internal economy of the country, their relative importance declined after the middle ages. The towns had steadily advanced in prosperity and now possessed the capacity to meet local requirements. The resident shopkeepers were supplied by wholesale merchants who used to travel all over England with droves of packhorses conveying great quantities of goods. The arduous existence of a 'travelling merchant' is depicted in the account given of a Lancashire merchant who lived in the early eighteenth century. 'He was from home the greater part of every year, performing his journeys leisurely on horseback. His balances were received in guineas and were carried with him in his saddle bags. He was exposed to the vicissitudes of the weather and to great labour and fatigue and to constant danger. In Lincolnshire he travelled chiefly along bridle-ways through fields where frequent gibbets warned him of his peril.' On the improvement of the turnpike roads the packhorses were replaced by waggons, and the 'travelling merchant' was succeeded by the 'commercial traveller' who rode out for orders carrying with him patterns in his bags.

The retail shops were of two kinds. In the metropolis and the more important towns they specialized in a single branch of trade, but elsewhere they were 'general' shops trafficking in all manner of wares. Thus Celia Fiennes, who rode through England on a side saddle in the reign of William and Mary, remarked that at Newcastle 'their shops are good and of distinct trades, not selling many things in one shop as is the custom in most country towns.' A provincial shopkeeper, William Stout of Lancaster, has fortunately left an autobiography which throws valuable light on contemporary business practices. Born in 1665 he sprang from yeoman stock: his father farmed a few acres. He received his education first at a dame school, then at the free school, and afterwards at a boarding school. When sixteen he was bound apprentice for seven years to a grocer and ironmonger, his father undertaking to pay a premium of £20 and to find his apparel. The shop was kept open until ten at night, though 'we were frequently called up at all times of the night to serve customers, [which] obliged us to have a bed in the shop.' Upon the expiry of his term he set up in business with a capital of £120 inherited from his father. He visited London to buy goods, paying each tradesman 'half ready money as was then usual to do by any young man beginning trade.' Altogether he furnished his shop with wares to the value of £300. He lodged in the shop of which the annual rent was £5, and boarded out at £5 a year for 'victuals and washing.' At the end of the first year he had made a profit of £50; at the end of nine years, upon giving up the retail trade, his 'clear estate' was £1,100. He became a wholesale grocer and supplied country shopkeepers. He also made unprofitable investments in 'adventuring' abroad, sending out merchandise to Virginia, Pennsylvania and Barbados. He retired from business when sixty-three years old worth £5,000, a substantial sum in relation to the purchasing power of the period, and he died at the age of eighty-seven.

Another class of vendors consisted of itinerant 'chapmen' who went from house to house selling by retail. They were frowned upon by the legislature from a general dislike of 'vagrant persons,' and viewed with strong disapproval by the resident traders since they escaped the burden of rent and rates; but they were acceptable to country dwellers who were spared the trouble and expense of a visit to the market town. The pedlars travelled either on foot or with horse, and carried a wide assortment of wares of which the following is a sixteenth-century list:

> 'What? dost thou not knowe that every pedler
> In all kinde of trifles must be a medlar?
> Specially in women's tryflinges.

Those use we cheafly above all things.
Gloves, pynnes, combs, glasses unspotted,
Pomanders, hookes and lasses knotted,
Broches, rynges, and all manner of bedes,
Laces, round and flat, for women's hedes.
Medyls, thred, thimbell, shers, and all such knackes.'

The foundations of an international trade had been laid
in the middle ages when connexions were established with
most European countries. In the sixteenth century it grew
considerably in volume and began to assume a world-wide
character. The exports of England penetrated into nearly
every part of the globe: her imports comprised the products
of four continents. A large portion of her population was
mainly dependent for its livelihood upon oversea markets.
Her commercial organization was highly developed on the
basis of companies, while the working of her credit system
and monetary exchanges reproduced in its essentials the
mechanism of modern business life. In short her economic
destiny appeared closely interwoven with that of other
nations, and in the age of mercantilism it was a common-
place that her 'prosperity and power depend on trade.' As
a seventeenth-century writer exclaimed: 'Trade is now become the Lady which in this present age is more courted
and celebrated than in any former.' Two outstanding developments stimulated the expansion of commerce and opened up
wider fields of opportunity to the entrepreneur. One was the
discovery of America and of a new sea route to India, which
created a fresh outlet for the energies of the mercantile class.
The other was the sense of nationalism, which became a
driving force to preserve economic independence by instituting direct trading connexions with countries hitherto monopolized by actual or potential enemies. In fact the efforts of
Elizabethan merchants to devise new channels of commercial
intercourse contributed not less to the security of England
than the exploits of Elizabethan seamen and the diplomacy
of Elizabethan statesmen. The success which crowned these

efforts is measured by the observation of the Venetian ambassador in the reign of James I that 'the English trade in all parts of the world with large capital;' and at the end of the seventeenth century England and Holland were coupled together as the two states which 'drive the greatest trades of all European nations.' England's foreign commerce was remarkable not only for the extent of her markets abroad but also for the variety of her exports and imports. This is convincingly demonstrated in a striking survey compiled by an Elizabethan merchant. A further token of progress was that the system of marine insurance, which was practised in the middle ages, was given a statutory basis at the beginning of the seventeenth century; while after the Restoration a famous 'coffee-house' (Lloyd's) became the meeting-place of the underwriters, whose name to our day perpetuates its memory.

Even a cursory glance at England's relations with the Continent shows how largely economics already entered into international politics. In the sixteenth century Spain occupied the foreground of the picture, in the seventeenth Holland, and in the eighteenth France. The first, Spain, was formerly one of the props of the English commercial system because she controlled or influenced the chief European markets for cloth; yet she was also the buttress of the Counter-Reformation, and this—together with her claim to appropriate the wealth harvested in South America, into which 'no other man ought to thrust his sickle'—produced a state of tension and then open war which was detrimental to trade. Holland was linked with England by close religious ties, and they shared a common aspiration in stemming the advance of the Counter-Reformation. Moreover Holland, the pattern of the nations, was constantly held up as a model to the English people and no other country has exercised a more profound influence on their economic development. Nevertheless these considerations did not prevent a succession of wars, since they were overridden by jealousies. The interests of the two states were everywhere in conflict. They were competitors in northern and south-eastern Europe, in the East Indies, in America and in Africa; the wealth garnered by the Dutch from fishing off the English coasts was a perpetual irritant; and the tariffs which they laid on English cloth in order to protect their own textile industry nourished the embittered feeling. The antagonism fostered by these grievances was reinforced when Holland seized the opportunity furnished by the Civil War to establish an undisputed ascendancy in the world's carrying trade, and it bore fruit in the acts of navigation and the three Dutch Wars. In the eighteenth century the French supplanted the Dutch in public estimation as 'our greatest and most dangerous rivals in trade.' Economic friction served to sharpen the edge of the national animosities which drew England and France apart, thus providing a conspicuous example of the interaction of politics and economics. The nature of the traffic, it was declared, enriched France 'whose power England ought not to increase;' and a tariff war paved the way for the second Hundred Years' War. In addition the belief that French imports exceeded English exports set the stage for a concrete application of the theory of the balance of trade.[1] The world was afforded the classic spectacle of protective tariffs carried to the point where they resulted in the almost complete eclipse of normal commercial relations between the two leading countries of Europe. After the Restoration the principal French products were either excluded or burdened with prohibitive duties; and during most of the eighteenth century Anglo-French trade was mainly in the hands of smugglers. To this impasse futile economic jealousies and the logic of protection inexorably led.

The unique prestige accorded to the merchants engaged in oversea trade reflects the exceptional appreciation in which this class of entrepreneurs was held. The public esteem was traditional, for in Anglo-Saxon times the merchant who thrice fared over the seas by his own means was

[1] See Chapter Six.

rewarded with the rank of nobility. In later times he had commercial agents, or 'factors' as they were called, in all parts of the world; but it was also a recognized feature of his training to travel abroad as a young man and make himself personally acquainted with the conditions of foreign markets. 'There are very few commercial houses,' it was said in the eighteenth century, 'but what send their sons abroad to inspect the state of the manufactures as well as to form connexions, and so promote the sale and extension of our manufactures.' It is significant that it was the normal practice in England, in marked contrast with the Continent, for the younger sons of gentlemen and 'sometimes of the nobility' to be 'bred' to trade 'without prejudice to their gentility.' High premiums, occasionally no less than one thousand pounds, were exacted from apprentices; and as a consequence they were largely recruited from the wealthier sections of the community. Individual merchants were often in command of considerable capital. The Venetian ambassador wrote home in the middle of the sixteenth century that among the Merchant Adventurers and Staplers 'there are many individuals possessed of from fifty to sixty thousand pounds sterling'—in terms of modern currency they were almost millionaires. The fact that merchants were commonly men of substance and credit meant that they were in a position to embark upon speculative undertakings. The American plantations provided an extensive field for investment, in which moneyed men sank and often lost their capital. The foundations of an empire in India were laid by a group of merchants at a meeting held in London in September 1599, presided over by the lord mayor, when it was decided to form an association to establish direct intercourse with India. English capitalists promoted other trading corporations such as the Eastland, Levant and Russia companies; they financed voyages to Africa which bore fruit in an immense accession of territory; and their efforts to capture the traffic in furs from the French resulted in the incorporation of Canada in the British Empire.

The growth of commerce, as evinced in the discovery of new markets and in the rapidly-expanding statistics of exports and imports, testifies to the existence of a vigorous and enterprising merchant class. 'The merchants of England,' it was affirmed in the seventeenth century, 'are an industrious people and lovers of trade. They do not upon small—no, not upon great—discouragements give it over.' None the less the communal system survived longer in the domain of foreign trade than elsewhere. The Englishman, like his mediaeval forebears, continued to conduct his business abroad not as an individual but as the member of a corporate body. He was bound by regulations of an all-pervasive kind which dictated to him in what places he might market his goods, in what quantities and with what stipulations. The many difficulties attendant on 'adventuring' abroad help to explain the success with which the companies engaged in 'feats of merchandise' asserted their exclusive rights long after individualism had emancipated itself in other directions. The circumstances of the age impelled merchants to assume the functions which are now the province of the state— guarding against the dangers of piracy at sea and robbery on land, presenting a united front against oppression and exploitation by alien potentates, maintaining embassies, and erecting forts. Thus the natural instinct of Englishmen to act in a corporate capacity, while it lapsed in the spheres of industry and agriculture, was strengthened in the sphere of oversea trade. Two types of companies were evolved—the regulated and the joint-stock. The broad distinction between them lay in the degree to which individual enterprise was tolerated. The regulated company was the older form of association; and its looser cohesion made it suitable for trafficking with countries where conditions were more settled. The joint-stock company was adapted for remoter lands where the normal risks of commerce were enhanced by political hazards. The posture of affairs might dictate an alternation of type—a company was sometimes regulated and at other times joint-stock. Every company had a territorial area assigned to it, in which the right of trading was restricted to its members.[1]

The regulated company was a corporation of merchants, each of whom traded on his own but was subjected to a common discipline—the 'old trade principles' laid down by the fellowship to which he belonged. Even the briefest survey of the 'common rules' of the Merchant Adventurers, the greatest of the regulated companies, discloses the narrow limits within which a merchant was confined in his operations. The by-laws covered all the aspects of trade. They stipulated that no member should sell his wares in any place inside the company's territory other than the 'mart' or 'staple' towns. Merchandise had to be shipped abroad in vessels chartered by the company, which sailed together at set times of the year. The continental market was held in appointed seasons during which commodities were offered for sale on certain days only in the week. A code of trading etiquette was prescribed—for instance, the enticing of customers was prohibited. More important still, a 'stint' fixed the volume of exports which a member might handle. The idea of a 'stint' was in accordance with mediaeval gild principles, it existed in the coal industry in the seventeenth century, and it is a feature of the modern cartel: hence it furnishes a remarkable illustration of the continuity of economic practices through centuries of growth and change.

---

[1] In the middle of the sixteenth century two companies, both regulated, existed—the Merchant Adventurers and the Merchant Staplers; before its close six new ones were established. The Russia Company (incorporated in 1555) was at first joint-stock and eventually regulated: in the eighteenth century, when the entrance fee had become nominal, it enjoyed a large part of Russia's foreign trade. The Spanish Company (1577, regulated) traded with Spain. The sphere of the Eastland Company (1579, regulated) was the Baltic lands—Scandinavia and Poland. The Levant Company (1581) alternated between joint-stock and regulated. The African Company (1585) began as a joint-stock and became regulated. The East India Company (joint-stock) received its charter on the last day of the sixteenth century. In the next century were founded the French Company (1611, regulated); the short-lived Canary Company (1665); the Hudson's Bay Company (1670, joint-stock) which traded with Canada; and the South Sea Company (1710, joint-stock) which had the monopoly of the English trade with the oversea empire of Spain under the Treaty of Utrecht (1713—the Assiento Pact).

The market was further controlled by the expedient of a restraint of shipping whenever the company wished to prevent a glut or produce a scarcity. Other regulations limited the maximum period of credit, imposed penalties on recalcitrant debtors, and endeavoured to maintain a high grade of quality by the exaction of penalties for wares found to be defective.

Although the chartered companies derived their privileged status from the king, they were destined one by one to succumb to the pertinacity of those who assailed the traditional structure of commerce in the name of economic liberty. The conflict between the companies and the interlopers or 'free traders' raised a thorny subject of controversy. It involved the crucial question whether communal discipline or individualism should gain the upper hand; or (as it was expressed in the seventeenth century) whether trafficking overseas could be 'possibly managed to the public and assured advantage of the commonwealth better by all English pretending merchants in a loose (which they call a frank and free) trade, than by merchants bred up in the mistery of this trade and associated together under order and government.' On behalf of the regulated companies it was claimed that they enjoyed 'ancient privileges' in foreign countries, which ensured them inviolability of person and property, speedy justice against natives, immunity from taxes and the right of autonomy. In addition they rendered public services by building 'many tall warlike ships,' by making loans to the state, by preventing frauds in the customs, and by continuing to buy goods when there was a stoppage of trade abroad. Above all, they established 'politic government' based on the ideal of a 'well-ordered and ruled trade.' This ideal, inherited from the middle ages and maintained down to the Revolution of 1688, embodied a philosophy of commerce in which 'adventuring' abroad was deemed a profession requiring training and experience, prices were kept at a high level, the standard of quality was guaranteed, and production was restricted. Upon these four fundamentals rested the communal organization of commerce.

The arguments in favour of an open trade show how the traditional outlook, embodied in the basic concepts, was being modified under the inexorable pressure of economic realities. The practice of endowing a company with exclusive privileges was bound to evoke the jealousy of those shut out from its limited membership. Freedom of trade, it was declared in the House of Commons in the reign of James I, 'is every man's inheritance and birthright.' Its denial infringed the 'Englishman's liberty'—a phrase which occurs in a fifteenth-century statute. 'The king's highway of trade should be opened unto all.' And those who hammered at the gates of the company—vociferating that 'all free subjects are born inheritable to the free exercise of their industry'—were supported by the testimony of facts, since behind the façade of a communal system which stood for equality of opportunity the forces of individualism were already in possession of the citadel. The bulk of the company's business was actually handled by a coterie of large traders who had managed to squeeze out the 'young beginners' and men of 'lower estates,' despite the 'order of stint' which was nominally designed to curb 'the overgrown and great-pursed merchant.' Moreover hostility to the competitive instinct, which was enshrined in the communal system, had considerably weakened with the passage of time. The growth of competition, 'all the world striving to engross all the trade they can,' gradually forced upon English merchants the conviction that they must make it the interest of other nations to deal with them by discarding the policy of high prices. The doctrine that nothing 'conduceth more to the enlargement of selling any commodity than cheapness' was a challenge to the mediaeval commercial concepts, and its eventual acceptance marked a fresh stage in the evolution of international trade. Thus against the regulated companies—the enemies of excessive competition, which flooded the market with goods and lowered prices to the benefit of foreign buyers

—were pitted the unlicensed traders, the 'active and industrious spirits,' opposed to the staple system, insistent that commerce should be left free to find its own channel, eager to seek out fresh places of traffic, and ready to reduce prices for the sake of quicker returns.

The triumph of individualism in its conflict with the regulated companies was delayed—as in the parallel case of industry—until after the Restoration, when Parliament inaugurated the policy of throwing open by stages the oversea markets which had hitherto been the close preserve of these companies.[1] Under the spur of provincial jealousy of the metropolis—which sought to make itself the focus of the economic activities of the kingdom, 'as if God had no sons to whom He gave the benefit of the earth but in London'—coupled with dislike of the companies' financial proceedings, the legislature had become converted to the view that the communal organization of England's trade with the European countries was no longer appropriate in an age when commerce had attained (so it was affirmed with pride) its present 'height of perfection.'

The joint-stock company was a corporate body, whose capital was provided by a number of shareholders who participated in the profits. The possibility of individual trading was not excluded, for private transactions might be permitted to the members in proportion to the amount of

---

[1] The oversea trade of the Merchant Staplers was extinguished by the embargo on the export of wool early in the seventeenth century, and they were confined to domestic trade. The Spanish Company had been dissolved in the reign of James I, and the French Company did not survive the Restoration. In the reign of Charles II Parliament on several occasions suspended the privileges of the Merchant Adventurers, whose trade was finally thrown open by the act of 1689. Yet though shorn of their monopoly they did not terminate their organization and retained their staple at Hamburg until 1807. The control of the Eastland Company virtually ended before the close of the seventeenth century; the South Sea Company lost its monopoly in 1807; the African Company was dissolved in 1821; the Levant Company surrendered its charter in 1825; the trade of the East India Company to India was thrown open in 1814 (except for tea), and the trade to China and the trade in tea in 1834; the Hudson's Bay Company yielded up its exclusive rights in 1869; the Russia Company kept up its own church and charitable institutions in Moscow until the revolution of 1917.

their stock. In a similar way a regulated company was not incompatible with corporate trading because groups of partners were sometimes formed. There was a rapid increase of the joint-stock system in the second half of the sixteenth century. Its merit was that it enabled capital to be drawn from a wide area: anyone was free to hold shares in the company whether 'skilled in trade' or not. The drawback of a joint-stock was that a member could not, with certain exceptions, carry on business as an independent merchant: he merely drew dividends on his investment as a shareholder. Hence it did not afford the same scope for individual enterprise as did the regulated company in spite of the restrictions which the latter imposed on its members. The joint-stock companies played an important part in the development of English oversea trade by opening up new branches of commerce in India, Africa and Canada, but they encountered the hostility of those who opposed the confinement of a lucrative traffic to exclusive corporations.[1] The case for the protraction of their monopoly beyond a limited period rested on political rather than economic considerations, namely, the peculiar situation which prevailed in non-European countries. This was notably the position with the East India Company, the greatest of the joint-stock companies, which originated as a mercantile body and grew into a sovereign power.

[1] The East India Company was also criticized on the grounds that it exported the precious metals to pay for Indian products, that it competed with the native woollen manufacture by its importation of calicoes, that it incurred losses of ships either at sea or taken by the Dutch.

Chapter Five

THE GROWTH OF INDIVIDUALISM

II. AGRICULTURE

The village community of the middle ages constituted an agrarian partnership. The occupiers of the soil were shareholders in an agricultural concern, and their 'shares' consisted of scattered strips of arable land together with rights of usage over the meadow and waste. For many hundreds of years the greater part of English society formed a co-operative commonwealth in which a detailed code of by-laws was laid down for its guidance by the rural courts. The routine of husbandry, the rotation of crops and the seasons of ploughing were settled by common agreement: the whole rhythm of village life was regulated in the public as distinguished from private interest. The realm was covered with open fields in which no man was 'truly master of his own,' and where the control was vested in an association of cultivators.

In the course of centuries individualism made great inroads upon the communal system. It attained its logical goal when in many places the partnership was dissolved, the village community became extinct, and the open field system with its customary and immemorial practices was obliterated from the countryside. The emancipation of the English farmer from subjection to 'the general will' was brought about by the spread of *enclosures*—a term applied to a variety of processes, namely, the consolidation of scattered strips into compact properties permanently fenced by hawthorn hedges, the substitution of large farms for small (termed 'engrossing' of holdings), and the curtailment of the common waste. These changes were incompatible with the survival of the traditional husbandry;

and as a consequence the system of intermixed ownership, joint labour and compulsory rotation of crops, which had been the basis of the old English village, either disappeared completely or underwent considerable modification.

The driving force behind the individualist movement was a new outlook on the land. Discarding the deeply-rooted concepts of social morality, it advanced the claim that agriculture should not be immune from the commercial spirit which dominated every other branch of the national economy; that the self-interest of the owner, and not an alleged national interest, should mould the course of agrarian development. Already in the later middle ages the new outlook was making itself felt, though it had not yet become articulate. Side by side with the disintegration of the manor another movement was slowly altering the face of English rural society. The march of capitalism was laying the foundations of modern England long before its dissolving influences were accelerated in the turbulent upheaval of the sixteenth century, when the flood-tide of catastrophic changes poured swiftly through the breach with unrestrained violence. The permeation of an individualist mentality was undermining the stability of the village community, relaxing the conservatism of agrarian life, and affording scope for the competitive instinct inherent in human nature to reassert itself. The prosperous tenant who added one strip to another, in disregard of the primitive equality of the original shareholders in the common fields, prepared the way for the capitalist entrepreneur who amalgamated one holding with another. The piecemeal exchange of strips between neighbours, and the transference of portions of the common waste to private ownership, furnished precedents for the growth of compact farms and the abolition of the cramping communal restrictions. Nevertheless the decisive influence which shaped the destiny of the rural community came not from within but from without: it was the impact of an expanding industry that set in motion the commercial forces which replaced a subsistence economy by a market economy.[1]

For centuries it had been considered axiomatic that the primary purposes of farming were to grow corn for the nation and to support on the land as large a population as possible. These were the twin postulates of agrarian economics in the light of which all rural questions were discussed and all rural changes approved or condemned. During the middle ages there was no serious challenge to these postulates. Feudal military obligations and the economic requirements of his estate combined to give the lord of the manor a motive for maintaining a numerous peasantry. In so far as there was a population problem, it arose from the shortage not from the superfluity of labour—at any rate after the Black Death; and even at other times the waste land was always at hand to provide an outlet for any natural increase of the country stock. It is true that corn was not the only product of the soil: wool was in regular demand abroad. However the Cistercians, who were notable producers of wool, established themselves in remote and sparsely-inhabited regions. There was, until the fifteenth century, no marked encroachment of pasture-farming upon corn-growing and the traditional balance in husbandry therefore remained unimpaired.

The growth of a native textile industry in the later middle ages created a new situation. The home market for raw materials expanded rapidly, and it had a profound repercussion on the fortunes of English agriculture. It drove a wedge between the two branches of corn production and wool production. The sheep-farmer no longer kept to remote regions or to the waste that was no man's property. He now invaded the corn-fields. The foot of the sheep turned sand

[1] An important contributory factor was the dissolution of the monasteries, when a considerable portion of the soil passed out of the hands of its conservative-minded owners. Speculation in land became widespread, and a moneyed class enriched by trade found opportunities for profitable investment in the purchase and exploitation of the great estates which were being brought into the market. The effect was to promote the more thorough utilization of the resources of the soil and of the mineral wealth beneath its surface.

into gold; but where the foot of the sheep passed, farmsteads were pulled down, cultivators of the soil were sent adrift, the open fields with their maze of strips were enclosed—and the landscape, economic, social and physical, was transformed. The successful wool merchant proudly displayed on the portal of his mansion the 'posie:'

'I thanke God, and ever shall,
It is the Sheepe hath payed for all.'

The fate of the victims of economic progress, submerged in the torrent which carried them away from their land, was inscribed in the lines of Oliver Goldsmith:

'The mournful peasant leads his humble band,
And while he sinks, without one arm to save,
The country blooms—a garden and a grave.'

The agrarian revolution was the most important event in the social history of the sixteenth century: it attracted attention to an extent which only finds a parallel in the religious changes. Society seemed in men's eyes to be drifting away from its traditional moorings into a welter of anarchy; and contemporary literature reveals how deeply the breach with the old order affected the imagination of the age. The feature of the movement which made the most vivid impression upon the public mind was the divorce of large numbers of the English peasantry from the soil—the depopulation of villages caused by eviction of tenants,[1] curtailment of agricultural employment and usurpation of the commons. When the land was turned into a sheep-run, the inhabitants rooted in the soil for generations were sent adrift (*lacrimose*) and farm-houses decayed. The passionate invectives against pasture-farming were filled with bitter denunciations of the grazier—the agrarian counterpart of the capitalist entre-

[1] Freeholders could not be evicted from their holdings, though they might be bought out. Copyholders (the successors of the villeins) did not acquire complete legal security until a later period; but if they held land by inheritance they might obtain some measure of legal protection. The curtailment of agricultural labour occurred when the lord converted his demesne into pasture.

preneur in industry. 'God gave the earth to men to inhabit,' said Tyndale, 'and not unto sheep.' 'Where,' cried Latimer, 'have been a great many householders and inhabitants, there is now but a shepherd and his dog.' Preachers quoted the words of Isaiah: 'Woe unto them that join house to house, that lay field to field, that they may be placed alone in the midst of the earth.' A popular proverb crystallized popular experience in one short and pregnant sentence: 'Enclosures make fat beasts and lean poor people.' 'I have heard,' said a writer, 'of an old prophecy that "Horn and thorn shall make England forlorn." Enclosers verify this by their sheep and hedges at this day. They kill poor men's hearts by taking from them their ancient commons to make sheep pasture of.' A ballad of the time ran:

> 'The towns go down, the land decays . . .
> Poor folk for bread cry and weep.'

The problem of the rural exodus was the more serious in an age when the poor laws laid restraints on the mobility of labour, and when gild restrictions and the insistence on apprenticeship hindered access to urban occupations. The injury inflicted upon the occupiers of the soil and upon agricultural labourers involved an ethical question whether a landowner was morally justified in putting his estate to any use that he thought fit. Sixteenth-century moralists were quick to perceive that the older conceptions of right and wrong were breaking down: in their stead was growing up the conviction that a man might do with his own as he would. More stress came to be laid on the rights of ownership than on its duties; and when land was thus treated primarily as a source of income to its owner, its real relation to the community was obscured.

Throughout the sixteenth, seventeenth and eighteenth centuries the course of English rural life was profoundly disturbed by the conflict between those who wished to preserve, and those who sought to disrupt, the traditional basis of agriculture. While the claim was openly made on behalf of the innovators that land was to be treated like any other commodity, the early mercantilist state[1] endeavoured to uphold the maxim that land stood in a separate category. It was one of the primary objects to sustain the English peasantry, to check the rural exodus, to prevent the displacement of the population from a traditional mode of life. Apart from the desire to avoid social unrest, considerations of national security reinforced the argument for official intervention because from the ranks of the husbandmen were recruited the defenders of the realm. 'Whosoever doth not maintain the plough,' said Cecil, 'destroys this kingdom,' for when military levies are raised 'we find the greatest part of them to be ploughmen.' Accordingly the government set its face against the commercialization of agriculture, that is, against the exploitation of the soil purely for purposes of profit without regard to the social consequences which might ensue. The urgency of the occasion was brought home by 'riotous and tumultuous' assemblies. A revolt in the reign of Edward VI under Kett the Tanner was provoked by the enclosure of the waste. Near the end of Elizabeth's reign a rising was planned in Oxfordshire, where it was rumoured that 'the commons long since in Spain did rise and kill all the gentlemen and sithence have lived merrily there. It was but a month's work to overrun England.' In the next reign occurred a revolt in the midland counties. The insurgents called themselves 'Levellers;' and they issued a manifesto in which they protested against encroaching tyrants who would 'grind our flesh upon the whetstone of poverty so that they may dwell by themselves in the midst of their herds of fat wethers.'

Under the Tudors a number of statutes were passed in restraint of sheep-farming. They endeavoured to limit the sheep which a grazier might own, and ordered that arable fields converted into pasture should be restored to tillage. The ministers of Charles I made a more determined effort

---

[1] The Civil War constitutes the dividing line between the early and the later mercantilist state.

to halt the agrarian movement, to maintain the corn-fields, and keep the villages intact. The famous decade 1630 to 1640 was marked by an unwonted vigour in all spheres of social policy, and a new spirit was breathed into the admini- stration of the laws. The government was engaged during these years in a sustained attempt to cope with the problem of destitution, but it was not content merely to relieve poverty; and it sought to strike at the very root of unemploy- ment in so far as this was due to the spread of sheep-farming. Unfortunately the fiscal taint sullied the monarchy's handling of economic affairs, and debased the pursuit of social justice into an ignoble lust for pecuniary penalties. The levying of fines offered a temptation to the official tribunals to seek opportunities for extortion, and thus discredited the whole reforming programme. However the root causes why the early mercantilist state failed in its agrarian policy lie deeper. The period during which it was seriously enforced was too short for any permanent results to be achieved; above all, the forces set in motion by the overwhelming impact of industry on agriculture were too strong. Henceforth the energies of the rural community were to be diverted into channels which might best satisfy the insistent require- ments of the urban population. When the authority of the monarchy waned, no further attempt was made to stem the current of economic changes. After the Civil War the state ceased to employ its influence to check the dissolution of the open fields, and no obstacles were put in the way of the promoters of enclosures. Once the aristocracy was placed firmly in the saddle by the Revolution of 1688, enclosures— so far from being condemned—were encouraged in a legisla- tive assembly of landlords, whose own needs were served by giving full reins to the claims of private interests. This striking difference between the eighteenth and the two pre- ceding centuries measured the momentous effects produced by constitutional changes upon the economic life of the country.

It is significant to observe that no sooner did the Great

Rebellion curb the power of the monarchy than the new outlook on the land was clearly articulated. The plea of economic freedom—tentatively urged by Sir Walter Raleigh in the last Parliament of Elizabeth when he said: 'I think the best course is to leave every man free, which is the desire of a true Englishman'—now found open expression in its widest implications. More than a century before Adam Smith published *The Wealth of Nations*, the gospel of self-interest was proclaimed. The ethical standpoint, from which economic questions had been discussed in the sixteenth century by men like Tyndale and Latimer, was definitely discarded. Another era, for good or evil, dawned when Lee, 'minister of the Gospel,' demanded to know whether land-owners might not with good conscience put their lands to the best advantage. Lee was not opposed to sheep-farming, since he was prepared to trust to the profit-making instinct to promote the public good. If there were a shortage of corn, he wrote, 'men will plough up their enclosed land for their own profit; it's an undeniable maxim that everyone will do that which makes for his greatest advantage.' The argument disclosed how far men's opinions had travelled when they were ready to accept self-interest and economic freedom as the natural basis of human society. The displaced rural inhabitants were bidden to migrate to other districts, where 'they might better benefit themselves and profit the public.' Formerly the social mischief attendant upon economic changes had dominated the whole discussion. Now it was thrust into the background: it was, somewhat cursorily, dismissed with the suggestion that the victims should find something else to do. And it was not only in this appeal to self-interest that the trend of opinion was revealed, and a challenge was thrown down to the orthodox canons upheld by the state. The revolutionary notion was also beginning to prevail that the crux of the agrarian problem was the best mode of investing capital in the land and not the best method of supporting people on the land.

The new standpoint completely triumphed. Henceforth

the use of land was to be determined by considerations of what was most profitable. The owner was encouraged to give free reins to the promptings of personal gain. The social injury which resulted from selfish indulgence no longer carried its former weight. Impressive consequences flowed from the inability of the early mercantilist state to restrain the movement which treated agriculture purely as an economic category, and ignored its other aspect as a way of life conducted on a traditional basis. They came to a head when the rapid acceleration of parliamentary enclosures gave full scope to commercial forces with little regard to their ultimate reactions.

The enclosing movement was a continuous process extending over many centuries. At no time in English agrarian history was it completely quiescent, though the degree of activity was more marked at certain periods than at others. Its progress depended upon a variety of influences, but the principal were geological, economic and psychological. The nature of the soil was an important element, since the open field system was less suited to light and sandy soils; proximity to urban markets brought into operation commercial reactions which stimulated improved methods of cultivation; and the conservative prejudices of the farming community might have a retarding effect. The purpose for which the land was used after it had been enclosed naturally varied according to circumstances. The enclosures of the sixteenth and seventeenth centuries had for their main object the conversion of arable into pasture. In sharp contrast the enclosures of the eighteenth century are commonly attributed to a different motive, namely, the desire to promote tillage. This view however is not supported by the price of corn, which remained too low for several decades to afford sufficient encouragement. It would appear that during the first sixty or seventy years at any rate a large proportion of the land enclosed was laid down to grass, so that the movement continued to function on its customary lines. Then towards

the end of the century and in the early decades of the nineteenth century enclosures were carried on more generally
for the purpose of increasing corn production. Several factors
now operated to give the plough the decided advantage over
the pasture. Take first the price of wheat. It averaged 36s.
a quarter from 1715 to 1765; afterwards it averaged 47s.
until the war with France (1793); for the rest of the century
it averaged 68s. while it even reached 126s. 6d. in 1812—subsequently it fell considerably but still remained high. The soar-
ing price of corn stimulated tillage, and enclosures were
pushed on in order to enlarge the area of arable cultivation
and improve the methods of husbandry. The second factor
was the growth of population, which was very marked during
the latter half of the eighteenth century—this greatly extended the demand for food. The third factor was the war
with France which cut off supplies of food from abroad.
The main source from which England drew corn in times
of scarcity was the Baltic, but now importation became
hazardous and unreliable. In an age when her population was
beginning to develop rapidly, England was thrown back on
her own resources; and to add to her difficulties, while the
first half of the eighteenth century was an era of good
harvests, the closing years witnessed a succession of deficient
harvests. The changed situation is reflected in the attitude
of writers who had hitherto decried the need for enclosures.
Now that an increase in the productivity of the soil was
recognized to be an economic necessity, the critics fastened
upon the methods of enclosures and the failure to take adequate steps to alleviate the situation of those injuriously
affected.

The procedure by which the dissolution of the open field
system was accomplished, either partially or completely, varied
at different periods. The oldest method of enclosure was the
initiative taken by individuals. It was a widespread practice
for open field farmers by purchase or exchange to build up
compact holdings. In addition the right of the lord of the
manor to occupy portions of the waste was recognized by

the Statute of Merton (1235), and it created a fertile source of controversy. The enclosure of the commons by the arbitrary action of the lords was a frequent occurrence in the sixteenth and seventeenth centuries when the development of sheep-farming created an inordinate land-hunger. Under the Commonwealth the 'Diggers' protested against this 'Norman tyranny.' 'Let the common people have their commons and waste lands freed. Break the Norman yoke of lords of manors. Seeing you took away the will of the king from enslaving lords of manors, take away the will of lords of manors from enslaving the common people.' They claimed that 'the common people' had a true right to plough up and dwell upon the commons since the whole land of England was 'a common treasury' to every one born in the land. More important than the spasmodic efforts of individuals was the corporate action of the community. Agreements between the shareholders in the open fields to enclose their land or divide the waste became the normal procedure in the seventeenth and first half of the eighteenth century. Yet the private agreement suffered from the defect that it required the unanimous consent of those implicated. To overcome the difficulty recourse was had to private acts of parliament[1] which were binding upon dissentients. Parliamentary enclosures started as a tiny rivulet, and in the second half of the eighteenth century were swollen into a torrent. There are barely a dozen examples in the Stuart epoch, they increased to over two hundred under George I and George II, and they exceeded three thousands during the reign of George III. In the opening decades of the nineteenth century they were almost as numerous as in the whole of the preceding century; and the destruction of the traditional system of husbandry was virtually completed before the accession of Queen Victoria. The promoters of a parliamentary enclosure nominated the commissioners who were

[1] A general enclosure act of 1801 made no change in the machinery—private acts were still necessary—but it grouped together in a single act various clauses common to private acts.

to redistribute the land. These commissioners were all-powerful. 'The property of the proprietors and more especially of the poor ones,' protested a contemporary, 'is entirely at their mercy; every passion of resentment and prejudice may be gratified without control, for they are vested with a despotic power known in no other branch of business in this free country.' A tribunal appointed by rich landowners was likely to give precedence to their interests; and even when there was no wilful injustice the small farmers and cottagers were injured by the failure of the legislature to lay down general principles for the commissioners' guidance. Arthur Young stigmatized the procedure of parliamentary enclosures as 'a composition of public folly and private knavery;' and the unpopularity in which the later enclosing movement became enveloped was largely due to complaints of mismanagement.

From the point of view of economic progress the dissolution of the open field system represented an advance in agricultural technique and—when its purpose was arable cultivation—a corresponding increase in the production of food for the nation. There is a consensus of opinion extending over many centuries that for the requirements of improved husbandry the individual occupation of land, with its opportunities for scientific farming, was superior to the system of intermixed ownership and communal control. But when we come to measure the far-reaching influence of these changes upon the structure of rural society, it becomes evident that a heavy price had to be paid for economic progress. The social consequences entailed by the agrarian revolution will best be seen if we trace the fate which befell the three classes of cultivators of the soil—the yeomanry, the capitalist farmers, and the cottagers.

The yeomanry held a unique position in English society. Contemporaries were unstinted in their praise; and it was never forgotten that from their ranks were recruited the archers who had conquered a kingdom on the plains of

France. The term yeoman was loosely used, but there is no question that it embraced copyholders and leaseholders in addition to freeholders. A more restricted usage of the term, however, was common; and it was often confined to those who cultivated their own land.[1] Not only was the status of the yeoman ambiguous but his income conformed to no fixed standards. Of some the proverb ran: 'A yeoman of Kent with one year's rent could buy out the gentleman of Wales and knight of Sscales [Calais] and a lord of the north country.' Others, like the 'statesmen' of Cumberland, occupied properties of scanty value. In contrast with the comparative uniformity which had prevailed under the manorial system, there was no longer anything in the eighteenth century which could be considered an average tenement. An endless variety of farms existed ranging in size from a handful of acres to hundreds and even thousands.

On social grounds the small farm was favoured by public sentiment; on economic grounds it was almost universally condemned. Even if the poor farmers knew how to farm well, they lacked the means to do so. Their holdings were stigmatized as 'the residence of poverty and misery;' and the crops were said to be inferior in quantity and produced at a proportionately greater expense. Their lot was one of hard labour and penurious living. 'They work without intermission like a horse and practise every lesson of diligence and frugality.' Nevertheless they were not without their defenders. A writer in 1775 deplored 'the destructive practice which has prevailed for near half a century back of demolishing small farms.' He claimed that they paid in proportion a higher rent than the large farms, though in the aggregate they needed more farm buildings and repairs. He also stressed the quality of the labour of the small holder; and it is now recognized that the most appropriate scale of production in farming depends largely on whether the nature of the produce demands more capital or more intensive labour.

[1] 'When I was a boy,' wrote Cobbett in *Rural Rides*, 'it was the common practice to call' those who paid rent farmers, and those who tilled their own land yeomen-farmers.

Again the small farm served as an agricultural ladder to give a spur to the industry of the ambitious labourer; and if its occupant worked hard his toil was sweetened by independence.

The decay of the yeomanry was a continuous process originally set in motion by the disintegration of the manor[1] and accelerated by the dissolution of the open fields. The land tax assessments indicate that the number of peasant proprietors had already greatly diminished before the last quarter of the eighteenth century. Contrary to the older view that the last quarter was the period of the 'agony of the yeomanry,' there was actually an increase of small occupying owners near the end of the century. This fact suggests that enclosure by act of parliament was less detrimental to the survival of freeholders than enclosure by voluntary agreement in earlier decades, when they were often prevailed upon to sacrifice their patrimony for a money payment. It may also be surmised that tenants threatened with eviction or a rise in rent purchased their farms doubtless at inflated prices. Yet not all tenants were offered the alternative, even if they had possessed the resources to avail themselves of it. They were in a more unfortunate position than the small farmer-owner whose consent was necessary to his own extinction. Originally, when the manorial system functioned, the class of tenants—though they were denied legal security—enjoyed practical economic security since their services were needed to cultivate the lord's demesne. The situation was transformed in the sixteenth century when the value of an estate came to depend upon the extent to which it was stocked not with men but with sheep, because legal insecurity was now reinforced by economic insecurity. This was the crux of the land problem, and so long as the landlords were allowed to retain their legal rights all expedients to safeguard the tenantry from expulsion were palliatives. The fundamental

---

[1] While the alienation of the lord's demesne (as was noticed in Chapter One) contributed to the formation of the yeoman class, its long-term effect was to create a general condition of economic insecurity.

error of Tudor statesmanship was the failure to give the English peasantry a clear legal title to the land. In consequence innumerable small tenants were evicted at the expiration of their leases, and property was concentrated in fewer hands. The author of *The Duty of a Steward to his Lord* (1727) counselled that an estate agent 'as much as in him lieth and without oppression should endeavour to lay all the small farms, let to poor indigent people, to the great ones.' He was to seize the opportunity 'as the heads of families happen to fall' to resume possession of the land instead of 'continuing the farms to the poor remains who may as well betake themselves to other employments.' His counsel, unlike that of many treatises on farming, does not appear to have been still-born.

The shrinkage in the number of small holdings heralded the triumphant progress of large-scale production, and the capitalist farmer now entered into the heritage of his poorer neighbours. He was not unknown in former ages, for he emerged as a typical figure in English rural society at least as early as the fifteenth century when the landowners gave up cultivating their estates and leased their demesnes to tenants. His importance increased as agriculture was called upon to provide raw material for an expanding industry and food for an expanding population. The eighteenth century established the predominance of capitalist farming with its large tenements worked by landless labourers; and thereby was created the agrarian setting which has continued to persist down to our own day.

The landlord's interest in amalgamating small tenements and letting them to men of substance is explained by their unsuitability for sheep-farming, and when land was enclosed for such a purpose it usually resulted in the consolidation of holdings. Furthermore the growth of a class of capitalist farmers seemed imperative in the interests of scientific farming. It was as hopeless to expect improvements from the small farmers, declared a contemporary writer, 'as it would be to gather pineapples from thistles;' and even if they had the inclination they lacked the capital. The substantial tenants alone possessed the resources for an advanced system of cultivation. Arthur Young depicted them in the most favourable light. 'All kinds of husbandry improvements are executed with spirit by these men. They drain all their wet lands, keep their fences in admirable repair, plough and harrow their lands thoroughly, and above all are rich enough at any time to purchase a sufficient stock of cattle.' In addition the large farm afforded greater opportunity for some division of labour, whereas on a small holding one man performed ten different operations in the day and acquired special skill in none.

The disappearance of the yeomanry and the substitution of large-scale production conducted on a capitalist basis were two of the outstanding features which changed the aspect of English rural society in the eighteenth century. A third feature was the growth of an agricultural proletariat, that is, a class of landless labourers entirely dependent on their wages. This class in respect of its size is peculiar to England: in no other country is the mass of the country folk so completely divorced from the ownership of the soil. In earlier centuries there were probably few farm workers who did not have a plot of land of their own or at least rights over the commons which served to supplement their meagre earnings. Moreover the thrifty person was placed in a position to work his way up in life and to extend the size of his allotment. In short the labourer was not a landless labourer and the village contained an agricultural ladder. The chief accusation brought by contemporaries against the agrarian revolution was the damage inflicted upon the poor by the eviction of cottagers and squatters from the commons.

No rural movement has attracted greater attention or excited more controversy than the enclosure of the commons. None has left behind it so permanent a legacy of bitterness, for to the present day the memory still survives of the commons which were 'stolen from the people.' From a legal standpoint the phrase is doubtless inaccurate, since the commons at no time belonged to 'the people' in the sense that they were public property which anyone was free to use. Their original purpose in a primitive economy was to serve as an adjunct to arable cultivation, and 'rights of common' were therefore attached to strips of land in the open fields. In practice their use was not confined to strip-holders, and the privilege was freely exercised by unauthorized persons. In the eyes of their critics the commons were the quintessence of all the defects ascribed to the traditional methods of husbandry. They were assailed as wasteful and inefficient. The cattle pastured on them were poorly nourished owing to their excessive numbers; they were liable to infection when herded together promiscuously; and scientific breeding was impossible. The commons were also alleged to be productive of great social mischief as an encouragement to idleness and beggary. Thousands of squatters settled upon them, erected a rude shelter, and lived as much as possible without labour eking out a precarious existence sometimes in dubious ways. It was the prevailing view that the commons were 'nurseries of thieves and horse-stealers' which created the poor by fostering idleness. One writer says of Epping: 'The undergraduates in iniquity commence their career with deer stealing and here the most finished and hardened robber retires from justice.' Admittedly some of the evidence is favourable to those who dwelt on the commons and worked for the farmers without being entirely dependent upon their wages. Nevertheless the prevalence of wide stretches of uncultivated land, given over to wretched cattle and to human beings scarcely less wretched, was hardly likely to be tolerated when the new urban population springing up in industrial centres called for a more economical use of the national resources; and their cultivation was urged as 'the very greatest object of British policy.'

It was a misfortune that the state took no steps to handle the commons on some uniform principle which might have safeguarded the welfare of those who were too weak to protect their own interests. In general the strict letter of the law prevailed. Owners of cottages with rights of common attached were entitled to a piece of land in exchange, though the allotment was often so small that it was practically of no use. Where the cottage was owned by the landlord, he received the compensation instead of the cottager. The squatters, who were devoid as a rule of any legal rights, received no compensation at all unless they could show some title. The loss of the commons deprived the poor of the means of keeping a cow and often even pigs or geese, and they now lacked opportunities for collecting fuel. In exceptional cases cottagers or squatters who had no legal claims were given a trifling sum of money, yet this was soon squandered; and if land were allotted instead of money it was frequently too small to be of any advantage. The result was to place the agricultural labourers entirely in the power of the capitalist farmer by depriving them of access to the land; and their social degradation proved a heavy price to pay for technical progress. 'Go,' said Arthur Young, 'to an ale-house kitchen of an old enclosed country, and there you will see the origin of poverty and the poor rates. For whom are they to be sober? For whom are they to save? (Such are their questions.) For the parish? If I am diligent, shall I have leave to build a cottage? If I am sober, shall I have land for a cow? If I am frugal, shall I have half an acre of potatoes? You offer no motives; you have nothing but a parish officer and a workhouse. Bring me another pot.'

As the social consequences of the agrarian movement gradually revealed themselves, a change became apparent in the views of those who had been foremost in their advocacy of the enclosure movement. Arthur Young, its leading champion, declared: 'By nineteen enclosure acts out of twenty the poor are injured, in some grossly injured. The poor in these parishes may say, and with truth, "Parliament may be tender of property; all I know is, I had a cow and an act of parliament has taken it from me." ' The Board of Agriculture, which at first was a semi-official committee of agriculturists, proposed—in order to meet the evils arising from enclosure of the commons—that a portion should be set aside and used for allotments. The proposal remained still-born; and only a negligible number of the enclosure acts made any provision for the poor. It was the general absence of such provision in parliamentary enclosures which made an economic necessity the source of social injustice. The explanation of contemporaries was that farmers did not approve of labourers renting land. They wanted it for their own, and they needed men who would devote themselves entirely to their master's service. In their attitude the farmers were supported by the landlords who doubtless wished to avoid the trouble of collecting small rents. The policy of both landlords and capitalist farmers seems to have been definitely to create a wage-earning class of landless labourers completely dependent for their livelihood upon their employers.

We must now look at another side of the agrarian revolution. This was the adoption of technical improvements in the system of cultivation as well as in the breeding of livestock.

After the decay of the manor the village community was released from the lord's control; and his administrative staff, which had the power to develop agriculture on progressive lines, was dissolved. As a result improvements in husbandry had to come from the initiative of individuals and depend upon the slow process of education for their adoption by the generality of farmers. If we could travel into the past on a time machine, we should be struck by the remarkable contrast which different parts of England presented in respect of agricultural technique even in the eighteenth century. Talk of improvements to a Buckinghamshire farmer 'and he laughs at you for a theorist; propose it to a Kentish one and he smiles at your talking of what he has practised a century.' 'When I passed,' said a famous agrarian expert (Arthur Young), 'from the conversation of the farmers I was recommended to call on to that of men whom chance threw in my way, I seemed to have lost a century in time or to have moved a thousand miles in a day.' His writings are filled with denunciations of the retrograde condition of English tillage, and he stigmatized the backward farmers as the 'goths and vandals' of the open fields. The extravagant methods of ploughing, for instance, are shown in the employment of six horses and three men to draw a plough, when it had been demonstrated that an efficient plough required only two horses and a man.

While small farmers remained wedded to their antiquated practices and handed on their patrimony to their children together with their notions of cultivating it, a fresh stimulus was given to English agriculture by a race of spirited proprietors and farmers. This race—whose improvements set a standard to the rest of the farming community although they were said to travel at the rate of barely a mile a year— existed before the eighteenth century, the period with which it is commonly associated. After the Civil War landed proprietors, in order to repair their ruined fortunes, 'fell to such an industry and caused such an improvement as England never knew before'—so wrote an enthusiastic contemporary. Under the Early Hanoverians farming became a fashion among men prominent in public life who had both energy and capital to exploit new ideas. George III had a model farm and welcomed the title of 'Farmer George.' Of Sir Robert Walpole, England's first 'prime minister,' it was said that 'he opened the letters of his farm steward' before state correspondence. We are told that Bolingbroke, 'propped between two haycocks, read Swift's letters uplifting his eyes to heaven not in admiration of the author but in fear of rain.' When Fox visited the Louvre, his mind was filled with the thought 'whether the weather was favourable to his turnips.' An archdeacon admonished a rector, who had planted a churchyard with turnips, that it must not occur again. He received the reply: 'Oh no! Mr. Archdeacon, it will be barley next year.'

This display of interest bore fruit in a series of technical improvements. The first comprised the new crops which came into general use—turnips (among other roots) and artificial grasses. Turnips were grown in sixteenth-century England as a garden plant.Their adoption for field-cultivation was due to the influence of the Flemings—'our first teachers' in the art of agriculture, as they were styled—but they were not widely sown until the eighteenth century. The importance of roots and artificial grasses cannot be over-estimated. They made it unnecessary to leave a large part of the soil fallow every year: instead it could now raise crops for keeping cattle alive in the winter and thus render fresh meat available throughout the year. Hitherto the nation had subsisted in the winter on salted meat; and the substitution of fresh for salted meat was responsible in part for the decline in the death rate and the consequent growth of population. The second outstanding improvement is that stock-breeding became a science. For centuries the value of sheep had lain primarily in their wool and the value of cattle in their milk or capacity to draw the plough, but as the population expanded the demand grew for beef and mutton. Bakewell breeded livestock directly for the butcher, and as a result the average weight for beeves, calves, sheep and lamb was greatly increased. Other contributions were made to the development of English agriculture —Jethro Tull drilled seed mechanically in rows instead of sowing it broadcast; Coke, the type of the capitalist farmer who sank money in the land, set the example of careful selection of seed and the use of artificial foods; inventors devised improved ploughs, threshing machines and all kinds of mechanical aids.

Chapter Six

THE FIRST PLANNED ECONOMY

CONTROL OF INDUSTRY, THE MERCANTILE SYSTEM, AND LAISSEZ-FAIRE

Control of Industry

To understand the economic ideas which prevailed in the past, we must view them in relation to the contemporary framework of society and not measure them by the changing standards of our own day. In the opening years of the nineteenth century it became the practice to fling scorn upon the old-fashioned principles which held sway in former centuries. 'The reign of Queen Elizabeth,' it was confidently proclaimed, 'though glorious was not one in which sound principles of commerce were known.' When this criticism was uttered the opposite conception of the province of the state had won almost universal recognition. The community had grown ripe for a larger degree of economic freedom and for greater elasticity in the working of the industrial system; it now relied upon the play of unfettered competition and enlightened self-interest to achieve social harmony. In earlier ages, when a widely different environment existed, the English people did not believe in an unregulated industrialism or that it was the duty of the government to abstain from interference with economic affairs. On the contrary, they were convinced that the divergence of public and private interests called for state intervention in order to protect the community from the harmful side of individualism. Two fundamental facts coloured their traditional outlook and attitude of mind. In the first place, industry was still conceived in the mediaeval light of a public service. It was an 'art'—we should now term it a 'profession'—and, on the lines of a modern profession, a code of conduct was laid down and suitable conditions were imposed designed to protect alike the interests of the public as consumers and of the skilled workers as producers. In the second place, the principle of communal control in the economic sphere was deeply-rooted in the historic consciousness of the English nation. There was never a time in the memory of men when the ideals of *laissez-faire* had reigned, or when men had been left at liberty in their pursuit of a livelihood. In the middle ages agriculture had been regulated by the village courts, industry by the craft gilds, commerce by the gilds merchant at home and by trading companies abroad. The Englishman was reared in a society in which his business was not his business alone, and in which his economic life was no less subject to supervision than his political or religious life.

The early mercantilist state inherited the communal traditions bequeathed by the middle ages. It came into existence in an era when profound changes were taking place in the industrial landscape. The growth of capitalism, the dispersion of the textile manufacture over the countryside, and the emergence of new enterprises outside the jurisdiction of the urban authorities, imperilled the whole structure of industry as it had been built up in the middle ages on a gild basis. Accordingly the intervention of the state was imperatively demanded if the time-honoured sanctions of a rigid industrial discipline were to be preserved from extinction. Public opinion was not yet prepared for the abandonment of the old order; and to avert its imminent break-up the central authority was impelled to assume wider responsibilities. Early mercantilist legislation was in its essentials nothing more than the application, on a national scale, of the orthodox practices which had been followed for several centuries by the municipalities.

In the sphere of industry the aim of the state was to bring capitalism under control. The industrial entrepreneur was subject to restrictions in six different ways. Firstly: he was bound by legal rates of wages. Secondly: pressure was exerted on him to keep his men at work. Thirdly: he could only employ trained artisans who had served an apprentice-ship. Fourthly: he must conform to a recognized standard of quality and dimensions. Fifthly: prices were sometimes fixed by public authority. Sixthly: his trade might be put into the hands of monopolists, who would either refuse him the right to continue in business or exact from him oppressive fees for doing so.

The grievance of low wages was as old as the capitalist system itself. It was voiced in a fifteenth-century pamphlet, *On England's Commercial Policy*:

'The poor have the labour, the rich the winning.'

The evil was accentuated by the failure of wages to keep pace with the advance in prices produced by the influx of American silver into Europe. A famous ballad in the time of Charles II recited:

'In former ages we us'd to give,
So that our work-folks like farmers did live;
But the times are altered . . .
We will make [them] to work hard for sixpence a day,
Though a shilling they deserve if they had their just pay.'

While the monarchy sustained its grip upon the economic life of the country, the regulation of working-class conditions was considered the province of the state. It refused to recognize the claim of the wage-earners to combine together in order to promote their interests, yet as a compensation it shouldered (in principle at least) the responsibility for safeguarding their welfare because it interfered in matters affecting wages, employment and technical training. The famous enactment known as the Statute of Apprentices (1563)[1] empowered the justices of the peace in every county and city to fix maximum wages, calculated to 'yield unto the hired person both in the time of scarcity and in the time of

[1] State regulation of wages goes back to the fourteenth century, though it was apparently limited to unskilled labour outside the craft gilds.

plenty a convenient proportion of wages:' later in the reign of James I was instituted the first minimum wage law on the English statute-book.[1]

The question how far the authoritarian regulation of wages existed in practice has been much canvassed. Wage assessments in one branch or another of industry have a continuous history for over two and a half centuries (1563 to 1824), and they have been revived in the twentieth century; but the machinery was most commonly put into operation in the first hundred years. Its efficient working depended primarily upon the hold which the central authority maintained over the local magistrates. Under Elizabeth and the Early Stuarts the government displayed a genuine solicitude for distressed artisans, and showed itself ready to support the interests of workmen against their employers, so that the procedure cannot be regarded as purely one-sided. Cases of intervention were especially frequent in the reign of Charles I when an active social policy was pursued. Apart from the discussion of the actual enforcement of wage control, the whole conception has been criticized on various grounds. Historians denounced it as an instrument for degrading and impoverishing the labourer: economists condemned it as a violation of the principles of *laissez-faire*: employers stressed the technical difficulties of a uniform scale: workers sometimes claimed that wages should be governed by merit. However we may reasonably draw certain broad conclusions. State control provided a safeguard against undue oppression. The occasions on which the wage-earners themselves pressed for official rates may be interpreted as an indication that it was not considered to work unfairly in their interests. Again it did not prevent a rise in wages since assessments which ran counter to the popular sentiment remained inoperative. 'The poor,' it was said towards the end of the seventeenth century, 'laugh at them and cry: "Statute work against statute wages." For laws will not make nor influence prices in open market.' Lastly the attempt to vary the remuneration of

[1] The act of 1604 applied to the woollen industry.

labour according to the cost of living proved unsuccessful, and a fall in prices enabled the working class to maintain its traditional standard of life with less effort. A later generation indeed flung scorn upon the orthodox theory of wages that the price of labour should be determined by the price of food. Instead the theory came to be held that wages depended, like other commodities, upon the economic laws of supply and demand.

We come next to the policy adopted in regard to unemployment. The growth of capitalism created the problem of unemployment as far back as the sixteenth century, for the more extended the market the greater is the liability to commercial fluctuations. The capitalist takes on fresh hands when trade is brisk and dismisses them when trade is dull. In addition the abnormal interruptions which we call commercial crises were already a prominent feature in the age of mercantilism. This explains why the early economists viewed with apprehension the rapid progress of industry. They saw clearly that England's commerce in becoming world-wide was affected by the vicissitudes of a world economy, and that the course of her economic life was profoundly distrubed by occurrences remote from her shores. Hence they preferred to see the prosperity of the realm broad-based on land rather than on the shifting foundations of trade. Even in the seventeenth century tariffs and wars were revealed as factors of cardinal importance. The efforts of 'the neighbouring nations in Europe' to establish their own manufactures made the continental market precarious; and their adherence to a protectionist policy furnished one of the main arguments for developing a colonial empire in order to provide an alternative market for English products. Moreover England seldom enjoyed a protracted spell of peace; and the industrial situation was adversely influenced by the succession of wars. They inflated certain branches of the national economy such as iron and shipbuilding, interrupted the normal channels of trade, disturbed the monetary exchanges, and brought in their wake unemployment and destitution. It is not surprising then that war was denounced as 'one of the greatest calamities.'

The attitude of the state towards unemployment has varied in different ages. Under the early mercantilist state the prevailing tendency was in favour of intervention. The period extending from the Civil War to the close of the nineteenth century was marked by *laissez-faire*. The twentieth century witnessed the revival of the principle of intervention though in an altered form. The reason for state action in the first epoch was partly that it carried on the traditions of the craft gilds, partly it was due to the fear of social unrest, and partly there was a genuine desire to protect 'the poor man's labour, his inheritance'—to quote a seventeenth-century phrase. The methods of official intervention were both legislative and administrative. The legislative method was to secure continuity of employment by insistence on long engagements. In the middle ages it was usual to bind workmen for lengthy periods, and the practice was given legal force in the Statute of Apprentices (1563) which enacted that no person should be taken into service for less than a year. The hiring of farm workers at the annual fair, or 'statute,' lasted into the nineteenth century and in some places it survives at the present day. A Yorkshire farmer in the reign of Charles I related that at one 'statute hiring' he 'heard a servant asked what he could do, who made this answer—

> "I can sowe,
>   I can mowe,
> And I can stacke,
>   And I can doe,
>   My master too,
> When my master turnes his backe." '

The administrative method was to find tasks for the unemployed or exert pressure upon employers not to turn their men adrift but to keep them in service. There are repeated examples of authoritarian intervention to warn employers against throwing their men out of work under penalty of a summons before the Privy Council. 'Those who had gained in profitable times,' the government admonished capitalist producers, 'must now be content to lose for the public good until the decay of trade was remedied.' One of the most memorable depressions in English history lasted several years (1620–24), when the export trade in cloth declined by one-third and unemployment was on a national scale. To deal with the situation merchants were ordered to lay in stock; manufacturers were protected by a moratorium from their creditors; and the magistrates were instructed to start relief works. Finally a royal commission composed of twelve persons was set up in 1622—the first of its kind to make a detailed investigation of the causes of unemployment. Its comprehensive report presents a contemporary analysis of a phenomenon destined to become a recurring feature of England's economic development.

The third restriction laid on industrial entrepreneurs was the obligation to employ trained labour. By making apprenticeship compulsory for all engaged in industry, the state supported the claim of qualified workmen to be protected against cheap labour, and the claim of consumers to be protected against unskilled workmanship—but a check was imposed on capitalism since it curtailed the supply of labour. The Statute of Apprentices, which invested apprenticeship with general legal sanction, remained on the statute-book for two and a half centuries (1563–1814). Its observance was primarily a matter of local custom, and there was an infinite variety of practices in different parts of the country. One example may serve to illustrate the dissensions provoked by breaches of 'the law Queen Betty made.' The bakers of Rye complained that in spite of 'good and wholesome laws' requiring 'each sort of people' to 'use the trade and living wherein they have been lawfully trained up,' brewers turned bakers without having served an apprenticeship 'contrary to all law, equity and good conscience.' The authorities finding that 'by no reasonable persuasion those brewers would leave baking,' and that the principal offender who baked and brewed 'is (God be thanked) grown to good wealth, and the whole company of the bakers thereby utterly impoverished,' issued a decree admonishing them that 'the state of a commonwealth is preferred before the private gain of a few.'

The economic functions of the state also embraced the sphere of production by prescribing the technical processes of manufacture. The minutest rules were framed regarding the nature of the materials, the use of mechanical appliances and the form of the finished products. Every branch of industry was in some degree brought under control, though the one chiefly affected by national regulation was the woollen manufacture upon which the legislature lavished unremitting care and attention. In order to ensure 'true making,' cloth had to conform to a certain length, breadth and weight: it was also forbidden to mingle different kinds of wool, or use various ingredients in dyeing, or employ mechanical devices such as gig mills and tenter-frames for finishing and stretching the fabric. The rules devised to establish a uniform standard of quality were not unjustified in earlier times at all events. It was a byword in the seventeenth century 'to shrink as northern cloth;' and the reputation which Bradford, now the metropolis of the worsted industry, had gained for fraudulent work may be gauged from a verse in a Methodist hymn:

> 'On Bradford likewise look Thou down
> Where Satan keeps his seat.'

There are sufficient indications that official supervision was needed with a view to foster elementary ideas of honesty and give credit to manufactures by the prevention of abuses; while it also harmonized with the gild tradition that industry should be 'orderly governed.'

Among the legacies bequeathed by the mediaeval gilds to the mercantilist state was the principle of price regulation. The conviction of consumers that price movements were due to the machinations of middlemen gave birth to a series of experiments intended to secure stability of prices. Commodities of which the price was fixed by the state at one period or another include cloth, silks, ale, wines and tea; but the conspicuous examples of continuity of policy were the two primary necessaries of bread and coal, for here a serious rise in prices easily assumed the proportions of a national catastrophe. Attempts to govern the price of bread, in what was known as the 'assize of bread,' extend from the thirteenth to the nineteenth century. They were intended, explained Davenant at the end of the seventeenth century, to 'give the common people the benefit of plenty,' the weight of bread increasing as the price of corn fell. He was not in favour of price regulation for all commodities and drew a distinction between those of a uniform character, such as bread, and those capable of improvement by 'skill, art and care.' In the former case he considered that limitation of the price 'may be for public advantage,' yet in the latter it was 'impracticable and a bar to industry.' Coal, like bread, came within the first of these two categories. No economic question in the seventeenth and eighteenth centuries agitated the public mind more persistently than the price of coal, and repeated though fruitless efforts were made by the authorities for over two hundred years to check its continuous advance. The extortions of coal merchants were lampooned in one of Crowley's 'Epigrams' on a sixteenth-century 'Colier of Croydon:'

'Men thyncke he is cosen to the Colyar of Hell.'

The sixth restriction on manufacturers—the ill-starred industrial experiments known as the patents of monopoly—was the most deeply resented of all the restraints placed on capitalism. Under the patent system the state bestowed the control of an industry on an individual or a group of individuals acting in a corporate capacity. The delegation of governmental functions to private persons seeking their own profit tended to create a kind of feudalism in industry.

Apart from the oppressive conduct of the agents whom the Crown employed in its projects for stimulating industrial development, the sincerity of its motives was mistrusted. A protectionist policy, intended to make England economically independent of foreign countries, was associated with a fiscal policy of finding new sources of income which would make the executive politically independent of the legislature. But the patents were so ill-managed that the sum extracted from the consumers was out of all proportion to the amount which reached the Exchequer, the greater part being intercepted by the monopolists. The fundamental defect of the patent system lay, in fact, in the malpractices of its administrators and even a good patent could be rendered noxious by the servants of the patentee. None the less there was another side to the patents, and it constitutes their true importance as an episode in English economic development. This side reflected a genuine desire to introduce new industrial arts. In the sixteenth century England was behind the Continent in several branches of industry, for example, cloth-finishing, glass-making, paper-making and mining. Her dependence upon other countries ran counter to the maxims of economic nationalism; and some of the patents at any rate were designed to free England from her handicaps, and make her self-sufficing so far as her natural resources permitted. The soap patent, for instance, provided that no foreign soap should be imported and that native soap should be made with home-grown materials. Similarly the salt and glass patents professed to encourage English manufactures. The fostering of infant industries is of course a normal objective in protectionist states, but nowadays it is accomplished by means of tariffs and subsidies. The peculiarity of the mercantilist methods was that they strove to achieve self-sufficiency by the prohibition of imports, coupled with the concession of exclusive privileges to an individual or company. Thus they vested complete control of the market in the hands of a single producer, because protection from external competition was combined with the suppression of independent enterprise at home: the invariable sequel was a considerable advance in prices.

We have sought to show that the claim of the state to regulate the industrial life of the community was in harmony with a deep-seated tradition. Another sign of the continuity of economic outlook is afforded by the survival of the craft gilds. It is sometimes the usage to speak of the 'decline of the craft gilds' after the close of the middle ages. It is true that they were deprived of their former predominance in the industrial order—both their power and prestige diminished —but they were able to perform some of their functions. The persistence of the gild regime is proved by the numerous grants of incorporation which both the Crown and Parliament made during the seventeenth century to newly-formed or old-established crafts. The erection of these companies indicates how strongly entrenched was the traditional idea of the corporate rule of industry. The dominating sentiment still supported in principle the exercise of authority in economic affairs. It held, to quote a contemporary view, that the craft gilds had 'worked great good in respect that the government of every artificer and tradesman being committed to men of gravity, best experienced in the same faculty and mistery, the particular grievances and deceits in every trade might be examined, reformed and ordered.' Various proposals were advanced in the seventeenth century for the general reconstitution of industry on the basis of trade associations armed with powers of control and search. They failed to materialize and in consequence the advancing tide of individualism swept on with unrestrained force.

The Mercantile System

During the space of three centuries England adhered to a commercial system known as the mercantile system, and we have long been accustomed to take our interpretation of it from *The Wealth of Nations*. Adam Smith was unquestionably a great intellectual force, but as in the case of other outstanding figures the real nature and extent of his influence have been obscured by legendary accretions and by the repetition of well-worn clichés. On several fundamental points it is necessary to reconsider afresh the current views— more especially, mercantilist opinion about money; the movement towards *laissez-faire* in industry; and the reasons for the adoption of free trade.

For many decades it has been regarded as axiomatic that the whole structure of mercantilist doctrines and policy was grounded upon a confusion of money with wealth. Yet it is, on the surface, a singular notion that a system of economic policy which endured for several centuries should have had its basis in pure fantasy; or that the business men of the seventeenth century should have entertained delusions about money and wealth which are patently absurd. It is possible to quote many representative authors from the early sixteenth century onwards, whose writings reveal clearly that money was not identified with wealth, and that its principal function—to serve as an instrument of exchange— was recognized in an unmistakable way. While occasional lapses and unguarded phrases may be found, the instructed opinion of the seventeenth century was interpreted by the historian of the Royal Society (in 1667) when he criticized the 'Spaniards in America' because their 'chief design' was the transportation of bullion, which was so profitable that they neglected 'many other of its native riches.' Nor was this enlightened attitude confined to a few thinkers in advance of their times. It was evinced in a parliamentary debate in the reign of James I when it was pronounced 'a general opinion that any kingdom that is rich in staple commodities must needs be rich.'

Admittedly one aim of mercantilism was the acquisition of the precious metals—not owing to any confusion with wealth but because they were indispensable as the mechanism of exchange at home and for the liquidation of the adverse balances which might arise in the course of foreign trade. Although credit instruments (bills, cheques and bank notes) were in use, paper money could not wholly take the place of metallic coins: after all, gold was retained in circulation in England down to the first world war. The precious metals had become more plentiful through the discovery of America, but mercantilist governments were moved by a genuine fear of the country lapsing into scarcity again; and their persistent anxiety was based on actual conditions. Currency difficulties were incessantly cropping up because the supply of circulating medium was not always adequate for the needs of industry and trade. Davenant—who enjoyed perhaps greater authority than any other seventeenth-century economist— voiced the real mercantilist viewpoint when he declared, on the one hand, that the 'true riches' of a realm consisted of industrious inhabitants and natural products; and on the other, that there must be enough money 'to keep the wheels of the machine in motion,' that is, for the payment of rent, wages, commodities and taxes. An insufficiency of specie to drive the nation's trade starved commerce of its 'radical moisture' and lessened its volume. Modern economists have expressed a similar idea that a substantial command of resources in the form of currency will help to render business easy and smooth.

The mercantilists were not only concerned to prevent a scarcity of money; they also wanted to keep its quantity ever increasing since a gradual rise in prices was favourable to industry. Indeed the mercantilist emphasis on treasure largely had its roots in the historical fact that the more abundant supply of the mechanism of exchange in the sixteenth century unquestionably served to lubricate the mechanism of production. In addition the government had an interest in expanding the amount of precious metals in circulation, for in time of war it was enabled to make essential purchases with a commodity universally acceptable. Hence the argument for a plentiful stock of money as the 'life of commerce' was reinforced by the needs of national defence, which demanded the sinews of war. One final consideration must not be overlooked. The currency system was ultimately part of a general protectionist system framed to obstruct the 'excessive import' of foreign commodities and ensure that the latter were paid for with native goods rather than with the money of the realm.

A famous controversy sprang up between two schools of thought as to the best method of conserving and augmenting the national stock of the precious metals. The bullionist school favoured restrictions on their export. The mercantilist school believed that the precious metals could be sent out of the country like any other commodity provided a favourable balance of trade, a surplus of exports over imports, brought money back into the country. The conclusion followed that the government should regulate not the flow of precious metals but the stream of commerce, directing it into channels which would secure a favourable balance of trade. With the virtual extinction of the bullionist school in consequence of a historic change in English monetary policy—when the export of bullion and foreign coin was legalized (1663)—the mercantilist doctrine triumphed and the balance of trade became the touchstone of national prosperity. Its practical influence was profound. It furnished the arguments for the severe curtailment of intercourse between England and France on the ground that the balance of trade with France was unfavourable to us;[1] and subsequently the partial revolt of economists against its teachings inaugurated the first phase of the free trade movement. The mercantilist theory of foreign commerce, while it marked an advance upon the crude doctrines of the bullionists, tended to foster a one-sided view of oversea trade whose value was measured by its balance rather than by its volume and character. To-day foreign commerce is vital to our existence because it supplies us with foodstuffs and raw materials. But until the nineteenth century England raised her own food supply and the raw material for her greatest industry, and banking and credit facilities were still incomplete; it was therefore natural that

[1] In place of French wines the consumption of port was encouraged by the Methuen Treaty (1703) with Portugal, with whom the balance of trade was in our favour.

foreign commerce should often be esteemed for the addition which it made to the stock of precious metals. It was the obvious means of accumulating gold and silver when a country had no mines of its own.

Nowadays we can understand the concern of the mercantilists to ensure a favourable balance with a more sympathetic insight than was displayed by their critics, the classical economists. An unfavourable balance meant a drain of gold abroad to pay for the excess of imports over exports; and a decrease in the quantity of money in a country caused changes in the general level of prices which might lead to an industrial crisis. It is no doubt true (as the orthodox economists averred) that in 'the long run' the gold will come back provided the fall in prices stimulates exports and diminishes imports. The mercantilists, however, were exercised with what happened in 'the short run,' that is, with the consequences entailed during a period of transition by a contraction in the volume of the currency. Adam Smith contended that no official 'attention' was needed to 'supply us with all the gold and silver' required; and on the strength of this assumption it has been the practice to regard mercantilism as based upon a fallacy. Actually the modern device of raising the bank rate, in order to protect the gold reserves, is only the counterpart of the methods adopted by the mercantilists to secure an adequate amount of the precious metals for the proper functioning of the economic mechanism. And the position was the more difficult in earlier centuries inasmuch as England could not freely import bullion from abroad owing to the embargo laid by certain European countries (for instance, Spain, and at one time even Holland) on the export of the precious metals. Moreover three great branches of foreign trade—East Indies, Baltic and Levant—depended on the export of bullion, of which the supply had necessarily to be replenished from other sources. Herein lay one reason for the importance attached to the balance of trade as 'a national object.' A favourable balance with one country enabled England to support an adverse balance with another country whose products were vital to her, such as iron and naval stores.

Pre-occupation with the subject of money has had the unfortunate effect of fostering a distorted conception of the mercantile system, and obscuring its more essential aspect as a planned national economy based on self-sufficiency. Mercantilism is town economy writ large. This means that the industrial and commercial activities of the community ceased to be organized on an urban basis, and local interests were merged in those of the country as a whole. The ascendancy which the towns enjoyed in remoter times lapsed when a national regime replaced a municipal regime as the mainspring of economic growth. The transition from the town economy which prevailed in Early England to the national economy dominant in the age of mercantilism had already made marked progress in the later middle ages. The process of unification, as it crystallized in the gradual concentration of economic forces in the state, is seen in a variety of directions—in the assimilation of municipal practices to a uniform standard; in the legislation which regulated on a nation-wide basis the woollen industry, the conditions of labour, the assize of bread, the assize of weights and measures, the currency and the customs system; in the break-down of the barriers to internal trade; and in the formulation of a common policy in external trade. Nevertheless, while the state represented a more comprehensive view of society now bound together in a community of economic life, it inherited the municipal armoury of ideas and weapons. It moulded itself upon the example set by the towns and applied the existing mechanism on a larger scale. The unit was no longer the borough with its genuine sense of solidarity though narrow range of vision, but the nation; yet the enlargement of the unit left unchanged the concepts in which the older structure was rooted, until they were modified under the insistent pressure of individualism.

A comparison of town economy and national economy

enables us to discern the continuity of economic policy. In the stage of a town economy every borough strove to become a complete entity, a self-dependent body. It displayed jealousy of other burghal communities towards which it conducted itself after the fashion of an independent city state armed with active powers of aggression and defence; it sought to establish a monopoly of industry over an extensive area; and it imposed trading disabilities on the strangers within its gates. In the stage of a national economy the body of tradition created by municipal practices was incorporated within the framework of state action. Its pivotal features, and especially the basic principle of exclusiveness, remained unaltered in so far as they implied the aim of self-sufficiency. The underlying idea was to consolidate the strength of a state by making it independent of other states in the economic sphere: in short it pursued a strategic economy based on power rather than a welfare economy based on abundance. The development of the national resources was designed to promote national security, and 'consideration of power' took precedence over 'consideration of plenty' (the antithesis is Bacon's). It should be observed that the notion of self-sufficiency—or autarky as it is now often termed—does not imply economic isolation, that is, the absolute severance of all economic ties with other countries. It does not, therefore, debar international trade. The mercantilist ideal was that a community should rely upon its own resources, agricultural and industrial, essential for its existence. This implied that normally it must produce its primary necessities in respect of foodstuffs and manufactured articles to the fullest extent possible, and it must also possess its own mercantile marine. In addition it should utilize foreign commerce to supply deficiencies which could not be made good at home, in return for the export of its own surplus products.

Accordingly the real kernel of the mercantile system lay in the protection of agriculture, industry and navigation; and the criterion applied to foreign trade was its reaction upon the other branches of the economic system. The accumulation of treasure was not one of the fundamentals of mercantilism. Its subordinate place in the mercantilist scheme may be gauged from the fact that the statute-book is burdened with innumerable acts relating to tillage and manufactures and shipping, but only one law of importance (1663) concerns treasure and it affirmed the right of export: previous to its enactment free trade in gold and silver had been in practice conceded through the issue of licences. No stronger proof is needed that the mercantile system was grounded, not on a confusion of money with wealth, but on the attainment of a balanced economy which in the interests of national security sought to achieve economic independence as the corollary of political independence.

To interpret mercantilism in the sense of economic nationalism does not involve the conclusion that it is necessarily a better system than its antithesis—international economic co-operation. The former aspires after self-sufficiency. The latter rests upon a more advanced principle, the world division of labour where each country concentrates its energies upon the pursuits for which it is best adapted and exchanges its surplus products for those of other countries— thereby affording the possibilities of a higher standard of life through a greater command over the bounty of nature and the resources of human skill. The following quotation from a seventeenth-century writer is worth pondering: 'To say, as many are apt to do, that England can live of itself without the assistance of any foreign nation is to give it not the least commendation beyond any other country. But to say, and that truly, that England by the industry of its inhabitants employed in shipping, plantations, mines, manufactures, pastures and tillage, doth not only abound in all sorts of commodities as native meat, drink, clothes, houses and coaches fit for the necessities, ease and ornaments of life, but can outvie most nations of the world for the vast plenty in varieties of wines, spices, drugs, fruits, silks, pictures, music, silver, gold, precious stones and all other supports of grandeur and delight, that is to speak it a truly civilized and glorious nation indeed.'

The resources of England, however, were inadequate to provide her with the raw materials required in certain industries, and her dependence upon alien sources infringed the cardinal maxim of the mercantile system. Hence the importance which was attached to the foundation of colonies, for they afforded the means by which foreign commodities could become 'native' to the realm: they opened up the vision of an empire knit together by economic ties in which each part sustained and nourished the whole, and the mother country and the colonies were made complementary to one another. Thus, in harmony with the fundamental principles of mercantilism, the conception of a self-supporting country eventually broadened into that of a self-supporting empire. The idea of imperial economic relationships was firmly entertained; and there was a consensus of opinion that the colonies existed to bring benefit to the parent state in consuming its manufactures, in employing its ships and in repairing its deficiencies in raw materials.

The legal structure of the mercantile system rested upon three pillars—the protection of industry, the corn laws, and the navigation acts.

The protection of native manufactures was not peculiar to mercantilism. It was an integral part of mediaeval state-craft, which in the course of the fourteenth and fifteenth centuries gradually crystallized in a succession of measures against imports. In essence it was an extension of the spirit which had led the burghers of each town to erect commercial barriers against every other town—the instinct to protection from being civic had become national. Apart from the pressure of vested interests, manufacturers and artisans alike, the basic motives for protection in the middle ages and the succeeding centuries down to the present day have always been the fear of unemployment coupled with the desire to foster infant industries. 'All the nations of Europe,' declared

The British Merchant (1713) in words that are scarcely less true to-day than when they were written, 'concur in this maxim that the less they consume of foreign commodities the better it is for them.' What is distinctive of mercantilism, as compared with earlier times, is the more systematic application of a protectionist policy in all spheres of the national economy in order to develop native productive sources of every kind, and it was due to the conscious pursuit of the ideal of self-sufficiency.

The mercantilists did not approve of all exports nor disapprove of all imports. They encouraged the export of manufactured articles but frowned upon the export of raw materials. It is true that the shipment of coal abroad was permitted (subject to a heavy duty) but the staple commodity of the realm, wool, was rigorously kept for the home market. The manufacturers claimed the right to monopolize the raw material produced at home, and they prevailed in their demand that it should not be sent abroad to feed the looms of their foreign rivals: 'so that we may not be killed with arrows from our own quiver.' The protection of the woollen industry was the most tenacious doctrine in the economic creed of the mercantilist state; and for two centuries it was a leading principle of English commercial policy to stop the export of the chief raw material. The embargo remained in force down to the third decade of the nineteenth century despite the persistent efforts of the wool-growers to secure its repeal. In the case of imports the mercantilists regarded as 'eminently bad' the wares which competed with home products; they deprecated 'things of mere luxury and pleasure;' yet they recognized the utility of commodities with which the nation could not dispense or which could be re-exported. On this basis was constructed a protective network of prohibitions and high tariffs on foreign manufactured goods, combined with the removal of duties on foreign raw materials: at the same time the export of most native products was stimulated by fiscal immunities —the remission or reduction of duties—as well as by the institution of bounties. The embargoes laid on the transportation of machinery and on the emigration of skilled artisans were other links in the chain of protection devised to safeguard the English producer as much as possible against his alien competitors.

The system of protection had its counterpart in the attempts to promote by direct means the domestic consumption of native manufactures. A strong agitation in favour of the compulsory wearing of English cloth sprang up in the seventeenth century. In the course of a parliamentary debate opposition was voiced on the plea that it was 'hard to make a law whereby we shall not know our wives from our chambermaids.' After the Restoration it was enacted that the dead must be buried in woollen cloth.

> 'Since the Living would not bear it,
> They should, when dead, be forc'd to wear it.'

Again when the cap-makers complained that men had left off wearing caps, Parliament ordered everyone above six years old 'except ladies and gentlemen' to wear 'a cap of wool' on Sundays and holidays, because the wearing of caps was 'very decent and comely.' The state endeavoured to regulate not only the apparel but also the diet of its subjects. After the Reformation the policy of 'Fish Days' was adopted, requiring abstention from meat on certain days in the week —'so the sea-coasts shall be strong with men and habitations, and the fleet flourish more than ever.' One fish, the herring, which played an important part in the fate of empires—the decline of the Hanseatic League and the rise of Holland—was held in particular repute as the 'king of fish.' 'No clothing comparable to the English bay nor pheasant excelling a seasonable English red herring,' was the verdict of Spaniards in the seventeenth century. And the housewife had at her command recipes for its preparation which ran into many scores.

Mercantilism, while it was at pains to stimulate manufactures, endeavoured to avoid a one-sided development of the national economy. Adam Smith's reflection—that the discovery of America and a passage to the East Indies by the Cape of Good Hope raised the mercantile system 'to a degree of splendour and glory which it could never otherwise have attained,' by making the towns of Europe become the manufacturers and carriers for Asia, Africa and America— led him to the conclusion that the object of mercantilism was to enrich a nation 'rather by trade and manufactures than by the improvement and cultivation of land.' Yet in the case of England, at any rate, it was perhaps the most instructive feature of mercantilism that it did not sacrifice agriculture to industry but sought to preserve something of a balance between them.

Tillage was considered one of the principal supports of the mercantilist state. It maintained people on the land in healthy employment, and freed the nation from dependence upon other countries for its food supply—'The realm doth more stand upon itself.' In harmony with this broad conception of the place of agriculture in the national economy, corn-growers were encouraged to raise grain sufficient to satisfy the public demand and furnish a surplus for sale abroad. The avowed object of agrarian legislation was to provide the requisite stimulus by permitting the export of corn and prohibiting its import except when prices became excessive at home. Yet under the Tudors and Early Stuarts the enactments which were nominally framed to safeguard the producer of food veiled a consistent determination to favour the consumer. The statutory price limit, at which the transportation of corn was allowed, was almost invariably below the price in the home market, so that legally no shipment was permissible. No doubt the main reason was the anxiety of the government to keep the price of corn low for the sake of the poor, partly from humanitarian motives and partly to prevent disturbances.

After the Restoration there was a complete reversal of the system which had been followed in earlier times: genuine protection was now accorded to the arable farmer. The change was due primarily to the ascendancy of the land-owning class. It was intended to promote the interests of the proprietor whose rents would benefit, and to give his tenants an assured market for their produce. It must be noticed, however, that the adoption of a new corn policy was facilitated by the advance in agricultural technique which raised the standard of husbandry and allayed the apprehensions of famine. From this time onwards, for a hundred years, it was believed that English agriculture could be relied upon to fulfil the nation's requirements. The new policy was enunciated in the act of 1670, which permitted the export of native corn whatever its price might be in the home market. Not less important was the principle laid down in regard to foreign corn. A high duty was imposed by the act of 1670 on imported grain when prices in England were low, and a low duty when prices were high. In other words, foreign corn could only be imported when native corn was dear. The result of these historic measures was to yield the corn-grower almost complete protection. He could freely export his own grain, and he was protected from alien competition unless prices here soared to famine heights. The corn law of the Restoration thus gave effect to the fundamental maxim of mercantilism that a country should aim at being self-supporting. The encouragement bestowed on the English farmer under the Later Stuarts went further, for the system of bounties on the export of corn was also inaugurated after the Restoration. It was then provided that a bounty should be paid on different kinds of grain when shipped abroad, so long as the prices at home did not exceed a stated figure. The purpose of the bounty was to ensure stability of prices, which would remove the farmers' fear of loss in the event of the market being glutted with a surplus of grain. It expressed the idea that the state should determine the nature of the economic activities of the community, encouraging some forms of enterprise by means of subsidies or bounties and discouraging others by the levy of duties.

Whether the achievement must be placed to the credit of economic statesmanship, or ascribed in part to favourable seasons and the progress of husbandry stimulated by the needs of an urban population, England became 'a famous kingdom for corn.' She had emerged from the stage in which the Venetian envoy could write home: 'In some places grain abounds, and there would be much more did not the natives shun fatigue.' Nor did she feed her own people alone. The statistics of the export trade register its growth and lend colour to the claim that England did 'feed other countries.' Even in the early years of George III's reign Arthur Young still clung to the belief that foreign nations might be induced 'to buy their corn of us than to cultivate it themselves.' In the last quarter of the eighteenth century, when the foundations of the mercantile system began to crumble, the increase of population led to the abandonment of the attempt to make England a self-supporting country. Nevertheless the protection of agriculture survived to the middle of the nineteenth century when the corn laws were at length repealed.

The navigation acts were intended to foster the growth of a mercantile marine: with this end in view they imposed the obligation to employ native ships. They were a legacy of the middle ages since the project of safeguarding the carrying trade dates from the fourteenth century. The navigation system was only intermittently enforced until the seventeenth century, when a comprehensive code was embodied in the famous enactments of 1651 and 1660 which provided the framework of English naval policy for nearly two centuries. The act of 1651 forbade any commodity to be imported from Asia, Africa and America except in English[1] ships; and from Europe except in ships belonging to England or to the country of its origin. The act of 1660 ordered that the master of an English vessel and three-fourths at least of its crew must be English; that all goods exported from or

---

[1] In these acts English included colonial.

imported into the colonies must be carried in ships owned by English subjects; that no 'enumerated commodities'—sugar, tobacco, cotton, etc.—should be exported from any colony except to another English colony or to the mother country. Subsequent measures extended the scope or relaxed the stringency of the navigation laws.

To form a just estimate of the mercantile system two things must be borne in mind. Part of the criticism directed against it is based upon an erroneous interpretation of its aims. Part reflects the inability to grasp the fact that a nation is a living organism whose growth is determined by historical conditions which the rulers of a community must take into account in their conduct of public affairs. In every phase of economic development the new is interwoven with the old; and the trend of statecraft necessarily depends upon the degree to which traditional influences still retain their potency. More fairly we can criticize mercantilism for pursuing objects which were mutually contradictory. The navigation acts were intended to promote a mercantile marine but they hampered industry and commerce upon which the carrying trade rested: the protection given to one branch of industry was often detrimental to other branches: the old colonial system served to limit rather than extend the capacity of the colonies to absorb the products of the mother country. Another valid criticism of mercantilist policy is that it looked with envy upon the prosperity of other countries—at one time Spain, then Holland, subsequently France; and it did not recognize that a trading nation benefits by having wealthy customers even if they are also competitors. Its standpoint was that of a merchant who sees his opportunity in the misfortunes of a rival. The conception of a fixed volume of trade implied that the economic progress of one state was achieved at the expense of others, and that its elimination would automatically enable its rivals to grasp a larger share for themselves. The elastic nature of trade warns us against such facile assumptions. The commercial jealousies between nations proved a fertile source of wars, for which a heavy price was exacted in the dislocation of industry, the increase of unemployment and the erection of workhouses.

When we turn from the aims to the achievements of the mercantile system we find a sharp division of opinion. The critics belittle its practical importance. They view its legislative programme as an empty futility which pursued a mirage, the accumulation of precious metals: they maintain that it diverted the national energies into channels where they were less profitably employed: they attribute to its operation the disruption of the first colonial empire. Another school of thought discerns in mercantilism a vital element in the explanation of England's industrial, commercial and maritime pre-eminence. It holds that the expansion of her industry and oversea trade, the supremacy of her naval power, and the building up of an empire bound together by political and economic bonds, all testify to the success and wisdom of mercantilist policy.

Our own estimate of the mercantile system starts with the recognition that England in the seventeenth and eighteenth centuries did make immense strides. The crux of the problem is to determine how far this notable advance was due to a planned economy. In general, economic effects are produced by the interplay of a variety of factors and it is difficult to measure the precise significance of any particular element. It is apparent that mercantilism does not furnish the sole or even the main explanation of England's industrial and commercial growth, because foreign countries lagged behind although they had recourse to similar expedients. Other influences besides legislative interference were at work, and they serve to show how intricate are the threads that weave the economic pattern. The first was the energetic and resourceful character of the business leaders, who were drawn from all sections of the community since trade was not considered a bar to 'gentility.' The second was the scope afforded to freedom of enterprise by the gradual relaxation of the traditional gild restraints. The third was the reign of law, 'the best inheritance that the subject hath,' which protected the liberty and property of the individual. The fourth was the stability of the political institutions and security from invasion—'Nature has given us the best frontier in the world,' observed an eighteenth-century writer. The fifth was the abundance of natural products—especially corn and wool—and the early exploitation of the mineral wealth in coal. The sixth was the geographical situation in relation to Europe and America combined with a multitude of convenient harbours. The seventh was the adventurous spirit which encompassed the globe and opened up new markets for manufactures. The eighth was scientific discoveries in agriculture and mechanical inventions in industry. The ninth was the settlement of aliens. The tenth was the flexibility of the fiscal system which kept the burden of taxes proportioned to the expanding wealth of the nation, coupled with the general disappearance of tolls in internal trade. The eleventh was the rise of a banking system which afforded opportunities for the deposit and employment of capital. The twelfth was the cumulative effects of centuries of uninterrupted economic growth. This impressive array of the factors which enabled England to outstrip her rivals in the race for industrial and commercial supremacy makes it impossible to assert that her economic ascendancy rested on the mercantile system. When a seventeenth-century writer affirmed that 'no nation in the world is naturally so adapted for a mighty trade of all sorts as England,' it was her natural advantages which he had in mind.

Nevertheless we must not under-estimate the genuine importance of the policy pursued by mercantilist statesmen. It can scarcely be questioned, for instance, that tariffs may materially assist an infant industry, though subsidies fulfil the same purpose without raising prices to the consumer. In the sphere of agriculture the institution of bounties on corn exported abroad achieved positive results in encouraging the farmers to retain land under the plough. If England became 'a famous kingdom for corn,' mercantilism may claim a portion of the credit. In other directions the results attained by legislative measures were more problematical. There are grounds for dissenting from the opinion—shared even by Adam Smith who considered them 'the wisest of all the commercial regulations of England'—that the acts of navigation stimulated the growth of shipping. Again in the treatment of Ireland, where the clamour of sectional interests produced a crop of repressive legislation, mercantilism conceived in the narrowest spirit yielded the fruits which for centuries embittered the relations between the two neighbouring countries.

One memorable feature of mercantilist policy was the old colonial system. Nothing that happened in the seventeenth century was more momentous in its consequences for the future destiny of mankind than the settlement of the New World by emigrants from the Old; but no one could foresee the incalculable significance of this impact of America upon Europe, and it was natural that the colonies should be viewed not as the nucleus of a new civilization but as the by-product of the old civilization. England's colonies were never intended to be like those of Ancient Greece, which cherished the sacred fire taken from the hearth of the parent state to remind them of their common origin, while they retained complete independence in the management of their domestic concerns. The English settlers in the New World also carried with them the sacred fire in the form of a knowledge of law and the ordered liberty that springs from law, but in addition they preserved an organic connexion with the mother country from which they were sprung. The 'Acts of Trade,' which governed the economic relations between England and her colonies, had injurious effects that were not always negligible. They failed indeed to check the growth of the woollen and iron industries in America, yet they had the unfortunate result of inducing the colonists, as Benjamin Franklin protested, to 'reflect how lightly the interest of all America had been estimated here when the interests of a few of the inhabitants of Great Britain happened to have the smallest competition with it.' They were condemned by the Elder Pitt who expressed his conviction that 'the whole commercial system of America may be altered to advantage. You have prohibited where you ought to have encouraged; and you have encouraged where you ought to have prohibited.' And Burke went to the root of the matter when he claimed that a great empire cannot be supported 'upon a narrow and restrictive scheme of commerce.'

None the less economic grievances were not the principal cause of the American Revolution. It is incorrect to say that England lost her first empire 'in consequence of an attempt to maintain the monopoly of colonial trade.' This notion now grown into a hoary legend is not supported by modern scholarship. In order to judge the system on which the British Empire was based for two centuries in a true historical perspective, it must be interpreted in the light of the services rendered to the oversea dominions. England furnished the plantations with their first settlers: she found the capital for their development: she ensured them a preferential market for their produce: she safeguarded their trade routes: she defended them from hostile attacks. Thus the old colonial system, though it assumed that the mother country was entitled to reap substantial benefits from her possessions, was far from being one-sided. Under it the colonies enjoyed reciprocal advantages in the shape of the protection, the credit and the market of the parent state. In one important commodity, tobacco, the colonists were given a monopoly of the English market at the expense of the English farmer whose interests were sacrificed. The ruthless destruction of tobacco-planting in England is a forgotten page of history. It took nearly a century to stamp it out; and the services of the militia and even of the regular troops had to be requisitioned year by year to trample down the growing crops. The maintenance of an unpopular policy in the face of widespread opposition at home was clearly due to the conviction that the prosperity of the plantations was bound up with the retention of their market in this country. All things considered it may be fairly debated whether—in spite of the subordination of their economic interests to the welfare of the motherland—they did not derive from the connexion ample compensation for the sacrifices which it entailed. The Declaration of Independence (which makes no reference to the 'Acts of Trade' beyond an allusion of doubtful significance) was born more of a sense of economic strength than of economic weakness.

Laissez-Faire

The growth of individualism was attended by practical consequences of the first magnitude. It not only bore massive fruit in the new economic structure of society described in a previous chapter but it also had a decisive influence in the domain of public policy. The entrepreneurs claimed a free hand in the management of their business; and owing to the pressure which they successfully exerted, the industrial system began to be liberated from state control as early as the seventeenth century, although the commercial system was not released from the stranglehold of tariffs until the nineteenth century. The one development emancipated the manufacturing class, while the other set free the mercantile class.

The age of mercantilism was the battle-ground in which was fought out the issue whether individualism should be allowed a free hand or kept rigorously under control. The issue was a momentous one for the future destiny of the English people. Every economic regime prescribes its own standards of conduct, and there was a fundamental difference in the basic concepts of the old order and of the new. The old order did not divorce economics from ethics, but judged economic behaviour by an ethical standard which took account of the social reactions. In subordinating sectional claims to the common good it reflected the current precepts of morality. Hence the insistence on righteous dealing between landlord and tenant; hence the view of commerce as the means to promote the welfare of the community and provide a 'sufficient' recompense to the trader; hence the doctrine of a 'just price' that was fair alike to producer and consumer; hence the efforts to extirpate the 'corrupt practices,' as they were styled, of commercial speculation which manipulated supplies with the object of forcing up prices; and hence the unsparing denunciation of enclosures for sheep-farming. The new order judged economic behaviour by the standard of enlightened self-interest; and this frank avowal registered a stage in the evolution of economic thought. The classical economists did not discover the 'economic man,' who pursues his personal gain. Indeed in the middle of the seventeenth century he had already inspired the bitter reflection: 'What does the merchant care, so that he be rich, how poor the public is?' Nor was there any novelty in Adam Smith's famous dictum which became the accepted postulate of his school of thought—'Man's self-love is God's providence.' The contention that public and private interests are ultimately identical had been anticipated nearly a century earlier by Sir Dudley North, when he claimed that 'wherever the traders thrive the public of which they are a part thrives also.' The new trend of opinion created the setting in which an insurgent individualism could work out its destiny unhampered by the traditional morality.

This revolution in ideas was not only a crucial departure from orthodox principles but it involved a choice between two conflicting ideals which seemed irreconcilable— economic progress and social stability. Sheep-farming provided England's greatest manufacture with its raw material, yet it caused the displacement of the tenantry from their ancestral holdings and flooded the peaceful countryside with swarms of beggars who were a menace to public order and private security. The growth of capitalism in industry degraded the status of the independent craftsman and created the wage-system. The expansion of commerce exposed England to the vicissitudes of a world economy, with its concomitants of commercial crises and unemployment. In short, economic change meant a loss of social security. The fundamental question was therefore raised whether the state could successfully control the rising tide of individualism; whether it could give scope to the free play of capitalist enterprise while ensuring that the pursuit of private gain was not detrimental to the community.

In its handling of the situation the monarchy stood unmistakably for the preservation of the old order—in the economic sphere not less than in the spheres of religion and politics. Without attempting to check the development of a capitalist class, it endeavoured to define its activities in order to prevent a violent breach with the usages of an ordered economic life. To this end it applied on a national scale the principles by which in the middle ages the corporate institutions—urban gilds and rural courts—had sought to regulate industry and agriculture. Statute law came to the rescue of local law: it reinforced a decaying custom which was breaking down under the pressure of economic forces. The position taken up by the Crown was one of the main reasons for the alienation of the middle class whose political self-assertion, born of a sense of economic power, was nourished and inflamed by specific grievances. By the side of the religious and constitutional struggles proceeded another struggle—a duel between the monarchy seeking to preserve the traditional framework of society, and an aggressive and progressive middle class bent on establishing its ascendancy. The issues at stake in the Civil War were not only those of the Crown versus Parliament and of the Established Church versus Nonconformity, but of a community conducting its economic functions on a disciplined if confined basis versus the entrepreneur following a lonely furrow.[1] The eclipse of the Tudor and Early Stuart regime was destined to usher in an era of economic freedom not

---

[1] Richard Baxter's analysis of 'the quality of the persons which adhered to the king and to the Parliament' implies that economic causes had a conspicuous share in determining the alignment of parties in the Civil War.

less than it inaugurated an era of constitutional and religious freedom.

We are confronted with the question: why did the monarchy fail to control the dynamic forces which shattered the corporate fabric of English society? Ultimately the explanation lies in the fact that the communal organization had for the time being exhausted its vitality. Its slower-moving mechanism was not sufficiently flexible to adjust itself spontaneously to the ever-changing needs of a people in whom the adventuring spirit of enterprise was never wholly quiescent. None the less subsidiary causes were in operation. One was the personal character of the monarchs. Queen Elizabeth sanctioned an elaborate code which turned local law (the custom of the locality) into national law (the custom of the country) by extending the scope of the age-old principles of wage assessment, technical training, a balanced economy [1] and relief of the poor; and the code remained on the statute-book for two hundred and fifty years. Her successors were signally unfitted for the planning and execution of a coherent policy; if their statecraft had been more enlightened, the breach between mediaeval and modern society might have been less irreparable. Moreover the economic problem became inextricably entangled with other problems which excited even more passionate feeling. The issue between the monarchy as the champion of the established economic order, and the rising middle class as its assailant, became involved with a widely different issue between the monarchy as the champion of the established religious order and the Puritan opposition. And yet a third issue was created when the monarchy, seeking to maintain its traditional position in the state, came into collision with the legislature which was encroaching upon the royal prerogative. Thus on one side was ranged the historic monarchy, defender of the national church and a corporate society; on the other side a representative assembly voicing the demand

[1] Limitations on the choice of apprentices in industry were designed to prevent the movement of labour from agriculture.

of the pioneers of individualism for religious and economic freedom. The interaction of religious and economic factors provided the mainspring of a constitutional movement which resulted in consolidating the ascendancy of Parliament and in freeing the capitalist class from control by the Crown.

The authority of the monarchy in the economic arena was impaired not only by its conflict with the religious and parliamentary forces arrayed against it but also by its alienation of the judicature. The common law of England was unfavourable towards restraints on individualism unless they were definitely sanctioned by immemorial usage; it was opposed to any fresh restrictions upon enterprise; and it disliked the exercise of the royal prerogative in economic affairs. 'The common law,' declared chief justice Coke in a memorable passage, 'hath so admeasured the prerogatives of the king that they should not take away nor prejudice the inheritance of any; and the best inheritance that the subject hath is the law of the realm.' The Crown, therefore, could not look to the law courts for support of its economic policy. Finally the monarchy was gravely handicapped by the absence of a trained civil service, which would have made it more practicable to curtail the field of capitalist enterprise. The strict regimentation of the economic system was viewed as the province of the state at a time when the machinery of government was primitive and a civil service of the modern pattern hardly existed. Nevertheless even if the Crown had been supported by a staff of professional administrators it could not have averted, though it might have modified, the establishment of a capitalist society. Alike in industry, commerce and agriculture, the foundations of the old order had been sapped by the subtle permeation of the spirit of capitalism. The mediaeval fabric still retained much of its old aspect, yet its vitality had been largely drained away until in reality there often remained little more than an empty shell.

The struggle between the monarchy and the middle class

175

lasted over a century: it might have proved more protracted but for the outbreak of the Civil War. The revolt against authority in the constitutional and religious spheres swept away the obstacles which had hitherto stifled the protests against authority in the economic sphere. The dissolution of the bonds which held society together had abiding consequences. A violent shock was given to institutions which had regulated the workings of the traditional system. When a settled government was at length established, it was unable to revive in their fullness the authoritarian sanctions which had enabled the monarchy to destroy or penalize enclosures; to bring pressure to bear on employers; to require local magistrates to provide work for the poor; to insist on technical training for artisans; to assess wages; to place individuals or corporations in charge of a branch of industry; and in other ways to superintend the economic life of the community. As the outcome of the Great Rebellion the movement towards *laissez-faire* acquired increasing momentum. In the relaxation of state control lies the untold economic significance of the Civil War.

From the Restoration, more than a century before the 'Industrial Revolution' or the publication of Adam Smith's *The Wealth of Nations*, the doctrine of economic freedom began to gain an increasing hold over the minds of the governing body. A number of factors were working in this direction.

In the first place, the development of capitalism and the stimulus of expanding trade had fostered and brought to maturity the nascent individualism of the middle class: already released from the jurisdiction of the craft gilds, it was grown ripe for the assertion of industrial liberty against the state itself. The business community now felt itself strong nough to claim the right to manage its own affairs withoute official guidance. In the second place, the new political system favoured economic emancipation since the monarchy could no longer exercise a restraining influence. The collapse

176

of the authoritarian regime proved to be the turning-point in the evolution of capitalism in England. It eliminated the one barrier which obstructed the path of the entrepreneur who was allowed henceforth a freer hand in industry. The constitutional order established at the Restoration and consolidated by the Revolution of 1688 created the framework within which a capitalist society could work out its destiny, unhampered by the control that the Crown had endeavoured to enforce. In the third place, the Civil War proved a powerful dissolvent of traditional ways of thought. The reaction against constituted authority extended inevitably to the economic field and encouraged a critical attitude towards state interference. The vigorous attack made by a group of Restoration writers upon restraints in internal trade and industry revealed the extent to which a growing body of public opinion had emancipated itself from many of the dogmas enshrined in the outlook of the age. In the fourth place, the trend of the judicial decisions given in courts of law was in favour of industrial freedom, and the judges were particularly potent in circumscribing the scope of the Statute of Apprentices and in undermining the legal position of the craft gilds. In the fifth place, the waning power of the Privy Council—whose multifarious activities, mirrored in its records, had pervaded every branch of the national economy—weakened irreparably the existing mechanism of administration. Once the government ceased to wield its former authority, the structure of which it had been the pivot began to disintegrate, and the economic functions of the local bodies in consequence largely lapsed.

The combined weight of all these factors produced an orientation of policy, which found expression in a definite advance towards *laissez-faire*. Parliament came directly under the influence of a capitalist regime which had successfully challenged the right of the Crown to limit its power, and now proceeded to demand its liberation from the shackles laid upon it by the legislature. Accordingly the old industrial code was allowed gradually to fall into desuetude.

The whole economic outlook of the eighteenth century was permeated by an encroaching individualism which insisted upon unfettered freedom of action, and imposed upon the government the course that it must pursue. Owing to this reversal of roles, the state renounced the right of dictating to entrepreneurs the terms on which they should employ their workfolk, and admitted their claims to make their own contract regarding the rates of remuneration, the length of service, the quality and supply of labour, and the nature of the products. Parliament pronounced the maxim in 1702 which was to mould its policy throughout the century—'Trade ought to be free and not restrained.' Fifty years later a parliamentary committee was appointed to inquire into 'the laws relating to trade and manufactures.' Its report, which constitutes a landmark in the progress of economic thought, indicated how drastic was the alteration in sentiment towards the enactments of a bygone age, 'perhaps well calculated for the times in which they were made, yet now become prejudicial to Trade in its present state.' In the traditional spirit of English institutional development piecemeal legislation, combined with the process of natural decay, sapped the foundations of the old order. Once the state abdicated its authority the relations of capital and labour entered on a fresh stage and ceased to be subject to the rule of law. Instead of the general conditions of employment being controlled by a superior power, they were determined henceforth according to the respective strength of the opposing sides.

The system of wage regulation survived the transformation of the political landscape, though in the main it was kept alive not by official pressure but by custom and usage—with the result that in the eighteenth century there was only intermittent action on the part of the magistrates, and wage assessment was not in constant operation as a regular procedure. The change of front on the part of the state was signally displayed in the year 1756. The weavers in the west of England appealed to the legislature to revive the system of wage regulation. In response Parliament re-enacted the Elizabethan statute on behalf of the woollen industry, but the next year it was induced to annul the measure. Its action was almost in the nature of an economic revolution. When wage control was openly abandoned in the premier industry of the country, the principles of *laissez-faire* received their first legislative sanction. In the case of unemployment the effect produced by the new outlook on industrial problems was more immediate. The Civil War brought to an end the practice by which employers were required by the state to keep their men at work in times of depression. The fact that the workers had no safeguard against dismissal threw them upon their own resources. They were forced to shoulder responsibilities which had hitherto been the province of the state, and to rely upon their own efforts for the maintenance of their standard of life. It is therefore significant that the change in public policy was shortly followed by the rapid growth of trade unions, which sprang into prominence as soon as the state loosened its grip upon economic life. Parliament also declined to lend its support to another part of the Elizabethan code—apprenticeship. While the system of technical training held its ground successfully in normal times, its survival was a matter of custom rather than compulsion. The disintegration of the apprenticeship system in its legal form paved the way for its dissolution in its economic form when the factory owners, indifferent to the claims of technical workmanship, sought only to buy their labour in the cheapest market. And finally the national regulation of industry, which was intended to standardize the production of staple wares, fell into disfavour. In actual practice it was found impossible to coerce the manufacturers into managing their business on the lines laid down for them. By the end of the seventeenth century the restrictions imposed by paternal legislation were fast becoming obsolete. It was drily remarked that 'as the worthy makers of those good laws are now asleep, so are their laws too.' The standpoint of the new age was indicated by Sir Dudley

North: 'Thus we may labour to hedge in the cuckoo but in vain, for no people ever yet grew rich by policies; but it is peace, industry and freedom that brings trade and wealth, and nothing else.'

While the state moved steadily in the direction of *laissez-faire*, it was not ready to cast to the winds all the cherished traditions which had inspired the legislation of an earlier epoch. Its action was not guided by any conscious theory of non-intervention but was largely opportunist. After the machinery for wage assessment was expressly discarded in the woollen manufacture, it was revived in several occupations—notably silk-weaving where it lasted until little more than a century ago. The right to fix the prices of bread and coal persisted and was reaffirmed in a number of statutes. None the less the trend of parliamentary thought was unmistakable: for good or evil the current had set towards free enterprise and freedom of contract.

The waning control of the state had its counterpart in the fate which overtook the craft gilds. For hundreds of years the latter had embodied a living tradition which enshrined the principle that industry should be regulated by corporate bodies, and that no one should pursue a skilled occupation who was not a member of one of these bodies. When, however, the entrepreneur emerged as the outstanding figure in the industrial life of the community, the craft gilds began to be considered an anachronism. In harmony with the individualist spirit of the age, they were now denounced as obstacles to the growth of trade. The corroding influence of capitalism upon the old industrial order was thus reinforced by the belief that the craft gilds hampered economic development through their efforts to exclude non-members from setting up in trade or working at a skilled profession, and through 'vexatious indictments' against those who engaged in a mistery to which they had not served an apprenticeship.

Other factors helped to make the decline of the craft gilds

inevitable. One was the failure to extend their authority to the outlying suburbs. Another was the rise of towns like Birmingham, Manchester, Leeds and Halifax, which were not wedded to 'ancient customs, franchises and liberties.' A third was that groups of capitalists sometimes exploited the gild organization to fulfil their own ends. Already in the later middle ages the control of the craft gilds had begun to pass to the richer members, who set at defiance two fundamental maxims of the gild economy—equality of opportunity for traders and care for the interests of consumers. Nevertheless it is noteworthy that the legislature did not venture to destroy the historic gild communities: the corporate tradition was too deeply-rooted in the national consciousness of the English people to allow of a frontal attack. Instead the craft gilds underwent a slow process of decay in which their life-blood was drained away in an atmosphere that was repugnant to their basic concepts. While no general act of parliament down to 1835 abolished their privileges[1]—and restraints on trade, real or nominal, still persisted in many places—the craft gilds found it increasingly difficult to enforce a strict observance. The law courts in the main ranged themselves on the side of industrial freedom; and the notable share which they took in fostering individualism may be fairly compared with their championship of political freedom. The fact that the common law, as a rule, favoured the removal of curbs on private enterprise was profoundly significant: as a consequence the main current of economic life swept by the traditional framework of a corporate society, unimpeded by any serious legal obstacles.

The trend towards *laissez-faire* after the Restoration demonstrates that there are no adequate grounds for assuming that Adam Smith converted England to the doctrine of industrial freedom, any more than that he converted England to the doctrine of the free exchange of goods.

[1] The Municipal Corporations Act (1835) authorized 'every person in any borough' to 'use every lawful trade and handicraft.'

Laissez-faire has a long history behind it. Even in the days when government control of industry was most active, it is difficult to determine the extent to which the manufacturing class submitted to it, since the repeated but futile efforts of the authorities to regulate the conduct of his business were met by the entrepreneur with passive resistance. In the absence of a civil service and an efficient system of inspection, it is certain that much of the industrial legislation was virtually a dead letter. The regulation of wages by the magistrates degenerated into a routine which rapidly produced a distinction between the legal rates sanctioned by authority and the market rates paid by employers. The institution of apprenticeship was undermined by the inclination of the law courts to weaken the checks which it imposed on individual enterprise; and in practice it was effective only when enforced by the custom of the trade. The famous assize of cloth, which fixed the dimensions of cloth, proved unworkable. It was found impossible to prevent the use of tenter-frames for stretching cloth and of gig mills for dressing cloth. Hence it is to the seventeenth century, and not to the 'Industrial Revolution' nor to *The Wealth of Nations*, that we must look for the movement towards *laissez-faire* in industry and for the cause of its triumph. Adam Smith only gave articulate expression to ideas in whose direction the leaders of industry had long been feeling their way. The belated repeal of the labour code in 1809 (in the woollen industry) and in 1813–14 (in other industries) was necessitated by the activities of informers and attorneys, who 'rummaged out' obsolete laws in the vain hope to stem the advance of the factory system. Its importance, therefore, should not be exaggerated as though it indicated that the legislature had suddenly surrendered itself to the influence of the classical economists. The relaxation of industrial restraints was already an accomplished fact upon which Parliament now proceeded to place the formal seal of legislative approval.

The control exercised by the state in the domain of foreign

trade survived long after its control over industry had virtually lapsed. The explanation lies in the united front which the entrepreneurs presented in their demand for *laissez-faire* in industry as contrasted with the cleavage of opinion in their ranks regarding external trade. The manufacturers insisted on protection against alien competition, and their views prevailed over those of the mercantile interests. The inauguration of free trade was delayed until the last quarter of the eighteenth century, when a commercial treaty with France [1] provided for the abolition of 'the prohibitions and prohibitory duties which have existed for almost a century between the two nations.' It is a common assumption that the adoption of a new commercial policy was due to the influence of Adam Smith. Actually among the forces responsible for the disintegration of the mercantile system and the substitution of a policy of plenty for the policy of self-sufficiency, *The Wealth of Nations* played a much smaller part than is usually attributed to it. It was not an abstract theory of international trade, nor a convincing demonstration of the fallacies of protection, that won over English industrialists to free trade. The real cause was the confidence which they had come to feel in their ability to meet foreign competition. The industrial interests still demanded protection, but they were content to dispense with *legal* protection once they enjoyed the *natural* protection afforded by their superior efficiency. In short the beginnings of the free trade movement in England were inspired by practical considerations; and theoretical arguments did not carry the weight with which they are generally credited.

[1] In 1786. An earlier attempt at free trade—when the tory ministry endeavoured to conclude a commercial treaty with France as part of the Treaty of Utrecht (1713)—had been unsuccessful.

PART III
THE AGE OF MACHINERY

Chapter Seven

'THE INDUSTRIAL REVOLUTION'

The romance of industry has its heroes no less than wars or voyages of exploration or empire-building. Men of inventive talent, thrilled by the great mechanical discoveries of a stirring age, were attracted into a field where glittering prizes dazzled the imagination. The spirit of adventure which had inspired the Elizabethan seamen in the sixteenth century now found expression in the longing to wrest from nature her coveted and closely-guarded secrets. The inventors opened a vital chapter in our island story, of which the pages are inscribed with a galaxy of momentous achievements: but their importance is not confined to England. Among the great events that have shaped the destiny of mankind, a distinctive place will always be assigned to the series of inventions which have subjected natural forces to the service of man. The historian sees in these inventions the climax of centuries of economic development. The economist is concerned with their effects which are writ large over the whole face of modern society. The inventions substituted for human energy the machine working under human guidance; and they have produced far-reaching consequences of which it is the purpose here to attempt some estimate.

It is tempting to dramatize great events; we picture them as thunderbolts emerging out of a clear blue sky; our minds are impressed by their apparent unexpectedness. Yet to the historian this attitude is profoundly untrue to historical realities. Where the popular imagination visualizes a swift transformation of the social or political landscape, the historian is conscious of a process of gradual change in which the old is blended almost imperceptibly with the new. Hence to view the 'Industrial Revolution' in its proper perspective, we must first discard the current clichés that

187

embody the traditional idea of the inventions and serve to distort their real significance.

According to the common belief the inventions constitute the starting-point of the present industrial society. They are generally regarded as the beginning of modern economic life, just as the French Revolution is regarded as the beginning of modern political life. The popular interpretation of the 'Industrial Revolution' traces to the introduction of machinery all the phenomena that we consider most characteristic of the nineteenth and twentieth centuries. Capitalism, factories, large-scale production, oversea markets, trusts, credit instruments, the alternation of booms and slumps, the proletariat and trade unions—these are supposed to have come into existence with the adoption of power-driven machinery not very much more than a hundred years ago. The state of England before the era of the inventions is painted in the stereotyped descriptions as that of a primitive regime in which there was no cleavage between capitalist employers and proletarian wage-earners, no world-wide commerce, no unemployment. Beyond the 'Industrial Revolution' the historians depicted centuries of slow and imperceptible growth during which the face of England remained almost unchanged. A static society slumbered in blissful unconsciousness of the dynamic forces which the invention of the steam engine was destined to let loose upon it. A fanciful picture, which has long passed for authentic history, of a backward community suddenly convulsed by uncontrollable economic impulses and upon which there descended a whirlwind of inventions bringing in their train the capitalist system, the factory system, the wage system, exploitation of labour and social strife.

Nothing more remote from historical truth can well be imagined than the prevailing misconception that the inventions of the late eighteenth century involved a violent breach with the past and effected an abrupt revolution in the tenor and rhythm of the national life. There is a wealth of material, as the foregoing chapters have abundantly shown, to demonstrate that England long before the inventions had a vigorous manufacturing and mercantile life of her own—in which striking resemblances to the modern pattern may be fairly set against the social dissimilarities born of the factory system. Much that is reputed novel in our present society is in reality deep-rooted. The older structure had already evolved many of the capitalist traits associated with the world of to-day; so that, when the invention of machinery ushered in a fresh epoch, it found a country prepared for its reception—where the entrepreneur was recognized as the mainspring of the economic mechanism and where belief in freedom of enterprise had crystallized into a dogma. In short it was in a nation organized on a capitalist basis that the inventions were brought to light. They were not the product of a primitive people absorbed in rural pursuits, but the mature achievement of an advanced community where industry and commerce had become a fruitful source of wealth. If we destroy the legend that the inventions suddenly revolutionized English society and gave birth to a new industrial order, we can at least put in its place a more rational interpretation in which the mechanical changes appear as a natural development in line with the course of historical evolution—the climax of centuries of steady growth.

The question has often been asked why the 'Industrial Revolution' came first to England. The explanation is commonly found in the expansion of her oversea trade with a far-flung commercial empire in America, India and Africa, which together with the Continent of Europe supplied markets for her manufactures. Admittedly the existence of markets abroad provided an incentive for the adoption of inventions: during the first half of the eighteenth century the value of exports from England increased 100 per cent. and the rate of progress continued to be rapid. However it is only a part of the explanation, since France also made notable commercial strides in the eighteenth century but was outstripped in the race for industrial supremacy. Nor would it be correct to infer that the French people were lacking in inventive talent: on the contrary, at one period they led the way in many of the industrial arts. We must take other essential factors into account.

In the first place, prior to the inventions English industry, commerce and banking were constituted on lines which served to make a large outlay on machinery and buildings a practicable as well as a profitable venture; nor could manufacturers have utilized the inventions if England had not accumulated sufficient capital for investment in productive enterprises. In the second place, there existed a class of entrepreneurs equipped with the requisite technical qualities and organizing abilities—and accustomed to large-scale production, the handling of labour forces, the utilization of credit instruments, the dependence on imported materials and the requirements of distant and varied markets. They were no less accustomed to latitude in the conduct of their business and infused with the spirit of enterprise, to which Dean Tucker bore testimony when he declared (1757) that 'almost every master manufacturer hath a new invention of his own and is daily improving on those of others.' In the third place, the growth of population in the hundred years following the Restoration failed to keep pace with the expansion of commerce and industry. The shortage of hands in the textile manufactures, combined with the comparatively high standard of wages, furnished English producers with an inducement to avail themselves of mechanical methods which would economize in the use of labour—a similar motive was not present in the same degree on the Continent. They had further incentives for the introduction of machinery in the shortcomings of the old hand-yarn products because manual spinning had many defects,[1] and in the rise of trade unionism which strengthened the desire

---

[1] The spinner often lacked skill and produced yarn which was neither uniform in quality nor firm enough to stand the strain of the loom; as a result the cloth was uneven in texture. The supply was also irregular.

of employers to be liberated from their dependence upon labour.

In the fourth place, the home market catered for a prosperous society where property was widely diffused, and whose standard of comfort was substantial without being luxurious. Side by side with a widespread middle class which consisted of manufacturers, traders and farmers, there ranged the better-paid sections of artisans and peasants. Voltaire on his visit to our country in the early eighteenth century was struck by the fact that 'the feet of the peasants are not bruised by wooden shoes; they eat white bread, are well-clothed;' and he could have added that they were learning to drink tea. Hume, who considered that 'a too great disproportion [of wealth] among the citizens weakens any state,' drew attention to 'the great advantage of England above any nation' in this respect, and he spoke of the 'riches' of her artisans. Unlike France the fabric of English society was composed of numerous layers which bridged the gulf between rich and poor, and made it relatively easy to move up in the social scale into a higher grade. A writer in 1767 remarked that 'in England the several ranks of men slide into each other almost imperceptibly; and a spirit of equality runs through every part of the constitution. Hence arises a strong emulation in all the several stations and conditions to vie with each other; and a perpetual restless ambition in each of the inferior ranks to raise themselves to the level of those immediately above them. In such a state as this fashion must have an uncontrolled sway. And a fashionable luxury must spread through it like a contagion,' since 'our luxury keeps full pace with our opulence.' This eighteenth-century picture of a fluid and progressive society throws a strong reflected light upon the conditions which were current in earlier times. The ability to rise from lowly beginnings is seen in the careers of two seventeenth-century entrepreneurs —Sir Ambrose Crowley the greatest ironmaster of the Stuart age who started life as a working blacksmith, and Peter Blundell one of its greatest clothiers who also sprang from the ranks. The strength of the movement to overcome class barriers is attested by the complaints that servants aped their superiors in luxury in dress, which put 'all degrees and orders of woman-kind into disorder and confusion,' while the master could not be known from his man except that the latter 'wears better clothes.' The more even distribution of wealth in England, as compared with the Continent, reacted upon the sphere of production. The nature of the market determines the nature of the productive processes, and the prevailing demand of the English people was for commodities which were sound and useful rather than flimsy and artistic. Such commodities could be manufactured by machinery without the loss of their essential qualities. Not only did the character of English wares lend itself to *machine* production, but the flexible trend of national consumption was responsive to *mass* production in a country where the population was increasing, wages were advancing and wants were elastic. The history of the United States demonstrates how a rapidly growing nation with a rising standard of life affords encouragement for the diffusion of new industrial methods and techniques.

In the fifth place, the early exploitation of the coal measures stimulated the progress of industry, for coal served as the fuel of numerous manufactures and as the driving-force of machinery. In the sixth place, all the varied influences (enumerated above[1]) which contributed to England's economic growth played their part in paving the way for the achievements of the factory age. To sum up—the 'Industrial Revolution' came first to England because she had expanding markets at home as well as abroad for her wares; because the nature of these wares was suitable for machine production; because the shortage, frequent inefficiency, relatively high price and organized power of labour supplied a motive to employ mechanical contrivances; because the necessary resources were available for investment; because there existed men of enterprise with the

[1] See Chapter Six.

energy to exploit novel methods; because it lay in the logic of centuries of development as moulded by a variety of contributory influences.

When does the age of the inventions commence? The decades with which the 'Industrial Revolution' is traditionally associated cover the period 1760 to 1830: but these dates are misleading. The events which are designated as the 'Industrial Revolution' constituted no sudden breach with the existing economic order but were part of a continuous movement which had already made marked advance. The famous inventions inseparably linked with the names of Arkwright, Watt, Stephenson and many others, were the climax of a long series of industrial experiments extending over two centuries. One important discovery, the knitting frame of William Lee for manufacturing stockings, showed that inventive genius was not altogether lacking even in the sixteenth century; and if, with this conspicuous exception, the earlier ages were barren of great technical achievements it was not due to want of ideas or energy. The eager search for improvements—reflected in an astonishing list of industrial patents—led Miege (1691) to claim that 'no nation has been more industrious than the English in mechanic arts, and the world to this day is obliged to them for many of their useful inventions and discoveries.' And Cary (1695) depicted a community in which 'new projections are every day set on foot, all which save the labour of many hands.' Nevertheless success in vital things eluded the grasp of the seventeenth century; and there was left as Fuller (a contemporary historian) observed: 'A new world of experiments to the discovery of posterity.'

Two impediments in particular retarded progress in the invention of machinery. Firstly: the fact that the initial stages are necessarily the slowest and most arduous. The idea of an invention may be grasped yet decades may elapse before it can be made to work. Lack of technical knowledge caused wealth laboriously accumulated to be dissipated in fruitless enterprises, where experience was painfully and dearly bought—though without them the discoveries of a later age would have been impossible. Secondly: the hostility displayed by the workers to labour-saving devices was a discouragement to inventive talent. Their aversion sprang from an inherited dislike of innovations, coupled with the fear that they would lose their means of livelihood. From the thirteenth century the introduction of machinery was a fruitful source of dissension, and the government frowned upon the 'abridgment' of labour in order to avoid social unrest. To disarm the popular opposition writers were at pains to correct what they called 'the mistaken notions of the infatuated populace who—not being able to see farther than the first link of the chain—consider all such inventions as taking the bread out of their mouths, and therefore never fail to break out into riots and insurrections whenever such things are proposed.' Accordingly the apologists for machinery were learning to use the familiar argument that cheapness stimulates the demand for commodities which in turn stimulates the demand for labour. Thus the poet Dyer, speaking of Paul's invention of spinning by rollers, bade the women spinners not to lose heart:

'Nor hence, ye nymphs, let anger cloud your brows;
The more is wrought, the more is still requir'd.'

It was as a result of the persistent efforts of innumerable pioneers that a generation before the accession of George III —the customary date assigned for the commencement of the 'Industrial Revolution'—there had already dawned the 'new world' confidently predicted in the previous century. Its golden promise was foreshadowed in a galaxy of outstanding achievements. In the first decade of the eighteenth century Abraham Darby smelted iron ore with coke; in the second decade Newcomen invented the steam engine to drain water from the mines; in the fourth decade Kay invented the fly-shuttle in weaving, and Paul invented spinning by rollers which Arkwright later developed; in the fifth decade Paul invented a carding machine for preparing wool, and Huntsman produced steel by what is known as the crucible process. It is not surprising then to find this picture of the industrial state of England in the middle of the eighteenth century drawn by Dean Tucker: 'Few countries are equal, perhaps none excel the English in the numbers and contrivance of their machines to abridge labour. In regard to mines and metals of all sorts the English are uncommonly dexterous in their contrivance of the mechanic powers. At Birmingham, Wolverhampton, Sheffield and other manufacturing places almost every master manufacturer hath a new invention of his own and is daily improving on those of others.' Thus in spite of obstacles economic society had not remained stagnant. It was continuously evolving, and the stage was being set for the coming of the factory age with its concomitants of power-driven machinery, mass production and the assemblage of workers under one roof.

The series of inventions, comprehended in the term 'Industrial Revolution,' took place in the textile and iron industries; they were accompanied by notable improvements in the system of internal and external transport as well as by an immense expansion of other branches of the national economy, especially coal-mining and engineering. We begin with the textile industries.

To understand the inventions which revolutionized the manufacture of textiles, it is necessary to grasp the nature of the main technical processes involved in the production of cloth. First of all the different qualities of wool in a fleece were sorted and cleansed from impurities. Then in the woollen industry the wool was carded (brushed) in order to disentangle the locks and straighten out and interlace the fibres. In the worsted industry the wool was combed instead of carded, the fibres were laid parallel with each other, and the long wool (the 'top') was separated from the wool of shorter staple (the 'noil'). The wool was now ready for spinning, in which either a distaff and spindle or a spinning wheel—the latter was known in this country at least as early as the fourteenth century—was employed to draw out and twist the fibres so as to form a continuous thread. The wool was converted into a thick coarse thread called roving, and the rovings were spun into a fine twisted thread termed yarn. Next came weaving. A piece of cloth is made up of longitudinal threads (the 'warp') intersected by transverse threads (the 'weft'). The process of weaving consists in inserting the threads of the weft between the alternate threads of the warp by casting a shuttle. When the cloth was woven it was fulled (in the woollen industry only), that is, thickened and felted, after which it was 'dressed' or finished—thus imparting a very smooth appearance to the surface.

Machinery had existed from early times in one of these processes, namely, in fulling. In the thirteenth century water-mills were used to thicken cloth, and they afford the first known example of the application of a motive force to the textile industries. All the other processes, carding, combing, spinning, weaving and finishing, were performed by hand. The era of the inventions was ushered in by John Kay, who was born in 1704 in Lancashire. In 1733 he patented the fly-shuttle[1] whose main feature was a new mode of casting the shuttle. By means of a lever, or 'picking peg,' it was driven to and fro across the warp mechanically without being thrown by the weaver's hand. The speed at which the shuttle could now travel gained for the contrivance the name of fly-shuttle. Robert Kay, a son of John Kay, afterwards invented the drop box which enabled the weaver to use a variety of shuttles, each containing a different coloured weft. The invention of the fly-shuttle permitted a weaver to dispense with assistance in weaving broadcloth: he ceased to be dependent on a journeyman whose irregular habits arising

[1] When Kay's fly-shuttle was introduced into the north of Ireland, the new process of weaving attracted large crowds and one woman 'was enthusiastic in her admiration of it. Clapping her hands, she exclaimed in Scoto-Hibernic phraseology: "Weel, weel! The warks o' God's wondtherful, but the contrivance o' man bates Him at last!" '

from idleness, intemperance or sickness, had often hindered his work. It also proved beneficial to the weaver's health; he was able to sit upright instead of having to lean forward, and was therefore less subject to breast disorders. Yet the work was apparently more strenuous, and the common or double-handed loom still had its advantages for older weavers.

Kay's ill-fated career is a melancholy illustration of the evil destiny which has pursued many of the English inventors: their lives have frequently been a series of disappointments, sometimes relieved by transitory gleams of success but more often shrouded in obscurity and gloom. The weavers of Colchester, where Kay lived, resisted the introduction of the fly-shuttle in the belief that innovations in the method of weaving would take from them their means of livelihood. Their opposition drove Kay to the north of England, and he settled in Leeds. Here he found himself in conflict with the West Riding clothiers, who adopted his invention yet refused to pay for it. Failing to maintain his invention against infringement—and his life threatened by a mob 'determining to hinder the wheel shuttles progress by killing of Mr. John Kay'—he retired to France where the French government awarded him a pension in return for his making shuttles. He died abroad about the age of seventy-five.

The next important invention was made in connexion with the spinning of thread. From time immemorial thread had been spun by hand, but in 1738 Lewis Paul—the son of a French refugee who had settled in this country—with the aid of a skilled mechanic, John Wyatt, invented a machine on which thread was spun without the aid of human fingers. The invention consisted of at least two pairs of rollers, one revolving faster than the other, which drew out the thread to the requisite degree of fineness. A mill was erected at Birmingham and another mill was afterwards started in Northampton. However the enterprise was successful at neither place. Paul was short of capital, and his letters to Wyatt reveal the straits to which he was often reduced in his desperate search to raise the necessary funds. Another reason for Paul's failure to achieve the commercial success which afterwards attended Arkwright's efforts in the same field was that his machine, though identical in principle, was inferior in point of construction. The subsequent fate of Paul's invention has given rise to much controversy; the problem is whether it entirely lapsed or whether it was revived in the next generation. One thing alone is certain: the practical application of automatic spinning was the work of Arkwright.

Richard Arkwright, one of the greatest captains of industry in this country and the most prominent figure in the history of the textile industries, was born in Preston in 1732. He was the youngest of thirteen children, and the impoverished circumstances of his parents threw him at an early age upon the world with none of the advantages of education to help him in the struggle for existence. He was apprenticed to a barber, and settled in Bolton where he obtained some reputation for his skill as a wig-maker. He had no knowledge of mechanics and no practical acquaintance with industrial processes, but he had a keen alert mind, an insatiable curiosity, and a genius for assimilating and developing the ideas of others. His natural gifts more than compensated for any deficiency of technical training, and he showed marked determination in pursuing his opportunities to the utmost. Among the manufacturers in whose midst Arkwright lived the shortage of yarn must have been a constant topic of conversation, and the wealth which awaited the fortunate discoverer of a new process fired the imagination of the poverty-stricken wig-maker. He was drawn irresistibly to mechanical experiments, and he came into contact with a clock-maker whom he employed to construct his apparatus. We cannot tell whether Arkwright's invention was the fruit of his own ingenuity, or whether he had stumbled by accident upon the secret of Paul's invention, or whether he was in any way indebted to any other inventor. All we know is that Arkwright came into possession of the secret which was destined to revolutionize the textile industries and create the modern factory system.

Arkwright had now reached the first milestone along the road which was to lead him to fame and fortune; but to achieve his goal took him many years of unwearied application and devoted labour. He was almost penniless, and his pecuniary difficulties were not completely overcome until he entered into partnership with two wealthy manufacturers at Nottingham, who had abundant resources at their command. In 1769 he took out a patent for his machine. This was known as the water-frame and its leading feature was the use of rollers. The roving, or thick coarse thread, was inserted between a pair of rollers placed in a horizontal position one above the other. These rollers revolved in contact, and as they revolved they compressed and drew the roving from the bobbins. Another pair of rollers revolving several times as fast received the roving from the first pair, and their rapid revolutions reduced the roving into a fine thread. A twist was imparted to the thread by means of revolving spindles, with which the roving was connected as it was drawn out of the second pair of rollers. The machine patented in 1769 was intended only for the final process of spinning—to convert the roving into a fine twisted thread (yarn). A few years later, 1775, Arkwright patented another invention which adapted the system of rollers to the first process of spinning—to convert the wool into rovings. He also invented a machine for carding wool by revolving cylinders in lieu of hand-cards. The series of inventions associated with Arkwright's name thus enabled all the preliminary processes of the cotton and woollen industries to be done by machinery instead of by hand. Henceforth wool could be carded, made into rovings, and spun into yarn without recourse to human fingers. The machine erected by Arkwright at Nottingham was driven by horse-power; then he built a mill at Cromford in Derbyshire where he employed water-power, and this gave his machine the name of water-frame; finally Watt's steam engine was applied to the cotton industry at Papplewick (Nottinghamshire) in 1785 and at Manchester in 1789. Through the use of steam the water-frame became known as the throstle.

Arkwright, unlike the majority of the inventors, won both fame and fortune. He received a knighthood at the hands of George III and was made high sheriff of Derbyshire. He reaped a rich harvest alike by the sale of his machines before his patent rights were cancelled, and by partnerships which gave him a controlling interest in numerous concerns. Among the men of the 'Industrial Revolution' he holds a leading place. It is true that he was not the original inventor of the mode of spinning by rollers, the pivot of all his other achievements; but he knew how to turn an invention to practical account. He was able to develop and bring to perfection the germs of the great ideas contained in the rude imperfect machines which he made the basis for his own creations. And his inventive faculty was combined with an unrivalled skill in business, shrewd judgment and a genius for organization. He was the founder of the modern factory system: not indeed that he erected the first factory in England, but he built up great business enterprises which formed the model for similar undertakings in every part of the country. In this way he inaugurated a new epoch.

The second of the great inventions in the spinning of cotton and wool was the work of James Hargreaves a weaver of Stand Hill near Blackburn, who about 1767 invented the spinning jenny. The merit of Hargreaves's invention was that it enabled spinners to use not one spindle alone, as had been the practice from time immemorial, but eight and ultimately as many as a hundred and twenty spindles at a time. The water-frame and the jenny differed in several respects. The water-frame, although originally employed to reduce the rovings into yarn, was subsequently adapted for all processes of spinning: the jenny was restricted apparently to the final process. Moreover the thread spun on the water-frame was harder, that is, more firmly twisted; and this permitted pure cotton cloth to be manufactured. Hitherto most cotton cloth had consisted of a mixture of linen and cotton to make it strong. Lastly the jenny was an implement which the artisan was able to work in his own cottage with his own hands: the water-frame was a machine which required more than human strength to give it motion. The difference between the jenny and the water-frame thus became the starting-point of a new economic order. The invention of the former was compatible with the retention of the domestic system of industry: the adoption of the latter brought in its train the establishment of the factory system.

Samuel Crompton, the inventor of the mule, first saw light at Firwood near Bolton in the year 1753. He was six-teen years of age when he learnt to spin upon the jenny and barely twenty-one when he started to make improvements, a task which occupied his leisure moments for the next five years. His patience and ingenuity were rewarded with success; but he was too poor or perhaps not enterprising enough to purchase a patent, and too diffident to protect his invention from prying eyes. Confiding in the liberal promises of the manufacturers, he yielded to their solicitations and disclosed the secret of his invention. No sooner was his machine in their hands than he was made conscious of the cruel deception practised upon him. In exchange for a secret which was worth a fortune to its possessor, the inventor obtained the paltry sum of £106; and many of the manufac-turers not only declined to pay the guinea or half-guinea to which they had pledged themselves, but even turned the inventor from their doors when he asked them for payment. This treacherous conduct rankled permanently in Cromp-ton's mind and clouded the rest of his days with gloom. After the lapse of many years Parliament recognized the claims of the inventor, one of the architects of England's industrial greatness, by giving him a grant of five thousand pounds.

Crompton, like Edmund Cartwright, was never able to use his inventive genius as a lever with which to raise up great business enterprises. His shy and retiring disposition was unsuited for the storm and stress of competitive life. He died in 1827, yet long before his death the mule had taken precedence of the water-frame and the jenny. His invention combined the principles of both Arkwright's and Hargreaves's machines:

'The forces of nature could no further go;
To make a third she joined the former two.'

It utilized the system of rollers which drew out and lengthened the rovings, as well as the spindles which served to impart the twist. The rovings as they came from the bobbins passed through the rollers to spindles placed on a spindle carriage—a movable box which ran on wheels. As the rollers gave out the rovings from the bobbins, the spindle carriage receded from the rollers, drawing out and lengthening the thread. This stretched the thread to the requisite degree of fineness and effected the necessary twist. Many improvements were afterwards made in the mule as practical experience brought to light its deficiencies. The most important innovation was the work of Richard Roberts, who invented an automatic or self-acting mule in 1825. The year in which water-power was applied to the mule was 1790. The mule produced finer thread than either the jenny or the water-frame, and rendered it possible to manufacture superior cotton fabrics.

The introduction of machinery in the manufacture of yarn removed the defects of hand-spinning. For one thing machine-spun yarn was more uniform in quality; it was also finer and stronger. Another result of machinery was to liberate the weaver from his dependency upon the hand-spinner; he now had an unlimited supply of material at his disposal. There was no longer a shortage of yarn, for it was estimated that a mule or a water-frame could provide material for about ten looms. Previously half-a-dozen spinners or more might be required to supply one loom. The scarcity of yarn had been an obstacle to the expansion of the textile industries, since an increase in the demand for cloth could not be met automatically by an increase in the output of thread. Now the position was reversed: instead of a shortage of spinners there was a shortage of weavers, and the invention of machinery in the weaving process seemed imperatively demanded. This was the achievement of Cartwright.

Edmund Cartwright, the inventor of the power-loom and the combing machine, was born in 1743 in Nottinghamshire. He entered the Church but a curious chance of fate changed the current of his life and embarked him on an inventor's career, which was destined to give him an enduring place among the creators of modern industry. He has himself related the story how he happened to be at Matlock in 1784 and 'fell in company with some gentlemen of Manchester, when the conversation turned on Arkwright's spinning machinery. One of the company observed that, as soon as Arkwright's patent expired, so many mills would be erected and so much cotton spun that hands could never be found to weave it. To this observation I replied that Arkwright must then set his wits to work to invent a weaving machine. This brought on a conversation on the subject in which the Manchester gentlemen unanimously agreed that the thing was impracticable; and in defence of their opinion they adduced arguments which I certainly was incompetent to answer or even comprehend, being totally ignorant of the subject having never at that time seen a person weave.' He then proceeded to invent a power-loom, for which he took out a patent in 1785.

Cartwright's faith in his machine was unbounded. With all an inventor's eager enthusiasm he sought to turn his discovery to practical account. 'May you weave your webs of gold,' wrote the poet Crabbe to him, but the wish remained unfulfilled and from the start misfortune dogged the inventor's footsteps. A Manchester firm erected a factory large enough to house five hundred power-looms, and a few were set to work as an experiment. The looms are said to have responded 'exceedingly well;' they wrought the work for half the amount of the wages paid to hand-loom weavers, and the latter threatened to destroy the mill. The threat was carried into execution and the mill was burnt down. As a result Cartwright found himself ruined, for no other manufacturer ventured on repeating the experiment. While his discoveries were destined to confer inestimable benefit upon the textile industries, the inventor himself reaped only a harvest of disappointments, though eventually he was awarded by the government a grant of ten thousand pounds. One reason for his failure to convert his discoveries into a source of pecuniary profit was the imperfect nature of his machines as they were first given to the world; another was the difficulty of protecting his patents against infringement.

Cartwright's fertile genius, restless energy and remarkable versatility were displayed in the range of his mechanical researches. His greatest achievement after the invention of a power-loom was the construction of a combing machine for combing wool—the most important preliminary process in the worsted industry. In his erection of a combing machine the inventor seems to have been guided by the same principle which underlies the mechanism of the power-loom: to imitate as closely as possible the movements of the hand but to substitute a mechanical force for manual labour. The genius of Edmund Cartwright pointed the way, yet fifty years were to elapse before the combing machine attained practical value and the requisite degree of perfection. Within a century of Cartwright's own invention the number of patents taken out in connexion with combing machines was nearly five hundred; and this affords convincing proof of the tenacity and zeal with which a long line of inventors—Heilmann, Donisthorpe, Lister, Holden and Noble—applied themselves to the problem.

The invention of machinery would have been robbed of much of its significance but for the discovery of a motive force with which to drive the machines. It was a fortunate coincidence that the year in which Arkwright took out a patent for the water-frame was also the year in which Watt took out a patent for the steam engine. The coincidence is a striking one though it was purely fortuitous, because in its origin the steam engine was devised for the purpose of draining coal-mines.

James Watt, the inventor of the modern steam engine, was born at Greenock in Scotland in 1736. When eighteen years old he was sent by his father to Glasgow to learn the profession of a mathematical instrument-maker. He found no one there who could teach him the craft, and so he proceeded to London where he remained for twelve months. Upon his return to Glasgow he endeavoured to set up in business, but was refused permission to open a shop by the gild of hammermen since he did not possess the qualifications of either patrimony or apprenticeship.[1] The University came to his rescue by allowing him to establish a workshop within its precincts, over which the gilds had no jurisdiction. Here his attention was drawn to the problem of the steam engine, and immediately it became the absorbing interest of his life.

The basic principles of the steam engine—the piston and the cylinder, the expansive force of steam and the creation of a vacuum by its condensation—were already known when Watt embarked upon his investigations. The engines invented by Thomas Newcomen had been in operation for a quarter of a century before Watt was born: they were used for pumping water out of coal, tin and copper-mines. However they suffered from the serious defect that they were wasteful of fuel; and Watt, when a model of Newcomen's engine came into his hands, speedily became cognizant of the defect. 'In the state,' he subsequently related, 'in which I found the steam engine it was no great effort of mind to observe that the quantity of fuel necessary to make it work would for ever prevent its extensive utility. The next step in

[1] I.e. he was neither the son of a burgess nor had served an apprenticeship in the borough.

my progress was equally easy—to inquire what was the cause of the great consumption of fuel: this, too, was readily suggested, viz. the waste of fuel which was necessary to bring the whole cylinder, piston and adjacent parts from the coldness of water to the heat of steam no fewer than from fifteen to twenty times in a minute.' He then tells how he conceived the idea of a separate vessel for condensation of the steam; and it was the notion of a separate condenser which furnished the solution of his problem. 'The idea came into my mind that as steam was an elastic body it would rush into a vacuum, and if a communication were made between the cylinder and an exhausted vessel, it would rush into it and might be there condensed without cooling the cylinder. The invention was complete in so far as regarded the savings of steam and fuel.' Shortly afterwards two friends of Watt happened to meet, and one observed to the other: 'Well, have you seen Jamie Watt?' 'Yes.' 'He'll be in fine spirits now with his engine?' 'Yes, very fine spirits.' 'Gad! The separate condenser's the very thing: keep it but cold enough, and you may have a perfect vacuum whatever be the heat of the cylinder.'

Between the conception of an idea and its practical application on a commercial basis there is a wide gulf; and many years were destined to elapse before Watt's invention attained maturity. One of his main difficulties was the want of competent mechanics to execute his designs. 'My principal hindrance in erecting engines,' he wrote, 'is always the smith-work.' The turning-point in his career occurred when he became associated with Matthew Boulton, a prominent manufacturer whose Soho works were near Birmingham. Boulton had the skilled workmen, the financial resources, the business acumen and the driving force, all of which were necessary to carry Watt's invention to a successful issue. Watt took up his residence at Birmingham in 1774, five years after he had taken out a patent for his invention which was still (as Boulton described it) 'a shadow as regarded its practical utility and value.' From this point onwards progress began to be rapid. Two engines were brought into use for pumping purposes, and a third was built for John Wilkinson's iron-works to blow the blast furnaces. Orders now came pouring in and the success of the steam engine was assured.

The next stage in the history of the steam engine was marked by efforts to produce rotary motion, in order that it might be employed for driving machinery. In 1781 Watt took out a second patent in which his engine was adapted for this end. Wind-mills and water-mills were affected by the vagaries of nature but the steam engine was independent. 'There is not a single water-mill now at work in Staffordshire,' wrote Boulton to Watt on one occasion. 'They are all frozen up, and were it not for Wilkinson's steam-mill the poor nailers must have perished; but his mill goes on rolling and slitting ten tons of iron a day, which is carried away as fast as it can be bundled up; and thus the employment and subsistence of these poor people are secured.' Yet Watt wished at first to discourage the orders for engines to drive machinery. 'Some people at Burton,' he informed Boulton, 'are making application to us for an engine to work a cotton mill; but from their letter and the man they have sent here I have no great opinion of their abilities. If you come home by way of Manchester please not to seek for orders for cotton mill engines, because I hear that there are so many mills erecting on powerful streams in the north of England that the trade must soon be overdone and consequently our labour may be lost.' The course of events showed that these apprehensions were unfounded. When Watt died in 1819 the steam engine was used for an infinite variety of purposes. Man had successfully harnessed the forces of nature to his triumphal chariot. The problem of production was now solved; and the stage was set for the inauguration of the mechanical age.

'I sell here, Sir, what all the world desires to have—Power.' The remark was made to Boswell, the biographer of

Samuel Johnson, during his visit to Boulton's works.[1] By the end of the eighteenth century the steam engines erected by Boulton and Watt—at first they acted as designers and consultants and later as makers of engines in their own foundry—numbered nearly three hundred: in textile mills, coal and copper-mines, canals, the iron industry, breweries and corn mills where the traditional mechanical contrivance of mill-stones was superseded eventually by rollers. The steam engine was applied to the blast furnace in 1776, to Wedgwood's pottery works in 1782, to a cotton mill (at Papplewick in Nottinghamshire) in 1785, to the printing press (*The Times*) in 1814, to river navigation in the twenties, and to railway locomotives in the thirties. It thus passed through three stages of development—draining water from mines, driving machinery, propulsion in traction. From being 'a giant with one idea,' as Coleridge called it in reference to its original purpose, it became the pivot of modern industry and transport. Nevertheless steam-power had not entirely displaced water-power which together with wind had long been utilized by industry[2] (even at the beginning of the present century some Yorkshire mills were relying upon steam and water or even water alone). At the middle of the nineteenth century steam-power was employed in the cotton industry only on a small scale, surprisingly enough; and its progress elsewhere was still more tardy. In this, as in other respects, the notion of a revolution which abruptly altered the industrial character of English society is not borne out by the facts.

While steam-power was thus slowly extending its kingdom, its supremacy was already being challenged by new forms of prime movers—gas, electricity and oil. Gas[3] was consumed by internal combustion engines in the sixties. Its introduc-

---

[1] The remark is also attributed (in *Richard Cobden's Speeches*) to Watt in his interview with George III.

[2] In the thirties of the nineteenth century the number of water wheels was three-fifths of the number of steam engines.

[3] Gas produced by coal had been used as an illuminant from the beginning of the nineteenth century.

tion enabled small manufacturers to install power-driven plant in their workshops: the change-over was particularly noticeable in the light metal industries during the seventies and eighties. The consequent decline of handicraft methods was accelerated in the last years of the nineteenth century when electric motors gave every producer the means to utilize power. Thus in many industries the handicrafts did not succumb to mechanical methods of production until in the closing decades of the century a cheap and easily-handled prime mover became available to those who had not adopted the practice of renting steam-power in a large establishment. An outstanding event was the discovery of a new motive force in oil which became the fuel of the automobile industry, began to supersede coal in ocean navigation, and ultimately made possible the conquest of the air. The consumption of oil expanded rapidly after the first world war when within a few years eight times as much oil was imported into England as before the war.

Two features of the 'Industrial Revolution' have been reviewed—the invention of machinery and the introduction of a motive force to drive it. We now turn to the third feature—the metals used for making the machines.

The production of iron and steel involves two main processes. The initial stage is to extract iron from the iron ore which comprises other substances. This is done by smelting the ore in a blast furnace with the aid of the carbon contained in coal or charcoal. The product is termed pig iron, and the subsequent stages depend upon the way in which it is afterwards treated. It may be poured into moulds in a foundry to make castings: it may be hammered in a forge until it becomes malleable (bar or wrought iron): it may be converted into steel by varying the proportions of the carbon content. Cast iron is described as 'hard but brittle,' wrought iron as 'soft but tenacious,' steel as 'strong and tough.' Corresponding to the various processes were the epoch-making metallurgical discoveries which ushered in an age of iron followed by an age of steel.

The first discovery was the most important since on it hinged all the rest. In the textile industries the invention of machinery had served to remedy the shortage of hands in spinning and then in weaving. In the iron industry the problem was the shortage of fuel. For hundreds of years iron ore was smelted with wood charcoal, of which there was an increasing scarcity due to the destruction of forests. Apprehensions of a timber famine promoted repeated efforts to substitute coal for wood in the production of pig iron. The task of smelting iron ore engaged the attention of inventors for two centuries; and although Abraham Darby achieved success early in the eighteenth century (1709), several decades elapsed before the new method was generally pursued. The next step was to utilize mineral fuel in place of wood charcoal for making bar iron. The twin processes which made this possible are associated with the name of Henry Cort (1783-4). One was puddling—melting the pig iron in a coal furnace and stirring it to remove unwanted elements; the other was rolling—passing the iron through rollers instead of employing hammers. Cort takes rank among the inventors because while he was not the originator he brought the two processes together. His career furnishes another illustration of the misfortunes which befell so many of the inventors inasmuch as he reaped small benefit from his experiments. Now that coal was used in all stages of iron production and the cost was considerably diminished, England no longer needed to import foreign iron: instead she became an exporter. The third development in the iron industry was the application of Watt's steam engine—first to the blast furnace (as early as 1776), then to the forge hammers, subsequently to the rolling and slitting mills. The fourth cardinal improvement was James Neilson's invention of the hot air blast in 1828. The consumption of coal in the furnaces was reduced eventually to one-quarter by his device of heating the air blast.

The introduction of high-grade steel in England was the achievement of Benjamin Huntsman who about 1740 invented the crucible process. Crucibles were clay pots which were subjected to such heat that the metal was freed from impurities. Crucible steel was more uniform in quality as well as harder than other kinds, and to this day the best steel is made in crucibles. However its cost limited its use to special purposes, and the production of steel which not only had strength and tenacity but also was cheap enough for general usage was deferred for more than a hundred years. Then in the latter half of the nineteenth century three fresh processes of steel-making marked the beginning of another phase in the industry. The first was disclosed by Henry Bessemer in 1856. It consisted in driving a blast of air through the mass of molten pig iron in a 'converter' in order to remove all the carbon, after which the iron was turned into steel by adding the requisite amount of carbon and other necessary elements. The second, the 'open-hearth' of William Siemens in the late sixties, afforded opportunity among its other advantages to test the metal in the furnace by samples during its conversion into steel. Both these processes suffered from the defect that they demanded non-phosphoric ores. The third process invented by Gilchrist and Thomas at the end of the seventies enabled steel-makers to eliminate phosphorus, and so use phosphoric ores which exist in great quantities. The term basic steel means that the phosphorus has been removed during the conversion: acid steel denotes that the ore itself in its natural state was largely free from phosphorus.[1]

In studying the effects of the inventions on English society certain important facts must be borne in mind. The expression 'Industrial Revolution' is apt to convey an erroneous idea of the rapidity with which the old economic order yielded place to the new. It is often assumed that the

[1] Iron ore is now also smelted by electricity. For the quantities produced by these different processes in recent decades, see Chapter Twelve.

inventions forthwith created the factory system and extinguished the domestic system. The mill-owners undoubtedly made their appearance very early in the cotton manufacture, where they erected buildings in which to house the water-frame; and their example was followed elsewhere. None the less the traditional structure held its ground successfully in some branches of the textiles even beyond the middle of the nineteenth century. In Yorkshire only half the workers engaged in the woollen manufacture were employed in factories as late as 1856; the rest continued to work in their own homes. Indeed the extinction of the domestic system in the woollen manufacture belongs to the closing years of the nineteenth century; while its decline has also been gradual in many other industries. To-day there still exist some survivals of the handicrafts working on the domestic basis. Hence the question arises whether the term 'revolution' is appropriate when applied, not to violent political changes, but to an economic process for which the ground had been long prepared and which in its actual operation proved to be decidedly more evolutionary than catastrophic.

There are several reasons why the introduction of machinery and the extension of the factory system proceeded more slowly than was formerly supposed. To begin with, some of the inventions were compatible with the retention of the domestic system. Here we must draw an important distinction between implements and machinery. An implement is a tool worked by hand; a machine is worked by power—it does the work under human guidance. An implement, therefore, can be used in the home; the machine must as a rule be used in a factory. Thus the fly-shuttle was an implement which gave the domestic weaver a better command over his instrument, namely, the hand-loom: similarly Hargreaves's jenny and at first Crompton's mule were feasible in cottage homes. Other inventions, again, from the start required power, such as Arkwright's water-frame, and in these cases factories were indispensable.

Hence the factory became essential only when a particular invention necessitated the use of power. In the next place, the inventions at the outset were often imperfect and it was not until they had been greatly improved that it became possible to apply them to industrial purposes. Technical factors were also responsible for the slow introduction of machinery; for instance, the tardy progress of steam-weaving in the woollen industry can be explained on technical grounds. The primary characteristic of woollen cloth is its felting property which enables the fibres to be interlaced during the fulling or thickening process: hence woollen yarn must be spun loosely. Weaving was thus rendered a more difficult operation since the threads were easily broken, and consequently the power-loom worked no faster than the hand-loom. In this peculiarity, rather than in the alleged conservatism of the woollen manufacturers as compared with the cotton manufacturers, we may find one of the main causes of the retention of the domestic system in the woollen industry during the earlier half of the nineteenth century. The power-loom was better fitted for worsted weaving, yet even here its adoption was belated owing to defects in the machinery and the fact that at first the saving in labour was not considerable. Nor were these technical obstacles confined to textiles. Wrought iron was not suited to the machine, so that in some metal trades mechanical methods of production were deferred until wrought iron came to be replaced by steel in the last decades of the nineteenth century. We must, therefore, avoid the assumption that the year in which an invention made its appearance was also the time when it was generally applied.

A further reason for the delay in utilizing machinery was the reluctance shown by employers to break away from their customary practices, whether through conservatism or the expense and trouble involved or fear of opposition on the part of their work-folk. It was particularly noticeable in the west country and in East Anglia. Moreover the domestic workers, when their resistance proved unavailing, pursued the fatal policy of 'lowering the dike'—that is, they submitted to repeated reductions of wages in order to compete in point of cheapness with machinery; the sacrifice they thus made retarded, though it could not avert, the ultimate extinction of hand processes. And finally, in Yorkshire, the small manufacturers showed marked flexibility. Instead of opposing the new methods they turned them to their own account. They preserved their status as independent producers by combining their resources and purchasing machinery for their common use. They formed co-operative societies and bought machines which they employed for certain purposes, while the remaining processes were carried on at home. Similarly the 'garret masters,' as they were called, in the Sheffield cutlery and the Birmingham light metal industries maintained a precarious existence in the face of factory encroachment by hiring the use of power in a large establishment. Thus the introduction of machinery did not necessarily involve a reconstruction of industry nor the displacement of the older forms of organization based on the workshop and the cottage. From all this it will be seen that the disappearance of the domestic system was gradual, and that its decay depended upon a variety of conditions, partly technical partly non-technical.

The adoption of mechanical improvements in the textiles was broadly as follows.[1] The fly-shuttle was accepted in Yorkshire in Kay's own life-time, but in the west of England it was delayed until the end of the eighteenth century. Hand-spinning in the cotton and worsted industries was generally superseded in the first decade of the nineteenth century, though in the woollen industry its survival was somewhat more protracted. The conquest of the hand-loom by the power-loom proved a much slower process than the conquest of hand-spinning by machine-spinning. In regard to hand-combing the middle of the nineteenth century may be taken as the period at which manual operations virtually became extinct.

[1] A fuller account is given in Chapter Twelve.

Another preliminary observation must be made: the evils attributed to the inventions were not wholly due to the introduction of machinery. They were caused in some measure by the circumstances of the period. It was a misfortune for England that, at a time when the tempo of economic change was being accelerated and the race was to the swift and the strong, the inevitable evils of the transition were aggravated by a succession of wars. First came the Seven Years' War, then the American War of Independence, then the Revolutionary and Napoleonic Wars. They had a detrimental effect upon trade and industry, and were partially responsible for the high price of food because it was difficult to import corn from the Baltic. This produced intense distress among the poor whose wages did not rise in proportion. Nor did the establishment of peace in 1815 bring with it plenty, for though foreign corn became available its importation was checked by the corn laws. Moreover Europe was too impoverished to buy our goods, while in addition the English labour market was flooded with many thousands of discharged soldiers and sailors. Further the currency was inflated with the result that its value was depreciated. At the same time there was an unparalleled growth of the national debt, coupled with a fantastical fiscal system since the succession of wars necessitated very heavy taxation. Again it was largely on account of the wars that a free hand was given to employers during the epoch of the inventions to transform the system of industry without any attempt at control or supervision on the part of the state. Economic forces were allowed to operate without hindrance, partly from the conviction that in the life and death struggle with France the production of wealth must over-ride all humanitarian considerations. It is improbable that, if circumstances had been normal, the government of the day would have shown its apparent indifference to the evils which attended the introduction of machinery. In short the dislocation of economic life helps to explain much of the prevailing distress; and the war atmosphere helps to explain the failure of the state to ameliorate the condition of the working class. Never-theless, while making full allowance for the character of the period, it would be a mistake to look for the explanation of the current social misery purely to the wars. Even had there been no wars, there would still have been great suffer-ing as the handicraft industries were slowly crushed to death beneath the weight of the overpowering competition of machinery. The suffering could alone have been averted by a frank recognition on the side of the community that it owed a duty to those who were the victims of industrial progress. But it was only very gradually that the community began to awaken to a full sense of its responsibilities towards them.

And lastly: the interpretation of the 'Industrial Revolu-tion' put forward in this book does not imply any desire to minimize the epoch-making status of the inventions. The stimulus given to the productive agencies by the application of mechanical power to industry and transport is a common-place; the increased command which man has acquired over the resources of nature merits the stress which is rightly laid upon it. These are trends whose importance no one will be tempted to belittle—but neither ought we to be tempted to magnify and distort their meaning by a false perspective which under-estimates the degree of economic development attained prior to the inventions. We must not let our minds be dazzled by the glamour of statistics. The true gauge of economic progress lies less in the scale of operations than in the fundamental adjustments which man makes in his efforts to satisfy his wants. From this standpoint the rise of indivi-dualism, and the far-reaching consequences which flowed from it, have a profound significance. For they show that the 'Industrial Revolution' was not a watershed, nor was it the genesis of a new industrial society composed of capitalist employers and proletarian wage-earners. Any history of the 'Industrial Revolution' which does not take due account of the facts that in England the industrial regime was already largely capitalist in character, and that the 'inventions'

were the creation not the creators of a capitalist society—
or which teaches that the English artisan was transformed
by the introduction of machinery from an independent
producer into a wage-earner—can only yield a fresh lease of
life to an historical myth.

The principal effect of the inventions on English society
was the shifting of the centre of gravity from agriculture to
industry. In the eighteenth century England was primarily
an agricultural country, although industry and commerce
had already attained considerable dimensions: in the nineteenth century she became primarily an industrial country.
Agriculture, though still one of the greatest branches of the
national economy, now occupied a subordinate position
when weighed in the balance against all the other branches.
The population to-day is mainly an urban population; it is
engaged chiefly in industrial and commercial pursuits. The
results of such a pregnant change have been conspicuous. It
meant first that the prosperity of the realm, instead of being
broad-based on land, was henceforth to rest on the unstable
foundations of trade. This in its turn meant that the mass
of the nation was for the future dependent for its livelihood
upon the existence of oversea markets, which were liable to
be closed against us at any moment on account of wars,
tariffs or other causes. Taking advantage of the opportunities
which the inventions had placed within her grasp, England
abandoned the attempt to produce her own food and built
up instead vast manufactures, exchanging her products for
food and raw materials from abroad. Hence her policy was
directed towards maintaining and acquiring markets to
supply her needs and absorb her surpluses; and in consequence the old conflict for empire developed into a conflict
for markets.

The next important outcome of the inventions was the
growth of the factory system as the predominant form of industrial organization. The factory system is of course much older
than machinery. In the sixteenth century, as we have seen,

a number of woollen manufacturers set up factories, and gathered servants and looms under one roof. We meet occasionally in the eighteenth century with textile factories but the practice was not general. Only in one industry is there any substantial evidence of a factory system before the time of Arkwright—namely, in silk spinning which used machinery worked by water-power, and here many hundreds were employed in a single factory. Apart from this exception the factory age began with the introduction of Arkwright's water-frame, which made the factory system an economic necessity; and in the face of economic necessity social objections were swept away. The establishment of the factory stage brought in its train two important changes in the capitalist system, as it had functioned in the domestic stage. One involved a transformation in the character of the employer. In the domestic stage he had owned the materials but not the instruments of production: he was therefore concerned with buying the materials and selling the finished product rather than with the actual processes. Now he owned both the materials and instruments, he carried on the work under his own roof, he made it his function to study and perfect in detail the whole business of manufacturing. The other change completed the destruction of the economic independence of the artisans, who in the domestic stage had owned the instruments of production and served more than one employer. Yet while the factory system thus rendered the wage-earner doubly dependent upon the capitalists, the balance was redressed—and more than redressed—by the fact that the concentration of the workers under a factory roof gave an immense impetus to the organization of labour in trade unions, and thus has placed them in an infinitely stronger position for bargaining on equal terms with the employer.

The most serious indictment laid against the inventions was their reaction upon the demand for labour. The use of machinery aroused vehement opposition from the workers, and one writer asked: 'Who does not consider the employment of machinery one of the greatest evils that ever befell the country?' Opposition was not confined to words. In the attempts made to prevent the introduction of machinery there was frequent recourse to violence, for example, the Luddite riots in 1812. The fury of the Luddites was directed primarily against gig mills and shearing-frames used to crop the loose fibres and impart a smooth surface to the cloth. A verse of the croppers' ballad ran:

'Great Enoch[1] still shall lead the van.
Stop him who dare! Stop him who can!'

At our time of day it is impossible to doubt the benefits which have accrued from mechanical methods of production. Machinery effects an economy of labour and cheapens the price of commodities; this in its turn stimulates the demand and so may ultimately provide more work than is at the moment actually curtailed. On the other hand, the invention of machinery meant at least a temporary displacement of labour; and it is no consolation to the workman, whose skill is rendered useless by some technical development, to know that at some distant date a larger number will be found employment in his industry. It would be unfair, then, to regard the hostility shown by the workers to machinery as wholly unreasonable. If the community had been prepared to undertake that no individual should suffer from changes imperatively demanded in the common interest, it would have been in a stronger position to denounce the anti-social policy of blocking economic change. Eventually the introduction of machinery greatly increased the demand for labour: it gave an immense stimulus to three industries—cotton, coal-mining and engineering. Each was already in existence but now grew to enormous dimensions. Accordingly machinery has provided the means for the employment and maintenance of a much vaster population.

What has been the result of the inventions not on the number but on the welfare of the wage-earning commu-

[1] The name given to the big hammer employed in the work of destruction.

nity? This is an important criterion of national prosperity, since the final test of economic progress is the situation of those upon whom the foundations of society must ultimately rest. Much of the criticism directed against machinery and the factory system is based upon a misconception of the conditions which prevailed in the older industrial order. Thus a common charge against the inventions is that they have made the worker into a machine-minder, killed the creative impulse, and destroyed man's pleasure in his work. But those who praise the old handicrafts overlook the fact that most of the operations, in the textiles at any rate, were already mechanical in character even before the use of machinery. In the textiles the processes of carding, combing, spinning, weaving and dressing, consisted in the monotonous repetition of certain movements of the hand. They afforded little or no scope for any expression of individuality, which is the justification of true craftsmanship. Another criticism was voiced by John Stuart Mill in his *Principles of Political Economy* (1848). 'Hitherto it is questionable if all the mechanical inventions yet made have lightened the day's toil of any human being.' Certain processes were even rendered more arduous as in the iron industry; others became less tedious and laborious as in power-loom weaving; in general it appears correct to say that machinery has relieved the workers of some of the drudgery of manual toil. Mechanical methods are more exacting than a handicraft in that they involve a more intense application to work, though against this may be set the greater opportunities for leisure. One undoubted advantage is that they have enabled tasks which were often unpleasant and unhealthy to be done by machinery instead of by hand; for instance, in the preparatory processes of the woollen and cotton industries. Hand-loom weaving itself was not necessarily an unhealthy occupation, yet prior to the introduction of the fly-shuttle weavers were liable to breast disorders. Moreover the erection of factories, while it subjected the mill hands to a novel and strict discipline, had its compensation in the fixed and far shorter hours ultimately imposed by the state; and from a health point of view it was better to carry on industry in large airy buildings, as later, rather than in crowded tenements where the same room had often to serve as a workshop and living place. Another thing is that the use of machinery raised the intelligence and improved the character of the industrial population, for it required of the worker both mental alertness and regular conduct. A feature of modern industry is the 'dilution of labour' whereby much of the skilled labour formerly expended on a product is superseded by the semi-skilled labour of operatives confined to repetition processes. Where artisans are recruited from the ranks of unskilled labourers, there is an improvement in the social scale as well as in the nature of the occupation. At the same time a fresh demand is created for skilled mechanics to fashion and adjust tools, to construct and keep in repair machines; and the increasing complexity of these operations makes a corresponding claim upon their intelligence. Similarly more skill is needed to build or work the modern liner than the wooden sailing ships of former days. Finally machinery has raised the standard of life of the community, because it has cheapened the price of commodities and afforded in the main a greater command over necessaries, amenities and luxuries. The population of England more than trebled in the nineteenth century, yet at the end of the century the masses were in a material sense better off than at the beginning.

In estimating the significance of the 'Industrial Revolution' we must not overlook the condition of those who remained outside the new economic order. In the case of the spinners the effect of machinery was that spinning as a cottage industry became extinct. The rural folk thus lost a subsidiary source of income since spinning had been carried on by women and children in almost every village throughout the country. It is true that the spinners were very poorly paid for their toil; in the seventeenth and eighteenth centuries England's greatest industry rested on the basis of sweated labour. Nevertheless spinning was a useful addition to the family income, and the loss of it meant that farm labourers became entirely dependent on their own scanty earnings in agriculture. Even more distressing was the situation of the hand-loom weavers. The story of their sufferings constitutes the most melancholy chapter in the history of the inventions. It is the classic example of the triumph of economic progress at the expense of social welfare.

At first the hand-loom weavers benefited by the inventions. They profited by the enormous output of yarn from the spinning factories, and as a result of the increased demand for their services they reaped a harvest of high wages. The muslin weavers of Bolton may be cited in illustration of their flourishing condition, though the prosperity of other weavers was much more subdued. 'The trade was that of a gentleman,' a witness informed a parliamentary committee. 'They brought home their work in top boots and ruffled shirts, carried a cane, and in some instances took a coach.' Many weavers at that time, we are told, 'used to walk about the streets with a five-pound Bank of England note spread out under their hatbands; they would smoke none but long "churchwarden" pipes, and objected to the intrusion of any other handicraftsmen into the particular rooms in the public-houses which they frequented. This prosperity did not continue, and few operatives endured greater privations than the hand-loom weavers of Bolton for the succeeding fifty years.'

Among the factors responsible for the distress of the hand-loom weavers the most important was the drastic fall in wages. The wages of a weaver in many cases declined (1797–1833) nearly 80 per cent. The report of the hand-loom commissioners published in 1840 showed that weavers all over England were earning from five to seven shillings a week, sometimes a trifle more but sometimes even less; they were also said to be out of work one-third of their time. The weavers' union estimated in 1828 that the minimum amount sufficient to keep a man, his wife and three children, was 15s. 8d. a week; and as the earnings of the weavers fell considerably below it, the commissioners reported that the condition of a pauper in the workhouse was superior to that of a weaver's family.

Some striking testimony as to the position of the hand-loom weavers in the neighbourhood of Huddersfield was given by Richard Oastler, the stalwart champion of factory legislation. 'I remember one particular circumstance that struck me very forcibly, for it was the very day when I read the speech of the king to this House in which he said: "The manufacturing districts are in a state of prosperity." On that very day I met with several of those weavers who were "manufacturing" operatives, and I questioned them very closely; and I found that on that day when they were said to be in such a state of "prosperity" those men—and those women too—were carrying burdens on their backs eight or nine miles to fetch their work and then had to carry them back again, and they were making from 4s. 6d. to 5s. 2d. a week clear wages.' In reply to the question: 'How many hours a day do the weavers generally work?' he answered: 'Those persons whom I have asked say from twelve to fourteen hours a day, but I am speaking of weavers in constant work. I very often find them going home without work at all. There are scores and hundreds of families in the district that I am now alluding to, to whom a piece of flesh meat is a luxury; it does not form a regular article in their daily consumption; they generally live upon porridge and potatoes, and they do not know what it is, many of them, very many of them, to taste flesh meat from year's end to year's end, except somebody gives them some. But as to their clothing they are clothed with rags, and their furniture is such as I am sure I cannot describe.'

Oastler's statements are corroborated by an overwhelming mass of evidence. The following is an official summary of the material laid before a parliamentary committee in 1834: 'A very great number of these weavers are unable to provide for themselves and their families a sufficiency of food of the plainest and cheapest kind; they are clothed in rags and indisposed on this account to go to any place of worship or to send their children to the sunday schools; they have scarcely anything like furniture in their houses; their beds and bedding are of the most wretched description, and many of them sleep upon straw; notwithstanding their want of food, clothing, furniture and bedding, they for the most part have full employment; their labour is excessive, not infrequently sixteen hours a day; this state of destitution and excessive labour induces them to drink ardent spirits, to revive their drooping spirits and allay their sorrows, whereby their suffering is increased; their poverty and wretchedness cause many to embezzle and sell the materials entrusted to them to be worked up, thus destroying the morals of the weavers.' The hand-loom weavers attributed their situation to a variety of factors, including the corn laws and the restoration of the gold standard. But the fall in their wages can be explained partially by other causes. The weavers were in competition with machinery. The power-loom was adopted only gradually yet it set the pace; and the ability of the power-loom master to undersell the hand-loom master forced the latter to cut rates of payment. Machinery was thus the great 'screw,' and the ever-present menace of its introduction sapped the weavers' will to resist. Again their weakness in bargaining strength was a fatal handicap in opposing reductions in their earnings. They were not organized in strong trade unions, for they were not concentrated under one roof like factory operatives and lived in isolation, their poverty could not stand the strain of a weekly contribution, and their instruments of production were their own property so that in a strike they mainly suffered. Moreover the ease with which hand-loom weaving was learnt made it a magnet for the destitute from all other classes. Farm labourers displaced by the agrarian changes from their traditional occupation, and Irish immigrants driven to invade the English labour market, flocked to the large industrial centres. Here they created a new race of hand-loom weavers accustomed to a lower standard of living and prepared to work at inferior rates of remuneration. In order to eke out their scanty resources the weavers put their children at an early age to weaving, thus involving them in the meshes of the same remorseless destiny in which they were themselves inextricably entangled.

The fate which befell the hand-loom weavers overtook also the wool-combers, who had formerly held the whiphand over their employers since their numbers were limited, their work demanded great skill, and they were not tied to one particular locality. Nevertheless they did not succumb without strenuous resistance. The most famous strike in their history broke out in 1825 and lasted five months. After its failure their condition underwent a rapid deterioration. Their sufferings were intense, they worked long hours in an over-heated atmosphere, and their toil was now wretchedly remunerated. The consciousness of their weakness constrained the hand-combers to adopt a humbler tone, which was in striking contrast with their proud and defiant attitude in the eighteenth century. In 1840 their union issued a statement which declared: 'Our lives have become miserable. We are compelled to work fourteen to sixteen hours per day, and with all this sweat and toil we are not able to procure sufficient of the necessaries of life wherewith to subsist on.' The hand-combers had clung to the conviction that Cartwright's machine would never prove workable, but the improvements made by a succession of inventors gave the death-blow to their fond anticipations. The only result of the ruinous contest of 1825 was to stimulate the introduction of machinery, which every day was increasing in its technical efficiency.

We have described the effects produced by the inventions upon the fortunes of the workers. The nature of the changes which took place in the structure of industry will be examined in a later chapter.[1]

The alterations brought about by the 'Industrial Revolu-

[1] Chapter Twelve.

tion' in the geographical distribution of the leading industries are noticed in connexion with those particularly affected.[1] A word, however, may be said here as to the general character of the movement and its broad consequences upon economic life. Although we speak of a migration of industry, it must not be interpreted to mean a movement of population *en masse* from the agricultural south to the industrial north. Contrary to what might be expected, the inhabitants of the southern counties did not diminish in numbers; indeed they increased though not at the same phenomenal rate. Before the advent of the railways which provided facilities for more distant journeys, the trend to manufacturing areas was in the nature of a rural exodus from adjacent shires. To this general statement the Irish immigrants are a conspicuous exception. One striking result of the migration of industry was the decay of country pursuits. We are so accustomed at the present day to associate manufactures with urban centres that we can scarcely conceive the extent to which they were formerly carried on in villages and townlets. In the eighteenth century probably every county in England had its local industries. The most widespread were textiles. Cottage spinning in particular was a valuable accessory to agriculture. It enabled the family of the farm labourer to eke out the miserable pittance earned by the principal bread-winner. This source of income, as was mentioned above, dried up when the introduction of machinery led to the general disuse of hand-spinning. In addition there was a great variety of dispersed trades including potteries, silk weaving, glove manufacture, straw-plaiting, paper-making and the rest. The general concentration in manufacturing districts extinguished many of these rural occupations. It thereby contributed to the decline of country life since the agricultural community was deprived of employments which had served to supplement its earnings in husbandry.

Chapter Twelve.

Chapter Eight

THE REVOLUTION IN TRANSPORT

The 'Industrial Revolution' was bound up with a revolution in the system of transport internal as well as external. Without improved methods of communications it would have been impossible for manufacturers to take full advantage of machinery. Markets were needed at home and abroad to supply the raw materials and to absorb the finished products; and to create new markets and expand old ones was primarily a problem of easy and rapid intercourse either by land or sea. Nothing is more vital to a country than adequate means of moving from one place to another, for facilities in communications are the arteries of commerce. We must therefore observe the notable developments by which the system of transport was rendered adequate for the burden it was now being called upon to sustain.

We begin with the roads. At the present day all branches of the public service are carried on by qualified officials supported by compulsory taxes. In early times they were performed by the people themselves. A mediaeval citizen, for instance, was required to undertake police duties, repair the town walls, pave the streets, make bridges. In particular the function of maintaining the king's highway was considered to be the duty of the local community as a whole. In the middle of the sixteenth century when the manorial courts and monastic houses had shed their former responsibilities, Parliament stepped in and enacted the famous law (1555) enjoining every parish to appoint annually two unpaid surveyors while the labour, tools and horses were to be provided gratuitously by the inhabitants. An occupier of land was to furnish a cart with horses and men; and every other person was to work on the highways or send a substitute for four (afterwards six) days in the year. This system of compulsory or 'statute' labour proved notoriously inefficient.[1] 'The days set aside for the performance of the statute labour,' commented an eighteenth-century writer voicing the general opinion, 'are considered as allotted to play and merriment.'

The condition of the roads gave rise to innumerable complaints. They were often little more than bridle paths and totally unsuited for wheeled traffic. Travellers, even judges on circuit, went on horseback; commodities of all kinds were borne by packhorses. In addition the highways were thronged with cattle, sheep and pigs, which kept the soft tracks in a permanently miry state. We have abundant evidence as to the 'execrable' character of English roads in the eighteenth century. Arthur Young branded the one road between Preston and Wigan in Lancashire in these words: 'I know not, in the whole range of language, terms sufficiently expressive to describe this infernal road. To look over a map and perceive that it is a principal one not only to some towns but even whole counties, one would naturally conclude it to be at least decent; but let me most seriously caution all travellers who may accidentally purpose to travel this terrible country to avoid it as they would the devil, for a thousand to one but they break their necks or their limbs by overthrows or breakings down. They will here meet with ruts which I actually measured four feet deep and floating with mud only from a wet summer; what, therefore, must it be after winter? The only mending it receives is the tumbling in some loose stones, which serve no other purpose but jolting a carriage in the most intolerable manner. These are not merely opinions but facts, for I actually passed three carts broken down in these eighteen miles of execrable memory.' Of the roads from London to Land's End it was said [2] that they were still 'what God left them after the Flood;' and of some of the main roads in Northamptonshire it was remarked [3] that 'the only way to get along in rainy weather

---

[1] It was abolished in 1835.   [2] In the eighteenth century.
[3] In the early nineteenth century.

was by swimming.' In the metropolis George II and his Queen spent the whole night in going from Kew Palace to St. James's Palace (a distance of eight miles) and once their coach was over-turned. In the middle of the eighteenth century it took the Edinburgh coach fourteen days, the Manchester coach and the York coach each four days, to reach London. The London-Oxford coach in a journey of fifty-five miles started at 7 a.m. and arrived on the evening of the following day. 'The increased speed with which everything connected with trade is transacted'—this was written in 1870—'is startling to men who remember the old times and ways. Time was, as men yet active in business well remember, when the Manchester merchant coming to Bradford [a distance of thirty-four miles] took three days for the outward and return journey in a post-chaise and pair of horses. The travellers by the Bradford and Manchester market express train would think chaos come again were they to return, if only for a month, to the habits of their immediate predecessors.'

The manifold consequences of this situation did not escape attention. It was recognized that defective communications hampered economic progress and rendered the carriage of commodities by land both difficult and costly. Henry Homer in 1767 wrote: 'The trade of the kingdom languished under these impediments. The natural produce of the country was with difficulty circulated to supply the necessities of those counties and trading towns which wanted [them].' The imperfections of the existing methods gave rise to the turn-pike system which embodied the principle that every person, other than foot passengers, ought to contribute to the repair of roads in proportion to the use he made of them. The turnpike system became common in the eighteenth century, and ultimately there were over eleven hundred bodies of turnpike trustees—the trustees being persons of local standing authorized by act of parliament to construct and maintain a road and to levy tolls. They administered eventually more than twenty thousand miles; while outside their sphere a vast extent of highways, several times as large, was still left under parish control. The turnpike roads made it feasible to use waggons in place of packhorses for the conveyance of goods; and Homer claimed that 'despatch which is the very life and soul of business becomes daily more attainable by the free circulation.'

Although the turnpike trusts were an improvement upon parish administration they suffered from numerous defects. The lack of centralized control resulted in a marked variation in the condition of the highways, which were too often confided to the care of incompetent officials or unscrupulous contractors. Road-making, in fact, was considered unworthy of the skill of engineers. For the sake of drainage the road was given a convex surface, but the convexity was sometimes so great that the sides are said to have sloped like the roof of a house; and the traffic fell on the centre which was speedily worn into ruts. The method of repairing was extremely primitive, since it was often nothing more than tumbling in large unbroken stones. Ultimately public opinion awoke to the fact that for centuries the methods of improving communications had been on radically wrong lines. Hitherto the idea had been to suit the traffic to the roads instead of suiting the roads to the traffic: hence the attempts of the legislature to regulate the character of the vehicles and the weight of their loads. No real progress was possible until highways were constructed and maintained on scientific principles. Development on these lines is associated with Telford one of the leading British engineers, and McAdam. The latter won a great reputation as a road repairer who sought to cover the surface with an impenetrable crust by spreading over it small broken stones uniform in size, which under the pressure of traffic would consolidate to form a smooth and hard surface.

The turnpike trusts were at the height of their prosperity in the thirties of the nineteenth century at the very moment when they were overtaken by 'the calamity of railways' and the consequent disappearance of the stage coaches, which had furnished immense sums in tolls. This ruined the trusts, which could no longer afford to keep the roads in repair. To meet the situation Parliament authorized the justices of the peace to subsidize the turnpike roads out of the highway rates. The parish was thus constrained both to pay toll (as hitherto) for using the turnpike road and also to contribute towards the cost of repairing it. Public feeling was inflamed; and in South Wales in 1843 occurred the Rebecca Riots in which the turnpike gates were destroyed. Then in 1864 came a complete change of policy. A committee of the House of Commons resolved that the abolition of the turnpike trusts would be both beneficial and expedient; and Parliament adopted the policy of terminating them as their legal term expired. Year by year they disappeared—in 1871, when tolls were ended in London, there still survived 854 turnpike trusts in the provinces yet in 1887 only 15 remained—until at the end of the century they were extinct. An entirely different system of road management came into operation. It was supported not by tolls but by a highway rate; it was administered not by self-appointed bodies but by the local authorities (the act of 1888 transferred the main roads to the county councils); it employed not amateurs but professional surveyors; it used not unpaid labour but a permanent staff of hired workers.

The universal discontent with the condition of the roads inspired attempts to utilize as much as possible an alternative method of transport, namely, the rivers. Experience, however, showed that river navigation was attended by serious drawbacks: rivers suffered either from an excess or from a deficiency of water, their course was irregular, they were not evenly distributed throughout the kingdom. Hence in the second half of the eighteenth century artificial waterways were made. They had certain advantages over natural waterways: they did not suffer from floods or droughts and they could be built where they were wanted. In view of the superiority of canals the delay in their construction requires some explanation. So long as corn and timber were the chief commodities for which carriage was needed, it did not seem profitable to embark upon expensive undertakings; moreover the necessary capital was not readily available in earlier times. In the eighteenth century the situation changed in both respects. The expansion of coal-mining and the iron industry made new methods of transport indispensable; and the accumulation of capital together with the advances provided by London bankers furnished the means for costly enterprises.

The era of canal navigation was inaugurated in 1761 when the duke of Bridgewater with James Brindley as engineer linked up the coal beds at Worsley with Manchester where the price of coal was halved, and subsequently linked up Manchester with Liverpool. Many other canals followed —among them the Grand Trunk connected Liverpool and Hull, that is, the west and east coasts. For several decades they enjoyed striking prosperity and their shares sometimes increased in value twenty-fold or more. None the less, although canals rendered a great service to the economic development of England, they were destined in their turn to be superseded by railways. The last canal was made about 1834, and from this time may be dated the period of their decline. The reasons for the decline are indicated in a report of a royal commission on canals (1909). 'Canals in this country were constructed upon no general scheme,' so that there was no national system of inland waterways, no through lines of communications, no uniform gauge. They are also inferior to railways in point of speed (a vital consideration where perishable goods are concerned); nor can they afford facilities for the extensive warehousing of materials. It should be observed that the decline was relative rather than absolute, since some canals continue to carry a considerable volume of merchandise. If canals and rivers in England occupy a very subordinate place in the system of transport as compared with the Continent, it must be remembered that in our country their purpose is served by the coastwise traffic from port to port.

In their origin railways, like canals, were connected with the coal industry. When coal began to be consumed in increasing quantities, one obstacle to its production lay in the difficulty of getting the mineral from the pits to the river. The first attempt to deal with the situation was by the construction of wooden rails. This was the starting-point of the railway and it was known in the sixteenth century. To secure traction four-wheeled waggons were drawn by a horse, sometimes preceded by a man with a bundle of hay which he held just in front of the horse to stimulate it to greater exertions. The next stage in the evolution of the railway was the substitution of steam engines for horses. A stationary engine was placed at the top of a slope and drew up or controlled the descent of the loads. This was the beginning of steam-power on the railways. The third development occurred when the Surrey Iron Railway between Croydon and the River Thames, a 'public' railway not connected with either collieries or canal navigation, was built in 1801. The trucks were drawn by horses, mules or donkeys. The company did not own the trucks, the notion being that railways were to be treated like canals—that is, the company provided the route and the users supplied the waggons or barges and paid tolls. Then came the Stockton and Darlington Railway opened in 1825: it furnished waggons for goods traffic and coaches for passengers. At first horse-power was contemplated, but the company was persuaded by George Stephenson to employ locomotive engines though horses were also used.

George Stephenson, who was born in 1781, began as an engineman in a colliery—the engine being worked to pump water out of the mine. He early displayed his talents and constructed a locomotive at Killingworth colliery in 1814. Other inventors—including Richard Trevithick who contrived a steam carriage to travel on public roads (1802) and a steam locomotive to travel on railroads (1804)—were seeking to solve the problem of utilizing the steam engine for purposes of locomotion. Nevertheless it was George Stephenson who by his perseverance overcame the mechanical difficulties: to him therefore must be assigned the credit of inaugurating the railway era. His great opportunity came with the formation of the Liverpool and Manchester Railway which was destined to give an immense stimulus to the growth of the railway system. The line was expressly conceived with the intention of competing with canal navigation owing to the discontent felt by traders with the waterway companies, which abused their monopoly by exorbitant charges and inefficient service. The directors agreed that 'horses were out of the question,' but it was an open issue whether the railways should have locomotives or stationary engines placed 'at intervals of a mile or two along the line to draw the trains from station to station by means of ropes.' Finally a prize of £500 was offered for a locomotive, which was won by George Stephenson with his 'Rocket.' The 'Rocket' attained a speed of twenty-nine miles an hour with an average of fourteen miles. After this trial (1829) the success of the railway was assured. The debate over the respective merits of haulage by horses, by stationary engines with cables and by locomotives lingered on for a few years: horse-power was still being used on some railways a quarter of a century later. None the less the practical problem of traction had been decided by the success of Stephenson's 'Rocket' in favour of locomotives. The Liverpool and Manchester Railway was opened in 1830. It was rapidly followed by the construction of railways in every direction.[1] Speculative finance in the thirties and forties bore fruit in a 'railway mania' with George Hudson—a linen draper who promoted the amalgamation of lines—cast for the role of 'railway king.' A prominent railway contractor was Thomas Brassey, whose experience of the economy of high

[1] The length of the railroad in the United Kingdom was 6,890 miles in 1851, and 22,078 in 1901.

wages added a crucial chapter to the works of the theoretical economists by demonstrating that low labour costs depended not on cheap wages but on efficiency.

The state[1] left the building of railways to private enterprise without attempting to devise a national scheme of communications consisting of great trunk lines in place of a series of disconnected lines serving particular localities. The opposition encountered by the railways was intense. 'It was declared that their formation would prevent cows grazing and hens laying. The poisoned air from the locomotives would kill birds. Houses would be burnt up by the fire from the engine-chimneys.' At the same time the consoling thought was that 'the weight of the locomotive would completely prevent its moving.' The *Quarterly Review* wrote in 1825: 'What can be more palpably absurd than the prospect held out of locomotives travelling twice as fast as stage coaches?' It was also asked: 'What was to become of coach-makers and harness-makers, coach-masters and coachmen, innkeepers, horse-breeders and horse-dealers?' As a consequence of this opposition inordinate expenditure was involved in acquiring the land from owners who extorted immense prices, as well as in securing parliamentary sanction. The total together with the cost of constructing the English railways exceeded sixty thousand pounds per mile or over four times the estimated amount expended in the United States.

The effects of the introduction of railways upon the economic life of the nation were manifold. The stimulus which they gave to trade was one of the main influences in the growth of industry. They enabled factories, wherever they were situated, to receive machinery, coal and raw materials at low rates. They provided facilities for circulating commodities throughout the land and easy access to the ports when goods were destined for foreign markets. Moreover the railway system furnished the means to concentrate the workers in any given place, bringing them from the

[1] For the policy of the state towards the railways, see Chapter Ten.

235

villages into the towns, and distributing them where they were most needed. And large industrial centres could not have developed in the north of England but for improvements in transport which allowed food to be brought to them quickly and regularly.

The working class gained in various ways. For one thing the railways came at an opportune moment since they helped to absorb the surplus labour in agriculture, and at the present day they afford employment on an extensive scale. For another thing they made labour in general more mobile by enabling the workers to move greater distances—an important factor in maintaining a standard wage. Then again the masses benefited by the cheapening of commodities consequent upon improved distribution, which put every district in a position to draw upon the whole kingdom instead of being restricted to the resources of the immediate neighbourhood. In particular the speed and low rates of railways rendered it possible to obtain fruit and vegetables at reasonable prices, and what were luxuries in the eighteenth century became almost necessaries. The railways, by creating opportunities for concentration in towns, must be held partially responsible for urban congestion and its corollary— slums; nevertheless in combination with motor omnibuses and cycles they have served in more recent decades to promote the development of suburbs and the gradual expansion of civic communities within wider territorial limits. Thus as a result of improved methods of transport, coupled with the diffusion of electrical power and the advantages of lower rents and rates, the pendulum is again swinging in the direction of a dispersion of industry. Lastly railways accelerated the decline of country life because they facilitated the rural exodus and the extinction of subsidiary industries, though they gave the producer of foodstuffs access to an extended market and therefore better prices than were prevalent in his own locality.

The story of the evolution of inland transport is not yet completed. Roads, rivers, canals, railways—and now again roads have come successively into the foreground. The automobile has brought about a return to the roads, which are entering into serious competition with railways both for passenger and goods traffic. Once more the maintenance of the roads has become a matter of great public importance.

The revolution in methods of transport embraced external as well as internal communications— with consequences of immeasurable significance. The growth of industry depended in an overwhelming degree upon the world economy both as the source of raw materials and as the market for the absorption of manufactured goods; while supplies of grain and meat had to be carried overseas to feed the vast population that was springing up in the urban centres of England. In vivid contrast with the beneficial effects produced on industry, English agriculture lost its former monopoly of the homeland and was exposed to the full rigour of the competition of virgin soils.

The nineteenth century was an era of outstanding developments in British shipping, both as regards changes in the material with which vessels were constructed (the replacement of timber first by iron and then by steel), and the utilization of a new motive force (steam instead of wind). In the opening decades the stimulus for improvements in ocean navigation came from the rivalry between England and the United States, for there was a prospect that the latter would win supremacy in the world's carrying trade. At the end of the Napoleonic wars the mercantile marine of the United States was half that of England, but at the outbreak of the American Civil War it was only about one-quarter of a million tons less. The advantage enjoyed by the United States was that she could draw upon cheap and abundant supplies of home-grown timber for shipbuilding, whereas England had largely to import her materials. A presidential message to Congress expressed the conviction that American shipping would soon outstrip that of any other nation. However in economics as in war there are surprises, and

England began to forge ahead. After the Civil War the American people devoted themselves to opening up the interior of their country by an immense construction of railways. Furthermore English shipowners—deprived of protection and forced to depend upon their own efforts—threw themselves into the competitive struggle with greater ardour, and produced a better and faster ship. Above all the iron age in shipbuilding was already dawning, and it was destined to transfer to England the advantage not only in material but also in power. Iron began to displace timber as the material for building ships at a time when the United States had not developed her metallurgical and engineering industries; while steam had commenced to compete with wind.

The introduction of iron was due largely to the scarcity of timber: yet it was many years before iron ships superseded wooden ships although they were lighter in weight and therefore could carry larger cargoes, they were more durable, and there was no limit to their size. (Steel was to prove still lighter and cheaper to work.) The prejudice against iron ships died hard. 'Don't talk to me about ships of iron,' said the chief constructor of a naval dockyard, 'it is contrary to nature.' While a canal barge was built of iron in 1787 more than two decades elapsed before iron vessels were employed in river and canal navigation, and another decade before they made sea voyages. Progress continued to be slow. When the navigation acts were repealed in 1849 iron-built ships were few in number. Iron in fact was not extensively used for either steamers or sailing ships until the third quarter of the century; the date of the first iron battleship is 1860. Not all steamers were of iron—small wooden steamships were launched as late as 1875; not all sailing ships were of wood—there were iron sailing ships at least as early as 1830 and they became very numerous a generation later; there was also a period of composite building—a mixture of iron and wood. Yet scarcely had iron won the victory over wood as the material for shipbuilding when it was challenged by steel.

A steel ship was built in 1858, but the price of steel delayed its adoption and in the eighties iron ships greatly preponderated. In the next decade the triumph of steel over iron was virtually complete. One result of the substitution of metal for wood was the transference of the shipbuilding industry from the south of England (the River Thames) to the northeast coast and to Scotland (the Clyde).

England was the first country to apply successfully in navigation not only a new material but also a new motive force. A great drawback to the sailing ship was its dependence upon the wind which made it unreliable. Before steamships plied with passengers on the River Thames, travellers from Gravesend to London [1] were often called upon to embark in the middle of the night, and after being six or eight hours on the water might be compelled to land at a considerable distance from their destination. The use of steam in place of sails as a means of propulsion in shipping virtually began with the *Charlotte Dundas*, a wooden steamboat built in 1802, which plied on the Forth and Clyde Canal. This led Fulton (1807) in America to build a wooden steamboat with a British engine for service on the River Hudson. Iron and steam were wedded in 1820 when an iron steamer was made in England. Ocean navigation under steam was tried in 1819 in an attempt to cross the Atlantic from the American side, though steam only served as an auxiliary power. The next year witnessed an effort to steam across the Atlantic from the European side: no particulars have survived of the exploit. Nearly two decades later (1838) four ships crossed the Atlantic under steam,[2] one of them taking fifteen days; in the same year Cunard and his partners were given a contract by the British government for the conveyance of the North American mails by steam. The sailing ship did not succumb without a long struggle. When British shippers were deprived of protection in 1849 only 5 per cent. of the mercantile marine was under steam. Sail tonnage continued to increase until it attained its maximum in 1865, steam tonnage rising

[1] A distance of 22 miles by land.   [2] One was built of iron.

to 15 per cent. of the total. In the seventies sail tonnage declined while steam tonnage forged ahead; the latter had grown ten times as large as the former before the advent of the first world war.[1] Thus, as in industry, the adoption of steam-power was slow and protracted.

Steamers were used for the conveyance of mails and passengers. In order to take cargoes, fuel economy was necessary both to avoid high freights and save bunker space. Two alternatives were possible—either to build a ship that would carry a great number of passengers and large cargoes to compensate for the heavy cost of working the ship, or to devise a more economical marine engine. A solution was first attempted on the lines of a vessel of exceptional tonnage, the *Great Eastern*, but the experiment was not successful. The other solution was the achievement of John Elder of Glasgow, who constructed steamers fitted with compound engines which reduced the consumption of coal to one-half; eventually the turbine lowered it to about one-sixth. This made the steamer a commercial proposition because a saving in coal meant extra cargo. At the present day coal, as the marine fuel, is being replaced by oil which occupies less storage and is more economical to work. Another important development was the motor ship fitted with internal combustion engines, of which an increasing number is now being built.[2] In these improvements marine engineering kept pace with the new materials of ship construction. Finally new types of vessels have been designed for special purposes—the conveyance of frozen meat, fruit and dairy produce (the first cargo of frozen meat came from Australia in 1880); and the transport of oil in bulk (the first tanker was made in 1886).

As befitted a maritime power whose walls for a thousand

[1] The approximate sail and steam tonnage was—1840 ($2\frac{2}{3}$ million sail: 88,000 steam); 1850 ($3\frac{1}{2}$ m.: 170,000); 1860 ($4\frac{1}{5}$ m.: 450,000); 1870 ($4\frac{1}{2}$ m.: $1\frac{1}{10}$ m.); 1880 ($3\frac{4}{5}$ m.: $2\frac{3}{4}$ m.); 1890 (3 m.: 5 m.); 1900 (2 m.: $7\frac{1}{2}$ m.); 1910 ($1\frac{1}{10}$ m.: $10\frac{1}{2}$ m.).

[2] The tonnage of motor vessels rose from 385,000 tons in 1924 to $2\frac{1}{2}$ million tons in 1938.

years were made of wood when her coasts were guarded by ships of English oak, England from the middle of the nineteenth century enjoyed an undisputed primacy in the production of mechanically-propelled vessels. In the years preceding the first world war she was responsible for three-fifths of the world's output of mercantile marine. The most serious competitor, the United States, had withdrawn from the race for supremacy in order to concentrate her energies on the opening up of the vast hinterland that stretched from her Atlantic seaboard to the Pacific Ocean. The predominance achieved by our shipbuilding yards was due to a combination of factors—the efficiency of the iron industry, the skill and inventiveness of engineers, the abundance of cheap coal. Yet England might not have maintained her ascendancy in shipping when other countries developed their steel industry and oil began to displace coal, if she had not attained the leading position in world commerce and world carrying trade. This position was owing to an enlightened policy which opened her ports freely to the goods of other nations, which gave access to all ships without flag discrimination, which financed business transactions in all parts of the globe. The shipbuilders had viewed the repeal of the navigation acts with gloomy forebodings, but within sixty years the merchant fleet had more than trebled. It mustered 2½ million tons in 1815 (100 per cent. sail), 3½ millions in 1850 (95 per cent. sail), 11½ millions in 1910 (9 per cent. sail), and 11 millions in 1938 (4 per cent. sail, 73 per cent. steam, 23 per cent. motor).

A fresh chapter in the history of communications has been opened up within recent years by the development of air transport. We stand on the threshold of a new era with its illimitable possibilities for good—and also for evil.

Chapter Nine

THE AWAKENING OF LABOUR

A pregnant consequence of the great inventions was the rapid growth of a class-conscious proletariat. The awakening of the English masses was a portent of momentous significance. It made the nineteenth century the seed-time of many movements which are only coming to full maturity in our own day. Almost all the modern manifestations of labour activity—the political party, trade unionism in its present structure, the co-operative societies —are to be traced to the same era. It was also the formative epoch of socialist thought. The ideas which were conceived as to the claims of labour became later the basis of the socialist creed.

It is often asserted that the 'Industrial Revolution' created in England the proletarian class, that is, a class which possesses no property and lives entirely upon wages. Thus Engels, an early socialist writer and friend of Karl Marx, declared that 'the proletariat was called into existence by the introduction of machinery.' Actually a wage-earning class has existed in England for hundreds of years. The invention of machinery did not establish for the first time the relationship of employers and employed: this relationship was already the basis of the industrial system. Nor did it initiate the antagonism of capital and labour: this antagonism was already acute particularly in the eighteenth century. Why, then, in the nineteenth century did the English working class become so keenly perceptive of its separate identity as a class and so determined to be master of its own destiny? The explanation is to be found in the effects produced by the inventions on the psychology of labour.

To begin with, the adoption of machinery brought in its train the factory system; and the concentration of great masses of workmen under a single roof quickened their sense of corporate interests. Engels has described the influence of factory and urban life in stimulating self-consciousness among working men. 'The workers,' he wrote, 'begin to feel as a class, as a whole; they begin to perceive that, though feeble as individuals, they form a power united; their separation from the bourgeoisie, the development of views peculiar to the workers and corresponding to their position in life, is fostered; the consciousness of oppression awakens, and the workers attain social and political importance. The great cities are the birthplaces of labour movements; in them the workers first began to reflect upon their own condition and to struggle against it; in them the opposition between proletariat and bourgeoisie first made itself manifest. Without the great cities and their forcing influence upon the popular intelligence the working class would be far less advanced than it is.' In the next place the 'Industrial Revolution' appeared to intensify the immemorial contrast between riches and poverty. Alike in industry and agriculture large-scale production challenged small-scale production, and as a result economic power was vested in fewer hands. Capital accumulated rapidly yet at the same time intense social misery prevailed. The situation seemed paradoxical. The spectacle of great wealth poured out by machinery, sharply accentuated as it was by striking inequalities in its distribution, provoked a fierce spirit of resentment and awakened the dormant feeling of class antagonism.

The ultimate consequences of the inventions have undoubtedly been, on the whole, beneficial. None the less progress has been achieved at a price, and a well-balanced view of the 'Industrial Revolution' will take into account both the price which has been paid and the gain which has accrued. Contemporaries however were, not unnaturally, mostly alive to the evils of the new industrial system; and in their eyes its disadvantages outweighed its merits. It was a common view that, bad as was American slavery, 'the white slavery in the manufactories of England was far worse.' Robert Owen asserted that the effect of all the 'splendid improvements' had 'hitherto been to demoralize society through the misapplication of the new wealth created.' Man, he cried, 'sees all around him hurrying forward to acquire individual wealth regardless of him, his comforts, his wants or even his sufferings.' We must indicate the nature of the evils from which the workers suffered, for they nourished the social unrest which found expression in a militant labour movement.

The first was the low price of labour. 'Half a million hand-loom weavers,' wrote Carlyle, 'working fifteen hours a day in perpetual inability to procure thereby enough of the coarsest food; English farm labourers at nine shillings and at seven shillings a week.' 'A great mass of our unskilled labourers,' observed Francis Place the devoted champion of labour, 'and a very considerable number of our skilled labourers are in poverty if not in actual misery. They live amongst others who are better off than themselves and they cannot understand why there should be so great a difference. To men thus circumstanced any, the most absurd, scheme which promises relief is eagerly seized and earnestly adhered to.' It was from the ranks of famished hand-loom weavers and others steeped in poverty that insurrectionary chartism recruited its most fiery supporters. Nevertheless the backbone of the militant labour movement was not the half-starved weaver, carrying on a hopeless fight against machinery, but the relatively prosperous factory operative. It often excited surprise that the best-paid workmen complained the most. 'No doubt of it!' exclaims Carlyle. 'The best-paid workmen are they alone that can so complain! How shall he, the hand-loom weaver who in the day that is passing over him has to find food for the day, strike work? If he strike work he starves within the week. He is past complaint!' The mill hands were better off yet (as Carlyle recognized) wages alone 'are no index of well-being to the working man.' Insecurity, in other words liability to unemployment, is even more demoralizing than poverty; and insecurity was the lot of the factory operatives. 'Their trade,' says Carlyle, 'now in plethoric prosperity, anon extenuated into inanition and short-time, is of the nature of gambling; they live by it like gamblers now in luxurious superfluity now in starvation. Black mutinous discontent devours them; simply the miserablest feeling that can inhabit the heart of man. English commerce with its world-wide convulsive fluctuations makes all life a bewilderment; sobriety, steadfastness, peaceable continuance, the first blessings of man, are not theirs.'

Poverty was the source of other evils. William Lovett, the chartist leader, tells of a visit which he paid to Spitalfields:[1] 'In whole streets that we visited we found nothing worthy of the name of bed, bedding or furniture; a little straw, a few shavings, a few rags in a corner formed their beds—a broken chair, stool or old butter-barrel their seats —and a saucepan or cup or two their only cooking and drinking utensils. Their unpaved yards and filthy courts, and the want of drainage and cleansing, rendered their houses hotbeds of disease; so that fever combined with hunger was committing great ravages among them.' And these conditions were general throughout the industrial north, for the official inquiries of the forties into the state of the towns gave an appalling account of the housing of the poor. A natural corollary of the social malaise was that intemperance, with its baneful consequences, was rife. We may quote a description from a contemporary writer, Lloyd Jones. 'Drink was the mainspring of enjoyment. When Saturday evening came indulgences began which continued till Sunday evening. Fiddlers were to be heard on all sides, and limp-looking men and pale-faced women thronged the public-houses and reeled and jigged till they were turned, drunk and riotous, into the streets at most unseasonable hours. On the Sunday morning the public-houses were again thronged that the thirst, following the indulgence of the night, might be quenched. When Church hour approached, however, the churchwardens with long staves tipped with silver sallied

[1] In London.

forth, and when possible seized all the drunken and unkempt upon whom they could lay their hands, and these being carefully lodged in a pew provided for them were left there to enjoy the sermon, whilst their captors usually adjourned to some tavern near at hand for the purpose of rewarding themselves with a glass or two for the important services they had rendered to morality and religion. In fact sullen silent work alternated with noisy drunken riot.' Such was some of the material out of which labour leaders strove to build up a stable and coherent labour movement.

Apart from the degradation produced by poverty, insecurity of employment, bad housing and intemperance, there were all the unsettling effects associated with a period of transition. In the eyes of contemporaries the foundations of society seemed in process of dissolution. The old social landmarks were being submerged in a torrent of industrialism; new classes were being formed and new relationships were being established between employers and employed. Three features in particular should be observed. The first was the complete collapse of the old industrial code instituted by the state for the 'well-ordering' of the working class—with the result that the latter was driven to depend upon its own efforts. The second was the increased importance of capital due to the installation of machinery, coupled with diminished opportunities for a wage-earner to attain mastership and economic independence. So long as the artisan had some prospect of improving his status, a permanent and efficient labour movement was impracticable. The leaders of the working men, with greater intelligence and capacity than their fellows, were constantly absorbed into the ranks of the employers. But the use of machinery required an amount of capital which the mass of operatives could never hope to acquire; and so the working class became more consolidated, more rigidly defined, and more conscious of a separate identity and of separate class interests. The third development was the growth of a vast industrial population employed in factories, workshops and mines, which had behind

246

it no corporate traditions to give it coherence and stability, and which was composed of the most diverse elements— handicraftsmen who had inherited a pride in their skill and semi-independence, agricultural labourers divorced from the steadying influences of country life, Irish immigrants accustomed to an inferior standard of existence. All these elements were mingled together in the large towns, each reacting on the other, creating intense social confusion, a sense of chaos and instability, out of which emerged a militant labour movement seeking blindly to accomplish far-reaching and even revolutionary designs. The moderating influence of education was absent. There was no compulsory school attendance. A number of day-schools were available for the children of working men but they were extremely unsatisfactory, and the teachers often lacked even elementary knowledge. In some towns mechanics' institutes afforded adults an opportunity for hearing lectures, which appear however to have been sometimes largely of a propagandist character.

The interplay of all these varied influences was responsible for a deep social cleavage; and the nation was arrayed into two opposing camps, employers and employed, each looking on the other as an enemy. Or rather one should say that two nations warred together within the confines of a single state. The 'complete separation of feeling between masters and men,' which began to arouse grave misgivings from the early decades of the nineteenth century, was partially due to the altered conditions of industrial life. Owing to large-scale production the masters no longer came into contact with their men, and this neutralized the possibility of friendly feeling between them. An enlightened employer of labour and a famous advocate of arbitration and conciliation, Mundella, has described the changed situation in these words: 'It is this hostile feeling between masters and men that is the cause of the mischief. In the old time when I was an apprentice, my master knew every man that he employed and knew his circumstances. When his wife was sick he helped him or lent him money or helped to send his boys to school. Now we employ thousands; we do not know their faces; they are "hands" to us, they are not men; there is no sort of mutual sympathy, and that is the top and bottom of all the mischief.' While there still remained anything of a patriarchal relationship between masters and men, there also survived a sentimental bond; but when they grew estranged, and the bond between them became purely a cash nexus, a clash was inevitable.

The conflict of capital and labour, though not a new phenomenon, was the dominating fact of industrial life throughout the nineteenth century. On the side of the men their leaders insisted that the interests of employers and workmen were irreconcilable. When Allan, secretary of the Amalgamated Society of Engineers, was asked by the royal commission of 1867 the question: 'Is it not the interest of the employer and employed to work together?' he replied: 'There I differ. Every day of the week I hear that the interests are identical. I scarcely see how that can be, while we are in a state of society which recognizes the principle of buying in the cheapest and selling in the dearest market. It is their interest to get the labour done at as low a rate as they possibly can, and it is ours to get as high a rate of wages as possible, and you never can reconcile those two things.' The doctrine that labour is a commodity to be bought and sold like other commodities was fiercely resented. 'Employers,' complained the author of *Tom Brown's School Days*, 'treated the labour of their men, which was in fact the lives of their men, on the same principles as those on which they treated a dead commodity. They most rigorously applied to it the same law of supply and demand as they applied to any other commodity, thereby putting the living man and inanimate things on the same footing.' For peace in industry, declared the spokesman of the miners, Macdonald, it is necessary that 'employers cease to treat their men as so much material in the market but treat them like men.'

On the side of the employers the feeling of suspicion and dislike shown by the men was largely reciprocated. Many of the early capitalists were sprung from the most ignorant section of the population, and they often abused their power. 'The old aristocracy of birth,' says Robert Owen, 'as I recollect them in my early days were in many respects superior to the money-making and money-seeking aristocracy of modern times.' For a long while employers resisted all proposals for arbitration with their men, because they considered that it would degrade and humiliate them to meet their workmen around a common board. Mundella declared that in some industrial centres he had heard the masters express their private opinions freely. 'One could hardly believe that they could be speaking of the same race when speaking of their workmen. The feeling that is cherished by some employers towards working men is so bad that it is the foundation of many of the strikes that happen.'

In these circumstances it is not surprising to find the conviction widespread that England was on the verge of a social revolution. This conviction explains the intense distrust exhibited by the governing class during the first half of the nineteenth century towards the aspirations of labour, and the adoption of a policy of intimidation and repression. And not until this conviction had died a natural death were the workers admitted to a share of political power. Here is one prophecy of an impending social catastrophe uttered by an acute if biassed observer. 'The middle class,' wrote Engels in 1844, 'dwells upon a soil that is honeycombed, the speedy collapse of which is as certain as a mathematical demonstration. The deep wrath of the whole working class [must] before too long a time goes by break out into a revolution in comparison with which the French Revolution will prove to have been child's play.'

What then was the solution of the social problem? Such was the question which agitated men's minds during the generation which followed the peace of 1815. Victorian optimism, the complacent feeling that everything was well with England, is a characteristic of the third quarter of the nineteenth century. In earlier decades there was ample recognition of the disease in the body politic, and the utmost variety of remedies was confidently propounded as the panaceas of all social ills. 'The poor patient,' Carlyle wrote, 'tossing from side to side' complained now of this now of that, while the physicians failed to agree among themselves. Let us observe the remedies that at one time or another engaged the attention of social reformers. They may be grouped under five heads: those proposed by the manufacturers, by the political economists, by the currency theorists, by the tory democrats, and finally those which found favour with the workers themselves.

The remedy of the manufacturers was free trade: repeal the corn laws, invite the whole world to exchange its grain for English products, and poverty will disappear. It is a curious fact that the proposal to repeal the corn laws, which meant a reduction in the price of bread, was strenuously resisted by a section of the working class.[1] The remedy of the political economists was Malthusianism. Human misery, they taught, was not the result of human injustice; it was due to the pressure of population upon the means of subsistence. Over-population was the prime cause of the economic malady; the supply of labourers must therefore be diminished, then 'the demand and the remuneration will increase.' This was to be done among other ways by a more stringent administration of the poor law and by emigration. In glowing colours Carlyle unfolded the great solution of the social problem—emigration. He depicted a world unpeopled, 'where Canadian forests stand unfelled, boundless plains and prairies unbroken with the plough; on the west and on the east green desert spaces never yet made white with corn; and to the overcrowded little western nook of Europe our terrestial planet, nine-tenths of it yet vacant or tenanted by nomads, is still crying: Come and till me, come and reap me! And in an England with wealth and means for moving such as no nation ever before had.' But to Malthusian teaching and its implications the workers turned a deaf ear.

[1] See Chapter Eleven.

Robert Owen, from whom all the labour movements of the age drew much of their inspiration, taught them to treat lightly its terrors. 'The reverse of the Malthusian doctrine,' he proclaimed, 'is true. Mankind are able to produce food in a geometrical ratio to their increase in number.' The third remedy, which was widely canvassed among a section of reformers, was the amendment of the currency. Society suffered, it was argued, from a shortage of gold to serve as the medium of exchange. Manufacturers were hampered because they could not obtain loans; workmen were unemployed or unfairly remunerated because they could not exchange their labour for money. In a word, shortage of currency meant economic stagnation; and conversely 'an increase of the currency quickens industry.' Thomas Attwood, the son of a banker and a prominent politician, proposed the creation of paper money whereby production could be made to balance effective demand; and Owen advocated the issue of labour notes.

The fourth remedy was that of the tory democrats, men like Michael Sadler, Richard Oastler 'the factory king,' Samuel Coleridge and Robert Southey. A passage from Coleridge's *Lay Sermons* will serve to illustrate their standpoint. 'Our manufacturers must consent to regulations; our gentry must concern themselves in the education as well as in the instruction of their natural clients and dependents; must regard their estates as secured indeed from all human interferences by every principle of law and policy, but yet as offices of trust with duties to be performed in the sight of God and their country.' The tory democrat based his philosophy upon the conservation of the existing fabric of society with its social gradations and economic distinctions of rich and poor, employers and employed; but he postulated also the principle of duties as the correlative of rights, the obligations of wealth and power as the justification of their privileges. Hence factory reform and the relief of poverty were the main planks in the social platform of tory democracy. To the mass of the workers the philosophy failed to commend itself because it ignored their demand for social and political equality. This explains also the failure of Disraeli's own vision of a 'Young England' party: it was incompatible with the wave of democratic sentiment which was beginning gradually to infiltrate all sections of English society.

The remedies which found most favour with the workers themselves were of three kinds. One was socialism—not state socialism but voluntary co-operation. State socialism means that the state owns and controls the instruments of production. Voluntary co-operation means that the workers organized in groups are to manage their own economic affairs. The second was parliamentary reform on the lines demanded by the chartists. The third was collective bargaining, that is, trade unionism. These proposed remedies represented attempts to solve the social problem from three different angles. The first (socialism) sought to dispense with the capitalist in industry: the second (chartism) endeavoured to capture the governmental machinery, and by the aid of political power establish economic ascendancy: and the third (trade unionism) was a recognition that the capitalist played a necessary part in production, or at any rate was too strong to be dislodged, and therefore the best thing to do was to strike a bargain with him. There was thus an acute division among the spokesmen of the working class as to the proper cure for the social disease; and the clash of the different schools of thought proved a fatal handicap in the efforts to establish a common front.

We may now consider more in detail the first two remedies propounded by labour leaders—socialism and chartism.[1]

England, and not the Continent, is the birthplace of modern socialism. The cardinal doctrines of the socialist creed—that labour creates wealth, and that profits are the 'surplus value' abstracted from labour—were first given to

---

[1] For the third, trade unionism, see Chapter Fourteen.

the world not by Karl Marx but by a small body of British thinkers in the second and third decades of the nineteenth century. From those writers Karl Marx drew his inspiration; and when—owing to an interval of economic prosperity—the memory of the early English socialists passed into oblivion, the Continent subsequently gave back to England the socialist doctrines of which this country was the original source and fountain-head. It was natural that England should be the birthplace of modern socialism. The latter was a reaction against the abuses of an unregulated industrialism, and these appeared earlier here than on the Continent where the adoption of machinery was delayed. The protest against abuses assumed two forms. Among the moderate elements it was confined to a demand for remedial legislation. Capitalism had revealed itself a potent force for good in so far as it promoted the increase of wealth; but also a potent force for evil in so far as it was left to exploit the industrial masses unshackled by any kind of control. Accordingly the moderate elements sought to limit the power of capitalism by factory reform, trade unionism and the institution of co-operative stores. But the more extreme elements endeavoured to eliminate the capitalist altogether, that is, they wanted to abolish completely the private ownership of capital.

Not only was modern socialism the product of British conditions: it was also in form and structure the creation of British minds. It was hewn by British hands out of materials supplied unconsciously by great British thinkers. Ricardo, whose authority in political economy was unquestioned—in line with John Locke and Adam Smith—had declared that labour was the cause of value; and although he did not mean what the early socialist writers thought he meant, his statement was eagerly seized upon and adopted by them as the basis of their theories. In their hands the doctrine that labour alone creates wealth received the narrowest interpretation because labour was regarded as purely manual or wage labour. The idea was popularly expressed thus:

'Wages should form the price of goods;
Yes, wages should be all;
Then we who work to make the goods,
Should justly have them all;
But if the price be made of rent,
Tithes, taxes, profits, all;
Then we who work to make the goods,
Shall have—just none at all.'

The theory of 'surplus value', which became the bedrock of Marxian socialism, was foreshadowed in the conception that the capitalist appropriated—in the shape of profits and rent —a large portion of the labourer's natural reward.

The socialists regarded competition as the source of all evil; and their remedy was co-operation in place of competition, associated enterprise instead of individualism. As the 'Christian socialists' afterwards expressed it: 'The watchword of the socialist is co-operation; the watchword of the anti-socialist is competition. Anyone who recognizes the principle of co-operation as a stronger and truer principle than that of competition has a right to the honour or the disgrace of being called a socialist.' In this sense of the term the father of English socialism was Robert Owen.

The career of Robert Owen passed through two main phases. In the first he appears as the successful manufacturer, the model employer devoted to the welfare of his workpeople, the ardent advocate of factory legislation, the pioneer of popular education—he was the founder of the first infant school in Great Britain—and the exponent of an enlightened philosophy. In the second he emerges as the apostle of a new social order based on the principle that the character of the individual is formed by his environment, and as the prophet of a new creed of co-operation in lieu of competition. His influence upon the evolution of the English labour movement cannot be over-estimated. The Radical poet, Ebenezer Elliot, wrote: 'You came among us—a rich man among the poor—and did not call us rabble. This was a phenomenon new to us.' It was not alone the sympathy that Owen exhibited to working men, alike in his creation of a model establishment at New Lanark which attracted world-wide attention, in his advocacy of factory reform, and in his schemes for the relief of the unemployed. It was also the fact that his teachings opened up before their eyes the vista of a better world and inspired them to resist the gloomy philosophy which saw salvation for the working class only in emigration and restriction of population. His passionate belief in the possibility of human progress, and in the attain-ment of a millenial state upon earth by the reconstruction of society on rational lines, profoundly influenced the thought and outlook of his countrymen; and even the doubts which have been cast upon the idea of progress have failed to eradi-cate human faith in its reality. He rendered, in any event, an inestimable service by inculcating the supreme lesson that human betterment is not beyond the scope of human control; and one solid—if unlooked-for—fruit of his career remains to the present day in the consumers' co-operative move-ment.

Owen assumed as an axiom that the state of society created in England by the 'Industrial Revolution' was utterly bad. He complained that industry and commerce were regarded purely as a source of wealth without regard to their political and moral reactions. Under a 'thoroughly selfish system,' as he termed it, there could be no true civilization. No permanent and substantial improvement in society was possible until the adoption of 'a superior mode of forming character and creating wealth.' Accordingly it was necessary to create 'entirely new surroundings' for the human race. This result was to be attained by life in a co-operative community, in which capitalism and the pursuit of individual competition were to be superseded by associated enterprise.

Many generous minds from antiquity down to our own era have conceived visions of an ideal commonwealth. Owen was not the first, nor has he been the last, to dream of a golden age for mankind. Yet in one respect he was more fortunate than other visionaries, in that several attempts were made in his own lifetime to clothe his ideas with the flesh and blood of reality. There were four main experiments at community-building. One was in Scotland; another in Ireland; the third in America where the prophet of communism himself tested the practicability of his own theories at New Harmony in Indiana (1825–28); the fourth and last in England at Queenwood in Hampshire (1839–45). One and all these Utopian projects failed. They imposed too great a strain upon human nature, and the old leaven of individualism proved too strong.

The early socialist movement bequeathed to the world as its unexpected legacy the consumers' co-operative movement. The community experiments had been conducted by moneyed men who had become converts to the new social system, so that the socialist programme appeared to depend for success upon the aid of wealthy philanthropists. But Owen's theories of society had fired the imagination of the working class, and a popular agitation sprang up spontaneously all over the country. It was this development which assured Robert Owen an enduring place in the history of the nineteenth century. If his career had resulted in nothing more than visionary projects for social regeneration and half-baked schemes for community-building, he would be remembered to-day as a dreamer who beyond his achievements at New Lanark had left behind him only a record of failure. In reality he gave birth, all unconsciously, to one of the most influential forces in modern industrial life.

The starting-point of the consumers' co-operative movement was the conviction of the masses that they must not wait, for an improvement in their condition, upon the willingness of the rich to provide capital for socialist experiments. They must work out their own salvation with their own hands and their own sacrifices, and gain thereby the additional recompense of being masters of their own destiny.

Inspired with this idea, groups of artisans began to form co-operative societies in order to procure funds for a community in which they could escape the thraldom of a capitalist regime. The funds were to be raised partly by subscriptions, partly by purchasing commodities for resale to their members and accumulating the profits. When Owen returned from America he found the movement in active operation—at one time the number of societies exceeded seven hundred—but the sanguine predictions of their promoters were not fulfilled and the associations of the thirties lapsed. Nevertheless the co-operative enthusiasm evoked by Owen's teachings bore permanent fruit, for a decade later the secret of success was discovered. In 1844 a general store was started at Rochdale with a capital of twenty-eight pounds by a body of co-operators who called themselves the 'Pioneers' and were only twenty-eight in number. The distinctive feature for which the 'Pioneers' became famous, although they were not the first society to adopt it, was the distribution of profits not among shareholders or employees but among members in proportion to the amount of their purchases. This avoided the mistake made by the old stores, which failed to draw custom because they had no special attraction for the public since the profits went to capital. The Rochdale plan was universally adopted by co-operative retail stores, which now number over a thousand (with a membership running into several millions)[1] and are linked up with two co-operative wholesale societies which also engage in production. The co-operative movement of the present day has diverged widely from the ideals contemplated by the co-operative enthusiasts of the thirties; and it may be questioned whether Owen himself would not disown the parentage of his off-spring. Apart from the fact that the community ideal is now generally discredited, the co-operative store foreshadows at best a consumers' paradise. The labour problem is not solved because the relations of employers and employees remain.

[1] In 1938 the number of co-operative retail societies in Great Britain was 1,124, and the membership exceeded eight millions.

Nor have these relations proved invariably amicable, though it is true that co-operators have been in many respects model employers.

Chartism was the first political expression of working class consciousness. It was a protest against the subordination of the masses—against a regime in which political power was vested in the hands of landlords and capitalists. Francis Place described it as 'a new feature in society produced by the increased intelligence of the working people.' John Stuart Mill termed it 'the first open separation of interest, feeling and opinion between the labouring portion of the commonwealth and all above them.' Chartism was thus essentially a class struggle, seeking the realization of its aims without the co-operation of other sections of the community. This is the broad historical significance of the chartist movement; and as the course of events was to demonstrate it was a movement born out of time. The workers lacked political sobriety, training and discipline, they lacked experienced and level-headed leaders, and they lacked a stable and coherent organization—all of which give to the modern labour movement its strength and solidity. After the collapse of chartism the working class abandoned for half a century the attempt to constitute itself a separate political party; and its leaders gave their allegiance to the principles of liberalism. Throughout the nineteenth century the middle class remained securely enthroned in its seat of power. At the end of the century political labour was resurrected as an independent entity; and this fresh development—pregnant with momentous economic consequences—is gradually unfolding itself before our eyes.

The 'Charter' itself was a political document. Its famous 'six points' were all political: manhood suffrage, equal electoral districts, vote by ballot, annual parliaments, abolition of the property qualification for parliament, and payment of members. The 'Charter' sprang from the disillusionment produced by the Reform Act of 1832, when the middle class obtained complete enfranchisement. The victory had been achieved with the co-operation of the mass of the working class, whose support was given in the expectation that the Reform Bill would be a 'stepping stone' to its own political claims. The government's determination to treat the Reform Act as a final measure, and not as an instalment, shattered the alliance between the middle class and the working class. In the eyes of the latter the change had only effected a transfer of power from one domineering faction to another. In consequence working men became utterly estranged; and their conviction that they had been used as tools to gain the franchise for others led them to establish a purely working class movement, in which they proceeded to challenge the newly-won political ascendancy of the middle class.

Nevertheless the driving force behind chartism, and the prime cause of the unrest which gave the movement its stern reality and threatened to bring England to the verge of revolution, lay in social rather than political grievances. Chartism was not in its essence a demand for electoral emancipation; but, as one of its most prominent leaders declared, it was 'a knife and fork question.' The acquisition of the franchise was not intended as an end in itself—only as the means to an end. Indeed it was the consciousness of the ulterior aims of the chartist movement that inspired the resistance to it. Not the 'Charter' but the fear of what lay behind it raised overpowering anxiety in the minds of the middle class. Macaulay, for instance, affirmed that he agreed with all the 'six points' except manhood suffrage, which he thought would imperil the security of property. This explains the paradox of chartism, namely, that the demands of the 'Charter' began to be conceded as soon as the chartist movement itself was extinct. Once the dread of a social revolution was removed, the opposition to political changes died away; and when in 1867 the working men in towns were enfranchised, the 'leap in the dark' failed to excite any serious apprehension.

The social programme of the chartists, unlike their political programme, was never stated with precision. There was nothing to correspond on the social side of the movement to the 'six points.' The reason doubtless was that, while they were united on the political platform, they were completely divided on the social platform. They were acutely conscious of the wretched condition of the people yet they produced no constructive platform. Carlyle could therefore with correctness define chartism to mean 'the bitter discontent of the working class,' for in its social aspect it was little more than a vague expression of intense unrest.

None the less some of the chartist leaders did commit themselves to concrete proposals, though they were mutually contradictory and destructive. In the ferment of ideas two main schools of thought emerged. The first was reactionary. It sought inspiration in a past which it idealized as the golden age of the English people: its cry was 'back to the land.' The agrarian projects were a protest against the economic order called into existence by machinery, which had developed the factory system and concentrated large bodies of operatives amidst unhealthy surroundings. The second school accepted as inevitable the changes which were taking place, and did not seek to stem the tide of industrialism that was fast submerging the old landmarks. Men like William Lovett saw the salvation of the working class not in a return to an idealized past but in co-operation, and above all in the education and moral up-lifting of the masses. Ultimately the conflict between the two opposing factions resolved itself into a conflict of ideas between those who treated the social problem as purely a bread and butter question, and those who put before themselves also a moral ideal. The nobler conception was expressed by Lovett in words which are still pregnant with meaning: 'Unless the social and political superstructure were based upon the intelligence and morality of the people, they would only have exchanged despotism for despotism and one set of oppressors for another.'

Apart from the main cleavage of opinion in the chartist

ranks, individual chartists cherished the most diverse aims. The movement, in fact, was a rallying-point for all those who had social grievances or panaceas for social ills. The assailants of the new poor law like Stephens, the opponents of the orthodox currency doctrines like Attwood, the supporters of voluntary co-operation like the 'Owenites,' the champions of factory legislation, the fiscal reformers who wanted to reduce the amount and shift the incidence of taxation—all these found a common meeting ground in the fight for political power. The disunion among the chartists extended to methods as well as to aims. The advocates of 'moral force' sought to pursue the path of orderly and constitutional agitation; they wished to achieve their objects through the spread of education and the growth of public sentiment. The advocates of 'physical force' believed in swift and dramatic strokes of action; they talked of armed insurrection; and their incendiary appeals to violence were responsible for serious outbreaks. The movement also was distracted by divided counsels and embittered personalities. Rival partisans, severed by antipathies of temperament and policy, created a schism in the party which no compromise could bridge.

In addition to the diversity of aims, methods and leadership which split the movement in twain, there was a fatal cleavage in the ranks of labour itself. The north and the south appeared, in an industrial sense, two different worlds. The workmen of the south, and more particularly London, represented the old craft traditions. They were skilled artisans, organized in unions which had maintained their privilege of exclusive membership and successfully resisted social degradation. A higher standard of life and experience of disciplined agitation, coupled with unique opportunities for instruction and discussion, gave them a superior character that stamped them as a kind of aristocracy of labour. In the north, on the other hand, a vast population had sprung into existence created by the new industrialism; and its turbulent and untamed character was the inevitable product of the harsh forces which shaped it. Uneducated, demoralized by excessive hours of toil, living amidst appalling insanitary conditions, and stung by a sense of injustice at the tyranny of the economic system, the miners and famished weavers of the north presented a seething mass of inflammable material which only needed the spark of fiery eloquence to set it ablaze. These were the men who made pikes, and learnt to drill, and attended torch-light processions, and awaited eagerly the call to arms.

The root cause of the failure of chartism was the progress of the working class, which relaxed the leaders' hold upon the people. In the fifties and sixties England emerged from the tribulations which had darkened her horizon; and as the sources from which the chartist agitation drew its chief strength—industrial depression and social discontent—dried up, those who had been attracted to the movement by specific grievances fell away from the chartist ranks. The political apathy of the workers, and their recognition of the middle class as their leaders and monitors, did not imply that they had abandoned all hope of raising their condition, or that they had sunk into a fatalistic acceptance of the existing regime. What really happened was that their energies were diverted into non-political channels; and they now sought to improve their position by means of two typically working class institutions, namely, trade unionism and co-operation. Thomas Cooper, a chartist leader, draws an effective contrast between the Lancashire workers of the chartist era and a generation later: 'In our old chartist times, it is true, Lancashire working men were in rags by thousands; and many of them often lacked food. But their intelligence was demonstrated wherever you went. You would see them in groups discussing the great doctrine of political justice— that every grown-up sane man ought to have a vote in the election of the men to make the laws by which he was to be governed; or they were in earnest dispute respecting the teachings of socialism. Now you will see no such groups in Lancashire. But you will hear well-dressed working men talking, as they walk with their hands in their pockets, of "co-ops" [co-operative stores] and their shares in them or in building societies.' The age of poverty and a keen interest in politics yielded to an age of prosperity and a keen interest in economics. Thus chartism declined—partly because Parliament now showed greater readiness to remedy the social grievances of the working class, thereby cutting the ground from under the feet of the chartist agitator; and partly because the wage-earners found another outlet for their energies in directions which seemed to promise more immediate and tangible fruits for their exertions and sacrifices.

In studying the history of the labour movement in the nineteenth century we are struck by an acute difference between the earlier and later decades. In the first phase— which ends in the middle of the century—labour appears as an insurgent force, full of revolutionary fervour, inflamed with a passionate sense of injustice and economic wrong. This is the epoch of England's social history, of which the burning passion becomes articulate in the pages of Carlyle. It is the epoch of revolutionary socialism, of communist experiments, of militant trade unionism, and of midnight assemblies of insurrectionary chartists armed with pikes and muskets: an epoch of grave unrest when contemporaries believed the whole frame of civil society 'to be breaking up.' The later phase—which covers the third quarter of the nineteenth century—presents a remarkable contrast. The revolutionary excitement had died down; labour had become the ally, or rather the handmaid, of liberalism; its feet were being trained to walk in constitutional paths; and Parliament, discarding the fashionable philosophy of an earlier generation—the 'dismal science' with its doctrines of *laissez-faire* and restriction of population—now displayed a greater willingness to make concessions to labour. The explanation of the contrast lies in the altered character of the general economic situation. In the opening decades of the century the working class suffered from all the evils associated with the industrial and agrarian changes, aggravated as they were by the long war with France. In the fifties and sixties the country entered upon an era of great prosperity due, among other factors, to the development of railways, the adoption of free trade and the increased output of gold. During these years of plenty working men turned away from the alluring vision of a socialist commonwealth. They devoted their efforts to building up on sound and moderate lines a stable and permanent trade union organization, and to covering the country with a network of co-operative stores. And when years of economic distress once more succeeded the years of plenty, socialist teachings again found a fruitful soil and the labour movement in England was reborn.[1]

[1] Socialism in England revived in the eighties—at a time of falling prices and trade depression—under the inspiration of Karl Marx.

Chapter Ten

THE REACTION FROM LAISSEZ-FAIRE

It has been shown in a previous chapter how the triumph of *laissez-faire* came in the eighteenth and not, as is commonly supposed, in the nineteenth century. It was the novel situation created by the introduction of machinery and the growth of the factory system that was responsible for an epoch-making departure in the national approach to economic problems. At first the state assumed an attitude of Olympian detachment, and did little or nothing to alleviate the distress which accompanied the transition from the old order to the new. The first prickings of the social conscience were stirred by the most helpless victims of the 'Industrial Revolution.' The children who worked at the machines in the factories often endured terrible hardships. As we turn over the leaves of the official reports on the employment of children in factories, abundant evidence of their sufferings confronts us on every page. A few concrete illustrations are worth any amount of general comments, and we will therefore glance at the statements taken down from the lips of the children themselves.

A boy employed in the carding-room of a mill at Leicester related his experiences thus: 'I am twelve years old. I have been in the mill twelve months. I attend to a drawing machine. We begin at six o'clock and stop at half-past seven. We don't stop work for breakfast. We do sometimes. This week we have not. We have generally about twelve hours and a half of it. I get 2s. 6d. a week. I have a father and mother, and give them what I earn. I have worked over-hours for two or three weeks together.' At Nottingham a witness fourteen years of age said: 'I have worked in Milnes's factory two years. We go at half-past five; give over at half-past nine. We sometimes stay till twelve. I asked to come away one night lately at eight o'clock being ill. I was told if I went I must not come again.' His father added: 'It's killing him by inches; he falls asleep over his food at night. I saw an account of such things in the newspaper, and thought how true it was of my own children.' A lad employed at Bradford stated: 'I first began to work before I was five years of age. It was a worsted mill. We used to begin at six o'clock in the morning and go on till eight o'clock, sometimes nine. My legs are now bent as you see.' (The knees, reported the commissioner, were bent dreadfully. The height of the boy, who was fifteen, was 3 feet 9 inches.) 'Got my knees bent with standing so long. Have asked my father and mother to let me stop away; they said they could not do with me laiking at home, there was so many of us laiking from not being old enough.' Another boy started life at a worsted mill near Halifax. 'I was hardly five when I went; I went in petticoats; got a shilling a week when I'd been about a month. We used to begin at six and I have wrought there while seven and eight and nine o'clock at night.'

Another evil connected with child labour was night work. 'We used to come at half-past eight at night,' said a girl fifteen years old, 'and work all night till the rest of the girls came in the morning.' In addition there were many complaints of ill-treatment. 'Kind words are God-sends in many factories, and oaths and blows the usual order of the day.' A little Scottish lassie aged thirteen told how 'when she was a child, too little to put on her ain clathes, the onlooker used to beat her till she screamed again.' It is fair to remark that those responsible for the brutal treatment of children were not the masters but a section of the workpeople themselves, in whose charge the children were placed. However the masters are not to be exonerated from blame, since it was their duty to ensure that their young employees were shielded from violence.

One result of the long hours was that children were robbed of sufficient sleep. 'A great majority of the children,' observed a commissioner, 'live from half a mile to perhaps a mile and a half and in some instances further from the place at which they work. The time therefore which is necessary to walk this distance must be taken into account as labour to a child, and that too of a distressing kind in winter-time to those who are very poorly clothed and are without shoes and stockings, which is the case in numerous instances. A fine is imposed if the party be not at work in time, and that too—in a great number of mills—bearing a most unjust proportion to the time lost. This severity produces a corresponding anxiety in both young and old to be at the mill in proper time; and in consequence children as well as adults are often called from their rest much sooner than is necessary in order to ensure their being at the mill when the bell rings. They have to dress and in many instances to put up the food which they require for the day, all of which takes up time, and which is so much abstracted from the needful hours of sleep. I have seen children, who have been thus too early called, sitting together in the ash-pit of the fires of the boilers placing their bare feet in the warm ashes and sleeping with their heads upon each other's shoulders until the bell rang, at which time they were expected to go to work.'

The long hours of labour, combined with an insufficiency of sleep, produced the inevitable effects: fatigue, sleepiness and pain causing deterioration of the physical constitution, deformity, disease, and deficient moral and intellectual instruction. 'I can have no hesitation in stating my belief from what I saw myself,' wrote a commissioner, 'that a large mass of deformity has been produced at Bradford by the factory system. The effect of long and continuous work upon the frame and limbs is not indicated by actual deformity alone; a more common indication of it is found in a stunted growth, relaxed muscle and slender conformation. There remains no doubt upon my mind that under the system pursued in many of the factories the children of the labouring classes stand in need of, and ought to have, legislative protection against the conspiracy insensibly formed between their masters and parents to tax them with a degree of toil beyond their strength. I have found undoubted instances of children five years old sent to work thirteen hours a day; and frequently of children nine, ten and eleven consigned to labour for fourteen and fifteen hours.' In view of this evidence it is not surprising to find the opinion prevalent that the factory children in England were worse off than the slaves in the West Indies. The earnings of young children were scanty in the extreme. Those who were six years old sometimes earned a bare sixpence a week, and the average wage of those ten years old was under two shillings in some districts.

At this distance of time—as we look back upon the controversy between those who were concerned only to exploit the economic potentialities of the inventions and those who applied a social criterion—the question springs to the mind: why did the government refrain from intervention? When we read of the horrors of infant slavery, the long hours of work of men, women and children, and the unhealthy state of many of the factories, we find it difficult to understand on what pretexts it was possible to offer any opposition to official control. We are driven to ask whether the 'Industrial Revolution' created a class of employers in whom all compassion was extinguished; but even so, we have still to explain why public opinion appeared so insensitive to the sufferings of the victims of economic progress.

In order to understand the psychology of those who resisted remedial legislation, two things must be remembered. Firstly: the conditions which prevailed under the early factory system were largely inherited from the industrial society which existed before the inventions. The reason why it was so hard to arouse the national conscience was that the abuses were deep-rooted, although sometimes they were now accentuated. For instance the gravest social problem of the day—the exploitation of child labour—did not originate with the introduction of machinery: on the contrary, children had long been accustomed to work at an earlier age and for less wages than the majority of those who were taken into the factories.[1] Inasmuch as child labour was an integral part of the older economy, the task of stamping it out in factories naturally became much more arduous. In the same way the protracted hours of labour were a legacy of the domestic system under which a working day consisted of twelve hours' toil. Secondly: the minds of the rulers of England were in the grip of the 'dismal' philosophy of the day, which found economic salvation in the rigid dogmas of *laissez-faire*; and these dogmas were likewise an inheritance from the past. The doctrine of non-intervention had been accepted in principle by the governing class for a century, so that it could not be discarded overnight. The reluctance to revert to the practice of state regulation measured the success with which the entrepreneurs had swayed public opinion in favour of industrial freedom. A signal illustration is afforded by the remark made in an official report in allusion to the demand of the hand-loom weavers that they should not be allowed to work more than twelve hours a day: 'Such remedies as these are so contrary to the principles of political economy that I scarcely need make any further comments on them.' Even attempts to protect children employed in chimneys were opposed on the ground that Parliament should not encroach on 'that great principle of political economy that labour ought to be left free.'

Public opinion was influenced against social reforms by other considerations. Many members of the legislature affected to believe that the evils of the factory system were greatly exaggerated. It was also maintained that conditions were worse elsewhere—in workshops, in the homes of the workers, and in industries other than cotton. The cotton manufacturers therefore remonstrated bitterly that their establishments were singled out for condemnation and state control. Yet there was an obvious advantage in beginning with this industry. It was least difficult to regulate because the factories assembled a large number of children

[1] An argument used in favour of the domestic system was that children could be employed at an earlier age than in factories.

under one roof. Publicity made it possible to gain an intimate knowledge of the industrial position, and the experience thus acquired was subsequently utilized over a wider area. Moreover the rapid growth of the cotton manufacture drew public attention to it much sooner than to the old-established occupations, and accordingly Parliament was more willing to take action. Then it began to be recognized that abuses were by no means confined to cotton; and the scope of factory legislation came to be extended to all textile industries and eventually to non-textile industries. As the favourable results grew conspicuous, it was easier later on to apply the principle to other fields. Another contention put forward the interests of the children themselves, who had to choose between work and starvation since their parents could not maintain them. It escaped notice that one reason why the parents were, as is alleged, unable to support their offspring was that their own wages were depressed by the competition of child labour. In addition it was urged that if children were given any leisure they would become idle and vicious. Here again it was not appreciated that education rather than manual toil was the proper method of keeping children occupied.

The most formidable argument against state interference with the conditions of labour was the plea that any proposal to reduce the hours of work would increase the cost of production and thereby drive trade out of the country. We should no longer hold our own in foreign markets, and the manufacturing population might be deprived entirely of its livelihood. Thus the misguided efforts to alleviate suffering must in the end only induce greater suffering. The first professor of political economy at Oxford, Nassau Senior, even went so far as to claim that the whole profit of factories was 'derived from the last hour;' hence if the working day were reduced by one hour and prices remained the same, net profit would be extinguished. When an early attempt was made to lessen the hours for children from twelve to eleven in cotton factories, a member of parliament objected on the ground that it would involve a diminution of over two million pounds in the total annual production. This won the retort from another member that it were 'better to give up the cotton trade altogether than to draw such a sum out of the blood and bones and sinews of these unfortunate children.' Apart from humane sentiment, the argument based on profit overlooked the fact that the cost of production does not depend upon the actual hours of labour but upon capacity; and experience has shown that the reduction of hours within reasonable limits makes the operative more efficient as well as more careful in the handling of machinery. Further some manufacturers were ready to accept shorter hours, and well-organized mills were ahead of statutory enactments. State regulation had the effect of protecting the good employers from the bad; it served to prevent the latter covering up their incompetency by the exploitation of their workpeople. In brief the industrial legislation which sprang out of the social problems created by the inventions was intended to reduce order from chaos, and to school the producers of wealth in the wholesome habits of discipline and self-restraint.

The force of circumstances proved too strong for the opponents of factory reform. We have seen that the early nineteenth century was an era of intense unrest when the old landmarks were being submerged in a torrent of industrialism and the frame of society seemed in process of disintegration. The need for extensive readjustments compelled the government to intervene once again in economic affairs. The drift towards *laissez-faire* was arrested, and the control of the state over the productive agencies was once more reasserted. As the evils evoked or intensified by the use of machinery attracted attention, they afforded a convincing demonstration that the accumulation of wealth in the hands of merchants or manufacturers was inadequate by itself to fulfil the requirements of national well-being. The invention of machinery had solved the problem of production, yet it still remained necessary to solve the problem of distribution and not merely ensure that wealth was distributed over as wide a circle as possible, but also that it was produced under conditions which did not degrade the mass of the community. Under the influence of this new conception the system of *laissez-faire* began to be assailed by those who believed that the only real wealth is life itself, from which it followed that to sacrifice the health and happiness of the nation in economic pursuits was to defeat the very object which the latter were designed to promote.

Other factors contributed to a change in public opinion, of which the full fruits are coming to maturity at the present day. The tentative efforts at reform were attended with a success which stimulated the activities of the social reformers, while the prophets of woe were discouraged to find that their predictions of national ruin were not verified. Experience has proved, said Lord Shaftesbury, that everything urged by the opponents of factory legislation 'has issued in the very reverse. Has ruin stalked over the manufacturing districts? Has capital quitted the country? Have your wages been reduced to the minimum of subsistence? Has the produce of cotton goods been diminished?' Furthermore one step involved another. Once the country put its hand to the plough it could not turn back, and the movement began to develop of its own momentum. Again prosperity mellowed the outlook of the governing class and rendered possible the experiments in social amelioration. In addition the tory party wanted its revenge for the repeal of the corn laws. Lord Shaftesbury wrote: 'The majority, that in 1847 gave victory to the old supporters of the [Ten Hours] Bill, were governed not by love to the cause but by anger towards Peel and the Anti-Corn Law League. Had not these passions interposed, there would have been no unusual humanity.'

We must not overlook also the chartist movement which focussed public attention on what Carlyle called 'the condition of England question.' The difficulty of securing factory reform had led the chartists to complain bitterly of Parliament's neglect to redress labour's wrongs. 'While our social evils have repeatedly been brought before you, you—whose duty it was to provide a remedy—have looked carelessly on. Your own commissioners have reported to you that thousands of infant children are doomed to slavery and ignorance in our mines and factories, while their wretched parents are wanting labour and needing bread.' And Carlyle wrote in a similar mordant strain: 'Read Hansard's Debates or the morning papers if you have nothing to do! The old grand question whether A is to be in office or B, Canada question, Irish Appropriation question, West-India question, Queen-Bedchamber question, game laws, usury laws, Smithfield cattle and dog-carts—all manner of questions and subjects except this [the condition of England question] the alpha and omega of all.' Within a few years after Carlyle in 1839 had denounced the legislature for its supine indifference to social issues, a new spirit manifested itself. 'With every session of Parliament,' affirmed Engels in 1844, 'the working class gains ground and in spite of the fact that the middle class is the chief, in fact the only, power in Parliament the last session of 1844 was a continuous debate upon subjects affecting the working class: the Poor Relief Bill, the Factory Act, the Masters and Servants Act.' Chartism stimulated the demand for state intervention because it impressed upon the national imagination an abiding sense of the grievances of the working class; it made impossible for the future the attitude of complacent acquiescence towards social ills. The insurgent movement of the thirties and forties taught the middle class a lesson which it has never forgotten. Hitherto it had displayed a marked reluctance to remedy the economic maladies of society, partly at any rate from a genuine conviction that they were outside the province of the state. 'If you attempt by legislation,' declared Cobden, 'to give any direction to trade or industry it is a thousand to one that you are doing wrong.' Now at long last the public conscience was awakened and from the forties onwards there has flowed a continuous stream of ameliorative legislation designed to raise the condition of the mass of the people.

The English middle class may therefore claim that, whatever the errors and limitations of its stewardship, it was not entirely unmindful of the welfare of those committed by the Reform Act of 1832 to its charge.

Finally, in this recital of the causes responsible for the new attitude of the state towards social problems, the conversion of the economists must be noticed. It came to be recognized that the national income depends, among other factors, on labour; and whatever increases the efficiency of labour ultimately increases the national dividend. Thus there was an economic as well as a humanitarian argument against *laissez-faire*. Excessive hours of work do not add to the production of wealth but tend rather to diminish it, as the experience of the nineteenth century and the recent scientific study of industrial fatigue have made abundantly clear. Similarly low wages may tend to be dear wages. The true facts of the situation were pointed out by Robert Owen as early as 1813, when he exhorted his fellow-manufacturers to devote greater attention to the welfare of their workpeople. 'Experience has shown you,' he told them, 'the difference of the results between mechanism which is clean, well arranged and always in a high state of repair, and that which is allowed to be dirty, in disorder, without the means of preventing unnecessary friction, and which therefore becomes and works out of repair. If, then, due care as to the state of your inanimate machines can produce such beneficial results, what may not be expected if you devote equal attention to your vital machines which are far more wonderfully constructed? Will you not afford some of your attention to consider whether a portion of your time and capital would not be more advantageously applied to improve your living machines?' A convincing proof that the system of *laissez-faire*, as it was carried out in the early nineteenth century, was wrongly conceived lies in the fact that—in spite of the legal restrictions imposed upon capitalists—the industry and commerce of the country, so far from languishing as was freely predicted, expanded by leaps and bounds.

The reaction in the nineteenth century against *laissez-faire* was unquestionably one of the most pregnant consequences of the 'Industrial Revolution:' yet the process of re-education was only very gradual. When the authors of an official report on child labour recommended factory legislation for the protection of children, they were careful to dissociate themselves from 'the pernicious notion'—so they termed it—'of the necessity of legislative interference to restrict hours of adult labour.' The employment of the young stood in a separate category because they were not 'free agents able to protect themselves,' as adult artisans were wrongly presumed to be. Cobden, for instance, wrote in a letter to a friend: 'As respects the right and justice by which young persons ought to be protected from excessive labour my mind has ever been decided, and I will not argue the matter for a moment with political economy; it is a question for the medical and not the economical profession. Nor does it require the aid of science to inform us that the tender germ of childhood is unfitted for that period of labour which even persons of mature age shrink from as excessive. In my opinion, and I hope to see the day when such a feeling is universal, no child ought to be put to work in a mill at all so early as the age of thirteen years.' On these grounds Parliament was induced to relax its system of *laissez-faire* in favour of a limited measure of industrial control designed in the interests of the weakest section of the community.

The outstanding feature of factory legislation was its patchwork character. No attempt was made to visualize the problem of child labour as a whole. On the contrary it was dealt with in piecemeal fashion as the glare of publicity brought to light one abuse after another. This method of seeking practical remedies when particular abuses became manifest is, of course, typical of English institutional development—though the result was that many evils were left to fester in obscurity half a century after similar evils had been stamped out in the better organized industries. The era of factory reform was inaugurated in 1802 by an act which was confined to apprentices in cotton and woollen factories. It restricted the hours of apprentices to twelve a day and forbade night work. In consequence the factory owners began to employ 'free' children instead of apprentices. The original mills were built in the country on the banks of streams, and they recruited their hands partly by applying to overseers of the poor for pauper children who were conveyed from all parts of the kingdom: some were even sent from London parishes to feed the cotton mills of Lancashire. But when steam was used as the motive force, the mills could be erected in towns where 'free' child labour was plentiful. The next act was passed in 1819 largely owing to the efforts of Robert Owen a pioneer of factory reform, although it fell short of his own proposals. Owen was among the first to perceive that the industrial system, despite its effectiveness in increasing the national wealth, had injurious reactions which could only be counteracted by legislative control. His own achievements at New Lanark had given to the world a shining pattern of the enlightened employer; and teaching by example and precept he sought to impress upon his fellow-countrymen the urgent need for the limitation of hours. Under this act, which was confined to cotton mills, no child under nine years old was to be employed; and those between nine and sixteen[1] not more than twelve hours a day exclusive of meal-times. Meanwhile official reports revealed to the nation the sufferings of children working in other factories. The act of 1833 prohibited the employment of those under nine,[2] and forbade night work for all persons

[1] Eighteen under an act of 1831.

[2] In 1835 children aged 8–12 formed 3.7 per cent. of the operatives in cotton, 6.7 in wool, 21.1 in silk. For those aged 12–13 the percentages were 9.3, 12.0 and 8.7. The limit of age did not apply to silk mills until 1844. The minimum age for the employment of children was progressively raised to fourteen years (in 1920).

Under the Factories Act (1937) and the Young Persons Employment Act (1938) the maximum number of hours of young persons in factories is 44 for those aged 14-16, and 48 for those aged 16-18. The minimum age below which young persons may not be employed in street trading (including the sale of newspapers) was fixed at 16 in 1933—though the local authorities may permit those aged 15 to be employed by their parents, where the latter are already engaged in street trading.

under eighteen in all textile factories. Those between nine and thirteen were limited to nine hours a day (or forty-eight hours a week); those between thirteen and eighteen to twelve hours a day (or sixty-nine hours a week). One and a half hours were allowed for meals, and factory inspectors were appointed to enforce the regulations. The appointment of inspectors was an important landmark since earlier legislation had been largely inoperative owing to lax administration; and it was primarily on their expert recommendations contained in annual reports that the factory code was built up.

Piecemeal legislation in curing one evil aggravated another —the employment of children underground. Parents who were not permitted to send their offspring into factories at an early age sent them into the coal-mines instead; they said that 'the boys refused to go to school and cried to be taken down the pit.' The children commenced from the age of five or six and were kept in the pit for twelve hours or more at a stretch, sometimes going at half-past three in the morning, sitting in the dark, opening and closing trap-doors as trucks passed, or dragging colliery tubs underground crawling on their hands and knees; young girls and women were similarly employed. Alexander Macdonald, a miners' leader and one of the outstanding figures in the history of trade unionism, has related his early experiences. He entered the mines when he was eight years old. 'The condition,' he said, 'of the miner's boy then was to be raised [awakened] about one or two o'clock in the morning if the distance was very far to travel. I had more than three miles. I was raised at two— never later than three' and remained in the mine until about five or six at night. There was no break beyond half an hour's pause for dinner 'to take your bread.' 'We had no rails in the coal-mines to draw upon, that is, tramways for our tubs to run upon. We had leather belts, and [had] to keep dragging the coal with ropes over our shoulders and sometimes round the middle. The state of ventilation was frightful. A very great deal of our drawing, as we call it, was in the dark on account of the want of ventilation. Of the boys who worked with me almost none are alive now. Deaths were caused by the carbonic acid gas in which we then worked and the degrading kind of labour and the long hours. The men worked as long as the boys'—likewise the women. In 1842 an act prohibited underground work of women and the employment of boys under ten.

The agitation for the restriction of hours was inspired, so far as men like Lord Shaftesbury were concerned, primarily by sympathy for the children but the operatives themselves utilized the agitation as a means of securing directly or indirectly a shortening of their own working day. When the act of 1833 limited 'young persons' to twelve hours a day, the factory owners had recourse to female labour. The men thereupon demanded a reduction of the hours of factory women; they fought the battle (it was said) behind the women's petticoats. Eventually in 1844 women's labour was curtailed to twelve hours a day; three years later the act of 1847 prescribed for women and young persons a maximum of ten hours. Thus after a struggle lasting a generation the Ten Hours Bill became law.

The next stage was the inclusion of the non-textile factories and workshops. Parliament was now ready to extend the scope of factory legislation in view of the evidence, which had accumulated in the protected occupations, that the output did not diminish as a result of shorter hours. In 1862 the children's employment commission was appointed to inquire into industries not already regulated by law. It was discovered that as late as the sixties children were being put to work at five or six years of age; and the hours were excessive—even sixteen a day. 'It is,' said the investigating commission, 'unhappily to a painful degree apparent through the whole of the evidence that against no persons do the children of both sexes so much need protection as against their parents.' The sanitary conditions were repellent in workshops and private dwelling places. Some trades were particularly unhealthy—for instance, lead poisoning in the pottery trade, while lucifer match-making was liable to cause a dreadful disease. In straw-plaiting the little ones were set a task at three years old. In the hosiery industry, where only 4 per cent. of the workers had been brought within the pale of the factory code, it was 'common for girls as well as for women to sit up all Friday night to work.' The children began at about four years of age, and were 'often kept up shamefully late on Thursday and Friday till eleven or twelve; mothers will pin them to their knee to keep them to their work.' Shirt-makers often toiled from 5 a.m. to 8 p.m.; and hand-workers in the boot trade from 7 a.m. to 10 p.m. Not in one but in all occupations which were unregulated by law the same evil practices were exposed; and from these revelations of abuses emerged a fact of cardinal importance, namely, that control of workshops was a social necessity no less urgent than the control of factories. Accordingly in 1867 two important measures were enacted. One covered establishments in which fifty or more persons were engaged in any manufacture; the other applied to any place in which less than fifty persons were engaged. In 1878 a new act, instead of applying a numerical criterion, distinguished between factories and workshops by the test of whether mechanical power was used. Apart from the shortening of the working day, factory legislation related to the enforcement of sanitary provisions, the fencing of machinery and precautions against diseases in particular trades. The hours of shop assistants were fixed at seventy-four a week in 1887—after the disclosure that some worked eighty-five—but the limit affected only young persons. The act of 1938 prescribed a maximum of forty-four hours a week for those aged fourteen to sixteen, and forty-eight for those aged sixteen to eighteen.[1]

The history of factory legislation shows how during the first half of the nineteenth century the state in its economic policy was groping its way. It could not lightly disentangle

[1] The hours of adult shop assistants were not regulated by law.

itself from the trend—now more than a century old—of *laissez-faire*; and in the absence of a clearly defined social philosophy it handled its problems, as it had done in the eighteenth century, in an empirical piecemeal fashion taking each on the merits of the case. Only slowly and reluctantly did the pressure of circumstances drive it to assume obligations for the maintenance of a minimum standard of working conditions in the industrial establishments that were springing up overnight. Yet looking back on the nineteenth century we may view it, not as the climax of *laissez-faire* (the common interpretation), but as an age in which the fabric of economic life was being reconstructed in preparation for an era that was to dawn in the twentieth century—the almost limitless extension of state functions into every sphere of the national economy. This new orientation was due to several factors—the influence of the humanitarians, the growing prosperity of the country, the momentum of events which once set in motion could not be arrested, and the political enfranchisement of the working class. It was in particular the widening of the suffrage that led Joseph Chamberlain to assert: 'We shall have to give a good deal more attention to what is called social legislation.'

The astonishing range of the government activities at the present day is reflected in the constitution of specialized departments concerned with agriculture, education, health, labour, transport and the rest. The state now embraces within its purview factories, workshops, mines, farming, railways, schools, universities, hospitals, sanitation, highways, lighting, libraries, parks, workhouses and other multifarious spheres: it is even a shareholder in a canal (Suez) and in an oil company. The fact that the state has at its command a highly efficient civil service enables it to undertake responsibilities which were beyond its resources in days when the administrative machinery was impotent to enforce legislation. These responsibilities fall into two categories. One group may be viewed as an expression of the principle which governed the creation of the factory code—the insistence on a basic standard of welfare. The other group was inspired by purely economic considerations. Something must be said on both these important categories.

A fresh epoch in the history of social legislation was foreshadowed when the state was brought to recognize that the concept of a national minimum already applied to hours of work could not stop short of a minimum of subsistence. The view that low wages are detrimental to the national interest was enunciated by the medical officer of the Privy Council, Sir John Simon, when he wrote in 1854: 'It is the public that, too late for the man's health or independence, pays the arrears of wages.' Towards the end of the nineteenth century the country was aroused to the fact that in spite of increasing prosperity a large portion of the population lived in a condition bordering on destitution. It was estimated that one-third of the working class in London lived in poverty, the figure for a provincial city (York) was approximately the same, while inquiries conducted in other towns disclosed poverty 'on a scale really appalling.' A committee of the House of Lords (1890) summed up the situation of the workers in the sweated industries in these words: 'Earnings barely sufficient to sustain existence; hours of labour such as to make the lives of the workers periods of almost ceaseless toil, hard and unlovely to the last degree; sanitary conditions injurious to the health of the persons employed and dangerous to the public.' At length in 1909 the principle of a minimum wage was embodied in the Trade Boards Act for the benefit of a few sweated industries though it was subsequently extended. In 1912 a minimum wage was established for miners. This was a noteworthy departure because the Trade Boards Act concerned the weakest section of the community, whereas the miners were highly organized. The latter were responsible for another achievement, the eight-hours day (1908):[1] hitherto legal regulation of hours had affected only women and children. A minimum wage was

---

[1] The hours of miners were reduced to 7 in 1919, raised to 8 after the strike of 1926, and reduced to 7½ in 1930.

instituted for agricultural labourers in 1924.[1] The measures devised in the pursuit of social security include also old age pensions, health insurance, unemployment insurance, and family allowances for the up-keep of growing children.[2] In short, recent legislation makes provision (it is claimed in an official handbook) 'against every one of the main attacks which economic ill-fortune can launch against individual well-being and peace of mind.'

Other things come within the compass of a national minimum. One is education together with meals and medical inspection for school children.[3] Another is housing and (closely connected) public health. The concentration of operatives in factories was responsible for the rise of large towns. The population of Leeds expanded between the beginning and middle of the nineteenth century from 53,000 to 172,000, and Bradford increased from 13,000 to 103,000. This unprecedented growth of urban centres brought in its train grave social problems. The accommodation provided for the new inhabitants was wretched in the extreme, and the government ultimately found it necessary to appoint a commission to inquire into the state of the towns. The report of the commission revealed an incredible situation. It gave the following account of the sanitary conditions existing at Leeds a hundred years ago (and they were equally bad elsewhere): 'By far the most unhealthy localities of Leeds are close squares of houses or yards as they are called, which have been erected for the accommodation of working people. Some of these, though situated in comparatively high ground, are airless from the enclosed structure and being wholly unprovided with any form of under-

---

[1] It was established in 1917, abolished in 1921, and restored in 1924.

[2] Old age pensions were instituted in 1908; health insurance in 1911; unemployment insurance in 1911 (at first on a limited scale but extended in 1920); family allowances in 1946. To-day the whole nation, and not wage-earners alone, are comprehended in these provisions.

[3] The act of 1870 created machinery for the provision of elementary schools. Elementary education was made compulsory in 1876 and free in 1891. Local authorities were empowered to provide meals in 1906. Medical inspection became obligatory in 1907.

drainage or convenience or arrangements for cleansing are one mass of damp and filth. In some instances I found cellars or under-rooms with from two to six inches of water standing over the floors. The ashes, garbage and filth of all kinds are thrown from the doors and windows of the house upon the surface of the streets and courts. The feelings of the people are blunted to all seeming decency, and from the constantly contaminated state of the atmosphere a vast amount of ill-health prevails leading to listlessness and inducing a desire for spirits and opiates; the combined influence of the whole condition causing much loss of time, increasing poverty and terminating the existence of many in premature death.' Reform proceeded on three lines: rebuilding individual houses when necessary,[1] clearing away slums,[2] and sanitary improvements—for the last of these the Public Health Act of 1848 created a central authority[3]—but executive efficiency lagged behind legislative aspirations.

In these ways during the course of the past century the doctrine of *laissez-faire* came to be abandoned in the sphere of welfare. It had served its historic purpose in advocating the free exchange of goods in commerce and the removal of obsolete restrictions in industry. Yet it had erred profoundly in postulating the free exchange of labour, that is, freedom of contract—the right of the employer to bargain with a workman without any external regulation. The individualists of the day were opposed to legislative interference with the freedom of adult labour whether in respect of hours or anything else—although as the report of a factory inspector pointed out: 'There can be no such thing as freedom of labour when from the redundancy of population there is such competition for employment.' Those who professed, not always with authority, to speak in the name of political economy discarded too hastily the traditional safeguards for the protection of the wage-earners. They failed signally

[1] The Torrens Act, 1868.   [2] The Cross Act, 1875.

[3] The Board of Health was short-lived and subsequently the responsibility was transferred to the Local Government Board and then to the Ministry of Health.

to understand that the requirements of a factory age made it imperative to institute fresh conditions of employment—relating to child labour, hours, wages, factory and workshop hygiene—which were not merely a revival but registered an advance upon the older principles of social morality. It is therefore not surprising that the 'political economists' incurred the stigma of being callous. Yet eventually the stark abuses of unregulated industrialism forced public opinion to recognize that maximum production may be purchased too dearly if human welfare is disregarded. Accordingly, while at first the government of the day was only concerned to facilitate the march of material progress, and to remove the obstacles which impeded the free play of industrial capitalism, the feeling steadily gained ground that something else was needed. Reluctantly the community was driven to acknowledge that it could not afford to be indifferent to an environment which went to the very roots of national existence. And the natural conclusion followed that it was incumbent upon the state actively to foster the general welfare by direct regulation instead of trusting to the operation of economic forces, such as unfettered competition, to achieve 'the good life.' As this conviction grew, there gradually developed the notion that it was the province of Parliament to legislate directly with a view to establish the foundations of social security.

The public consciousness became increasingly permeated with a new concept which replaced that of *laissez-faire*—the concept of a 'national minimum,' a minimum standard of well-being to which every person was entitled irrespective of his or her position in the industrial order. The concept could be defended on the ground that it was the best method of increasing production, or on the ground of preserving the nation, or on the ground of humanitarianism; but whatever the reason for its acceptance, it has become a cardinal postulate of social morality. It was foreshadowed by Macaulay when he declared: 'Never will I believe that what makes a population stronger and healthier and wiser and

284

better can ultimately make it poorer. If ever we are forced to yield the foremost place among commercial nations, we shall yield it to some people pre-eminently vigorous in body and mind.' The principle of a 'national minimum' found expression in factory acts designed to secure a minimum of leisure and safety, in education acts designed to secure a minimum of instruction, in trade boards acts designed to secure a minimum of remuneration, in public health acts designed to improve the health of the people, in old age pensions and insurance against unemployment, and in other measures of remedial legislation. All these strands of social policy were inspired by the doctrine (to quote Joseph Chamberlain in 1885) that 'government is only the organization of the whole people for the benefit of all its members; and the community may and ought to provide for all its members benefits which it is impossible for individuals to provide by their solitary and separate efforts.'

In the eternal flux of human affairs the cycle of the ages often brings mankind back to an earlier standpoint. The exaggerated individualism of a past age has been profoundly modified by the principle that it is the duty of the community to ensure for its members, one and all, a minimum of well-being. With an infinitely superior equipment, and a more conscious sense of purpose, this country is returning to an older tradition—the regulation of economic life in the spirit of social harmony and justice.

Other fields in which the authority of the state has been exercised are in some respects more significant. Perhaps the most instructive episode in the reaction against *laissez-faire* in the nineteenth century is furnished by the policy adopted towards the railways. The measures which were concerned with social welfare might be explained on humanitarian grounds. No such explanation could be offered for the control of the railways—except in the framing of safety provisions, which were also extended to shipping in a stream of enactments improving the situation of the seamen in regard to wages, medical attention, accommodation, and the rest. The interference of the state in a sphere where purely economic considerations were alone involved was a landmark in the momentous conversion of the business community from the rigid doctrines of non-intervention. The fact that the traders had been exploited by the canal companies gave grounds for apprehension that, if the railway companies obtained a monopoly, they would abuse their position in the same way. In order to safeguard the public interests, Parliament embarked on the wasteful policy of sanctioning competitive lines and fostering rivalry between the companies. The refusal to establish central direction and secure co-ordination of lines was castigated by Porter in his *Progress of the Nation*: 'The *laissez-faire* system—which is pursued in this country to such an extent that it has become an axiom with the government to undertake nothing, and to interfere with nothing, which can be accomplished by individual enterprise or by the associated means of private parties—has been pregnant with great loss and inconvenience to the country in carrying forward the railway system.' However the companies themselves came to appreciate the necessity for amalgamating their lines to ensure through traffic. The prospect foreshadowed the growth of great monopolies acting in concert for the fixing of railway charges. The complaints of traders compelled Parliament to intervene, and the Railway and Canal Traffic Act (1888) laid on the Board of Trade the duty of revising railway rates. Not only were maximum charges imposed but subsequently the companies were required to justify any proposed increase up to the authorized maximum.[1] The reaction from the traditional viewpoint became complete when in the present century the government actively promoted the amalgamation of railways into four groups.[2]

The first world war (1914–18) gave a marked stimulus

[1] This was in 1894. Maximum rates had been fixed the previous year. The act of 1844 laid down that one train must be run daily carrying third-class passengers at a penny per mile. The train was known as 'the parliamentary.'

[2] In 1921. They passed into public ownership in 1948.

to the movement away from *laissez-faire*, because it necessitated an immense extension of interference in all branches of the national economy. Although the end of the war was soon followed by the abolition of many forms of control, the broadening of state activities continued unabated. The mercantilist device of giving bounties (direct financial subsidies) to foster the development of particular industries was now revived notably in the case of agriculture (sugar beet, etc.) and in the construction of houses for the working class. Opinion on the merits of such a practice may be divided, but there can be no question as to the wisdom of official encouragement of scientific research in industry. Another consequence of the war was that the nation grew accustomed to intervention in the economic sphere. Moreover government departments had regulated industry, commerce, shipping and finance, and thereby acquired a corporate experience which is seldom wholly lost and can bear fruit when a fresh change in public policy should provide the occasion. This change materialized immediately after the second world war (1939–45). Now dawned the era predicted by Lord Randolph Churchill half a century earlier: 'The labour interest is now seeking to do for itself what the landed interest and the manufacturing capitalist interest did for themselves when each in turn commanded the disposition of state policy. Our land laws were framed by the landed interest for the advantage of the landed interest. [We are coming] to a time when labour laws will be made by the labour interest for the advantage of labour. The regulation of all the conditions of labour by the state appears to be the ideal aimed at.' A government came into power (1945) with the avowed intention to embark upon a programme of nationalization. The post office, telegraph (in 1870) and telephone system (in 1911) afforded a precedent, while proposals for state ownership of the railways had long been mooted. Lord Londonderry recommended in 1836 that after a term of years the railways should revert to the public; an act of 1844 provided that after twenty-one years the state could purchase any railway constructed subsequent to the act; the policy was again advocated before the royal commission of 1865 and on other occasions. The nationalization of the Bank of England, of the coal-mines, of transport, of gas and electricity,[1] must be taken to mean that the state is no longer content to exercise control but now seeks to acquire ownership in spheres hitherto the province of private enterprise.

Nationalization in England (except in the case of the post office which is administered by a government department) assumes the form of public corporations. This promises to be her specific contribution to the constitution of a new economic order. A public corporation is an organ of the state which is not bureaucratic:[2] it is moulded in the shape of an autonomous self-governing institution. It differs from a government department because it is managed not by civil servants but by nominees of the government who enjoy independence within the terms of their charter. As a non-profit-making organization with no shareholders and serving the interests of the community, it fulfils the purpose of nationalization: as an autonomous body it is shielded from political influence, ministerial vacillation, Treasury control, and conventional procedure. The public corporation, although it has only come into prominence within recent decades, can be traced back to the middle of the nineteenth century. A port authority was established by an act of parliament in the fifties to own and operate the docks at Liverpool: it functioned as a public service which was not carried on for profit-making. The port authority at London, whose members are partly elected by users of the docks and partly nominated by public authorities, came into existence in 1909. Other docks managed on similar lines include Glasgow and Leith. Private commercial enterprise, however, is not completely excluded either as regards ownership of wharves and warehouses or employment of dock labour. After the first world

[1] These were measures of the labour government which assumed office in 1945.
[2] The term 'bureaucracy' is here used in its original sense of a body of government officials appointed by government and directly engaged on government work.

war there followed the Forestry Commission, the Central Electricity Board (created to construct and administer a system of main transmission lines interconnecting the principal generating stations), the British Broadcasting Corporation, the London Passenger Transport Board, and various other agencies. In these institutions the practical genius of the English people is seeking to work out a compromise between individualism and collectivism, based on the conception of a national economy controlled and guided in certain of its branches by professional corporate bodies acting on behalf of the community.

The public corporation furnishes an alternative both to private enterprise and to state enterprise. There is yet a fourth form of enterprise—municipal trading (sometimes called municipal socialism). The urban authorities, moved by practical considerations and not by political predilections, have constructed harbours, docks, markets, working class dwellings and baths; they operate water,[1] gas, electricity and tramway undertakings; they provide entertainments; even a bank and dairies figure among their interests. In general the municipalities have confined themselves to services which are in the nature of a monopoly.

In one sphere of national life—the relief of the poor— state intervention has had a continuous history extending over many hundreds of years.

As the law of England now stands, an obligation is imposed upon the responsible authority to give aid to any person who is destitute. The virtual right of the indigent to receive succour in case of need is implicit in the whole series of poor law enactments stretching back to the middle ages. It constituted a degree of recognition on the part of society that it had a duty, however imperfectly fulfilled, towards its impoverished members. It was not an accident that the creation of a national system of poor relief was the work of the sixteenth century. Firstly: England was now definitely

[1] Water-works were operated by a municipality in the sixteenth century.

committed to a capitalist regime with its unsettling impact upon security of employment. Secondly: the conversion of arable land into pasture flung upon the countryside those who had hitherto been safely anchored to the plough. Thirdly: the price revolution pressed with peculiar hardship upon that section of the community whose income was most inelastic. Fourthly: England often suffered in earlier ages from famine, and corn prices easily soared to panic heights in times of dearth. In the face of an advancing tide of pauperism, combined with the break-down of religious and voluntary agencies, no government could hold itself aloof. The main principles of the social policy were laid down by stages; and eventually the different strands of poor law legislation were woven into a single texture in the act of 1598, a temporary ordinance perpetuated in the more famous act of 1601. Henceforth down to our own day the responsibility rested upon the local authorities to afford relief to the indigent out of a local fund raised by compulsory taxation. These legislative measures for the relief of destitution were supplemented under the early mercantilist state by administrative measures for the prevention of destitution in so far as this was due to unemployment or a rise in the cost of living.

The Civil War in destroying the power of the Privy Council shattered the machinery of centralized control and so established the independence of the parish. After national uniformity—the ideal of the monarchy—disappeared, each parish was left to go its own way. Another important change was the abandonment of the practice by which work was provided for the unemployed. These twin developments created the framework within which poor relief was administered for nearly two centuries. The consequence of parish autonomy was the increased restraints placed on the mobility of labour by the Law of Settlement (1662), which embodied in a statute the traditional right of the parish to expel all new-comers likely to become chargeable. The consequence of the failure to find employment for the able-

bodied was the institution of the modern workhouse—one
of the most debated and least happy features of English
social policy. The workhouse became the Mecca of poor law
reformers, who promised themselves that the assemblage
of the poor within its walls, without distinction of age or sex,
would be an effectual method of relieving the aged and
impotent, employing the able and industrious, reforming
the idle and profligate, and educating the young in religion
and industry. There was a rapid growth of workhouses in
the early eighteenth century, and an act of 1723 sanctioned
the 'workhouse test' by which relief could be refused to any
applicant who declined to enter the workhouse. Subsequently
the act of 1782 explicitly authorized the payment of outdoor
relief to the able-bodied poor whose earnings were considered inadequate. At the close of the eighteenth century
when the cost of living advanced sharply, this method of
supplementing wages by a parochial allowance proportioned
to the current price of bread and the size of the family was
general.[1]

The English poor law became the target of much adverse
criticism. It grew into a fashion to condemn the practice of
giving relief as a source of demoralization in inducing the
indigent to believe that—however improvident and idle
they might be—the parish was 'bound to find' them.
Benjamin Franklin, when visiting London, expressed the
trend of opinion when he wrote: Repeal the act of 1601 and
'St. Monday and St. Tuesday will soon cease to be holidays.
Industry will increase and with it plenty.' One of the first
tasks taken in hand by the reformed House of Commons was
the amendment of the poor law. An outbreak of rioting
among farm labourers in the south-east of England in 1830
was the immediate occasion of the appointment of a royal
commission to inquire into the working of the system. Its
famous report appeared in 1834. Starting from the premiss

---

[1] It was known as the 'Speenhamland system,' because the scales instituted
by the Berkshire magistrates at a session held in Speenhamland (1795) were
widely adopted.

that 'as the poor's rates are at present administered they operate as bounties on indolence and vice,' it made three outstanding recommendations. (1) That a central board should be established 'to control the administration of the poor laws,' and to frame regulations which 'shall as far as may be practicable be uniform throughout the country.' (2) That parishes should be incorporated into unions for the purpose of providing common workhouses. (3) That the 'most essential of all conditions is that [the situation of the individual relieved] on the whole shall not be made really or apparently so eligible as the situation of the independent labourer of the lowest class;' accordingly 'except as to medical attendance all relief whatever to able-bodied persons or to their families, otherwise than in well-regulated work-houses where they may be set to work, shall cease.' None of these recommendations embodied a new principle. The first sought to put an end to the autonomy of the parish by restoring the authority of the executive exercised down to the Restoration by the Privy Council. The second and third, the institution of workhouses covering a wider area than the parish together with the 'workhouse test,' had been anticipated in the act of 1723.

The Poor Law Amendment Act of 1834 gave effect to the proposals enunciated in the report. It created a central authority in the shape of a poor law commission, whose members were styled 'the three kings of Somerset House' since they were not placed under a minister responsible to Parliament. The commission was intended to be an independent and non-party organ of government, though the experiment of a public department uncontrolled by the legislature proved a failure.[1] The function assigned to it was to frame regulations for the six hundred unions which were now substituted for the fifteen thousand and more parishes hitherto the poor law units. The administration of

---

[1] In 1847 the department became the Poor Law Board presided over by a minister; in 1871 it was merged into a new ministry, the Local Government Board.

each union was vested in the hands of a board of guardians; and this replacement of appointed magistrates by a network of elected bodies, concerned with the relief of destitution, was regarded by contemporaries as a 'domestic revolution.' The phrase was not without justification: the novel method of national control operating through elected local boards set a precedent for other public services such as health and education.

The 'new poor law' represented an attempt, inspired by the best of motives, to raise the working class out of the degradation into which the old poor law had helped to thrust it. The 'Speenhamland' system of supplementing the scanty earnings of labourers by parochial allowances, while it was well-intentioned, served to pauperize the rural community. It was virtually a subsidy to employers of labour, who were relieved of the responsibility of paying adequate wages; it discouraged hard work since the less a man earned the more he received from the parish; it enabled the improvident to multiply their numbers and so caused further deterioration in their condition; it placed a heavy burden upon the shoulders of those who were themselves often barely solvent. None the less the reformed method of treating destitution was bitterly assailed. Its basic concept was that no able-bodied person was to receive any relief unless he or she entered the workhouse.[1] The rigid application of a hard and fast rule of this nature was clearly indefensible. All social principles must be governed within due limits by circumstances, if they are to avoid the infliction of undeserved suffering. The new system was first introduced into the country districts where it met with little opposition; but the attempt to administer it in the industrial north coincided with a trade depression, and then a storm burst which at one time threatened to bring the kingdom to the verge of civil war. Two men led the agitation against the 'Bastille,' as the workhouse was termed—Richard Oastler who won renown as the opponent of child labour in factories,

---

[1] Relief in the pauper's own home was still given to the impotent poor.

and Stephens a Nonconformist minister whose fiery eloquence roused his audiences to a fever of frenzy. Their incendiary appeals to violence exhorted the masses to resist by armed force. The style of Stephens's oratory is illustrated in the following passage: 'I have never acknowledged the authority of the new poor law and I never will. I will lay aside the black coat for the red, and with the Bible in one hand and a sword in the other—a sword of steel not of argument—I will fight to the death sooner than that law shall be brought into operation.'

To understand the depth of the passions provoked by the Poor Law Amendment Act, it must be remembered that in the eyes of the poor they had a legal claim to relief by right of inheritance when unable to work or to find employment —not relief doled out in a workhouse but efficient relief in their own homes. Their case rested on the argument that the mediaeval Church had been endowed with land in order to enable it to alleviate distress; therefore the dissolution of the monasteries placed upon their successors the duty of supporting the poor. Nevertheless it was not an abstract sense of injustice which inspired the opposition to the poor law. A labour leader Holyoake, who lived through the greater part of the nineteenth century, has pointed out (with perhaps some exaggeration) the contrast between the beginning and the end of the century as he knew it. 'Now the mass of the people do not expect to go to the workhouse and do not intend to go there. But through the first forty years of this century almost every workman and every labourer expected to go there sooner or later. Thus the hatred of the poor law was well-founded. Its dreary punishment would fall, it was believed, not upon the idle merely but upon the working people who by no thrift could save nor by any industry provide for the future.' The new poor law was denounced as a capitalist conspiracy to force workmen to accept whatever wages their masters offered them, because refusal would mean starvation or the workhouse. This view was not borne out since the level of wages was maintained: but those who had real grounds for apprehension were the hand-loom weavers condemned by the competition of machinery to earn a miserable pittance in spite of arduous toil. For these men the supplementary allowance from the parish was a matter of life and death, and any attempt to force them into the workhouse and separate them from wife and children was bound to excite the most violent resentment. It was, in short, a vicious circle. The low wages paid to many thousands of poverty-stricken workers made inevitable some system of outdoor relief, yet the latter helped to keep alive the evils which it sought to remove. It enabled employers to sweat their workpeople and to ignore the prime necessity of organizing their businesses on proper lines; while it exposed the independent workman to the competition of cheap and subsidized labour. However the vehement agitation against the new poor law attained its object. The manufacturing areas of Lancashire as well as Yorkshire were exempted from the operation of the 'workhouse test' during the years of depression, and then followed a remarkable outburst of prosperity in which the stormy issues of a troubled decade ceased to have their former importance and the social tension was relaxed.

Thus, contrary to the expectations cherished by the authors of the report of 1834, it proved impossible to ensure national uniformity in the relief of destitution. The central authority framed directions but the boards of guardians could not be coerced into obeying them because they enjoyed financial autonomy. One defiant board was sent several letters every week, 'which it threw under the table.' In the rural districts where the granting of allowances in aid of wages was held to lower the earnings of the independent farm labourer, its cessation had a beneficial effect on wages—especially since railway construction had now begun to open up fresh avenues to employment. In the manufacturing districts, on the other hand, the commission was constrained to acknowledge that it was 'not expedient absolutely to prohibit outdoor relief even to the able-bodied.' This signal admission only recognized, as we have seen, the facts of the situation. Accordingly, instead of the 'workhouse test' under which the able-bodied were refused relief except in the workhouse, there was adopted the 'labour test'—that is, outdoor relief was given provided the applicant performed a task such as stone-breaking.

In another direction the march of events diverged widely from the recommendations of the report. In place of a 'general mixed' workhouse in which all classes of indoor paupers were relieved under the same roof and the same officials, the report had contemplated a number of specialized institutions—completely separate buildings, each under its own officials, each housing a different class (the aged and impotent, children, able-bodied females, able-bodied males), and each treated in the mode appropriate to the character of its occupants. The central authority was content to establish in every union a single 'union workhouse' to serve as a receptacle not only for the able-bodied and their dependents but for the sick, the aged, deserted children and mental defectives. In the opening years of the twentieth century three-fifths of the workhouses were still of the 'general mixed' type, and served (it was rightly said) as a 'deterrent to the decent not to the work-shy.' 'The principle of separate and appropriate management,' advocated in the report, belatedly received full recognition in all its implications in our own day.

As the nineteenth century proceeded in its course, the growing reaction from *laissez-faire* bore fruit in a revulsion of feeling against the principles of 1834.[1] In part this was due to their very success in abolishing the allowance system in supplement of wages. In part it was owing to a consider-able decline in destitution as a result of the increased prosperity of the country—in the middle of the nineteenth century 5 per cent. of the population received relief as paupers, while at the end of the century the percentage had

[1] Namely, the principles of 'less eligibility' and the 'workhouse test.'

been halved.[1] In part it was caused by the recognition that a principal source of pauperism was irregular employment. Above all, public opinion was gradually converted to the view that something more than deterrence was needed to deal with those whom misfortune or misconduct made a burden on society. A vicious circle of poverty, crime and punishment, was broken when the conception of preventive and curative treatment became the basis of a new social philosophy out of which emerged public services of momentous significance. Expression was given to the change of sentiment in the majority and minority reports of a royal commission (1909). Both recommended the replacement of the boards of guardians by county councils and urban councils, the abolition of the union as the poor law unit, and the disappearance of the 'general mixed' workhouse. Here agreement ended. The majority report wished to preserve 'unity in the administration of relief,' though 'public assistance authorities' appointed by the county or municipality were to supersede the elected boards of guardians. The minority report advocated the break-up of the poor law —by placing children of school age under the education committee of the county or municipality; the sick, infirm and infants under the health committee; the mentally defective under the asylums committee; the aged under the pensions committee; together with a national scheme for the unemployed covering insurance, labour exchanges and timing of government orders. The act of 1929 abolished the boards of guardians. Their functions were transferred to county and urban councils which appointed public assistance committees, while the latter in turn set up local committees. The general procedure was to 'take out of the poor law' services affecting health and children, but leaving to the committees the aged and infirm, destitute workmen and vagrants.

The poor law report of 1834 had rejected out of hand the

[1] In England and Wales. On the eve of the first world war it had fallen to 2 per cent. On the eve of the second world war it had risen to 3 per cent.

proposal 'to promise subsistence to all, to make the government the general insurer against misfortune, idleness, improvidence and vice' as 'objectionable in principle.' The new trends of thought now discernible in social legislation—designed to ensure a minimum of well-being—mark a notable departure from the standpoint of a century ago. We no longer consider it a fair assumption that poverty is always the fault of the poor. It is recognized that poverty may be due to economic maladjustments—that the poor may be the victims of the imperfect mechanism of the industrial apparatus, or the victims whose wrecked careers strew the path of human advancement.

In concluding this account of the reaction against *laissez-faire*, two quotations may be contrasted on account of the instructive differences which they disclose in their conception of the province of the state. At the opening of the nineteenth century—when *laissez-faire* was enthroned as the fashionable philosophy of the day—a president of the United States, Thomas Jefferson, delivered an inaugural address in which he said: 'With all these blessings what more is necessary to make us a happy and a prosperous people? Still one thing more, fellow citizens, a wise and frugal government which shall restrain men from injuring one another, shall leave them otherwise free to regulate their own pursuits of industry and improvement, and shall not take from the mouth of labour the bread it has earned.' A British official handbook in current use reflects the spirit of the modern age. 'The first duty of government is to protect the country from external aggression. The next aim of national policy must be to secure the general prosperity and happiness of the citizens. To realize that aim two courses of action must be followed. The first is to foster the growth of the national power to produce and to earn with its accompanying opportunities for increased well-being, leisure and recreation. The second is to plan for the prevention of individual poverty resulting from those hazards of personal fortune over which individuals have little or no control. Neither of these courses of action can be effective alone. In a community whose earning power was seriously impaired by its failure to use its people and resources effectively—that is to say, by unemployment or inefficiency—it would be impossible to avoid widespread individual poverty whatever special measures were adopted. But it is also true that a nation with a high power of production would not have solved its problem if it included any appreciable section of people who were in want, whether through loss of individual earning power due to ill-health, unemployment or old age, or through inability to provide properly for their children. Only when this problem is also solved has a community achieved genuine social security.'

Chapter Eleven

THE FREE TRADE MOVEMENT

There is a marked contrast between England's industrial policy and commercial policy in the nineteenth century. The trend of the former was from *laissez-faire* to protection, when the state began to re-establish its control over the economic life of the country; the trend of the latter was from protection to *laissez-faire*, when by gradual stages free trade superseded mercantilism.

The free trade movement occupies one of the most significant chapters in English history, and by its repercussions throughout the world it assumes a leading place among the great formative ideas that have shaped human progress. Its basic principle was the antithesis of the mercantile system: it postulated 'plenty' instead of 'power.' In place of the doctrine of economic nationalism in which each country pursued the mirage of self-sufficiency, it substituted the doctrine of the international division of labour in which each country devoted itself to the products for which it was best suited and exchanged its surplus for the products of other nations. At the opening of the nineteenth century two notable branches of the mercantile system had already been discarded—the regulation of the currency by an embargo on the export of precious metals, and the conception of a 'well-ordered' trade on the basis of chartered companies. Four other branches still survived, and their gradual elimination constitutes the history of the free trade movement. These were the protection of native manufactures by tariffs or even absolute prohibitions; the protection of shipping by navigation laws; the protection of agriculture by corn laws; and the old colonial system which treated the colonies as subservient to the mother country and controlled their trade.

The best example of the protection of native manufactures is afforded by the woollen industry which down to the nineteenth century was our greatest industry. In order that clothiers might have an abundant supply of raw material at low prices, the export of wool was forbidden: in order that they might have the undisputed possession of the home market, a prohibitive duty was laid on foreign cloth while certain foreign textiles were excluded. In the same way less important industries were safeguarded by an elaborate and complicated system of tariffs. Agriculture was shielded by virtually prohibitive duties on the importation of wheat and other grains; foreign livestock (cattle, sheep, swine) and all kinds of meat were not admitted. The campaign for emancipating commerce from its shackles made an auspicious start at the close of the eighteenth century, when Pitt concluded a commercial treaty with France in 1786. The ground had been prepared long before Adam Smith by a group of seventeenth-century economists who found in the theory of the 'general balance' of trade (that total exports should exceed total imports) an effective weapon with which to counter the views of those who condemned the trade with any particular country from which imports exceeded exports. Moreover they had anticipated the main arguments in favour of free trade by demonstrating that it was the means to stimulate industrial efficiency and ingenuity, foster a mercantile marine, lower the cost of living, reduce the price of materials, promote the international division of labour, and establish friendship between states. Already at an early date they taught the doctrines that 'the whole world as to trade is but as one nation;' that 'trade is in its nature free, finds its own channel, and best directeth its own course;' that 'England never throve by trade but while she was an universal merchant;' that those who seek to promote the consumption of their own native products 'by an universal discouragement of foreign goods will find themselves in process of time to have little or no trade, and that their own commodities shall remain a drug upon their hands.'

The outbreak of war with revolutionary France wrecked the course of the free trade movement for a generation. It was revived by a petition presented to Parliament in 1820 which was drafted by Tooke the economist and signed by merchants of the city of London. This famous manifesto enunciated the principles of free trade and demanded the abolition of all restrictions on imports which were imposed in the interests of industry, unless they were required for revenue purposes. It affirmed: 'That freedom from restraint is calculated to give the utmost extension to foreign trade and the best direction to the capital and industry of the country. That as no importation could be continued for any length of time without a corresponding exportation direct or indirect there would be an encouragement, for the purpose of that exportation, of some other production to which our situation might be better suited. That a policy founded on these principles would render the commerce of the world an interchange of mutual advantages, and diffuse an increase of wealth and enjoyments among the inhabitants of each state.' The manifesto made a deep impression, and the first step was taken (1824) to break down artificial barriers by allowing the export of native wool. It was a remarkable change in English commercial policy, since for two centuries it had been an article of faith to prevent the transhipment of wool as the raw material on which the chief industry of the kingdom depended. In the following year the duty on foreign cloth was reduced from 50 to 15 per cent. By the withdrawal of protection from the woollen industry, which had always been considered the staple manufacture of the realm, the state threw to the winds the most tenacious doctrine of its former economic creed.

After so striking a departure from mercantilism, the way lay open for a general application of free trade doctrines. The progress of the movement is to be traced in the reform of the fiscal system associated with the names of Huskisson, Peel and Gladstone. Huskisson asserted that 'whenever you give a free scope to industry, to the stirring intelligence and active spirit of adventure, you are in fact opening new roads to enterprise.' Yet he himself was not a free trader in the full sense of the term; he favoured a limited degree of protection. The drift of his policy was to do away with absolute prohibitions and to reduce duties, though the latter were kept high enough to prevent foreign goods from seriously competing with home manufactures; in the case of no commodity was the protective duty higher than 30 per cent. Subsequently a marked stimulus was imparted to the agitation in favour of free trade by the investigations of a parliamentary committee on import duties. Its report (1840) disclosed that 1,150 different articles were liable to duty: of these 9 yielded £18½ millions out of a total of £22 millions. The committee therefore proposed that duties should only be levied on a small number of articles in order to 'facilitate the transactions of commerce, benefit the revenue, diminish the cost of collection, and remove the multitudinous sources of complaint and vexation.' Thus the revision of the tariffs was prompted less by the doctrinaire advocacy of free trade than by the conviction that the complexity of the fiscal system retarded the progress of industry.

The responsibility for giving effect to the committee's recommendations fell upon Peel, who declared that if imports cause unemployment then our exports must do the same elsewhere. The simplification of the tariffs in the budget of 1842 proceeded on the following lines—the removal of prohibitions; the reduction of duties on raw materials to 5 per cent. at the most; the reduction of duties on partially manufactured articles to 12 per cent. at the most; and the reduction of duties on manufactured articles to 20 per cent. at the most. The budget of 1845 went beyond the reduction of duties by sweeping them away on several hundred imports as well as on all exports. In 1846 the duty on manufactured articles was lowered to 10 per cent. and at the same time the cotton, woollen and linen industries ceased to be protected. It was this budget, also, which doomed the corn laws. Gladstone continued Peel's policy of abolishing or reducing duties. In 1860 England concluded a commercial treaty with France; as a result duties on manufactured articles were abolished with a few exceptions.[1] Henceforth the fiscal system was virtually reconstructed on the basis of raising revenue. The disappearance of protective tariffs meant that the historic commercial policy of utilizing the mechanism of the customs to promote industry was now discredited.

In the parliamentary debates on free trade it is apparent that abstract economic doctrines played a negligible part. Practical considerations were responsible for the rapid progress of a movement which in the space of two or three decades completely reversed the traditional principles of commerce that had persisted for several centuries. One was the discovery that the national revenue actually benefited by a scale of moderate duties. A chancellor of the Exchequer acclaimed 'the seeming paradox that a larger revenue might be obtained from smaller duties;' but a hundred and fifty years before Swift had enunciated the maxim that in the arithmetic of the customs two and two make not four but often make only one. Another weighty factor was that English manufacturers in general (the silk industry was a conspicuous exception) no longer feared foreign competition at home or abroad. 'In ingenuity, in skill, in energy,' exclaimed Peel, 'we are inferior to none. Our national character, the free institutions under which we live, the liberty of thought and action, an unshackled press, combine with our natural and physical advantages to place us at the head of those nations which profit by the free interchange of their products. And is this the country to shrink from competition?' The beneficial consequences which flowed from the adoption of an enlightened policy were reflected in the expansion of our exports in the face of hostile tariffs. Numerous commercial treaties in the sixties contained the

[1] These were flour, sugar, gold and silver plate, alcoholic drinks, manufactured tobacco, cards and dice. Flour, sugar and plate were subsequently exempted.

'most-favoured nation' clause, by which English goods were admitted by other states on terms at least as favourable as those conceded to similar imported commodities. Moreover experience was to demonstrate that free trade in widening the scope of our oversea markets afforded a larger measure of security: if one temporarily failed, another supplied its place—for instance, when the American Civil War interrupted trade with England, the latter was able to find compensation elsewhere. Lastly the protection furnished by high tariffs was delusive since they encouraged evasion by smuggling, which was practised on an extensive scale in the seventeenth, eighteenth and early nineteenth centuries.

The corollary of a free commerce was a free carrying trade. The first serious breach in the navigation system— which for many centuries had sheltered the mercantile marine from its competitors—was made by the secession of the American colonies, because it was no longer possible to insist that American produce must be carried in English (including colonial) vessels. Accordingly in 1815 ships belonging to England and the United States were accorded similar treatment by the abolition of discriminatory duties upon their cargoes. Then in 1822 the colonies were allowed to trade with foreign regions direct instead of sending their goods first to England, though their trade with the motherland was still confined to English (including colonial) ships. Three years later the government was empowered to conclude commercial treaties which extended the principle of reciprocity to other nations besides the United States, and permitted them to export their commodities to England without having to pay the additional duties levied on goods brought in alien ships. The alternative, declared Huskisson, lay between 'reciprocity of intercourse or retaliation of exclusion.' The various modifications introduced into the working of the system paved the way for the final repeal of the navigation code in 1849. Peel, addressing the House of Commons, rested his case on the unfavourable attitude of the colonies, on the demands of European countries, on the 'complicated claims' arising out of reciprocity treaties, and on 'the mutilated and shattered state of the navigation laws as they now exist.' Accordingly British ports were thrown open freely to foreign ships; and in 1854 the coasting trade was thrown open. This change in mercantile policy meant primarily that England was exposed to American competition; but owing to the introduction of iron ship-building, she was enabled to preserve her maritime supremacy.

The mercantile system had contemplated not only a self-supporting country but also a self-supporting empire. It was natural therefore that the reaction against mercantilism should extend to the policy of maintaining the colonies in a state of economic dependency upon the motherland. The reaction was assisted by a revulsion of public sentiment after the loss of the American colonies. The celebrated remark of a French statesman, Turgot, now appeared justified: 'Colonies cling only until they ripen.' It was thought that Canada, when she felt strong enough to stand alone, would follow the example of the United States and cut herself adrift from England: meanwhile the latter had the cost of protecting and administering possessions which would remain faithful only so long as it seemed to their advantage. Even in the seventeenth century there was an under-current of feeling against the foundation of colonies on the ground that, at a time when England was under-populated, she could not afford the drain of men and capital. And it could be argued that, for the sake of the dependencies themselves, it might be best to let them go their own way. The United States made rapid strides after she obtained her indepen-dence, while the territories which still adhered to us made but slow progress. In the forties of the nineteenth century a new interest in colonization was awakened as a result of the efforts of Wakefield, whose writings attracted public attention. He urged that the Empire could be utilized to absorb the surplus population, and his views were given prominence in the pages of John Stuart Mill. Subsequently Seeley published his lectures on *The Expansion of England*, in which he contended that our oversea possessions were to be regarded not as distinct from but as an integral part of the parent state; and he stressed the defects of the old colonial system in order to show that the American Revolution was the result of those defects instead of a natural law that colonies must break away. Thus the ground was prepared for a quickening of public sentiment at home, which in the early years of the twentieth century deepened into enthusiasm. Nothing contributed more to strengthen the Empire than the development of ocean navigation, which drew the remotest regions closer to the motherland. Then the dominions became valuable both as producers of food and raw materials and as a market for manufactured goods. In return for the protection which they received, they instituted preferential tariffs; while England, although keeping steadfast to her policy of free trade and refusing to tax imported food, furnished capital at favourable rates. The two world wars powerfully reinforced the ties of sentiment and the consciousness of a common heritage.

The most memorable as well as the most dramatic episode in the history of free trade was the repeal of the corn laws. In this question—'the keystone of protection' so it was termed—the champions and the assailants of the old order joined issue. The removal of protective tariffs aroused little controversy, not because English manufacturers had been converted by the economists to an enlightened philosophy of commerce, but because they were confident of their ability to hold their own in the world's markets. The corn laws stood in a different category. They were the bulwark of the landlord interest, whose economic and political ascendancy was now being successfully challenged by the industrial and commercial interests. Moreover they expressed a deep-rooted instinct that England should raise the food needed to feed her people and not depend upon external sources for the necessaries of life. Over the battle of the corn laws was fought out the momentous decision whether the country should remain faithful to the traditional system of a self-sufficing economy or discard economic nationalism and fling wide the doors to the imports of the whole globe.

The early history of the corn laws has been sketched elsewhere. They entered upon a new phase after the Napoleonic wars when English agriculture found itself in a critical situation. The high price of corn during the war had encouraged farmers to cultivate every scrap of soil available, and to borrow money from the banks in order to pay extravagant sums for land; rents had risen; landlords had sunk capital in improvements. With the coming of peace prices fell sharply. In 1812 the price of wheat was 126s. 6d. the quarter; in 1815 it was almost halved. As a consequence farmers became insolvent, tenants threw up their holdings, the number of small owners diminished, land went out of cultivation, bankers were forced to call in their loans. It was in these adverse circumstances, when the system of agriculture seemed on the verge of collapse, that the corn law of 1815 was passed. This famous measure, the solitary relic of a corn policy which had persisted for several centuries, prohibited the importation of foreign corn so long as the price of wheat at home did not rise above 80s. It was definitely a protective measure, designed to keep the price of corn at a level considerably above the world price, whereas earlier corn laws were probably not a serious factor in raising prices. In 1828 the principle of a sliding scale of duties was instituted under which the duty varied according to the price of grain; it was 20s. 8d. when the home price of wheat was 66s. a quarter and 1s. when it was 73s. or upwards.[1] The enactment of 1828 was the corn law against which the Anti-Corn Law League directed its fulminations. It should be noticed that preferen-

[1] When wheat was under 66s. the duty rose by one shilling for every shilling the price fell. There were similar sliding scales for other grains. The sliding scale was revised in 1842. Under 51s. a quarter the duty was 20s. and as the price rose the duty fell.

tial treatment was accorded to the colonies in the various corn laws.

The repeal of the corn laws was the achievement of the Anti-Corn Law League under the leadership of Richard Cobden and John Bright. 'It is necessary for the concentration of a people's mind that an individual should become the incarnation of a principle.' Thus wrote Cobden; and so successfully did he embody the principle of free trade that in Peel's view 'the name which ought to be chiefly associated with the [repeal] is the name of Richard Cobden.' In 1838 the prime minister, Lord Melbourne, had informed all petitioners for the repeal of the corn laws that 'they must look for no decided action on the part of the government until they had made it quite clear that the majority of the nation were strongly in favour of a new policy.' The price of wheat had then risen to 77s. a quarter, and Manchester accepted the challenge. The Anti-Corn Law League was formed (1839) in place of a previous organization which had made little headway. The prospects of success at the moment did not appear rosy. The landlords displayed the utmost determination to resist the attack upon the last stronghold in which they were now entrenched. The founders of the League were told: 'You may as well try to over-turn the monarchy;' while Lord Melbourne declared that the proposal to repeal the corn laws was the most insane proposition which ever entered a human head. The House of Commons still representing in the main the landed interest refused to take into consideration petitions against the corn laws. However the reform of Parliament had opened the way for movements to organize public opinion and by constitutional agitation bring pressure to bear upon the legislature. Inspired by the example of the Catholic Association which had achieved Catholic Emancipation a decade earlier, the League actively bestirred itself. Subscriptions poured in and large sums of money were collected to conduct a propaganda campaign. 'Tons' of tracts were distributed: hundreds of public meetings were held in town and country. The League sent missionaries throughout the length and breadth of the kingdom. These missionaries encountered much local opposition from vested interests: sometimes they were denied the use of a hall on the ground that they would make the labourers discontented, and sometimes they were roughly handled. Cobden believed that a moral and even a religious spirit must be infused into the question of the corn laws; and that, agitated in the same manner as slavery had been, 'it will be irresistible.' It was in this atmosphere that the case for and against the corn laws was debated.

Take first the arguments for their maintenance. The landowners found themselves in a difficult position after the conclusion of peace in 1815. During the war they had sunk capital in the soil, and some had mortgaged their property to raise money for improvements. They were now menaced with ruin if war prices were permitted to fall to a peace level: as Disraeli observed, they were tortured by 'visions of deserted villages and reduced rentals.' The claim was also made that their rank in society involved them in obligations and responsibilities which subjected their estates to special burdens. In the eighteenth century Pitt had pronounced a warm panegyric on the landowners 'who form the lime which binds and knits society together, on whom in a great measure the administration of justice and the internal police of the country depend, from whom the poor receive employment, from whom agriculture derives its improvement and support, and to whom of course commerce itself is indebted for the foundation on which it rests.' In the next place the corn laws were an insurance against undue dependence upon foreign countries, and stress was laid on the danger of excessive reliance upon sources of food supply which in time of war could be cut off. Finally it had always been the traditional policy of England to foster a rural population. In brief, if legal protection—which had existed for several centuries—were discarded, then free trade in grain would be detrimental to the landed interest by causing a fall in rents; it would hurt farm labourers by reducing opportunities for employment; it would be fatal to the nation as a whole since land would go out of cultivation and as a consequence the area devoted to arable production would proportionately shrink.

On the other side a formidable array of arguments was marshalled against the retention of the corn laws. The latter belonged to an age in which the wealth of England lay in her fields and the mass of the inhabitants followed the plough: an age when the encouragement of tillage even if at the expense of the urban population might be considered defensible. But in the nineteenth century the centre of economic gravity had shifted. The wealth of England now lay in her factories and workshops, and the artisan and the trader emerged into the full light of day as the typical figures of English life. In the altered circumstances the corn laws appeared to be purely a class measure which was beneficial to a single section of the community—the landowners—yet was harmful to the rest. The crux of the controversy was the claim that the protection of agriculture should be judged by its reaction upon industry and commerce. The effects on industry were injurious in the extreme. The poverty of the people was attributed to a bread tax 'levied for the benefit of the richest portion of the community.' Cobden pictured the intense privations that have left an indelible stamp on the 'hungry forties.'[1] 'He knew of a place where a hundred wedding rings had been pawned in a single week to provide bread, and of another place where men and women subsisted on boiled nettles.' The age of the 'common man' was foreshadowed in Peel's pronouncement that 'the real question at issue is the improvement of the social and moral condition of the masses of the population; to this great question the mere interests of landlords and tenants were subordinate.' Bread was the main article of consumption for the vast proportion of the realm which earned a subsistence by

---

[1] In 1840 the average price of British wheat per quarter was 66s. 4d. (in August it touched 72s. 6d.); in 1841—64s. 4d.; 1842—57s. 3d.; 1846—54s. 8d.; 1847—69s. 9d. (in June it touched 92s. 10d.).

manual labour—often constituting more than one-half of its expenditure. Accordingly the first step towards improving the standard of life of the working class was the removal of the tax on bread, in order to leave artisans and farm labourers with a larger margin for meat, dairy produce, fruit and manufactured goods.

The mischief done by the corn laws was not confined to the home market for industrial products; the oversea market was also severely curtailed. It was contended that other nations were unable to buy English commodities except in return for their corn and timber. We were compelling them to develop their own manufactures because they could not afford to buy ours. Moreover foreign competitors were declared to enjoy an advantage since the cost of living was lower abroad. The Manchester remedy for unemployment was 'to invite all the world to become our customers by opening our ports to their products in exchange.' The free entry of corn into England would stimulate tillage in grain-bearing countries, keep their labourers on the land, and check the growth of their industry. In exchange we should export more goods and so employ more labour, which would serve to raise wages.[1] Thus in the eyes of their critics the corn laws were productive of a three-fold evil. They contracted the domestic demand for native wares owing to the poverty of the people; they checked the expansion of the foreign demand owing to our refusal to buy food abroad; and—a vital consideration for an island power with scattered dominions—they had an adverse influence upon the mercantile marine whose existence was bound up with the fortunes of the carrying trade.

The opponents of the corn laws were at pains to show that they were not 'advantageous to agriculture.' They did no good either to the farmer or the labourer. The farmer did

---

[1] This contention has been questioned on the ground that the growth of English exports before the repeal was greater than immediately afterwards. But after the earlier rapid rise further progress would naturally slacken at first. Also foreign states could not immediately readjust their economic system to the new orientation in English commercial policy.

not benefit by high prices which meant high rents—'the corn law is a rent law.' Nor was there any assurance that prices would remain high, for legislation could not prevent a fall where it could not control the size of the harvest. When the harvest was abundant prices slumped: they were 96s. 11d. in 1817, 44s. 7d. in 1822, 68s. 6d. in 1825, 39s. 4d. in 1835, 70s. 8d. in 1839, and 50s. 1d. in 1843. Protection thus failed signally to secure steady prices, and the farmers considered stability their primary interest. Wide fluctuations in prices rendered farming a highly speculative business. A deficient harvest resulted in famine prices and so induced the farmer to cultivate inferior soil; the next year a good harvest might bring prices down and ruin him. Furthermore the corn-grower, though he might profit by the duty on grain, had to pay for the protection of any feeding stuffs bought for his cattle. In addition other branches of agriculture were discouraged by the high price of bread, which curtailed the public demand for meat and dairy produce. Above all the protective system was condemned on the ground that it led to bad farming because it promoted inefficiency. The salvation of agriculture, it was insisted, lay in improving the standard of farming by working with adequate capital. 'How is it,' asked Cobden, 'that in a country overflowing with capital, where every other pursuit is abounding with money, when money is going to France for railroads and to Pennsylvania for bonds, when it is connecting the Atlantic with the Pacific by canals, and diving to the bottom of Mexican mines for investment, it yet finds no employment in the most attractive of all spots, the soil of this country itself?' Insufficiency of capital was the root cause of the farmer's distressed condition; repeal the corn laws and landowners would be forced to develop the resources of the soil in order to increase its yield. The more all countries freely exchanged their commodities with one another the richer they became, and the more the consumer could afford to buy bread as well as other food. Under the stimulus of a growing demand the output of agriculture in England would then be increased by compelling the application of fresh doses of capital and labour to the land. Hence the conclusion was drawn that the only way for farming to become permanently and naturally prosperous was not by artificial expedients, such as protective tariffs, but by a larger circle of international exchange.

The wretched plight of the English farm labourers was adduced in evidence that the corn laws brought no benefit to this impoverished section of the rural community. Their low wages did not fluctuate according to the price of wheat; and as they spent a larger proportion of their earnings on bread than did any other class, they suffered most from a precipitous rise. 'I be protected,' a labourer is quoted as saying, 'and I be starving.' It was estimated that less than thirty shillings a year on manufactures (except shoes) were expended for a whole family. 'We have exported more goods to Brazil in one year than have been consumed in a year by the agricultural peasantry and their families.' Their poverty was shown also in their dwellings, of which some were stigmatized as 'worse than the wigwams of the American Indians.'

While the advocates of repeal relied upon the strength of their destructive criticisms, the governing factor in the final analysis was the growth of population. The corn laws could not be debated merely from the angle of how far English agriculturists were able to feed the existing population, but whether they could cope with the needs of a rapidly expanding population at reasonable prices. It was imperative to enlarge the area of supply; and though the production of home-grown wheat had been increased by the enclosure of the waste, it was necessary to draw upon external sources in order to obtain abundance of food at the 'natural' world price. It was not less vital to provide employment for the new recruits to industry, and this meant winning access to foreign markets by our willingness to accept their agricultural produce.

The struggle between the champions of the corn laws and

their assailants developed into a class struggle between the landed and the industrial interests. The landowners displayed a sympathetic regard for the condition of the operatives in the factories. The manufacturers were distressed at the condition of the labourers in the fields. Cobden confessed that 'the cotton lords are not more popular than the landlords,' and the abuses of the factory system discredited the cause of the free traders. One section of the working class, in whose eyes the real enemy was not the corn laws but capitalism, was hostile towards the Anti-Corn Law League which was mainly composed of capitalist employers. The chartists resented the free trade agitation inasmuch as it distracted public attention from their own campaign for an extension of the suffrage. Again their belief in the iron law of wages—the theory that the labourer received only a subsistence wage, of which the amount was determined by the price of the necessaries of life—led many chartists to infer that it was a matter of indifference to the working class whether the price of bread was high or low. Placards were posted at Manchester with the following notice: 'Why do these liberal manufacturers bawl so lustily for the repeal of the corn laws?—because with the reduced price of corn they will be enabled to reduce the wages of working men so that they may compete with foreigners who live upon potatoes.' Cobden sought to meet the damaging accusation that factory owners might cry 'cheap bread' but they meant 'low wages.' He contended that the repeal of the corn laws in extending our foreign trade would create a demand for labour and so raise wages. He exposed the fallacy that low wages and cheap labour are synonymous, and claimed that the highly-paid labour of England was the cheapest in the world.

For a time Peel was able to resist the pressure of the League owing to a succession of good harvests, but in 1845 and the following year the potato crop in Ireland was a disastrous failure, and the 'potato plague' prevailed also in England. 'It was the rain,' said Morley, 'that rained away the corn laws.' His famous dictum meant only that the crisis furnished the immediate occasion. In the eighteenth century the government had been accustomed in time of famine to throw open the ports temporarily. Peel recognized that the state of public opinion made such a solution impracticable, for it would have been impossible to reimpose the corn laws after a term of suspension. It was the work of the League in preparing the country for a more radical treatment that turned a freak of the weather into a *deus ex machina*. The act of 1846 provided for the abolition of the corn laws in 1849. For three years a new sliding scale of duties was imposed under which foreign wheat paid 4s. when the price per quarter rose to 53s. and upwards. Then in 1849 a nominal duty of one shilling per quarter was levied for registration purposes on imported wheat and other grains: in 1869 even this duty was abolished. In his resignation speech Peel uttered these memorable words: 'It may be that I shall leave a name sometimes remembered with expressions of good will in the abodes of those whose lot it is to labour, and to earn their daily bread by the sweat of their brow, when they shall recruit their exhausted strength with abundant and untaxed food the sweeter because it is no longer leavened by a sense of injustice.'

In the short space of seven years the determined efforts of the League had been crowned with victory in the face of difficulties that seemed insuperable; and it had shattered a structure which was considered as safe as the monarchy. What was the reason for its success? Peel himself contended that his proposals for the repeal of the corn laws were a logical development of those principles which had governed his revision of the tariff in 1842. 'You could not long continue,' he said, 'to apply different principles in respect to agriculture from those you had applied to other articles of commerce.' His conversion was no doubt sincere, yet it was probably stimulated by one very important circumstance. The League was all the more potent since it represented the force of public opinion outside a House of Commons which was unrepresentative of the nation. The total number of the electorate was about three-fourths of a million or one-seventh of the male population. Manchester, which had double the value of the property of Buckinghamshire, returned only two members while Buckinghamshire had no less than eleven. It is said that when Peel heard of the fall of King Louis Philippe, he exclaimed: 'This comes of trying to govern the country through a narrow representation in Parliament without regarding the wishes of those outside. It is what this party behind me wanted me to do in the matter of the corn laws, and I would not do it.' The awareness of Parliament that it was not broad-based, that it represented only vested interests, sapped its powers of resistance to the demands of the League.

When appraising the significance of the repeal of the corn laws a distinction must be drawn between the immediate and ultimate effects. In a broad view the repeal was the coping stone of the edifice of free trade: it marked the final stage in the struggle against mercantilism. Henceforth for nearly a hundred years England discarded the system of economic nationalism—on which the fabric of her agriculture, industry and commerce had been reared—in favour of international co-operation. The momentous change of policy eventually had profound repercussions upon the fortunes of the farming community, though its true inwardness was hidden from most contemporaries. They stressed the fact that the corn-grower, while deprived of artificial protection, continued to enjoy the 'natural' protection afforded by his proximity to the home market. Wheat might be more cheaply raised abroad, but the cost of freight and insurance must be added to its price. They believed that no land in England would be thrown out of cultivation—and for a generation their optimism was well-founded. Another consequence of the repeal was the transference of power from the landed interest to the industrial and commercial interests.

This aspect of the free trade movement as a class struggle[1] was frankly recognized: Cobden himself described the agitation as 'eminently a middle class agitation.' The middle class had successfully asserted its claim to a share in government, but the fight for the Reform Act was only the first phase of its conflict with the aristocracy. The second phase was the fight against the corn laws, whose retention would have meant that the middle class enjoyed the semblance not the substance of political power. The issue at stake involved the crucial question as to which section of the community should occupy the chief place in the national economy. Cobden avowed openly that 'the conflict was not merely a battle about a customs duty; it was a struggle for political influence and social equality between the landed aristocracy and the great industrialists.' The repeal of the corn laws was thus the complement of the Reform Act, because economic power was the logical fruit of political power. Deprived of their former ascendancy in the state the landowners were relegated to a subordinate position. Not indeed that they had lost their power to retaliate. They had their revenge on the manufacturers by passing the Ten Hours Act of 1847 on behalf of the operatives in factories: but the day of their supremacy had passed from them beyond recall. The stage was now set for the dawn of a fresh era in the annals of English society— 'a bagman's millenium.'[2]

In the eyes of its leading exponent the triumph of free trade transcended the narrow grounds of national self-interest or mere changes in political balance. It held out the golden promise that it would 'promote the enduring interests of humanity,' 'alter the relations of the world for the better,' and prove to be 'the only human means of effecting universal and permanent peace.' The conception of free trade as

---

[1] The conflict of interests between agriculturists as primary producers and industrialists as consumers of food and raw material had persisted for centuries. 'The landed and trading interests are eternally jarring,' exclaimed an old writer.

[2] The phrase was scornfully applied to Cobden's policy. The term *bagman* denoted originally a commercial traveller who carried samples in his bags.

the basis for a new international order, both economic and political, deepened immensely its significance. On the economic side the belief prevailed that an enlightened commercial system would be universally adopted, and that the circle of exchange would be progressively widened until the whole earth was comprehended in its embrace. On the political side there was the conviction that in free trade had been discovered a principle which would liberate mankind for ever from the scourge of wars, since the lust of conquest would die away when men could freely exchange the fruits of their labour without let or hindrance. The mists of hostility which now divided the nations would be dissipated in the sun-lit atmosphere created by the sense of an indivisible unity of interests springing from material well-being. For a brief moment, pregnant with destiny, this vision of the future seemed justified: but only for a brief moment. With the proverbial blindness of contemporaries Cobden, despite his insight, had failed to grasp the significance of the mighty force which was to dominate the next hundred years, turn the Continent of Europe into a shambles, and effectually counteract the influence of free trade doctrines. It was the force of nationality, which pursued in a distorted form served only to raise fresh barriers among the peoples of the earth.

The free traders had cherished the belief that all governments would eventually follow England's example and adhere to the principles of a progressive commercial system. If their aspiration had not been darkened all too soon by an intractable fate, recent history might have worn a different aspect: it is at least probable that the two world wars would have been avoided. But the aftermath of the Franco-Prussian conflict (1870) shattered the high hopes that mankind would beat its swords into ploughshares and concentrate its energies upon the peaceful interchange of its products. The trend towards free trade was soon reversed. When the Anglo-French commercial treaty of 1860 lapsed, it was not renewed: in Germany the chancellor Bismarck, in spite of his categorical assertion that a war of tariffs was worse than a war of cannon balls, embarked upon a protective policy: in the United States protectionist banners were inscribed with the slogan—'Protection against the pauper labour of Europe.' Disappointment at the backsliding of other countries caused a revulsion of feeling in England, where the swing of the pendulum was producing an inevitable reaction against the enthusiasm of the preceding generation. The new orientation was manifested in a revival of the plea for reciprocity. When in the free trade debates Disraeli had asked Peel whether he believed that he could fight hostile tariffs with free imports, his argument for the retention of tariffs—as a bargaining weapon to extort concessions—was rejected by those who refused to 'make the folly of others the limit of our own wisdom.' Subsequently Disraeli, now prime minister, was constrained to admit that 'practically speaking reciprocity whatever its merits is dead.' Yet in the eighties the notion was once more advanced that we should use the power of retaliation and fight tariffs with tariffs. The great depression of this decade created a pessimistic sentiment—which has periodically recurred during her long history—that England had lost her lead among the industrial nations. Lord Randolph Churchill declared that iron and silk were dead, coal languishing, cotton seriously sick, the woollen industry at its last gasp. Out of the conviction that English commercial supremacy was on the wane,[1] the protectionist movement was reborn in the foundation of a Fair Trade League which gave articulate expression to the demand for a tariff on foreign manufactures. Its propaganda was fortified by the campaign of Joseph Chamberlain who believed that imperial preference would strengthen the Empire by reinforcing natural ties of sentiment with the material bonds of economic interests. Even while the issue of free trade was still undetermined, the warning had been uttered that 'by the withdrawal of the substantial advan-

[1] Actually in 1913 our oversea trade attained its pinnacle.

tages which bind [the colonies] to your distant authority, you will yourselves take the first step towards severing the connexion.' Although the ground was being prepared for the coming changes, the reaction against free trade appeared to make little headway notwithstanding the fact that the first world war revealed the extent to which the country had become dependent upon the importation of vital commodities—synthetic dyes, drugs, optical instruments. It was not, as will be seen later, until England was in the throes of a world-wide depression that in a wave of panic she abruptly discarded an enlightened commercial system which had conferred inestimable benefits upon her people, and had served as a beacon of light to mankind.

Chapter Twelve

THE NATIONAL ECONOMY (1815–1914)

I. Industry

In the hundred years that lie between the end of the Napoleonic wars and the first world war England entered into her full economic heritage. She occupied a unique position. The inventions gave her the start of all her competitors and machinery poured into her lap a seemingly inexhaustible store of wealth. In the nineteenth century she stood pre-eminent as the leading commercial nation on the face of the globe, as the possessor of the largest mercantile marine, and as the universal banker, insurance and commission agent. Her population enjoyed a standard of living higher than that of any other European country. Her surplus wealth fertilized the barren places of the earth and promoted material progress in backward lands. She was the pioneer of free trade, her doors were thrown wide open to the imports of both hemispheres, and she imposed no customs duties on foreign commodities other than those levied for revenue purposes. After the abolition of protective tariffs in industry, the corn laws in agriculture and the navigation acts in shipping, she appeared to have renounced once and for all every vestige of the mercantilist doctrine of economic nationalism with its concept of self-sufficiency. By the teachings of her economists and the practice of her statesmen she upheld the enlightened doctrine of a world economy with its concept of specialization; and she exhibited a shining example of the blessings of international trade. The pursuit of a far-sighted economic policy based on the free exchange of goods, coupled with the energy of her people, the mildness of her political institutions and the absence of domestic turmoil, enabled English society to reap in ample measure the harvest which was the fruit of the ingenuity of its inventors, the organizing ability of its entrepreneurs and the skill of its artisans.

The remarkable expansion of the national economy in the nineteenth century will be shown in the present chapter by a survey of the salient features of the principal industries.[1]

If the cotton mills 'lately erected in the neighbourhood of Manchester' were 'suffered to destroy our woollen and stuff [worsted] manufactures, they will prove the most fatal discoveries ever made in Old England.' The panic-stricken warning was uttered in 1782 when the woollen manufacture had enjoyed for seven centuries its proud status as the premier industry of the realm and one of the pillars of the state. Within a few decades wool was dethroned from its eminence by its upstart rival, and the claim advanced nearly half a century later could no longer be contested that 'cotton by the magnitude of its manufacture must justly rank as the staple trade of this kingdom.' Norwich, once the metropolis of the worsted industry and the greatest manufacturing town in England, was now displaced by Manchester the metropolis of the cotton industry—of which Camden had written in the reign of Elizabeth that it excelled in 'the glory of its *woollen* cloths which they call Manchester cottons.'

The 'Industrial Revolution' had notable effects upon the location of the woollen and worsted manufactures. In marked contrast with cotton which has always been in the main associated with a single county (Lancashire), they were

[1] The distribution of the industrial population in some of the principa occupations in Great Britain is indicated (approximately) in the census returns as follows. In 1851 (population 21 millions) agriculture absorbed $1\frac{3}{4}$ m., building $\frac{1}{4}$ m., cotton $\frac{1}{4}$ m., woollen $\frac{1}{4}$ m., coal $\frac{1}{5}$ m., iron 80,000. In 1901 (population 37 m.) agriculture absorbed $1\frac{1}{2}$ m., manufacture of metals, machines, conveyances $1\frac{1}{4}$ m., coal $\frac{3}{4}$ m., cotton $\frac{1}{2}$ m., woollen $\frac{1}{4}$ m. In 1931 (population 45 m.) agriculture absorbed $1\frac{1}{5}$ m., metals, etc. $2\frac{1}{4}$ m., coal $1\frac{1}{5}$ m., cotton $\frac{1}{2}$ m., woollen $\frac{1}{4}$ m.

A comparison of the census returns of 1881 and 1931 shows the proportions engaged in the principal industries per 10,000 occupied. (The figures for 1931 are given in brackets.) Fishing 48 (30), agriculture 1,250 (567), coal 343 (554), manufacture of metals, machines and conveyances 728 (1,145), cotton 408 (281), woollen 198 (118).

For the numbers engaged in the principal industries and services on the eve of the second world war, see Chapter Fifteen.

in former ages carried on all over the country—whereas at the present day they are concentrated mainly in the West Riding of Yorkshire. In East Anglia, its most ancient and long its principal centre, the worsted industry is practically extinct. The west country—the seat of the broadcloth manufacture on which the fame of English textiles rested down to the nineteenth century—still makes the finest woollen cloth, but of it may be said: 'Its glory hath departed.' This migration is usually ascribed to Yorkshire's mineral assets. The explanation overlooks the fact that industrial expansion started in the north before the great inventions made iron and coal indispensable. The dormant energies of the backward northern regions were being quickened to new life in the eighteenth century by the resourcefulness and adaptability of a thrifty and hardy people. Contemporaries accounted for their rapid progress on the ground that the price of labour was lower and that wealth 'had not produced indolence.' The cheapness of Yorkshire cloth, combined with a very colourable imitation of its competitors' products, enabled the West Riding to gain command over markets at home and abroad. The early Yorkshire clothiers were therefore not without justification when they boasted—even before the days of machinery— that, 'in spite of fate,' the woollen manufactures would 'come into these northern counties.' The 'Industrial Revolution' assured them the final victory in the task which they had taken upon themselves to wrest from the east and west of England their industrial pre-eminence, largely owing to the fatal delay in the introduction of machinery in the old-established seats of the textiles. The reasons for delay were twofold—firstly the conservatism of the workers who claimed a vested interest in the processes and were able to prevent, or at any rate retard, the use of machines which destroyed this vested interest; and secondly the want of enterprise on the part of the manufacturers who lacked the energy displayed by their Yorkshire competitors. The latter were stimulated by the proximity of the Lancashire cotton industry to discard the traditional organization of the woollen industry, and develop it on the lines of the factory system. 'While the men of Leeds and Huddersfield,' wrote a hand-loom commissioner in 1839, 'were constantly in their mills and taking their meals at the same hours as their workpeople, the clothiers of Gloucestershire, some of them, were indulging in the habits and mixing with the "gentle blood" of the land.' The failure to keep pace with the needs of the time enabled Yorkshire—which showed greater power of adaptation to the changing industrial order—to reap the first-fruits of the inventions, to forge ahead, and to consolidate its position.

Another change, destined to have a profound influence on the economic development of a newly-discovered continent, took place in the sources of our wool-supply. For hundreds of years the raw material of England's greatest industry was mostly raised at home: but by the end of the seventeenth century the quality of native wool had deteriorated owing to the breeding of larger sheep in place of the 'ancient small breed.' 'So long as Englishmen are fond of fat mutton, they must not expect to grow fine wool.' As a result manufacturers became increasingly dependent upon foreign wool. At the beginning of the nineteenth century the quantity of imported wool was about 8 million lb.; at the middle 74 millions; at the end 560 millions.[1] Originally the main source was Spain, then Germany, and eventually Australia. When the first fleet sailed from England for New South Wales in 1787, it took on board at the Cape of Good Hope some sheep of the Spanish breed. The oak springs from an acorn. A handful of sheep, twenty-nine in 1788, increased to ten thousand within fifteen years. Australia sent us 100,000 lb. of wool in 1820 and nearly 40 millions (over half the total quantity imported) in 1850.[2] Meanwhile the manufacturers had been forced (1824) to abandon their age-old opposition

[1] In 1913—806 millions; in 1938—881 millions.
[2] In 1840 Australia sent 10 millions and Germany 22 m. In 1850 the corresponding figures were 39 m. and 9 m. In 1913 Australia and New Zealand sent 446 m. out of a total of 806 m.

to the export of home-grown wool in return for the removal of a heavy duty recently imposed on imported wool. The export of domestic wool grew at a much slower rate; but in 1850 it reached 12 million lb. and in the early twentieth century 38 millions[1]—approximating to one-third of the estimated total clip.

The manufacturers, who yielded up their monopoly of the native raw material with grave misgivings, had predicted that if foreign nations were able to procure English wool to mix with their own the export of woollen goods from this country would immediately cease. Never was a prophecy more signally falsified. Owing to the perfection of the machinery and the skill of the makers who had now to depend upon their own ingenuity in place of artificial protection, the oversea trade was not destroyed; notwithstanding the competition of the cotton industry, woollen exports in the course of the nineteenth century trebled in value. Inevitably there had been a decline in the proportion of woollen exports to total exports. In the middle of the seventeenth century the former accounted for nearly two-thirds, in the early eighteenth century for almost one-half, in the early nineteenth century for one-sixth, in the early twentieth century for one-thirteenth of total exports.[2] Moreover it must be remembered that (unlike the cotton industry) the domestic market is far more important than the foreign market: about two-thirds of the output were absorbed at home.

In spite of the growth of the woollen manufacture in the nineteenth century the numbers employed did not expand. The reason lies in the adoption of mechanical methods which made possible an immense increase in the volume of production without an increase in the volume of human labour. Indeed the numbers returned in the census of 1851 (one-quarter of a million) were approximately those recorded

[1] In 1938—30 million lb.
[2] In 1854 woollen exports amounted to £10½ millions (total exports £97 m.); in 1900 to £24 m. (total £291 m.); in 1913 to £38 m. (total £525 m.); in 1938 to £27 m. (total £471 m.).

half a century later.[1] The first example of the application of a motive force to the textile industries is afforded by the use of fulling mills for the purpose of thickening woollen cloth; they were forbidden in London as early as the thirteenth century. Gig mills which raised the nap on cloth in the finishing processes were prohibited by statute in the sixteenth century. Surprisingly enough they were employed in the west country long before opposition was overcome in Yorkshire where most kinds of machinery were introduced more easily than elsewhere. The cloth-finishers also objected to shearing-frames for cropping the nap, which were worked by power and effected a great economy of labour. Yet though the shearmen put up a stiff fight against machinery they failed, despite their strong organization and the Luddite riots, to prevent the displacement of manual operations by mechanical contrivances in the opening decades of the nineteenth century. At the other end of the industry, where the women and children could offer no resistance, the preliminary processes were being more rapidly revolutionized. This was especially the case in the spinning of worsted yarn: Arkwright's 'frame'[2] began to be used in the West Riding of Yorkshire in 1787, and within a quarter of a century hand-spinning was being generally superseded in the worsted manufacture.[3] In the woollen manufacture, on the other hand, yarns are spun on mules which came more slowly into general use.

The most important stage in the making of cloth is weaving, and here the power-loom only very gradually ousted the hand-loom. Technical reasons delayed the introduction of steam-looms, which established their predominance much earlier in the worsted than in the woollen branch. Yorkshire in 1835 contained under seven hundred

---

[1] At the middle of the nineteenth century about 40 per cent. of the operatives were outside the factories.

[2] At the present day worsted yarns are still spun on some modification of the frame.

[3] The general adoption of the combing machine in the worsted manufacture was deferred owing to its technical imperfections for another three decades.

power-looms in woollen weaving and more than four times as many in worsted weaving. Lancashire, however, had eleven hundred power-looms which could weave wool; the west country possessed only a handful. In the middle of the nineteenth century the number of power-looms in the United Kingdom had mounted to over fourteen thousand in the woollen industry and almost forty thousand in the worsted industry; in the closing decade of the century the numbers were respectively sixty-two thousand and sixty-seven thousand. Thus as late as the eighties there still remained numerous hand-loom weavers; and then, except for occasional survivals and revivals here and there, hand-loom weaving—the oldest of the handicrafts—succumbed irrevocably to the machine. In general we may say that the progress of machinery in the woollen and worsted industries was influenced less in the north by the storm of hostility which it sometimes evoked than by the degree of its technical efficiency. In the west country and East Anglia, on the other hand, popular resistance was a determining factor in the maintenance of the traditional methods. 'The opposition that we generally meet with in introducing machinery is so great that until the Yorkshire manufacturers have stolen the article away from us we are almost afraid to introduce it.'

The phenomenal rise of the cotton industry was the outstanding feature of the 'Industrial Revolution' that impressed itself most vividly upon the imagination of contemporaries. Indeed it was mainly responsible for the invention of the phrase, which however appropriate in the case of cotton was certainly misleading when it was subsequently applied to the whole industrial scene—since even after the nineteenth century had run a third of its course the factory population of England, the mill hands, was not much more than 5 per cent. of the working population.[1]

---

[1] I assume the working population to have been about one-third of the total population. (It is erroneous to compare the mill operatives with the *total* population.)

The cotton industry had already existed for two centuries, although not until the introduction of machinery did it eclipse in importance the staple manufacture which was now rapidly outstripped by its younger and more vigorous rival. Of its place in the national economy something will be said in the following paragraphs: its place in the international economy may be gauged from the fact that in the early decades of the present century it comprised two-thirds of the world's mule spindles, one-fourth of the looms, and half the value of the yarns and fabrics exported from the principal countries. Equally significant for the national economy and the international economy was its influence on English commercial policy, since the 'cotton lords' were mainly instrumental in forcing upon the landlords the repeal of the corn laws.

The growth of the cotton industry can best be measured by the imports of cotton, for it depended entirely upon external sources for its raw material. Here the statistics are astronomical, and they account for the wonder with which the English people viewed the spectacular elevation of an industrial Cinderella to a pinnacle of greatness. At the beginning of the eighteenth century the quantity of cotton was 2 million lb.; in the middle 3 millions; while in the last decade it soared to nearly 30 millions. At the beginning of the nineteenth century it reached 56 millions; in the middle it approached 700 millions; and on the eve of the first world war it exceeded 2,000 millions.[1] The chief source of supply in the eighteenth century was the British West Indies; they sent us 75 per cent. and the United States less than 1 per cent. By the twenties of the following century the United States contributed 75 per cent. of a much vaster amount, and the proportion remained generally constant.[2] Thus the United States became the principal purveyor of the raw material

[1] Imports doubled between 1850 and 1860. In 1938 the quantity was 1,200 million lb.

[2] The American Civil War caused a cotton famine in Lancashire.

for England's leading industry, just as half a century later she became the principal purveyor of England's bread. An important source is also Egypt: fine counts of yarn are spun mainly from Egyptian cotton, and coarse or medium counts mainly from American cotton.

The statistics of the consumption of cotton afford some idea of the effects flowing from the inventions:[1] but they are not a measure of the total value of the finished products. For this we must look at the export trade as a partial criterion, because the practice of ascertaining the output of an industry by means of a census of production started only in the present century. Even export values are not an accurate gauge of the volume of trade owing to changes in the level of prices. (The price of cotton goods fell considerably in the first half of the nineteenth century with the return to the gold standard and the cheapening of production through improved mechanical methods.) Yet two things stand out with crystal clearness. One is that the cotton industry more than any other English industry became an export industry since it depended upon markets abroad for the absorption of no less than three-fourths of its output. The excessive disproportion between the internal and the external market was an element of insecurity which was ignored in the nineteenth century but bore its fruits after the first world war. The other significant fact is that the exports of cotton yarns and piece goods constituted a substantial percentage of total exports— amounting to one-half of the value in the early nineteenth century and about one-quarter a hundred years later.[2] Like the woollen industry in the days of its primacy, the cotton industry thus made a unique contribution to England's oversea commerce. In 1912 an English economist declared that 'the export trade in manufactured cotton goods from this country is in money value the greatest

---

[1] The inventions did not affect the position of Lancashire as the main seat of the cotton industry. It contains four-fifths of the operatives.

[2] In 1854 cotton exports amounted to £31½ millions (total exports £97 m.); in 1900 to £70 m. (total £291 m.); in 1913 to £127 m. (total £525 m.). In 1938 they had declined to £49 m. (total £471 m.).

export trade in manufactured goods of any kind from any country in the world.' A decade later one of the vicissitudes of fortune, which are visited upon industries as well as upon men, had brought disaster to the cotton mills.[1]

The number of operatives engaged in the cotton manufacture, as in the parallel instance of the woollen manufacture, is not a criterion of its growth; for they were just as numerous in the middle of the nineteenth century (approximately half a million) as they were at the close.[2] Yet in the interval the increased efficiency of machinery doubled the output of yarn and cloth per operative. The absence of vested interests, in contrast with the woollen manufacture, facilitated the introduction of machinery into an undeveloped industry. Moreover the cotton mills resembled the gold fields of California and Australia in their attraction for adventurous spirits, who flocked from other occupations and from all parts of the country to exploit a new source of wealth; and these men showed determination as well as ruthlessness in the haste with which they discarded the traditional methods of production. Arkwright's patents were cancelled owing to obscurities in the specification; Hargreaves was unable to protect his patent from infringement; and Crompton disclosed the secret of his invention without taking out a patent. Thus the water-frame, the jenny and the mule soon became the common property of the manufacturing world. The hard thread spun on the water-frame made it possible to dispense with linen in weaving cotton cloth and to make cotton calicoes; hitherto pure cotton goods had not been manufactured on a large scale. The mule, which yielded a softer and superior yarn than the water-frame, enabled England to produce the finest cotton fabrics, and so the cotton industry was transferred from India to Lancashire. At the present day cotton is spun either on the mule operated by men, or on the ring-frame (a modification of the water-frame) operated generally

[1] See Chapter Fifteen.
[2] In 1851 they numbered 470,000 in Great Britain (372,000 in England and Wales).

by women. While ring spindles spin a greater weight of yarn, mule spindles (which are three times as numerous) spin a better quality.

Machine-spinning rapidly established itself in the cotton industry in the last quarter of the eighteenth century, though hand-spinning survived well into the next century—indeed hand-mules had not wholly disappeared in the eighties. The adoption of weaving machinery lagged considerably behind spinning machinery mainly owing to technical deficiencies. Yet in part also it was due to the stubborn resistance of the hand-loom weavers who clung to their instruments at the price of increasing deterioration in their standard of living, whereas the women and children engaged in spinning were impotent to resist and alternative employment was afforded them by the yarn factories. Cartwright's power-loom was introduced (1791) into the cotton industry by a Manchester firm a few years after its invention; the weavers threatened to destroy the mill and it was burnt down. The set-back deferred further hazardous experiments for a time but in the opening decade of the nineteenth century power-looms began to be erected—in 1806 Manchester had its first steam-weaving factory. In the thirties they began to multiply fast; Lancashire had over sixty thousand and neighbouring counties nearly half as many. The number of hand-loom weavers at the same period is a matter of conjecture; it may have been as high as two hundred thousand or more. Speaking generally, half the workers in the cotton industry were outside the factory in 1835; about one-third still remained outside in the middle of the nineteenth century; and the domestic weavers had not been completely absorbed at the turn of the century. An illuminating fact which shows that the traditional organization of industrial society only slowly yielded ground even in the classic hearth of the 'Industrial Revolution.'

'A pretty engine' was the designation applied by an eminent engineer, Smeaton, to Watt's steam engine. He declared

that neither the tools nor the workmen existed to manufacture so complex a machine with sufficient precision.
Boulton conveyed the comment to his partner who had
suffered painful experience of its truth in his protracted
experiments; and it required at the time (1776) exceptional
faith to believe that these handicaps would be successfully
overcome. The tools used in the construction of the engines
were rude—with the result that the machines were constantly
breaking down; and (as Boulton also complained) 'the want
of proper men to work our engines' brought discredit upon
the new contrivances. The introduction of the steam engine
and of power-driven machines was thus delayed by imperfect
workmanship; and the creation of an engineering industry,
which could cope with the requirements of a mechanical
age, was the necessary complement of the great inventions.
Without it machinery would have remained a pretty toy—
an intellectual curiosity like the visionary projects of Roger
Bacon and Michelangelo. It was the mechanical engineers
of the nineteenth century who made possible the practical
application of the ideas which had been conceived in the
eighteenth century.

In order to lay the foundations of an engineering industry,
the first essential was the provision of trained mechanics.
When in the middle of the eighteenth century Campbell
wrote an account of the various industrial occupations of
his day, he referred to engineers who were employed in
making engines 'for raising of water' to drain mines or
supply reservoirs; but he added that 'the business is at present
in few hands.' It is noteworthy that Brindley who inaugurated the era of canal navigation was a millwright, and that
Telford a road-maker was a stone mason; while textile
manufacturers were often forced to construct their own
machines, employing for the purpose all kinds of artisans.
The second essential was to devise machine tools. At the end
of the Napoleonic wars, according to a contemporary
William Fairbairn, 'the whole of the machinery was executed
by hand. There were neither planing, slotting nor shaping

333

machines; and with the exception of very imperfect lathes and a few drills the preparatory operations of construction were effected entirely by the hands of the workmen.' As a consequence the machines were unsatisfactory and their defects caused frequent stoppages of work. The indispensable preliminary therefore, if machines were not to be deficient in the adjustment of their parts, was the fashioning of automatic machine tools designed to ensure precision of measurement and fitting. With this important development—the making of machine tools to make machinery 'with a degree of accuracy which the unaided hand could never accomplish' —are associated the names of numerous pioneers. When William Fairbairn delivered his presidential address to the British Association in 1861 he was able to claim that 'everything is done by machine tools,' to whose exactitude 'our machinery of the present time owes its smoothness of motion and certainty of action.'

The way was now prepared for the rise of engineering firms which specialized in machinery and so relieved textile firms of an irksome responsibility. In the course of the nineteenth century the scope of engineering science was widely extended, and to-day embraces generally the manufacture of finished articles composed of metal—machinery, prime movers, mechanically-propelled vehicles, tools. An industry limited in the eighteenth century to engines for pumping water out of mines became the pivot of all production in fields, factories and workshops which used power-driven machines, of all forms of transport which did not depend on horses or wind, of all lighting and heating which required gas or electricity. Its position in the national economy is also indicated by the fact that between the two world wars nearly one and a quarter million persons were engaged in its various branches.[1]

The engineering industry was the youngest of the great industries which have dominated modern economic life. It

[1] The census of 1851 entered 48,000 'engine and machine makers' in Great Britain (42,000 in England and Wales).

334

was virtually the creation of the 'Industrial Revolution' since it was called into existence by the substitution of steam-power for water-power, animal-power and human-power. Moreover it utilized the products of the metal industries, especially iron and steel, so that its progress was governed by the advance made in metallurgy. It thus affords an admirable illustration of the extent to which the various branches of the national economy—iron, steel, coal, engineering and the whole range of manufacturing processes—served to react upon each other at every phase of their evolution. Accordingly we notice next the history of iron and steel.

The immense expansion of the iron industry—where the number of workers increased from eighty thousand in the middle of the nineteenth century to over half a million seventy years later[1]—was rendered possible by the use of mineral fuel in place of wood in all stages of production. The result was that England, equipped with an abundance of coal, ceased to be dependent for iron upon the countries which had an abundance of timber. On the contrary she sent large quantities of iron abroad in addition to providing the vast amount needed at home for machinery, railways and shipping. In pig iron the giant strides of the statistics recall those of cotton. It is estimated that in 1740 the output was 17,500 tons; the beginning of the nineteenth century registered a tenfold increase with the demand for munitions of war; in the middle of the century it rose to $2\frac{3}{4}$ millions; at the end it reached 8 millions; on the eve of the first world war it attained its maximum of $10\frac{1}{4}$ millions; and then after the war came (as with cotton) the turn of the tide.[2] England was now in a position to export both pig and bar iron to other nations far in excess of the quantity which she took from them: high grade Swedish iron, however,

---

[1] Great Britain. For the use of coal in the iron industry, see Chapter Seven.
[2] On the eve of the second world war the quantity was $6\frac{3}{4}$ million tons. (These statistics refer to the United Kingdom.)

still remained in demand for making crucible steel. Yet while imported iron formed only a negligible fraction of her total consumption, she became increasingly dependent upon imported ore which was twice as rich in metal as native ore. In the early seventies imported ore was only one-thirteenth of the amount raised at home: in 1913 it had risen to one-half and this meant that 50 per cent. of the home production of pig iron was obtained from foreign (mainly Spanish) ore—for the latter though smaller in quantity had the same metal content as the much larger domestic supply.[1]

An age of steel succeeded an age of iron; and the transition robbed England of the metallurgical pre-eminence which she had enjoyed for the first three-quarters of the nineteenth century. Steel had notable advantages over wrought iron, in which we had hitherto excelled—it was harder, it was stronger, it was easier to machine, and it was cheaper because it could be produced on a larger scale. Thus it came to displace wrought iron in the metal-working trades except for special purposes. In the seventies our production of steel was about half a million tons;[2] on the eve of the first world war it had multiplied fifteen-fold, but it was only one-tenth of the world production of steel which had risen from one million tons to no less than 75 millions. Our proportion of the world production of pig iron similarly declined from nearly one-half to about one-eighth. England was outdistanced by her competitors, the United States and Germany, for two main reasons. The Thomas-Gilchrist process[3] facilitated the use of phosphoric iron ores in America and in Lorraine. Moreover

[1] The quantity of iron ore produced in the United Kingdom in 1938 amounted to nearly 12 million tons. The metal content averaged 30 per cent.

[2] The production of steel in the United Kingdom was (in thousand tons)—110 (1868), 329 (1871), 1,778 (1881), 4,904 (1901), 6,462 (1911), 10,398 (1938).

The quantities of steel produced by the main processes in 1938 were as follows (in thousand tons)—

Converter (Bessemer)		Open Hearth		Electric
Acid	Basic	Acid	Basic	
164	431	1,665	7,731	223

Thus about three-fourths were produced by open hearth basic.

[3] See Chapter Seven.

England had been first in the field of metallurgical discoveries and she paid the penalty of the pioneer in being saddled with obsolete plant, while those who started later were enabled to install the most up-to-date methods. Not until the depression of the eighties did acute competition from abroad compel the primary producers to scrap machinery and embark upon the capital expenditure entailed by the extended size of the industrial unit. Nevertheless the exceptional position which the English makers of wrought iron had once occupied was denied to the English makers of steel.

The iron industry resembles the woollen industry before the nineteenth century in its dispersed and migratory character. Its centres have risen and fallen not haphazardly but in accordance with its requirements in fuel and material. At first it was established in the midst of forest regions, for instance Sussex, where it procured wood for making charcoal. Eventually the local timber supplies were exhausted, the iron works were starved out, and they moved to the midland counties. When mineral fuel replaced wood, and the blast furnace was worked by the steam engine instead of by water-power, the ironmasters were relieved of the necessity to cling to forests and streams, and they could erect their furnaces elsewhere. South Wales and Staffordshire grew important—in 1830 they accounted for four-fifths of the total production of pig iron. Those seats of the iron industry were located near the coal-fields because it was cheaper to carry ore to coal, which was greater in weight. Then the situation was reversed. Improvements in the blast furnace considerably lessened the consumption of coal; the Bessemer process demanded non-phosphoric ores which were found in Cumberland and Furness; and the quantity of imported ore rapidly increased. For these reasons the steel-makers in the third quarter of the nineteenth century moved to the north-east and the north-west coasts.[1] Thus changes in the geographical

[1] In 1913 the north-east coast accounted for three-eighths of the pig iron produced in Great Britain; South Wales and Staffordshire had sunk to about one-sixth.

distribution of iron and steel works corresponded to the advances made in metallurgy.

The manufacture of finished articles in the metal industries was localized in particular districts. Sheffield was the historic centre of the cutlery trade, famed for hundreds of years for its knives. In the first half of the nineteenth century its population trebled. The small masters, threatened with extinction by the rise of the new industrial system, managed to survive by hiring the use of power-driven machinery; and they 'amazingly multiplied' (as a contemporary remarked) though cutlery factories were now making their appearance. Even to-day machinery has not completely displaced handicraft operations. A pocket knife may be handled forty times in the various processes which it undergoes, a table knife eighteen times, a pair of scissors thirty-two times. One notable development with which Sheffield is associated is the manufacture of 'special' steels, that is, alloys of steel which contain other minerals (for example stainless steel). This has benefited the engineering industry by providing it with tools suitable for specific purposes such as high speed. Birmingham had been for several centuries engaged in fashioning small metal wares. The traditional skill of its artisans and the proximity of coal and iron, coupled with freedom from gild restrictions and immunity from the disabilities imposed on Nonconformists in corporate towns, combined to attract a growing population which in fifty years (1801–1851) more than trebled. It furnished an extensive variety of goods which embraced articles of brass, guns, jewellery, buttons and other staple products. Machinery came far later to the finishing branches in the light metal trades than it did to the material on which they worked. There were exceptions as in the case of pin-making, but in general much of the labour was manual. A French observer wrote that machinery was only an accessory of manufacture and that everything depended on the skill and intelligence of the operative. We have already seen how the wide adoption of power was delayed until the last quarter of the nineteenth century.[1] Indeed the nail industry—where fifty thousand nailers (men, women and children) are said to have been occupied in Staffordshire in the third decade of the century—was still producing hand-made nails under the domestic system in the closing decade.

Coal in the nineteenth century was 'king.' It enjoyed the primacy among English products once held by wool. Its uses already extensive in earlier ages were now greatly augmented. Apart from the domestic requirements of a rapidly increasing population, coal was needed for smelting iron ore with which to make machinery, for driving machinery by steam-power, and for railways and shipping to distribute the fruits of machinery in markets at home and abroad. The importance of coal can scarcely be over-estimated. It was responsible for some of the principal developments connected with the 'Industrial Revolution.' The original purpose of the steam engines was to drain the coal-mines: the original purpose of the railways was to link up the mines with the coast: the original purpose of the canals was to convey coal to an inland market. Coal became the basis of every industry and the life-blood of transport both by land and sea; it furnished a very valuable export; it enabled ships to carry outward cargoes and thereby reduced freight costs for return cargoes of food and raw materials; its waste products were being turned to various industrial projects.

The immense growth of coal-mining kept pace with the demands made upon it. The statistics of the upward trend are impressive even in an age pre-eminent for its statistical peaks. At the beginning of the eighteenth century the estimated annual output was about $2\frac{1}{2}$ million tons; in the middle it was nearly twice as much; and at the end it was four times as much. Official returns do not actually commence until the fifties of the following century when the output rose above 60 million tons; it soared to 225 millions in 1900

[1] See Chapter Seven.

and to 287 millions (its maximum) in 1913.[1] No anxiety was felt that the supply of coal might soon approach exhaustion. The apprehension expressed in the seventeenth and again in the nineteenth century had been allayed by the estimate that the coal reserves of the United Kingdom were ample for centuries to come. The quantity shipped abroad grew until in 1913 it was more than a quarter of the entire production, and it was responsible for an increasing proportion of the value of total exports.[2] The number of all persons engaged in coal-mining also expanded rapidly at the same time: it approached 200,000 in the census of 1851 and was five times as large in 1913.[3] The annual average output per person occupied in the industry was 260 tons in 1913 and 287 tons in 1938. Variations in coal output are determined by circumstances such as the age of the mine, the greater depth and difficulty of the seams, the reduction of hours, the increase of workers at the surface of the mine. Moreover marked differences in the efficiency of management and in the adoption of mechanical equipment were inevitable when there existed nearly 2,500 coal-mines belonging to approximately 1,400 separate undertakings.[4] Of these about one-half employed each a hundred or fewer persons and produced 2 per cent. of the output; one-quarter employed each more than a thousand persons and produced over 80 per cent. of the output. Mechanical methods in mining found their way into the pits by stages—first for winding, then for hauling the coal in conveyors from the hewer to the bottom of the shaft, but virtually not until the

[1] In the United Kingdom. (The coal output for England and Wales alone was 245 million tons.) On the eve of the second world war it was 227 m. in the United Kingdom (and 197 m. in England and Wales).

[2] In 1860 coal exports were 7¼ million tons (out of a total production of 80 m.), and they accounted for 2¼ per cent. of the value of total exports. In 1913 they were 77 m. (out of 287 m.)—10 per cent. of the value of total exports. In 1938 coal exports had declined both in quantity (36 m. out of 227 m.) and in their share of the value of total exports (8 per cent.).

[3] In 1851 the number in England and Wales was 185,000; in 1913—965,000 (and 1,105,000 in the United Kingdom); in 1938—701,000 (and 791,000 in the United Kingdom).

[4] In 1924.

present century for hewing.[1] The crux of the situation lies in the fact that a coal-mine is a wasting asset; the duration of its productivity is limited, and when it is worked out it is closed. This affects capital expenditure for equipment on mines approaching extinction.

An increasing measure of state regulation was applied to coal-mining in the course of the nineteenth century: it has culminated in the nationalization of the mines in our own day (1947). It was largely due to the policy of the miners' unions, which sought to achieve their purposes by legislative action—it is significant that the first two labour leaders to sit in Parliament were miners. The intervention of the state was also necessitated by the bitterness of the relations between the mine-owners and their employees. No other industry has equalled coal-mining in the intensity of labour unrest. It has been officially estimated that the aggregate duration of disputes 1907–25 (excluding the war years), reckoned in working days, was greater than in all other industries combined; and out of the coal strike of 1926, which lasted for seven months, developed a general strike.[2] The environment in which the colliery workers lived was not conducive to good feelings towards their employers. Housing conditions were often deplorable. The old mining village, according to one description, 'consists of cottages poorly constructed, frequently overcrowded, with inadequate sanitary arrangements.' Friction over wages was chronic. Under one system which was widely prevalent, wages fluctuated according to the selling price of coal, rising and falling on a sliding scale. Under another system, adopted after the first world war, wages and profits were assigned fixed proportions of the proceeds. State interference in the coal-mines began with the prohibition of women's work underground and the restrictions on child labour.[3] These were an extension of factory legislation to the special conditions of the mines, but other

[1] Coal-cutting machines accounted for 1½ per cent. of the total output in 1901, for 19 per cent. in 1924, for 42 per cent. in 1933.
[2] See Chapter Fourteen.   [3] See Chapter Ten.

measures went beyond the factory code—the legal right conferred on the miners to appoint their own checkweighers in order to ensure correct weighing of coal, the curtailment of the working day for adult males, and the institution of a minimum wage in a highly organized industry.[1] The severe depression in coal-mining between the two world wars led the government to undertake a notable departure from *laissez-faire* traditions when it set up machinery for restricting output, regulating prices, promoting amalgamations,[2] and establishing public for private ownership of mineral rights.[3] Finally in 1947 the coal-mines passed into the hands of the state.

Two industries, gas and electricity, did not exist before the nineteenth century—they represented new forms of power, lighting, heating and traction; while a new textile (rayon)[4] foreshadowed an age in which natural products would be supplemented or replaced by artificial substitutes. The use of gas as an illuminant started about 1800 when William Murdock lit up the works of Boulton and Watt at Soho.[5] It was adopted for street lighting, introduced into the home both for lighting and heating, and in the sixties served as the fuel for internal combustion engines. Experiments in electricity were made near the end of the eighteenth century, but so long as it was generated by a battery the quantity was restricted; the dynamo provided ample generation by mechanical methods. Of all human discoveries electricity has the widest range in the uses to which it can be turned: its potentialities indeed seem infinite. It provides homes with the means for lighting, heating and cooking. It furnishes industry with power which can be transmitted over long distances, thus facilitating the dispersion of factories fed from a remote source (a power station) in

---

[1] See Chapter Ten.   [2] The act of 1930.
[3] The act of 1938.   [4] For rayon, see Chapter Fifteen.
[5] Murdock used gas for lighting in his own house in the last decade of the eighteenth century and at the Soho works in the first decade of the nineteenth century.

place of the former urban concentration. With it trains and trams can run, and instantaneous communication can be achieved by telegraph, telephone and wireless. Nevertheless the progress of electricity was retarded by the fact that gas was first in the field and that coal was cheap and abundant. It was utilized for telegraphy in the thirties and for the telephone in the seventies but for other purposes only on a small scale in the eighties; its extended application for domestic lighting and power supply was delayed until the closing decade. Electric traction also came near the end of the nineteenth century. The omnibus had made its appearance in the streets of the metropolis in the twenties and the tram in the sixties; the one was introduced from France, the other from America. Both were horse-drawn but steam trams and steam omnibuses were not unknown. In the opening years of the present century electric trams were displacing horse and steam trams, though Oxford still retained its horse trams until 1914. Steam, moreover, was being challenged on its classic hearth since the London underground railway was electric and surface trains were beginning to be electrified. To meet all these varied uses of electricity there grew up a very considerable industry engaged in the manufacture of generators, motors, lamps, stoves and other domestic apparatus.

A dual interest attaches to the silk industry. It preserved the system of state regulation of wages as late as the third decade of the nineteenth century—the solitary survival of a practice once the law of the land. Further it was the only important manufacture which proved unable to dispense with protection. In the eighteenth century foreign silk goods had been prohibited; but when the free trade movement started on its course no industry could hope to remain unaffected. However in the case of silk the wind was tempered to the shorn lamb, and prohibition was replaced in 1824 by the maximum possible duty of 30 per cent. At the same time the high duty on imported raw silk was reduced from 5s. 6d. per lb. to 3d. and the reduction in the cost of the material together with improved machinery in the throwing mills enabled English producers to lower their prices. Subsequently the Cobden Treaty with France (1860) abolished the duty on foreign silk goods, and native textiles were exposed to the full blast of alien competition. As a result imports of silk broadstuffs in the early years of the twentieth century were nearly five times as large as home production, which gave employment to but one-fourth of the number engaged in it fifty years previously. Coventry, one of the principal centres, turned to the making of bicycles in which it gained renown, thus affording an apt illustration of the tendency of free trade to divert the national energies into the most fruitful channels. Yet one branch which was a recent development prospered, namely spun silk, a waste product whose potentialities were successfully exploited by Lister the inventor of a combing machine. As in other textiles, machinery was introduced first into the preliminary processes—in the case of silk this was the throwing process where factories using power were erected half a century before the advent of cotton spinning factories; but hand-looms continued to be kept by Macclesfield firms in the eighties. Thus side by side with the factories there persisted a domestic system in which the 'master' who owned the silk gave out the material to an 'undertaker' who employed journeymen to do the weaving. The 'undertaker' took one-third—'to repay him for the winding, warping, shoproom and looms' (so it was explained)—and the weaver two-thirds of the price paid by the 'master.' The adoption of power-loom weaving was stimulated by the removal of protection, which made it all the more necessary to introduce up-to-date methods of production.

The hosiery industry was at first confined to the manufacture of stockings ('hose'), although it has now other products knitted in the same way as stockings by a chain of loops—in contrast with cloth which is woven (interlaced)

344

with warp and weft. It enjoys the distinction of being the first textile in which the processes were revolutionized by an English invention, the knitting-frame of William Lee in the reign of Elizabeth. This was a hand-frame and it was not generally displaced by power-frames until the latter part of the nineteenth century. Another textile, linen, never took firm root in England; instead it became established in Ireland which, as Strafford had planned in the early seventeenth century, was thus compensated for the discouragement of a woollen industry that could not have competed successfully with its English rival.

Any survey of English industries must include a reference to building and earthenware. Building ranks among the most ancient of economic activities, and it has afforded scope—more especially in edifices consecrated to religious uses—for some splendid manifestations of human art. Alike in its materials, as in architectural form, building has evolved through the ages; but the old materials were never completely superseded by the new, and mud huts existed together with structures of timber, stone and brick, while in the past fifty years the steel-frame building has made its appearance. Campbell's *The London Tradesman* (1747) shows that in his day there was a class of master builders, doubtless recruited mainly from bricklayers, who either work for others or 'launch out into building projects of their own which frequently ruin them.' It was those speculative builders who found in the rapid urbanization of the nineteenth century their opportunity to create a jerry-builder's paradise though the conditions were far from being all of their own making. The number of workers engaged in building was nearly half a million in the middle of the nineteenth century[1] and twice as many at the end.

Another ancient occupation was the potter's craft: among others the museums of Peking, Athens and Constantinople exhibit treasures of surpassing beauty. In England a manu-

[1] In Great Britain. (It was 400,000 in England and Wales.)

facture, which had already made considerable headway,[1] flowered into the artistic productions of a great master-potter who built upon the foundations laid by his pre-decessors. Josiah Wedgwood (1730–95) at the age of twenty-eight set up on his own, and in the course of a highly successful career he erected a large earthenware factory together with a village for his workmen which he named Etruria. A monument to his memory claims that he 'converted a rude and inconsiderable manufactory into an elegant art and an important part of national commerce;' while his biographer asserts that 'dissatisfied with the clumsiness of the ordinary crockery of his day, he aimed at higher finish, more exact form.' It is at least unquestionable that the technical and ornamental improvements which Wedgwood effected in English earthenware carried his products all over the Continent.

The changes in the structure of English industry during the nineteenth and twentieth centuries have been less revolutionary in scope than those which occurred in the manufacturing processes. Neither factory organization, nor large-scale production, nor joint-stock companies, nor integrated concerns, nor combines to suppress competi-tion, were new when Watt's steam engine was given to the world. The changes that took place were more in the nature of an acceleration of tendencies already at work. In the aggregate they have served to modify the character of English society, but the transformation has been the result of piecemeal and gradual developments parallel to those which at all stages of economic evolution have con-tinuously and subtly altered the aspect of the industrial landscape. The main features with which we are here con-cerned are the enlargement of the size of the business

[1] The fine white English earthenware 'was just reaching perfection.' Chelsea china in the middle of the eighteenth century is described as 'the finest ever made in England.' This was porcelain made of soft paste. Spode and others manufactured a porcelain made of hard paste and bone ash

unit, the increase of joint-stock companies, the trend towards the elimination of competition, and the growth of the factory system.

One of the misconceptions about English economic life arises from the belief that small-scale production was the invariable practice before the epoch of the great inventions, and that in the nineteenth century it was almost entirely superseded by large-scale production. In fact we think of modern industrial society in terms of the mass creation of standardized articles and the assemblage of thousands of wage-earners under the same roof. Attention has already been drawn to the error of the view that large-scale production was unknown or exceptional in earlier times: great undertakings constituted a recognized feature of the extractive and manufacturing industries, and in a variety of occupations there existed a class of capitalist employers engaged in a substantial way of business. Here it remains to consider how far the conventional picture corresponds to the realities of our own age.

It is undeniable that enterprises giving employment to vast numbers of workers are common to-day. Nevertheless the 'representative firm,' if any was found to exist, would diverge considerably from the pattern usually conceived of it. Actually there is an indefinite gradation of firms whose staffs range from a handful of employees to many thousands. This can best be shown, first, by examining the situation as it prevailed at the middle of the nineteenth century. Fortunately evidence is available, for the census of 1851 asked employers to state the number of their operatives. The inquiry was answered by nearly 130,000 masters who had almost three-fourths of a million people on their pay-roll. The returns are illuminating because they serve completely to dispel the notion of a society dominated by large producers. About one-third kept no hired workers or made no return of any, and simply stated that they were masters. Of the remaining 87,000 employers there were (approximately) 76,000 with 1 to 9 employees, 9,000 with 10 to 49 employees, 1,000 with

50 to 99 employees, 900 with 100 to 349 employees, and 228 with 350 or more employees (the last category had in all 85,500 employees).[1] Under fifty persons were employed by 605 out of 1,188 cotton manufacturers; by 853 out of 976 woollen manufacturers; by 84 out of 127 worsted manufacturers; by 161 out of 236 silk manufacturers; by 3,157 out of 3,322 builders; by 609 out of 677 engine and machine makers; by 267 out of 310 earthenware-makers; by 6,741 out of 6,752 tailors; by 10,285 out of 10,354 shoemakers; by 1,976 out of 1,991 millers; by 5,048 out of 5,049 blacksmiths. Three hundred or more persons were employed by 136 cotton, 23 woollen, 13 worsted, 16 silk, and 10 earthenware manufacturers, as well as by 6 builders, 17 engine and machine makers, and 3 shoemakers.[2]

We may next look at the results of an investigation conducted nearly a hundred years later (1935). It concerned over 53,000 firms engaged in industry, of which each hired over ten persons, with a total of approximately seven and a quarter million employees. Rather more than one-half kept less than fifty, but they accounted for only one-ninth of the total number and produced only one-tenth of the total net output. Firms comprising less than five hundred accounted for nearly half the total employment. About 1,000 firms had a thousand and over; as few as 100 firms had five thousand and over. A closer analysis of the figures

[1] The employers in England and Wales who made a return in 1851 numbered 129,002 (of whom 41,732 stated only that they were masters); the employees numbered 727,468.

Number of men	Number of employers	Number of men	Number of employers
1	24,345	30–39	878
2	19,243	40–49	514
3	11,177	50–74	681
4	7,624	75–99	348
5	4,108	100–149	390
6	4,178	150–199	236
7	2,093	200–249	135
8	2,044	250–299	88
9	1,140	300–349	65
10–19	5,826	350 and	228
20–29	1,929	upwards	

[2] See Table on following page.

Total number of Employers	Number of Employees																					
	1	2	3	4	5	6	7	8	9	10–19	20–29	30–39	40–49	50–74	75–99	100–149	150–199	200–249	250–299	300–349	350 and upwards	No men or number not stated
Blacksmiths, 7,331	2,470	1,565	555	217	88	47	27	22	11	31	12	2	1	0	1	–	–	–	–	–	–	2,282
Builders, 3,614	151	266	278	321	198	312	154	193	85	701	271	126	101	77	36	24	9	8	5	1	5	292
Cotton Industry, 1,670	46	35	24	35	38	35	18	20	14	124	104	55	57	85	87	97	82	57	39	23	113	482
Earthenware Industry, 378	36	32	22	27	18	19	9	12	5	31	23	21	12	3	4	15	4	2	5	3	7	68
Engine and Machine Makers, 837	77	75	68	63	38	45	27	23	31	90	30	27	15	21	13	6	3	3	5	3	14	160
Millers, 2,394	664	483	272	178	88	75	47	40	22	84	15	7	1	9	4	2	–	–	–	–	–	403
Shoemakers, 17,665	3,444	2,572	1,363	867	432	492	192	191	107	444	115	46	20	31	7	12	9	5	2	0	3	7,311
Silk, 272	15	15	15	16	14	18	3	4	2	22	15	13	9	9	20	14	7	5	4	3	13	36
Tailors, 10,991	2,330	1,522	900	581	275	309	156	152	83	343	61	22	7	10	0	1	–	–	–	–	–	4,239
Woollen Industry, 1,107	109	90	74	73	47	78	17	18	12	156	94	52	33	28	13	23	26	8	2	2	21	131
Worsted Industry, 154	6	8	7	4	5	1	1	5	1	20	13	4	9	9	3	9	6	3	0	1	12	27

349

reveals instructive information on the distribution of the wage-earning population and the scale of production at the present day.[1]

It is evident that after a century and a half of power-driven machinery and factories the small producer in England has not been expelled from the industrial field. He still holds his own, just as the 'one-man' business continues to survive in the face of the competition of the large stores. A more intimate sense of the modern position can be conveyed better by a brief review of particular branches of industry than by a bare statistical abstract. In coal-mining about one-half of the undertakings counted each a hundred or fewer workers. In iron and steel there is a marked contrast between the primary and finishing processes. The blast furnace increased its capacity from an average annual output of 3,500 tons in 1840 to 30,000 tons in 1913. Some of the ironmasters of a century ago seem to have had several hundred men; but the new steel works involved a much greater concentration of capital. A score of firms in recent decades was responsible for nearly three-fourths of the output of iron and steel; while an integrated concern with coal and iron mines, furnaces and manufactures may employ as many as sixty thousand hands. The light metal industries present a very different picture. Here there remains even to-day plenty of room for the small producer. He has persisted in the cutlery trade side by side with factory establishments; in jewellery the average firm numbers twenty-five persons; in many of the hardware trades the unit of production has kept small.

Among textiles the cotton industry was conducted from

[1]No. employed	No. of firms	No. employed	No. of firms	No. employed	No. of firm
11–24	17,609	300–399	1,084	1,500–1,999	198
25–49	14,147	400–499	606	2,000–2,499	111
50–99	9,459	500–749	865	2,500–2,999	55
100–199	5,814	750–999	405	3,000–3,999	80
200–299	2,218	1,000–1,499	414	4,000–4,999	51
				5,000 and over	101

These figures for 1935 are taken from Leak and Maizels in *The Journal of the Royal Statistical Society*, N.S., vol. 108, parts I–II.

the start on a large scale in the spinning factories which
housed the water-frame. In the early years of the nineteenth
century a firm might employ hundreds and sometimes more
than a thousand mill hands. However the distinctive feature
of cotton undertakings is their degree of specialization.
Two-thirds of the operatives are in the service of firms
carrying on either spinning or weaving but not both together;
and each branch contains hundreds of concerns varying in
size. This feature of the cotton industry is shared by the
worsted industry where combing, spinning, weaving and
finishing are usually (though not invariably) organized separ-
ately by independent firms. In the woollen industry, on the
contrary, all the processes are frequently in the hands of the
same firm, and the material does not change ownership at successive stages of manufacture. The woollen business is managed
as a rule on a smaller scale than the worsted business and
accordingly it comprises fewer employees: between the two
world wars nearly one-fourth of the establishments had less
than twenty-one operatives, and nearly two-thirds accounted
for barely one-sixth of the total number of workpeople engaged in the manufacture. The engineering industry, in
marked contrast with the United States, is also characterized
by small-scale production although there are some substantial
undertakings. In the middle of the nineteenth century
two-thirds of the 'engine and machine makers' employed
under ten men: less than a score reached three hundred or
more.[1] In recent years an official report has spoken of 'the
very large number of relatively small firms that exist—each
with a separate organization, separate establishment charges,
separate buying and selling arrangements, and each producing a multiplicity of articles.' In shipbuilding we may
find a builder with over five hundred on his pay-roll early
in the nineteenth century but the average unit was still
small, and the absence of uniformity has persisted down to
the present day.

In general it appears that at all times and in all industries

[1] In the eighteenth century Boulton employed about 700 persons.

business units of varying sizes have prevailed. There exist many large enterprises yet in number (though not in volume of employment) they are often exceeded by small manufacturing firms. The increase in the scale of operations is responsible for a notable development in industrial technique. There is nothing new in principle about the mass production of standardized goods: it was the aim of the legislature for hundreds of years to force standardization upon the makers of textiles. Modern engineering science has facilitated—as well as necessitated—the application of mass production methods to an unparalleled extent. The automobile industry affords the most conspicuous example of 'flow production,' in which articles under construction travel along a conveyor and receive their component parts from each mechanic in turn until the process of assemblage is completed.

The growth in the size of an undertaking is dependent upon the concentration of capital. An entrepreneur seldom has the resources which will enable him to embark upon an extensive outlay: he must therefore seek a loan from a bank or form a joint-stock. The bank provides as a rule short-term advances for the purpose of supplying circulating capital. The joint-stock company, unless it is a private firm confined to a few persons, makes it possible to draw fixed capital from a wide field of investment. The joint-stock system, as we have seen, is at least as old as the sixteenth century; but its adoption was retarded partly by the Bubble Act of 1720 which required every joint-stock company to possess a charter, and partly by the indefinite liabilities of shareholders. The Bubble Act was repealed in 1825; while the privilege of limited liability was expressly conceded in 1855 (with some exceptions) and made general in 1862.[1] Family businesses at once began to utilize the much coveted opportunity to turn themselves into joint-stocks, and the practice continued in later decades. In other cases any person

[1] Limited liability had been established for certain trading companies in the seventeenth century.

was at liberty to purchase shares with his liability limited to the extent of the shares which he held.

The importance of joint-stock companies in the national economy is impressively demonstrated by the fact that between 1885 and 1925 the capital employed in them increased over nine-fold.[1] They have been one of the prime causes of the expansion in the size of the business unit. The ability of the general public to invest savings in industry, in commerce and in transport, enables a concern to determine the scope of its operations without being unduly hampered by financial stringency. The enlargement of an undertaking is brought about in different ways. It may be horizontal— that is, it extends the field, without varying the nature, of its processes. It may be vertical—that is, it takes in other stages of production. Thus in iron and steel a company may own collieries and iron mines, so that it can charge its furnaces with its own fuel and ore to make the steel which it converts into finished products. Integration is also a feature of the woollen industry—in contrast with worsted and cotton where independent firms specialize in a single process. Other consequences of the joint-stock system must be noticed. For one thing, the risks of an industrial or commercial enterprise are spread over a greater number of people. For another, a joint-stock company can effect economies in the costs of production by widening the scope of its activities rather than by cutting wage rates. During the 'Industrial Revolution' the low wages, long hours and insanitary conditions of the early factories were, partially at least, due to the inventions being largely exploited by men who had sprung from the ranks and were often hampered by inadequate means. On the other hand the personal relationship, which can subsist between employees and an employer

[1] From £482 millions to £4,470 m. Allowance must be made for the change in the value of money. Moreover when private firms are converted into a joint-stock there need not necessarily be any investment of fresh capital. On the eve of the second world war the number of joint-stock companies registered in England and Wales was 13,018 public companies (with a paid-up capital of £3,801 m.) and 134,843 private companies (with a paid-up capital of £1,741 m.).

z

who both possesses and conducts the business, becomes impossible when possession is vested in hundreds and even thousands of shareholders. Hence the result of joint-stock companies has been, as it were, to make capital impersonal and to deepen the cleavage with labour. Lastly the effect of a joint-stock is to separate the ownership of capital and the functions of management. The capitalist who furnishes the resources, and the entrepreneur who directs the under-taking, cease to be identical when the ownership of capital grows diffused. This does not mean, however, that the real control of a company passes into the hands of its managerial staff—a conclusion which has been too hastily drawn. Its policy may be shaped by a shareholder or group of shareholders either by reason of the extent of their holding in the company or their ability to influence the voting of other shareholders.

We are accustomed to think of the nineteenth century as the age in which the spirit of competition reigned supreme. The truth is that 'pure' competition has rarely if ever existed, and even 'imperfect' competition has often been conspicuously absent. There are clear indications to support Adam Smith's statement that 'people of the same trade seldom meet together but the conversation ends in some contrivance to raise prices.' We have seen that compacts to restrict output and control prices have a continuous history from the opening of the seventeenth century when they first began to excite adverse comment. In the nineteenth century there is similar evidence of combinations. We hear of associations to lay down the tariffs ·of fire insurance offices (1858) and to determine the price of soap (1867); witnesses before parliamentary committees in the seventies and eighties testified that price agreements were 'a universal practice' or 'the practice of nearly all the main trades.' We even meet in the eighties with an arrangement of English, Belgian and German makers of steel rails to divide the export trade: the international scheme was short-lived but it was followed by others to fix prices, curtail output and delimit

354

marketing areas. In the present century an official report has drawn attention to the presence of over five hundred associations of producers in this country 'all exerting a substantial influence on the course of industry.' One object which all combinations—extending from informal understandings ('gentlemen's agreements') to formal contracts or amalgamation into trusts—share in common is to regulate output and maintain or raise prices. Nevertheless numerous industries and services still remain largely immune from associations, such as textiles, building (including shipbuilding), boots and shoes, automobiles, etc.

In recent decades public opinion in England has grown less unfavourable to industrial combinations. It is recognized that concerns in which a great amount of fixed capital is invested and overhead charges are proportionately heavier, and in which price-cutting militates against the maintenance and replacement of expensive equipment, may be constrained to enter into agreements that will provide an assurance of stable prices and regular output, as well as facilitate co-operative research, diminish the costs of distribution and promote export selling agencies. Furthermore it may be found necessary to eliminate the redundant capacity of an industry by extinguishing small and inefficient plants; and under the name of rationalization this is widely advocated as a means of avoiding economic wastage. Accordingly between the two world wars the government itself took steps to bring about fusions in the coal, iron, steel and shipping industries, and it exerted pressure upon undertakings to reorganize themselves in more efficient units, cheapen costs of production, and limit competition. Especially notable was the amalgamation of the railways into four large groups and of the joint-stock banks into five companies with official encouragement. The reconstitution of industries and services on a basis which involves co-operation and the concentration of resources measures the vast difference in the standpoint of our own times and of a hundred years ago towards competition.

355

Perhaps the most convincing demonstration that English economic society has grown by the process of unceasing change and adaptation, in which the old is blended almost imperceptibly with the new, is to be found in the persistence of the usages and practices of by-gone ages. Throughout the nineteenth century and down to the present day there have survived traces of two earlier stages in industrial evolution —one when the consumer was his own producer; the other when he came into direct contact with the producer whom he supplied with material. These two historic stages had once been widely prevalent. Thus Eden writing in 1797 declares that country folk in the north of England manufactured almost every article of dress except shoes and hats. Linen thread and woollen yarn, after being spun at home, were sent to weavers and dyers 'so that almost every family' had an annual supply of linen and woollen cloth. Doubtless in other parts of England the same custom had prevailed in rural districts where the services of the local professional weavers were requisitioned whenever the weaving was not done in the home. The first stage has not yet altogether disappeared, for instance, bread may be baked or jam made or (now extremely rare) beer brewed at home. The second stage is far from being extinct. It is not unknown for tailors and dressmakers to use the customer's cloth; within living memory bakers were accustomed to work up the customer's flour, while millers ground the customer's corn; it is still the regular practice—though here the producer furnishes the material—for working watchmakers, shoemakers, cobblers, carpenters, house-painters, glaziers, plumbers and black-smiths to execute the customer's orders. There still persist also many survivals of the old handicrafts even where machine production has become predominant, such as hand-loom weaving, hand-made shoes, watch-making, processes in the cutlery and other light metal trades. Nor has factory production completely displaced home production. Tailors and dressmakers give out cloth to be made into fabrics; iron is supplied to skilled outworkers who produce hand-wrought nails of good quality on their forges; the manufacture of twine and nets is a domestic occupation; and other examples could be multiplied. If our industrial system to-day wears in many of its parts something of the air of a museum piece, it at least affords proof that economic change as a rule is gradual in development.

In the hundred years of freedom from great wars, which England enjoyed after a long drawn-out conflict with France in the eighteenth century and before the briefer but more deadly conflict with Germany in the twentieth century, the energies of her people were absorbed in the pursuits of industry and commerce. An ever-increasing stream of riches poured from her mines, her furnaces and her factories in the shape of coal, engineering products and textile fabrics which she exchanged for raw materials and for foodstuffs—corn, meat, butter, tea, sugar and fruits brought in her ships from all the regions of the earth. In the growing prosperity of the country the working class shared with other sections of the community. Its progress was revealed in the shorter hours of labour; in the advance in wages real as well as nominal; in the more abundant and varied articles of consumption; in the marked decline of intemperance; in the influence exerted upon social habits by the spread of education; in the mounting deposits of savings banks;[1] in the provision—made by friendly societies (whose number even in the eighteenth century ran into thousands) with several million members—for the casualties of life; in building societies to enable working men to own their homes;[2] in the institution of holidays; in the facilities for cheap travel; in the amenities afforded by public authorities, such as libraries, parks, etc.

Broadly speaking the standard working day in the nine-teenth century exceeded ten hours during the first two

[1] Deposits in post-office savings banks in the United Kingdom rose from £5 millions in 1864 to £140 millions in 1901 and to £509 millions in 1938.

[2] The number of houses in England and Wales in 1851 was 3½ millions (the population was 18 m.); 6¾ m. in 1901 (32½ m.); 9½ m. in 1931 (40 m.).

quarters; it fell to ten during the third quarter and nine during the last quarter, where it remained for several decades until it was reduced to eight after the first world war. This generalization takes no account of overtime, variations between seasons, and work done at home or in non-industrial occupations. The state did not regulate adult male labour for nearly a hundred years until in 1908 it established an eight-hours day for coal-miners. Indirectly, however, factory legislation on behalf of women and young persons served to limit the working day for men. The act of 1847 restricted the hours of women in the textile industries to sixty a week; this was lowered to fifty-six and a half in 1874. In other industries the operatives were able to profit by the tide of prosperity in the seventies to secure fifty-four hours (for example, the engineers and builders in 1872); but young shop assistants were required to work as many as seventy-four by the act of 1887. It must be added that hours of labour throughout the nineteenth century were longest under the system of industry which had prevailed for centuries, namely, the domestic system carried on in the homes of the workers.

The complexity of wage-payments, where uniformity is lacking in the methods and standards of remuneration, does not easily lend itself to a summary statement. In general it may be said that money wages rose sharply during the early years of the nineteenth century when the country was at war and the currency was inflated. Subsequently they fell until in the thirties and forties they became nearly stationary. The third quarter of the century registered a marked improvement in the condition of the working class, for wages increased over 40 per cent. Some of the advance was forfeited in the depression of the eighties, but the lost ground was more than regained before the end of the century. The upward movement was accelerated during the first world war, and finally raised wages 70 per cent. above the pre-war (1914) level. Attempts have been made to compile index numbers of money wages for different industries. They

358

suggest that the chief gain in wages during the second half of the nineteenth century was made in cotton—roughly 100 per cent. as compared with 70 per cent. in building; 60 per cent. in agriculture; 50 per cent. in worsted,[1] coal, engineering, iron and steel.[2]

Nominal wages as measured in terms of money tell only half of the story: it is necessary to ascertain real wages as measured in terms of purchasing power. In other words wage movements must be correlated with price movements. During the war with revolutionary France prices soared. A cost-of-living index has been constructed and its indications may be used tentatively to show the trend of prices. Taking 1790 as the base year (100), the general level of prices mounted to 170 in 1800 and attained its highest point (187) in 1813; then in spite of occasional setbacks it continued to recede until it touched 83 in 1850. The decline was due to the cessation of government spending, the return from a paper to a metallic currency, the cheapening of production by machinery, the reduction of tariffs, the repeal of the corn laws, and the changes in the system of transport. It is significant that during the first half of the nineteenth century exports increased over 600 per cent. in volume but only 60 per cent. in value. During the next quarter of a century came the turn of the tide, and prices resumed their upward trend. The advance is usually attributed to the gold discoveries in California (1847) and Australia (1851) which multiplied the annual world output of gold. In the early seventies prices fell more rapidly than they had risen: the slump in wholesale prices brought them to a point where they were lower at the end of the century than at the middle. The output of gold remained unchanged but England now ceased to be the only country whose currency was based on the gold

---

[1] In the woollen industry it was 60 per cent. These percentages of wages in the mass only furnish general indications. As prices were rising, the percentage of increase in real wages was much less.

[2] A government inquiry listed the average earnings of adult men in a full week in the early twentieth century as follows: pig iron 34s. 7d., engineering 32s. 4d., cotton 28s. 8d., woollen and worsted 26s. 8d.

standard, and the use of gold for industrial as well as currency purposes was also expanding. Other factors must not be overlooked—the drop in wheat prices was due to the opening up of the middle west in the United States, cheap steel was made possible by new processes, the costs of ocean transport were reduced by improvements in navigation. Then as the century drew to a close the annual production of gold was greatly enlarged with the development of the South African mines. Prices again rose though money wages lagged behind, and this explains the social unrest in England just before the first world war. When these changes in the general level of prices are taken into account, they lead to the broad conclusion that real wages were rising throughout the nineteenth century (except in the opening decade); and according to one statistical estimate they were nearly doubled between the middle and end of the century. The expansion in the purchasing power of the great mass of the community is reflected in the volume of imported foodstuffs (bread, butter, cheese, tea, sugar, eggs, meat).[1] If the price of bread is taken as a measure of the consumer's command over the necessaries of life, it appears that the retail price of the four-pound loaf of household bread in London was roughly as follows—15d. in the first two decades, 10d. in the next two, 8½d. in the next three, 8d. in the seventies, 6½d. in the eighties, after which it proceeded to fall to 5½d. or less.[2]

The standard of life of the working class cannot be gauged alone by the wages, nominal or real, of the male head of the household: contributory if indeterminate elements are the

[1] The quantities of imports in lb. which were retained for home consumption per head of the population in 1850 (and in brackets in 1900) were as follows—butter 1·30 (9); cheese 1·38 (7½); wheat and flour 81·76 (244); sugar 24·79 (87); tea 1·86 (6); eggs, number 3·84 (49); tobacco 1 (2); bacon and ham in 1850—1·41; meat in 1900—54.

For the quantities in 1913 and 1938 see Chapter Fifteen.

[2] In the first decade of the twentieth century the retail prices of food (per lb.) were as follows—tea 1s. 4d. to 1s. 8d., sugar 2d., butter 1s. 2d., meat (British) 7½d. to 9d., meat (imported) 4d. to 6d., milk (quart), 3d. to 4d., coal (cwt.) 9½d. to 1s., potatoes (7 lb.) 2½d. to 3½d., flour (7 lb.) 8d. to 10d., bread (4 lb.) 4½d. to 5½d.

earnings of its other members. In former centuries a widespread industrial pursuit, cottage spinning, enabled women and children to supplement the family income. When the source dried up, new channels of employment were created. Of these one was the textile factories, for the cotton and woollen industries always absorbed many more women than men. In addition women were occupied in the silk and hosiery manufactures. There also came into existence factories in non-textiles, for instance, chocolate, biscuits, jam, tobacco. Further opportunities for women's work were furnished by the cycle, motor and electrical industries. Commerce provided careers as book-keepers, secretaries, clerks, typists, shop assistants. The importance of women's place in the economic life of the country is indicated by the fact that, according to the census returns 1881–1931, they accounted for about 30 per cent. of the total number engaged in industry.[1] The most numerous of all women's occupations was domestic service: in the middle of the nineteenth century it claimed almost a million women,[2] or nearly double the number of female operatives in the textiles. At this period the common wage for a general servant in London was about ten pounds a year, besides board and lodging; before the first world war it had risen to twenty pounds; in recent years it has increased in greater proportion than the remuneration of any other form of service. Although domestic service has continued to grow with the expansion of the population,[3] it is now expected to attract a diminishing number owing to changes in social habits and the multiplication of other outlets for women's work.

[1] In Great Britain.
[2] Great Britain. The total includes general domestic servants, housekeepers, cooks, housemaids and domestic nurses.
[3] According to the census returns (Great Britain) female indoor domestic servants numbered 1,271,000 in 1921 and 1,471,000 in 1931.

Chapter Thirteen

THE NATIONAL ECONOMY (1815–1914)

II. AGRICULTURE, COMMERCE AND FINANCE

Agriculture

A review of the fortunes of English agriculture must be prefaced by some reference to the factor which was the mainspring of its development—namely, the growth of population.

The most arresting feature of English society during the nineteenth century, and the underlying cause of the transformation in England's economic situation, was a momentous change in the rate of natural increase which upset the traditional balance between agriculture and industry and forced this country to rely on international trade for its daily bread. In former ages the population seemed almost stationary, though it was perhaps 50 per cent. larger at the end of the eighteenth century than at the beginning. When the original census was taken in 1801 England and Wales contained approximately nine millions; the first decade added one million, the next five decades two millions each, and the next four decades three millions each—the total in 1901 was $32\frac{1}{2}$ millions while in 1938 it was $41\frac{1}{4}$ millions. The reasons for so startling a phenomenon have been much canvassed. The common explanation that it was the effect of the 'Industrial Revolution'—a 'response to increase in skill'—fails to account for a similar trend in countries which were not exposed to similar influences. The determining element was not a rise in the birth rate (it actually diminished during the nineteenth century[1]), but a fall in the death rate due to an improvement in the health of the nation as a result of a better water supply and drainage system,

[1] In England and Wales the average annual birth rate was 34·1 per thousand of the population in 1851; 28·7 in 1901; 15·1 in 1938. The average annual death rate was 21·8 in 1851; 17·2 in 1901; 11·6 in 1938.

the abolition of famine, the substitution of fresh for salted meat in winter, and the decline in diseases such as smallpox and fever. (The statistics of infantile mortality, however, showed a deplorable wastage of human life. In the seventies of the last century one infant in six died; at the beginning of the twentieth century one in seven; on the eve of the second world war one in twenty.)

At the present day the prospect of a stationary or even a declining population is causing considerable apprehension. Yet at one time a growth of population was commonly associated with a growth of destitution—an opinion to which Malthus gave classic expression in his famous *Essay on Population*. It was natural therefore that the rapid advance made in the nineteenth century should be viewed with misgivings. In reality the extent to which a country is over-populated depends not on the numerical size of the population but on the flexibility of the economic system, that is, on its capacity for expansion sufficient to absorb the surplus without undue strain. The aftermath of the Napoleonic wars which bequeathed a legacy of inflated industries, a depreciated currency and heavy taxation, combined with the transition from handicrafts to mechanical methods of production, heightened the difficulty of making the necessary readjustments in order to meet fresh demands for employment and food. Accordingly public attention was drawn to emigration as a panacea for the social ills of the age. A leading economist, John Stuart Mill—whose *Principles of Political Economy* together with Adam Smith's *The Wealth of Nations* formed the economic bible of successive generations of Englishmen—laid down that the 'exportation of labourers and capital from old to new countries, from a place where their productive power is less to a place where it is greater, increases by so much the aggregate produce of the labour and capital of the world. It adds to the joint wealth of the old and the new country what amounts in a short period to many times the mere cost of effecting the transport. There needs be no hesitation in affirming that colonization in the present state of the world is the best affair of business in which the capital of an old and wealthy country can engage.' He added: 'There is hence the strongest obligation on the government of a country like our own with a crowded population and unoccupied continents under its command to build, as it were, a bridge from the mother country to those continents [by facilitating emigration] without cost to the emigrants themselves.' However before Mill wrote, a parliamentary committee (1826) had recommended colonization as a remedy for the redundancy of population and the government responded by providing money for the purpose. This followed the lifting of the embargo in the previous year (1825) on the emigration of artisans, who were now accorded the same legal 'liberty to go abroad as other classes of the community.'

The movement overseas assumed substantial proportions, though it is not possible to indicate the number of English emigrants during the first half of the nineteenth century because the returns do not specify the nationality before 1853. The total number (including Scots and Irish) who left the shores of the United Kingdom averaged 20,000 a year in the twenties, 50,000 in the thirties, and 120,000 in the forties (the decade of the Irish famine). In the fifties English emigrants averaged 64,000 annually (the Irish 125,000), in the sixties 65,000, in the seventies 100,000, in the eighties (the decade of the depression) 150,000, in the nineties 110,000.[1] On the eve of the first world war the excess of emigrants over immigrants was a quarter of a million.[2] The continuous stream of emigrants overseas not only from the British Isles but also from the Continent of Europe meant that in the nineteenth century the Old World exported men as well as goods and services. It was the sub-

---

[1] These are not net emigration figures since there was also immigration.

[2] The numbers of passengers leaving the United Kingdom for countries out of Europe in 1913 were—British 470,000 and aliens 232,000 (total 702,000). The numbers arriving from countries out of Europe were—British 228,000, aliens 145,000 (total 373,000). The total net emigration was one-third of a million.

sequent drying up of the outflow that created problems of the first magnitude.[1]

The growth of population was accompanied by a change in its composition—a change fraught with untold significance. If English society had remained preponderately rural, it would have been necessary to cultivate inferior soils in order to increase the production of home-grown food: the consequence would have been a deterioration in the standard of living. What actually happened was the reverse: an expanding population enjoyed a higher standard because it switched over from agriculture to industry and commerce. In other words English society in the last hundred years became preponderately urban. In the middle of the nineteenth century half the population was concentrated in or around towns, in the eighties two-thirds, at the end of the century three-fourths, after the first world war four-fifths. It was this trend that led a writer as early as the seventies to exclaim: 'This country is becoming every ten years less and less of a farm, and more and more of a meadow, a garden and a playground.' In the following paragraphs we shall trace the process by which the English countryside was turned from 'a farm' into 'a meadow and a garden.'

The history of English agriculture in the nineteenth century falls into two distinct periods each covering fifty years. The repeal of the corn laws was the watershed which separated one system of agrarian economy, whose structure rested on the basis of artificial protection, from another system stripped of its legal monopoly of the home market and exposed to the full blast of world competition. The general conditions which prevailed in the first period have been described in the chapter on the free trade movement. Here it may suffice to recapitulate that the combined influence of a growing population, depreciated currency and a succession of bad harvests, caused corn prices to soar to unprecedented heights. The subsequent relapse threatened

[1] See Chapter Fifteen.

landlords and farmers with ruin since they had entered into commitments of which the 'real' burden was now augmented by the rise in the value of money. To meet a precarious situation a corn law was enacted expressly designed to keep domestic prices above the international level, and the ensuing controversy was only finally stilled with the total repeal of the protective legislation. Yet while the free trade debates fill the canvas, there is another side to English agriculture in the first half of the century. It was required to support a community which was doubled in the period, for the amount of imported food was usually small. Although the general population was growing fast the rural element expanded at a much slower rate. The great increase in production must therefore be attributed to other causes—the cultivation of the commons, the application of capital in improving the soil and in drainage, a more advanced technique, superior implements, better rotation of crops. Unfortunately agriculture is liable to vicissitudes which are beyond the farmers' control, and a deficient harvest at home spelt famine prices and starvation for the toiling masses. Under the corn laws of 1815–46, as we have seen,[1] wide fluctuations in the price of wheat were a normal occurrence. Wheat was the bread of the English people, the staple article of diet, the largest item in the household budget—and so its price was a matter of national concern. England had reached a stage in her economic development when she needed regular and continuous supplies as well as a price level that did not resemble a fever chart. In the second half of the nineteenth century a changed commercial policy enabled her to draw upon the resources of the whole world to supplement the produce of her own fields; and English agriculture now passed into a new phase.

The effects produced by the repeal of the corn laws were widely different from those which the landed interest had gloomily anticipated; they were also different from what the free traders had optimistically predicted. On the one hand

[1] See Chapter Eleven.

366

agriculture was not ruined: on the other hand there was for a generation no appreciable decline in the average annual price of wheat,[1] which during the space of three decades was only a few shillings below the 'hungry forties.' However the general price level was rising, so that the real fall in wheat was masked. Furthermore the wide fluctuations normally ceased—a notable exception was the Crimean war—when our ports were thrown open to the grain of other lands. But the arresting feature is that, while English husbandry had been in a depressed condition before the repeal, subsequently it entered upon what is often regarded as its golden age—in spite of the fact that grain was cheaper. Its prosperous condition was shared by all classes of the rural community, for the value of land, rents, profits and wages moved upwards. The explanation seems to be that the farming interest, deprived of legal protection against foreign grain, began to pull itself together and endeavoured to meet external competition by reliance upon its own efforts. This counsel had been given to it by James Caird who published in 1849 a pamphlet bearing the significant title: *High Farming the best substitute for Protection*. Like Arthur Young whose tours eighty years earlier are a classic, he made a pilgrimage of farming. He was struck, as his eighteenth-century predecessor had been, by the fact that 'the successful practices of one farm or one county are unknown or unheeded in the next.' It is certainly astonishing to learn that, in the decade of the Great Exhibition which revealed to the world England's industrial progress, 'within a couple of miles of Brighton may be seen in use every day' wooden ploughs drawn by six oxen, an operation 'infinitely more cheaply executed by one man and two good horses.' Accordingly Caird sought to impress upon farmers the lesson

---

[1] The average annual price of British wheat per quarter was 56s. 8d. in 1840–45 and 52s. 10d. in 1846–77. In the year of the repeal (1846) the average price was 54s. 8d. and the following year it was 69s. 9d. The annual average was 43s. in 1848–52, and 65s. 3d. in 1853–57 (the rise of 50 per cent. was due to the Crimean war). The annual average for the next twenty years (1858–77) was 51s. 4d.

that their salvation depended not on 'the crutch of legislative protection' but on raising the standard of husbandry. He urged them to make the best of the situation arising from a 'policy which whether for good or evil is now the law of the land,' and to use the resources which still remained—'capital, skill and the mutual co-operation of landlord and tenant.' Caird believed that a condition had arisen where capital could be more profitably exploited in other ways than 'in further attempting to force our poorer class of soils' to grow corn—since it was cheaper to obtain the surplus from the richer lands placed within our reach by 'the beneficient principle of free trade.' Instead farmers were advised to concentrate upon meat and dairy produce. The 'vast development of industry' increased the income of the general body of wage-earners and rendered possible a more extensive consumption of animal food—meat, cheese and butter—with a consequent advance in prices leading to a rise in landowners' rents, tenants' profits and labourers' wages. The advice did not fall on deaf ears. The large farmer, who hitherto had been interested primarily in wheat production, now combined it with meat and dairy produce: herein lay the strength of English agriculture and the source of its prosperity for the next thirty years.

This does not tell the whole story, for the abolition of the corn laws also accelerated technical progress, which was henceforth to serve in lieu of protection. The farmers set themselves to make their industry profitable by a greater outlay of capital and the employment of scientific methods. An outstanding improvement was the drainage of land on which several million pounds were expended. Parliament in repealing the corn laws provided public loans on favourable terms to landowners for drainage and reclamation (that is, bringing the waste land under cultivation). Another improvement was due to chemistry, which analysed the composition of soils and discovered artificial manures capable of making good their deficiencies and replacing the substances abstracted by particular crops. Chemical manures enabled fertility to be maintained with less expense and in a more convenient form. The combination of agricultural practice with agricultural science was one of the notable differences between agriculture before and after 1850. The third change was the adoption of labour-saving machinery which reduced the costs of production. A writer in the seventies observed with approval a 'striking feature of agricultural progress in the last twenty years'—namely, the introduction of reaping machines and steam ploughs. Although the threshing machines were known a century before in the northern parts of England where in Cobbett's day they were 'turned by steam engines,' they found their way into the south at a slow rate. The steam plough lagged behind the steam threshing machine for reasons doubtless connected with the size of the farm. In the early years of the present century labour-saving machinery was extensively used on English farms, while the exigencies of the second world war led to the wide acceptance of motor tractors.

In recounting the factors which help to explain the apparent anomaly that the repeal of the corn laws ushered in an era not of disaster but of prosperity, mention must be made of the reduced cost of transport due to the railways. The farmers were able to buy more cheaply their requirements such as machinery, manures and feeding stuffs for cattle; at the same time they could sell more cheaply their own produce, corn and meat, and gain access to the new markets opened up to them. It is noteworthy, however, that even agrarian experts attributed the progress of English farming 'beyond all efforts of agriculturists' primarily to free trade, whose influence in promoting industrial prosperity was bound to have favourable repercussions upon the rural community. In contrast with the view so stoutly upheld in the eighteenth century by Arthur Young, it was now maintained that the fortunes of agriculture and industry were intimately related.

The organization of English rural society in the nineteenth

2 A

century was described by Caird in a book entitled *The Landed Interest*. His account, written in 1878 for the benefit of foreign readers, is substantially true of the whole century. He sets out the subdivision into landowners who furnish the fixed capital in the way of buildings and derive their income from rents; the tenant-farmers who direct cultivation and provide farm-stock, implements and circulating capital; and the labourers who cultivate the land as employees of the tenants and are paid wages. Caird spoke of the landowner or squire in much the same terms as Pitt had done nearly a hundred years earlier.[1] 'He takes a lead in the business of his parish, and from his class [are selected] the magistrates who administer the criminal affairs of the county and superintend its roads, its public buildings and charitable institutions,' and from his class also are largely recruited 'the learned professions, the Church, the army and the public services.' The distribution of landed property in the United Kingdom had been investigated a few years earlier in *The New Domesday Book* (1874), which showed that about a quarter was owned by twelve hundred persons and about a half by seven thousand four hundred.

Next to the landowners came the farmers. Their importance in the rural economy is indicated by the fact that the great bulk of land was cultivated not by the owners but by their tenants. In Caird's day only one-eighth of the soil was farmed by its owners; subsequently between the two world wars occurred a remarkable change when the ratio rose to one-third. The circumstances which favoured the large farm in the eighteenth century persisted in the following century. Thus in the census report of 1851—embracing approximately 215,000 farms (five or more acres) with an aggregate of twenty-five million acres—about one-third of the farms had a hundred or more acres and covered four-fifths of the total acreage, while one-thirteenth of the farms had three hundred or more acres but they covered as much as one-third of the total acreage.

[1] See Chapter Eleven.

The late nineteenth century witnessed an attempt fostered by the state to increase the number of small farms—to re-create an English peasantry which, as in earlier centuries, might have a stake in the soil of their country. Agrarian reformers urged the necessity of instituting an agricultural ladder in order to keep labour on the land and check the rural exodus—and the chief rung of an agricultural ladder is a small holding to which the farm labourer who sought independence could aspire. The Small Holdings Act of 1892 laid down that county councils should establish small hold-ings, the state providing money for buying the land but the new owner paying immediately at least one-fifth of the price. It failed, partly because the county councils were dis-inclined to carry out their duties, partly because they did not have powers of compulsory purchase, and partly because small holders did not wish to sink all their available capital in buying a farm. The law of 1907 was intended to remedy these defects—firstly, by enabling the Board of Agriculture to take action in cases where the county council was negligent; secondly, by giving the county council the right of compul-sory purchase; and thirdly, by affording adequate facilities for tenants as well as for owners. Yet the measure did not prove very successful since it made no provision for strangers in want of local ties with the county where their application was lodged, nor for those who lacked the neces-sary experience and capital. Altogether before the first world war it furnished land for about fifteen thousand appli-cants and the area comprised about two hundred thousand acres, so that the public authorities have now become large landowners.

The lowest place in the agricultural hierarchy was occu-pied by the labourers. Their only capital, said Caird, lies in 'the furniture of their dwellings, their well-acquired experi-ence in all the details of husbandry, and the bodily strength to use it.' Half a century earlier William Cobbett had commented on the 'furniture' and 'dwellings' as he found them in some places: 'Look at the miserable sheds in which the labourers reside! Look at these hovels made of mud and of straw; look at the bits of chairs or stools, the floor of pebble, broken brick or of the bare ground; look at the thing called a bed; and survey the rags on the backs of the wretched inhabitants.' As regards 'bodily strength' Caird declared that 'till a recent period' wages were often 'below the means of maintaining' it, with the result that two men at low wages were kept to do the work of one well-paid labourer. He attributed the scanty remuneration of the farm labourers to lack of education and immobility—if they left the parish they risked the loss of relief in illness or old age. Their position only changed when a more extended area (the union) was substituted for the parish as the poor law unit, when the development of industry and transport increased the demand for men, and when the facilities afforded by steamships for emigration drew off the surplus rural stock. Above all, farmers were forced by the upward trend of wages— general in all industries—to use machinery; in turn this led to still higher wages of which the cost was compensated by superior skill and greater economy of labour. The evidence of statistics confirms the view that the condition of the farm worker markedly improved after the repeal of the corn laws. At the middle of the nineteenth century wages in some southern counties were scarcely more (at seven shillings a week) than they had been eighty years earlier when Arthur Young made his famous tours; but in the industrial north they were twice as high.[1] The disparity supported Peel's contention in the free trade controversy that they depended not on the price of agricultural produce but on the degree of proximity to manufacturing centres which offered alternative employment. The progress achieved by the end of the century is shown in the fact that the lowest rate (14s. 6d. in Oxfordshire) was double the lowest rate of the fifties, while

[1]	West Riding	Lancashire	Gloucestershire	Dorset	Oxford	Norfolk	Sussex
1767-70	6s.	6s. 6d.	6s. 9d.	6s. 9d.	7s.	8s.	8s. 6d.
1851	14s.	13s. 6d.	7s.	7s. 6d.	9s.	8s. 6d.	10s.6d.

the highest rate was treble.[1] In addition to payments in cash the farm labourer received allowances in kind. He also benefited greatly by the fall in price of his staple foods when they were imported freely from abroad. Money wages continued to rise in the twentieth century, and between the two world wars a minimum wage was instituted.[2]

In the economic affairs of nations as of individuals there is no assurance of permanence. With the late seventies came the turn of the tide: an era of prosperity yielded place to an era of depression. The effects of the repeal of the corn laws hitherto beneficial now began to work themselves out in an adverse influence upon rural society. The new situation was the result of two factors—the employment of steamers in ocean navigation, coupled with the opening up of the middle west of America by means of railways, enabled the United States to flood the English market with wheat. This was not due to a higher degree of efficiency. Caird affirmed (1878) that the average produce of wheat per acre was greater in England than in other countries: but henceforth it was brought into competition with wheat raised on the more fertile—because virgin—soils in the New World, where the produce per acre (though it was smaller) involved less labour and so was cheaper. Moreover the natural protection afforded by distance, which the English farmer enjoyed so long as it cost 11s. a quarter to send wheat to England, lapsed when grain was carried across the Atlantic under steam: by the nineties the cost had sunk to two-fifths and a decade later to a fourth. In the year of the repeal (1846) we imported 10 million cwts. of wheat and flour (of which $3\frac{1}{2}$ millions came from the United States), and 32 millions in 1860 (9 millions from the United States); in the late seventies there was a sharp advance in the upward trend which reached 68 millions in

[1] The general rise in agricultural wages in the second half of the nineteenth century is estimated at 60 per cent.

[2] Wages rose from 28s. (1924) to 34s. 7d. (1938); after the second world war there was a substantial advance. For the minimum wage, see Chapter Ten.

1880 (45 millions from the United States), and 96 millions in 1892 (61 millions from the United States).[1] The consequence was a drastic fall in price which in the eighties tumbled down by 20s. (the equivalent of 40 per cent.[2]), until it finally touched bedrock in 1894 at 22s. 10d. The result was seen in bankruptcies among farmers of whom many lost their capital, in remissions of rent even up to 50 per cent. (the average between 1878 and 1894 was nearly 25 per cent.), and in the reduction of wages of agricultural labourers. Confronted with this situation the English farmers began to lay down arable land to grass. The arable area diminished from fifteen million acres in 1871 to nine millions on the eve of the second world war; the permanent grass increased from eleven millions to sixteen millions. There was a decline in root crops, green crops, barley, and above all in wheat—in the seventies three and a half million acres were under wheat but two generations later the wheat acreage had shrunk to one-third.[3]

The conversion of arable into pasture had a profound significance, for it made the English people dependent on external sources for their food. Down to the last decade of the eighteenth century England was not completely divested of the status which she had enjoyed under the Roman Empire when she was styled 'the granary of the north,' since she still continued to 'feed other countries.'[4] For another six decades down to the repeal of the corn laws she continued to feed her own people, and the quantity of imported wheat was small. Then the pendulum began to swing in the opposite direction. In the latter half of the nineteenth century wheat imports multiplied tenfold. In the fifties one loaf out of four

[1] In 1913 we imported 123 million cwts.; the share of the United States (43 m.) declined to one-third; while nearly half (58 m.) came from Canada, India and Australia. In 1938 we imported 108 m.

[2] Between 1870 and 1877 the annual average price of British wheat per quarter was 52s. 10d. It fell in 1878–83 to 44s. 5d.; in 1884–92 to 32s. 6d.; in 1893 to 26s. 4d.

[3] It was $1\frac{1}{5}$ millions in 1931, but subsequently recovered to $1\frac{4}{5}$ m. in 1938. (The total area of England and Wales is approximately 37 m. acres.)

[4] See Chapter One.

came from abroad, in the seventies two out of four, in the eighties three out of five, in the present century four out of five.[1] Meat and dairy produce show a comparable position. Imports were negligible until free trade unlocked our ports and artificial refrigeration was adopted. Beef was brought from the United States in the seventies[2] and mutton from Australia in the eighties; eventually no less than three-fifths of our meat supply came from abroad. The immense growth in the consumption of imported food per head of the population is noticed below.[3]

Unable to meet the competition of corn or the inferior qualities of meat raised overseas, the English farmer concentrated his energies on those commodities in which external competition was powerless to injure him. Pasture-farming (no longer, as hitherto, combined with corn-growing) together with market-gardening now entered into their own. The very cheapness of grain, which was so detrimental to the corn producer, gave the producer of other foodstuffs his golden opportunity, because the fall in the price of bread left the industrial population with a larger margin for a more varied diet. The result was an expanding demand for meat, milk, butter, eggs, fruit and vegetables. In the case of meat the rising prosperity of the kingdom created a market for the best quality; great progress was made in the technique of stock-farming, and English pedigree cattle became famed throughout the world. Caird had claimed that in quality and quantity of livestock our country enjoyed superiority. Half a century later an official court of inquiry reached the conclusion that 'at no time has the livestock of Great Britain been of such high standard. In this respect it still holds a premier position.' Another branch of pasture-farming was dairying, and in the supply of fresh milk and cream the native producer possessed a monopoly. Simultaneously

[1] Home production of wheat in the United Kingdom amounted to 44 million cwts. in 1884, 29 m. in 1901, and 20 m. in 1931. It recovered to 39 m. in 1938 under the influence of a subsidy (see Chapter Fifteen).

[2] Argentina became the largest source of imported beef.

[3] Section on Commerce in the present Chapter.

the increased consumption of fruit and vegetables, eggs and poultry, resulted in more attention being paid to market gardening. Under the stimulus of these altered conditions, agriculture began to revive, and after the turn of the century it was described by a competent authority as 'sound and prosperous.' The recovery of farming from the depression of the nineties was reflected in a rise in the price of agricultural produce—even wheat rose almost 50 per cent. above its former bedrock price.[1] The momentous reversal which took place in public policy towards agriculture in recent decades will be shown in a later chapter.

The change in the system of production was accompanied by a numerical decline of English rural society, for tillage employs more labour than pasture-farming. During the first half of the nineteenth century the number of persons engaged in husbandry had continued to expand—though at a slower rate than the general population—owing to the enhanced demand for cereals on the part of a rapidly growing nation. When the corn laws were repealed, there were approximately a quarter of a million farmers and one million labourers in the fields. A century later the number of farmers remained the same but the number of employees had been halved. The decline in the wage-earning population was due mainly to the replacement of manual labour by machinery and to the contraction of the arable acreage. Subsidiary reasons for the rural exodus were the economic opportunities and social amenities of the towns, the lack of cottages, the reduction in juvenile employment. Yet the migration from the country was in general compulsory rather than voluntary: it was caused by the falling-off in the demand for agricultural labour. The course of events thus demonstrated the truth of Caird's observation (1878) that English 'agriculture is no longer influenced by considerations of the means of finding employment,' but seeks 'the largest produce at the least cost

[1] In 1894 it was 22s. 10d. Then it moved upwards and in 1913 it reached 31s. 8d. In 1934, during the great depression, it fell to 20s. 9d.—a figure unknown for centuries; but by 1938 it had risen about 40 per cent.

—the same principle by which the power-loom has supplanted the hand-loom.'

Commerce

The reconstruction of English agriculture in the nineteenth century was dictated by the new orientation of policy, which completely discarded the conception of a self-sufficing economy. England ceased to expect her farmers to feed her. 'Our foreign trade,' it was now proclaimed, 'enables us to add the food resources of other countries to our own.' Commerce thus assumed added importance when it was required to furnish the very necessaries of existence. It is not surprising then that the growth of industry was accompanied by a notable expansion in the volume of exports and imports. Exports were essential to provide employment for a population which increased from nine to thirty-three millions in the course of a hundred years, as well as to pay for imports in the shape of food and raw materials. At the same time our dependence on markets abroad meant that our national economy was exposed to vicissitudes in the world economy which were largely beyond our control. This element of instability was not a novel phenomenon but the area of its repercussions was widened and the gravity of its consequences proportionately deepened.

The exports of native produce, according to the values declared by merchants, advanced only slowly in the first half of the nineteenth century; the volume had grown immensely but values were depressed by the fall in prices due to improvements in methods of production. In the second half exports soared from £95 millions in 1855[1] to £291 millions in 1900 and to £525 millions in 1913. The impressive rise of 80 per cent. in the opening years of the twentieth century, in the face of acute foreign competition, was a signal refuta-

---

[1] The year 1855 is taken because the method was now adopted of valuing *imports* on the basis of their computed real values (instead of the widely different basis of official values). The values of *exports* had long been those actually declared by merchants—a practice extended subsequently (1870) to imports.

377

tion of the frequent jeremiads of ruin and decline. The importance of the external trade is shown by the fact that we shipped abroad almost one-third of our industrial output in 1907. Cotton manufactures held pride of place. They were followed in order of importance in 1855 by woollen manufactures, iron and steel, hardware and cutlery, haber-dashery, coal, etc.; and subsequently in 1913 they were followed by iron and steel, coal, woollen manufactures, machinery, chemical products, etc. Textile yarns and fabrics (cotton, woollen, linen, silk, etc.) accounted for 56 per cent. of the total exports in 1855 and 35 per cent. in 1913. The United States continued for a long time to be our largest customer: she took about one-fifth of our exports in 1855, but only about one-twentieth in 1913. Then came in 1855 India, Germany, France, Australia, etc.: in 1913 the order was India, Germany, Australia, the United States, France, etc. The proportion of exports taken by the Empire from the mother country in the latter half of the nineteenth century remained stationary at one-third. After the first world war the Empire's portion rose to 45 per cent.[1] and the Ottawa Agreements lifted it to 50 per cent.

The imports reflect the epoch-making change which had taken place in the national economy. Before the nineteenth century England raised at home bread to feed her people and materials to feed her staple manufacture. Now she is dependent on other countries for four-fifths of the wheat and three-fifths of the meat, for the whole of the cotton and nine-tenths of the wool, for more than a third of the iron ore, for all the petroleum and rubber, for most of the timber—and the list can be extended. In coal alone are the native resources sufficient for her needs. In order of importance our principal imports in 1855 were cotton, grain and flour, sugar, oils, timber, wool, etc., and subsequently in 1913 grain and flour were followed by cotton, meat, oils, wool, timber, sugar, etc. In the space of two generations imports

[1] Average of the years 1927–29. For the Ottawa Agreements, see Chapter Fifteen.

increased five-fold in value (£143 millions in 1855, £523 millions in 1900, and £769 millions in 1913). One-fifth of the imports came from the Empire in 1855–1900; the proportion rose to one-fourth in 1913 and to two-fifths between the world wars. The United States sent us about one-fifth of the imports: she was followed in 1855 by Germany, India, France, Netherlands, etc., and in 1913 by Germany, India, France, Argentina, Russia, etc. The growth in the consumption of imported foodstuffs is especially noteworthy because it was directly owing to a rise in the standard of living of the masses. In the second half of the nineteenth century[1] per head of the population eggs were multiplied thirteen-fold, butter seven-fold, cheese five-fold, tea and sugar over three-fold, wheat three-fold, tobacco[2] two-fold; imported beef and mutton, formerly negligible in amount, became a staple article of diet.

On the eve of the first world war England's external commerce, encircling the globe with a 'golden girdle,' attained its highest pinnacle. Her share of international trade accounted for no less than one-sixth of the world's imports and one-seventh of the world's exports. The commanding position which she enjoyed was due to a variety of factors. One was the policy of free trade. In the long run imports are paid for by exports; and when our doors were thrown wide open to the goods of other nations the latter were enabled to purchase our goods in return. The second was the high quality of many native wares. The reputation acquired in earlier ages was abundantly maintained when handicrafts were superseded by mechanical production. The third was the investment of capital overseas, which served the dual purpose of promoting exports and opening up new territories to provide us with food and raw materials. Long before the nineteenth century it was an established practice to export capital abroad. The colonies became a field for

[1] For the quantities imported per head of the population in 1913 and 1938, see Chapter Fifteen.

[2] On the eve of the first world war a writer commented that 'English women hardly smoke at all.'

379

enterprise from their foundation, and moneyed men sank considerable sums in them. It was asserted early in the eighteenth century that we 'supplied foreign princes, lent money upon bottomry [on the security of the ship] and upon commodities in all countries, the remittances from whence swelled the balance of trade so much in our favour.' Later in the century native capital was invested in French water and canal concerns and even in the Crimea; while Boulton and Watt frequently received payment for engines sold to foreign buyers in the form of shares in foreign companies. In the nineteenth century opportunities for international lending multiplied, and we acquired an interest in railways and other large undertakings throughout the world. It was estimated in the eighties that our investments of capital abroad amounted to £1,500 millions.[1] Moreover London as the world's money market financed short-term transactions on a scale which knew no national frontiers. England then had a standing similar to that now held by the United States, and John Bull was depicted as 'throned on his money bags.' In addition exporters and importers were furnished with the financial facilities needed to conduct their business all over the earth; while they also had at their command a mercantile marine which, owing to the existence of a universal network of coaling stations, could penetrate into every part of the globe.

The fourth factor which influenced the development of English commerce was that the 'Industrial Revolution' started in this country, and manufacturers profited by the priority which they enjoyed. The rotary steam engine, most of the machinery in textiles, many of the machine tools in engineering and new processes in steel-making were British inventions; and for a time they gave the industries concerned a semi-monopolistic position. There is, however, a tendency to exaggerate the importance of a temporary advantage. After all our oversea trade reached its climax at a period

[1] Giffen's estimate. The estimates for earlier decades are unreliable. Those for the present century are given in Chapter Fifteen.

when the United States and Germany were in the front rank
of the industrial nations; no doubt there was a change in
our situation relative to our competitors but the aggregate
volume of our exports enormously increased. Furthermore,
in spite of efforts to prevent the emigration of skilled artisans
or the transport of machines,[1] the secrets of the 'Industrial
Revolution' soon leaked out abroad. The secretary to the
Board of Trade told a parliamentary committee of inquiry
in 1840: 'We find in France that the principal foremen
in the cotton factories are from Lancashire; you find it in
Belgium, in Holland, and in the neighbourhood of Liège.'
In Vienna 'the directors and foremen' in the cotton mills
were 'chiefly Englishmen or Scotsmen from the manufactories of Glasgow and Manchester.' He added: 'You find
British capital going into Belgium, France and Germany to
a very great amount; and this very British capital employed
there producing manufactures' which competed with our
own exports. Nevertheless if other nations borrowed from
England in the first half of the nineteenth century, she in
turn borrowed from them in the second half; for instance,
the United States led the way with high-speed tools in
engineering, with sewing machines used in clothing factories,
and with machines for boot-making.

The organization of oversea commerce had already
crystallized into its modern essentials at the dawn of the
nineteenth century. London retained the ascendancy which
it had invariably claimed over its provincial competitors,
the outports, although the condition of the latter had im-
measurably improved since the seventeenth century. Bristol
was no longer second on the list because she had yielded
her place to Liverpool, while Hull came third. 'Free
trade,' in one of the older usages of the term, was now established in the acknowledged right of all persons to trade freely

---

[1] The legal restrictions on the emigration of artisans, imposed in the seventeenth century, were removed in 1825. The embargo on the export of machinery,
which also dated from the seventeenth century, was modified in 1825 when
the Board of Trade was given a discretionary power of relaxing the law against
the export of specified kinds of machinery, and it was finally abolished in 1843.

abroad without being a member of a privileged company. Several companies still preserved a monopoly within their sphere of influence, which they were doomed to lose within a few years.[1] As in former centuries commercial intercourse with other countries was conducted mainly by merchants, but some manufacturers sold direct to customers instead of employing the services of intermediaries. Merchants have always been accustomed to specialize in markets—as well as in commodities—and the practice continued notably in the case of cotton goods which were taken by different vendors according to the market for which they were intended. Merchants also fulfilled an important role in the structure of credit. The system of making advances to those who handled a commodity at each stage of production and distribution was applied to external in addition to internal commerce. Bankers and brokers financed merchants, who in turn gave credit to the other links in a chain which led ultimately to the producer overseas.

Similarly the channels of domestic trade have not undergone any radical alterations in the past hundred and fifty years, though the scale of operations is much enlarged. Fairs long ago ceased to enjoy the importance which they once possessed, yet weekly markets still furnish an opportunity for the sale of country produce. The Municipal Corporations Act of 1835 affirmed the legal right of all persons to set up shop without being a member of a gild—it made *de jure* what was already substantially *de facto*. The number of middlemen kept pace—perhaps more than kept pace—with the increasing complexity of the economic system due to the growth of population, to urban concentration, to expanding prosperity, and to the catering for special tastes and needs. The consumer became dependent for almost all his requirements upon the retailer, who sometimes bought direct from the makers, but more generally was supplied by wholesalers with the variety of produce covering his shelves. Co-operative societies with branches in the suburbs and

[1] See Chapter Four.

joint-stock multiple shops grew prominent in the second half of the nineteenth century, yet neither they nor the large departmental store have squeezed out the 'one-man business.'

Finance

Down to the nineteenth century the English currency system was one of bimetallism—that is, both gold and silver were legal tender; but in 1816 silver coins were made legal tender to the value of forty shillings only, and beyond this amount payments could be demanded in gold. Three years later another act of parliament provided that Bank of England notes, which were declared inconvertible in 1797 during the war with France, should gradually become convertible into gold. The transition period ended in 1821 when the Bank completely resumed payment in specie. The return to a metal currency met with considerable opposition. Attwood, a prominent advocate of a paper currency, urged that an abundancy of money would stimulate economic activities. 'Let the circulation be kept on so ample a footing as shall create a greater demand for labour than labour can possibly supply.' It is evident that there is no novelty in the current theories of 'full employment,' nor is there any substantial difference even in the proposed methods of achieving it. Attwood and his 'currency men' failed to carry conviction for proposals 'which few understand and all who did condemned' (so alleged a contemporary).

England was now on the gold standard, a term which means that the national currency is convertible into foreign currencies at fixed rates of exchange in gold. Her policy of free trade in gold—the absence of restrictions on its export— enabled her to attract gold whenever she needed it by the device of raising the bank rate. When the Franco-Prussian war broke out in 1870 she still remained the only state to adhere to the gold standard, but in the next few years her example was followed by the United States and the chief European countries. The first world war forced

England to create an inconvertible paper currency; then in 1925 the gold standard was again restored on the basis of the pre-war parity.[1] 'No one would dream of disturbing the settlement so arrived at,' it was authoritatively affirmed; within three years of this confident prediction the settlement had been shattered.[2]

The early history of banking has been sketched in a previous chapter. At the opening of the nineteenth century the sole joint-stock bank was the Bank of England, which enjoyed the right to issue notes. The right was shared, not by other London banks which had discontinued the practice, but by country banks now numbering nearly four hundred. A new era in banking was ushered in by the act of 1826 which permitted a joint-stock bank, without limitation as to the number of persons comprising it, to be set up outside a sixty-five mile radius from London; and these country joint-stock banks opened branches. Next came the act of 1833 which acknowledged the claim of corporate bodies in London itself to conduct banking functions except the issue of paper money: the first to take advantage of the opportunity was the London and Westminster Bank founded in 1834. The Bank Act of 1844 completed the series of legislative measures which formed the basis of the modern structure of English banking. This famous enactment embodied the principle that the amount of 'bank money' (bank notes) which may be issued should be regulated by the amount of gold held in the Bank of England. It laid down that the latter might issue notes up to fourteen million pounds against securities, and that any excess must be against coin and bullion. No other banks could issue notes other than country banks already exercising the privilege, and they were limited to the total of their current issue. Their rights lapsed if they became insolvent or were absorbed by another bank: in such cases the Bank of England could increase its own issue to a corres-

---

[1] The gold sovereign, however, was not restored to circulation.
[2] In 1931. See Chapter Fifteen.

ponding extent. The aim was to curtail the use of bank credit in times of speculation and trading booms. On three occasions in the nineteenth century the Bank Act was suspended owing to a financial crisis. The first was in 1847, the year of the 'railway mania,' when there was over-speculation in the shares of railway companies; it was also the year of a dramatic collapse of corn prices which were nearly halved, causing the failure of corn firms, banks, bill-brokers and others. The reserves of the Bank of England were depleted, so the chancellor of the Exchequer (1847) authorized it to enlarge the amount of its discounts and advances by issuing, if necessary, notes in excess of the statutory limitation. The sanction helped to relieve anxiety and restore public confidence. The second crisis occurred a decade later (1857). Originating in the United States, it invaded other national frontiers. The chancellor again empowered the Bank of England to violate the Bank Act in order to assist banks and bill-brokers. This was the sole occasion on which the Bank reluctantly decided to avail itself of the permission to expand the note issue beyond the legal maximum. The third crisis came in 1866. Impending war on the Continent produced a panic in which crashed, among other financial houses, Overend and Gurney who failed for several million pounds. Although the chancellor approved a breach of the Bank Act, no issue of uncovered notes was required. Upon the outbreak of the first world war in 1914 the Bank Act was a fourth time suspended.

One important change in the banking world was not indebted to legislative action. Nothing has contributed more to the security of the English banking system than the consolidation of a great number of small institutions—liable to be caught up in the whirlpools of a financial storm—into a few units of towering strength. The number of country banks grew in the first two decades of the nineteenth century from 386 to 781, but by 1841 it had fallen to 321 and it continued to fall. The rate of mortality was alarmingly high: between 1815 and 1830 over 200 banks became insolvent owing to

2 B

speculation with inadequate resources or to overlavish lending to customers. However in the eighties the private banks mustered 250, though henceforth they were more rapidly absorbed by the joint-stock banks and only about a dozen survived when the first world war started. The joint-stock banks underwent a similar shrinkage. None was in existence (except the Bank of England) before 1826, but there were 32 at the end of 1833 and 115 in 1841; they increased slightly in later years until in the present century the leading joint-stocks banks amalgamated into five great corporations, and few independent banks are now left. The English banking system thus presents a marked contrast with that which prevails in the United States, who has not hitherto favoured the building up of great financial houses equipped with immense resources and a nation-wide network of branches. One other development must be noticed. The cheque system is as old as the seventeenth century: an enormous application in modern times made it possible to economize in the use of a gold currency and subsequently of a paper currency.

Down to the nineteenth century taxation[1] was mainly indirect: it was levied in the form of customs duties on commodities entering the country or in the form of excise duties on commodities produced within the country. Edmund Burke claimed that 'our taxes for the far greater portion fly over the heads of the lowest classes.' Yet in the middle of the eighteenth century it had been estimated that a labourer paid over 6 per cent. of his scanty earnings in taxes on beer, salt, sugar, leather, soap, candles, tobacco, etc. Although some held the view that such taxes stimulated him to greater

---

[1] In earlier ages Crown revenue was derived from a variety of sources—the royal estates, feudal dues, taxes on movables (fifteenths, tenths, subsidies), customs duties, profits of justice. Two important taxes were instituted in the seventeenth century. One was the excise (intended to compensate for the abolition of feudal dues). The other was an income tax on real and personal estate, which survived almost entirely as a land tax. Other taxes, analogous to a property tax, included hearth-money, window tax, taxes on servants, carriages, animals, etc.

exertions, others contended (even as early as 1641) that 'the poor man's food should be free of all charges.' The 'second hundred years war' in which England was engaged with France necessitated huge increases in national expenditure and a corresponding advance in taxation. Much of the distress which prevailed during the 'Industrial Revolution' was attributed to the pressure of taxes. Thomas Paine in his *Rights of Man* spoke of the spectacle of youth going to the gallows and age to the workhouse, and he attributed the wretched condition of the people to wars and the taxes which they involved. It is noteworthy that a president of the United States in his inaugural address (1801) depicted the ideal state as one which did not 'take from labour the bread that it has earned.' During the first half of the nineteenth century the fiscal burden continued to fall heavily on the labouring population; and it was rendered still more oppressive when the corn law became a tax on bread.

The accepted theory of public finance was the theory of diffusion. It was believed that the weight of taxation was lightened by spreading it over as wide an area as possible. Accordingly taxes were raised on every conceivable commodity. The multitude of impositions with which all classes in the community were visited was immortalized by Sydney Smith. After enumerating the various duties which a man had to pay at each turn his description ends as follows: 'The dying Englishman pouring his medicine which has paid 7 per cent. into a spoon that has paid 15 per cent. flings himself back upon his chintz bed which has paid 22 per cent. makes his will on an eight-pound stamp and expires in the arms of an apothecary who has paid a licence of a hundred pounds for the privilege of putting him to death. His whole property is then immediately taxed from 2 to 10 per cent. Besides the probate large fees are demanded for burying him in the chancel. His virtues are handed down to posterity on taxed marble, and he is then gathered to his fathers to be taxed no more.' The reform of the fiscal system, described elsewhere, led to the reduction and eventually to the abolition of many hundreds of customs duties during the forties. It was accompanied by the sweeping away of excise duties on commodities produced at home, until there only remained a handful which included liquor and patent medicines. Taxes on journals, on paper and on windows disappeared together with licences for the sale of tea, coffee, cocoa, etc. It was estimated by a writer in the eighties that as a result a wage-earner with a family now paid about 7 per cent. of his income in taxes in this decade as compared with 16 per cent. in the forties.

To fill the gap created in the national budget by the drastic curtailment of indirect taxes, another mode of taxation was revived. The income tax had been instituted by Pitt near the end of the eighteenth century: with reluctance since it involved (in the words of Adam Smith) 'an inquisition more intolerable than any tax.' Pitt had sought to avoid the income tax—so he explained to Parliament in 1797—because it required 'such an investigation of property as the customs, the manners and the pursuits of the people would render odious and vexatious.' He conceded that 'if the amount of every man's property could be ascertained, it would be a most desirable thing to make the people contribute to the public exigence in proportion to their wealth. But there existed no means of ascertaining the property of individuals except such as were of a nature that could not be resorted to.' Instead therefore he adopted 'a tax upon general expenditure.' Nevertheless he found himself constrained by the insufficiency of the yield of the taxes on consumption to impose in 1799 an income tax which necessitated 'a scrutiny of property in every point of view highly objectionable. Incomes under £60 a year were exempt; at £60 and over the rates varied; at £200 and over the rate was two shillings in the pound. The tax was described as 'a great temporary exertion' to finance the war with France. Pitt asserted that in all previous wars 'the mode of raising money has been that of borrowing and leaving to posterity the burden of paying principal and interest.' Accordingly the income tax in its origin was designed to avoid lasting burdens by bearing the pressure for a short time. After the conclusion of the war Parliament forced an unwilling government to drop it (1816).

First used as an instrument of war finance, the income tax was restored in the forties in order to carry into execution the free trade programme of liberating commerce from the stranglehold of tariffs. In altered circumstances the mantle of Pitt now fell on Peel. In his turn he explained to Parliament the need for 'subjecting the opulent classes to the imposition of an income tax out of consideration for the permanent prosperity of our manufactures.' Yet even free traders, while they accepted the position as the lesser of two evils, shared the general aversion for 'those men with sharp noses and ink bottles at their buttons, who have gone prying about your houses and at your back doors to learn how many dinner parties you give in a year and to examine and cross-examine your cooks and foot-boys as to what your style of living may be.' Peel restricted the income tax—revived in 1842 at the rate of sevenpence in the pound—to a duration of three years, which would afford an opportunity of remedying 'a great public evil,' the deficit in the revenue caused by his commercial reforms.

Successive chancellors of the Exchequer protested their firm determination to abolish the income tax but meanwhile kept it in existence by renewals for limited periods. For half a century it continued to make its last but one public appearance in the national budgets. At length in 1874 it hovered on the very edge of the abyss in what now seemed a genuine farewell performance, for in that year the rate almost touched vanishing-point (twopence in the pound). However the tax-payer was once more disillusioned when it rose again. At the beginning of the first world war it stood at fifteen pence and at the end at six shillings in the pound; in the second world war, which brought within the net many millions of wage-earners, it soared to ten shillings[1] while on higher incomes

[1] These rates are subject to various allowances; and a minimum amount and a fraction of earned incomes are exempt.

there was in addition a progressive sur-tax. Thus after a long and chequered career the income tax had become a principal pillar of public finance.

Fed by two mighty streams of taxation, one direct and the other indirect, the state revenue expanded enormously with the ever-increasing prosperity of the country. Not only did the budget grow in size but it changed in character: from being primarily concerned with the defence of the realm and the payment of interest on war debts, it developed into an engine for redressing inequalities of wealth and carrying out a far-reaching social programme. The arid statistics of national expenditure are invested with a fresh significance, when they are used to interpret the trends in public policy. Prior to the long war with revolutionary France (1793) taxation produced about £19 millions. After the conclusion of peace until past the middle of the nineteenth century the amount settled down on a basis three times as large. The interest on the national debt absorbed about £28 millions or one-half, the defence services (army and navy) £15 millions, the collection of the revenue £4 millions; and so there remained only £10 millions for all other disbursements. In the latter part of the nineteenth century expenditure began to move upwards, and by the end it had exceeded the £100 millions mark. The Victorian age which regarded thrift as a moral duty was passing away and with it the pursuit of rigid economy in the conduct of the public finances. The first decade of the new century inaugurated an era of rapid growth in state spending—the amount rose to £150 millions in 1910 and almost reached £200 millions on the eve of the first world war. One cause of the increase was the enlarged civil service, of which the charge (£54 millions[1]) was over twice as high in 1913 as it was at the opening of the century—a notable indication of the extent to which the state was now exercising control over the lives of its citizens. Another cause was the burden of the defence

[1] Civil service expenditure includes civil departments, education, justice, public works, etc.

services which in the same period nearly doubled. A portentous element in the situation was the swiftly mounting outlay on social services especially education and old age pensions. After the first world war the budget totalled £800 millions or four times its pre-war size. The interest on the swollen national debt, pensions and expanding social services all absorbed immense sums; moreover the general level of prices had risen by about two-thirds, and this also contributed to swell the cost of the civil and defence services.[1]

The public attitude towards state expenditure has undergone a striking change. In the middle ages articulate opinion was insistent that the king 'should live of his own' and avoid taxing his subjects: in the seventeenth century the legislature showed the utmost reluctance to unloosen its purse-strings: in the eighteenth and nineteenth centuries a frugal administration was the nation's ideal. When the force of circumstances compelled governments to start an epoch-making departure from the traditional concepts, the 'disastrous expansion of the national expenditure' was viewed with dismay. Chancellors of the Exchequer found themselves confronted, as one of them deplored, with 'a universal demand for more and more expenditure every year for every conceivable object, all of them excellent objects but all of them pursued absolutely without regard to their cost.'

The change of sentiment was not wholly due to the 'excellent' or at any rate the apparently necessary 'objects' which presented themselves before a harassed Treasury. Two other factors were at work. One was psychological. During the first world war the nation became accustomed to an unprecedented pouring out of public money—separation allowances for the wives and children of service men; pensions for the disabled, widows and orphans; subsidies to keep down prices; high wages of munition workers; money gratuities

---

[1] In 1938 on the eve of the second world war the budget amounted to £1,006 millions. The defence services absorbed £254 m.; the civil services £431 m. (this included education £65 m. and pensions £43 m.); and the national debt £232 m.

391

to the demobilized. The golden manna had dropped on millions of families, and after the lavish outlay of the war years a return to cheese-paring economy was no longer tolerated. The other factor was the growing influence of a school of thought which taught the doctrine that it was incumbent upon the state to redress the inequalities between wealth and poverty, and to use the fiscal weapon as the means of effecting a social revolution—improving the distribution of the national income by taking from one class to give (in the form of social services) to another. The twentieth century repudiated the belief entertained by earlier generations that it was 'perhaps beyond the power of human legislation to correct' inequalities of property.[1] Pitt, in expounding this view to a House of Commons which was not likely to dissent from his argument, explained that the inequalities 'arise from our social state itself; and the correction of that order we cannot, as we ought not, attempt to alter. It would be a presumptuous attempt to derange the order of society which would terminate in producing confusion, havoc and destruction, and with a derangement of property terminate in the overthrow of civilized life.'[2] But in 1798, when all this was said, the mass of the nation had nothing to do with 'human legislation' except to obey it; in recent decades it has embarked upon the experiment of creating a new civilization through the medium of taxation, and the outcome still lies hidden in the womb of Time.

Although the yield of taxes grew prodigious, its real burden cannot be measured by its volume in terms of money. It depends upon the proportion which government expenditure bears to the national income: but here we enter into the

---

[1] In 1937, prior to the second world war, 44,452 persons had an annual income exceeding £2,000 but not exceeding £3,000; 20,269 persons = £3–4 thousands; 11,187 = £4–5 th.; 6,729 = £5–6 th.; 4,344 = £6–7 th.; 3,015 = £7–8 th.; 3,876 = £8–10 th.; 4,298 = £10–15 th.; 1,619 = £15–20 th.; 796 = £20–25 th.; 413 = £25–30 th.; 444 = £30–40 th.; 164 = £40–50 th.; 232 = £50–75 th.; 85 = £75–100 th. Lastly 99 persons exceeded £100,000 a year. In all 102,022 persons exceeded £2,000 a year.

[2] Hume believed that a state was weakened by 'a too great disproportion [of wealth] among its citizens.'

realm of conjectures. In the decade following the Napoleonic wars the national income was estimated at £300 millions;[1] in the forties at £500 millions; in the eighties at nearly £1,300 millions; at the turn of the century at £2,000 millions; and between the two world wars at £4,600 millions.[2] On the basis of these computations it would appear that the income of the community had grown something like fifteen-fold within the space of a hundred years, while oddly enough the budget also was fifteen times as large.[3] We are thus led to the arresting conclusion that the proportion absorbed by the state (about one-sixth) was approximately the same in the twenties of the nineteenth century as in the corresponding decade of the following century. But between the beginning and end of the period government expenditure lagged behind the national income, which in the second half of the nineteenth century was expanding fast; at the close of the century the proportion had sunk to one-twentieth. The Gladstonian principle of finance aimed at keeping down the burden of taxation and leaving money to fructify in the hands of its owners, in contrast with the current principle which favours the substitution of communal for individual spending. Then the trend of public policy was sharply reversed; and after the first world war the proportion again recovered to one-sixth.

Another valuable conclusion emerges from a study of the national debt. It was nearly nine times as large after the war of 1914–18 as it was after the war with France a century

---

[1] Parnell, *On Financial Reform* (1830), cites the following estimates: at the Revolution of 1688—£43 millions; Arthur Young (1776)—£100 millions; 'of late years'—£300 millions.

[2] The second and third estimates are Giffen's, the fourth is Bowley's, and the last is a Treasury estimate.

The sources of income *assessed for income tax* in 1937 were as follows—ownership of land and houses £573 millions; occupation of land £47 m.; government securities at home and abroad, and interest £293 m.; other dominion and foreign securities £86 m.; manufacturing and extractive industries £485 m.; distribution and transport £505 m.; finance and professions £217 m.; salaries assessed annually £965 m.; weekly wages of manual workers £820 m. See also Chapter Fifteen.

[3] From over £50 millions to £800 millions.

earlier, yet it constituted a smaller percentage of the total resources of the realm.[1] A third inference may be drawn from the estimates of the annual income of the community. The income (in terms of money) per head of the population quintupled in a century although the population itself had trebled.[2]

[1] The national debt was £262 millions in 1792 on the eve of the war with France. At the end of the war it was £885 m. In 1900 it had dropped to £629 m., but the Boer war raised it (1903) to £771 m. On the eve of the first world war it was £661 m., on which the interest was £25 m. After the first world war it fluctuated round about £7,700 m., on which the interest was £357 m. In 1938 it was £8,301 m., on which the interest had fallen to £232 m.

[2] The national income was estimated at £300 millions in the twenties of the nineteenth century, and at £4,600 millions a hundred years later.

Chapter Fourteen

THE NATIONAL ECONOMY (1815–1914)

III. The Organization of Labour

Side by side with the enlarged scope of industrial capitalism in the national economy proceeded its counterpart—the organization of labour. England was the birthplace of trade unionism. In our country it has enjoyed a continuous existence of two and a half centuries, and now occupies a unique position among the forces that shape and mould modern economic life.

The 'Industrial Revolution' did not give birth to the trade union movement. The conflict of capital and labour is far older than the age of machinery. History records examples of strained relations between employers and employed, which often equal and sometimes surpass in bitterness those afforded by the nineteenth century. In one form or another 'social unrest' has manifested itself for six hundred years. The workman's labour is a perishable commodity; he cannot withhold it for long or he may starve. This creates a situation favourable to exploitation, and from mediaeval times down to the present day the energies of the working class have been consumed in the effort to maintain and improve the standard of life. We meet with embryonic organizations confined to wage-earners—the journeymen or yeomen gilds—as far back as the fourteenth century: yet not until the beginning of the eighteenth century did there emerge a genuine trade union movement. Its tardy development was due to two main causes. While the craftsmen as a body were being transformed into a permanent group of wage-earners, the road to independence and mastership still lay open to the more enterprising among them; and so long as it was possible for a certain number of the hired workers to become masters, a stable association was out of the question. The leaders with more vigour and capacity than their fellows would constantly

395

be absorbed into the higher ranks of the industrial hierarchy. Furthermore the state at first assumed the function of guaranteeing 'a convenient proportion of wages.' It denied the right of working men to determine the conditions of their labour, yet it did not disclaim some responsibility for safeguarding the welfare of the masses.

In the later seventeenth century the obstacles which had hindered the evolution of trade unionism were rapidly disappearing. The prospects of attaining mastership had considerably diminished for all except those who were born to inherit or achieve leadership. Simultaneously under the influence of a full-fledged economic individualism fostered by the development of capitalism, there was a change of public policy. The state began to adopt a different attitude towards industrial problems and allowed the protective code of an earlier epoch to fall into disuse. Capital and labour were now left free in a large measure to pursue the paths marked out by their destinies. The workers were constrained to rely upon their own resources, and shoulder responsibilities which had hitherto been the province of the state. The beginnings of trade unionism must therefore be traced to the growing importance of capitalism, which not only narrowed the avenues to economic independence but was also emancipated from the shackles of an external authority in all relations with labour. It is at any rate significant that the Revolution of 1688, which brought to a final close the era of benevolent autocracy, should have been followed within a few years by an outburst of trade union activity; and this sudden eruption occurred in those industries where capitalist influences were strongest, and where a permanent body of wage-earners imbued with the consciousness of class interests was most firmly entrenched. The conclusion seems inevitable that we must associate the origin of trade unionism in England not with the introduction of machinery and the expansion of the factory system but with the movement successfully engineered by capitalism in the eighteenth century towards *laissez-faire*.

Although trade unionism was a well-established feature of English society prior to the 'Industrial Revolution,' it admittedly received an immense impetus from the changes set in motion by the great inventions. Machinery reduced the operatives to a complete dependency upon their employers, while concentration under one roof made it easier for them to combine together. Nevertheless the right of labour to organize was only very gradually conceded by the state. The movement did not commend itself to the governing class; and in 1799 the combination act made it illegal for the workers to act together in the pursuit of their economic interests. Henceforth any person who joined with others to increase his wages, or decrease his hours, was liable to be charged before a single magistrate (perchance one of his own employers) and, if convicted, sent to prison for three months. The same penalty was imposed if he attempted to persuade someone to leave his work, or if he refused to work with another person. He was also compelled to give evidence against himself—a violation of one of the fundamental maxims of English jurisprudence. The statute was modified the following year, when two magistrates were to act instead of one and they must not be engaged in the same occupation as the defendant.

In connexion with these famous measures it must be noticed, at the outset, that the principle of prohibiting trade unions was not new. There already existed numerous enactments directed against combinations in particular industries. The novelty of the law of 1799 lay in the fact that it was a general law—it penalized all combinations in all industries. Moreover earlier statutes had been framed on the notion that the regulation of wages and apprenticeship was the function of the state, and that trade unions could not be allowed to override and supersede the proper legal machinery. The combination act of 1799 was not framed on this understanding, for Parliament had grown definitely opposed to the regulation of wages or apprenticeship. Indeed it was largely prompted by political motives. The French Revolution had created a panic, and the government dreading a revolution condemned associations of working men partly from the fear that they would be concerned with political objects. At the same time the operatives themselves put forward claims which in the altered circumstances of the age were clearly impracticable. They demanded the prohibition of machinery and the revival of obsolete laws which limited the number of apprentices and required a seven years' apprenticeship. Prohibition of machinery would have meant economic stagnation. The insistence on a long apprenticeship took no account of the ease with which many technical operations could be learnt. And in view of large-scale production it was no longer possible to restrict the number of employees that a master might engage. Hence by associating itself with a reactionary policy trade unionism seemed to be incompatible with industrial progress.

The modern history of trade unionism may be divided into four periods. The first (1800–1825) was the period of legal repression when trade unions were banned by the law of the land. The second (the twenties and thirties) was the period of militancy and revolutionary tendencies, mainly inspired by the doctrines of the early socialists. The third was the period of construction and organization, and it culminated in the legislative achievements of the seventies. The fourth was the period of the succeeding decades, when unskilled labour was brought within the scope of the trade union movement which now entered into its full heritage as the representative body of the workers. Trade unionism thus followed natural lines of development. Emerging from obscurity and oppression it rioted at first in its newly-found liberty, but finally settled down to the work of building a stable and permanent edifice—gaining its reward in complete legislative and social recognition.

The outstanding figure in the first phase was Francis Place to whose devoted efforts, aided by Joseph Hume in the House of Commons, the repeal of the combination acts was mainly due. For several years Place worked to procure the repeal yet he worked almost single-handed. The rank and file of trade unionists did not believe that success was possible, and they fastened their hopes for an improvement of their condition upon an extension of the franchise. At length in 1824 Parliament set up a committee to inquire into the question, and this provided an opportunity for stating the case in favour of repeal.

The strongest argument was the oppressive character of the eighteenth-century statutes. The mere act of striking was construed as an infringement of the law. When the Scottish weavers went on strike in 1812, the justices found their demands reasonable; nevertheless the leaders were sentenced to imprisonment. If workmen went in a body to lay their grievances before a master they could be prosecuted for combination; if they agreed to leave his service in consequence of a reduction in wages they were liable to imprisonment; if they held a meeting—even at the employer's request—they had broken the law and were subject to its penalties. Another criticism was that the statutes were unfair: they did not deal out justice with an even hand. Nominally they applied to masters as well as men; in practice it was notorious (as Adam Smith pointed out) that the masters combined with impunity for the purpose of regulating wages. A prosecution was bound to be ineffectual since the law did not compel the masters, as it did the men, to give evidence against each other. Furthermore the combination acts had a pernicious influence because they embittered the relations of capital and labour. They created an atmosphere of suspicion and discord. The men smarted under a sense of grievance. They felt that they were not at liberty to dispose of their labour to the best advantage, and they looked upon their employers as oppressors. The settlement of disputes was also made more difficult. The men were afraid to go to an employer with their complaints for fear of prosecution; instead they met in private and decided on a strike or had recourse to violence. As trade unions were unlawful, the best men remained in the background and refused to hold office. Acccordingly the extremists took the lead, and there was greater likelihood of outrages. On their side the masters were tempted to take their stand on the high ground of the law and to show less inclination for compromise.

Convinced by the evidence placed before it the parliamentary committee recommended the repeal of the combination acts; and a bill was hurried through both Houses in 1824—'almost,' says Place, 'without the notice of members within or newspapers without.' As a result trade unions sprang up everywhere accompanied by an epidemic of strikes, due partly to an unwonted sense of freedom, partly to a rise in the cost of living. This aroused the employers who had been taken by surprise, and pressure was brought to bear upon the government to re-enact the statutes. Another committee was appointed; but the workers, though they had done little to win the repeal, now exerted themselves to retain it. So successfully was the case of the men presented before the committee that it dared not propose the re-enactment of the statutes. Instead it recommended that the common law, which had also been abrogated in favour of trade unions by the act of 1824, should be restored. The effect would have been to make all associations illegal; so an exception was proposed in favour of meetings held to discuss wages and hours of labour. These recommendations were embodied in the act of 1825, which legalized trade unions solely for the specific purpose of settling wages and hours. Their other activities were still illegal—for example, efforts to limit the number of apprentices, to intervene in the master's conduct of his business, to prevent the employment of non-unionists, to induce any man to leave his work by threats, intimidation or insults. For the next half century the legal position remained unchanged.

The repeal of the combination acts inaugurated the militant phase of trade unionism. Attempts on the part of employers to suppress trade unions had exposed the weakness of isolated unions and discredited the ordinary methods of collective bargaining. Moreover in 1832 Parliament had been reformed but power was given only to the middle class, and the restricted scope of the Reform Act seemed to show the futility of political agitation. The result was that organized labour became for a time enamoured of socialist aspirations. It is at this stage in the history of the labour movement that the two streams of socialism and trade unionism commingled. For one brief moment, indeed, it appeared as if the trade union structure would be captured by Robert Owen and completely diverted from its traditional lines of development. He laid before working men 'a plan of organization by which they might in a short time emancipate themselves from the thraldom of their present condition.' The 'plan' in his own words was as follows: 'I now give you a short outline of the great changes which are in contemplation and which shall come suddenly upon society like a thief in the night' though without violence or injustice. 'It is intended to include all the working classes in [one] great organization. All individual competition is to cease; all manufactures are to be carried on by national companies. All individuals of the specific craft shall become members, and these shall include all producers of wealth or whatever contributes to knowledge or happiness.' Henceforth, he proclaimed, 'there shall be no more masters, no more servants.' According to the ambitious scheme with which Owen now dazzled the vision of the trade union world, associations of producers were to supersede the capitalist organization of society, and the workers in each industry were to own and control that industry.

To give effect to these ideas there was formed in 1834 the Grand National Consolidated Trades Union, which was designed to unite all the manual workers of the country in one national society. It was attended at first with remarkable success, being rapidly joined by over half a million members including many thousands of agricultural labourers and women. Its exact policy was obscure. The executive apparently contemplated the gradual transformation of trade unions into co-operative associations, for it recommended the unions to employ their members and to open shops for the mutual exchange of their products; presumably it was intended for each union in this way to get the whole industry into its hands. A general strike was also contemplated, and its actual occurrence in our own times gives added interest to the picture drawn by an optimistic advocate. 'There will not be insurrection; it will simply be passive resistance. The men may remain at leisure; there is, and can be, no law to compel them to work against their will. They may walk the streets or fields with their arms folded; they will wear no swords, carry no muskets; they will present no multitude for the Riot Act to disperse. They merely abstain, while their funds are sufficient, from going to work for one week or one month; and what happens in consequence? Bills are dishonoured, the Gazette teems with bankruptcies, capital is destroyed, the revenue fails, the system of government falls into confusion, and every link in the chain which binds society together is broken in a moment by this inert conspiracy of the poor against the rich.' However the general strike never materialized. Instead the Grand National Union found itself involved in sectional disputes over wages and hours, and in those disputes its energies were largely frittered away. In March 1834 occurred the famous incident of the trial and transportation of the six Dorchester labourers for administering an oath. It created everywhere a great sensation and dealt a fatal blow at the Grand National Union. The employers seized the opportunity to destroy it by dismissing men who would not sign the 'document' (as it was called) in which they were required to dissociate themselves from the trade union movement. The Grand National Union thus disappeared, its members deserting it in thousands.

Although the trade unions had been brought within the pale of the law they still remained outside the social pale.

Public opinion was almost unreservedly hostile. The lord chancellor openly declared in 1834 that 'of all the most pernicious devices that could be imagined for the interests of the working classes as well as the interests of the country at large, nothing was half so bad as the existence of those trade unions.' The question then arises: what were the causes of their unpopularity?

The first ground of complaint against the trade unions was their secrecy. The privacy in which they shrouded their proceedings, and the oaths they imposed, were inspired originally no doubt by motives of safety in an era when it was illegal to hold meetings; but critics of the unions declared that secrecy was favoured because it influenced the minds of the ignorant. The ceremony of initiation into the society was designed to impress the superstitious fears of uneducated members. A pamphlet published in 1834 describes the reception of members into the Wool Combers' Union. The scene, we are told, is usually the first floor of a tavern and the time eight or nine in the evening. On one side of the apartment is a skeleton, above which is a drawn sword and a battle axe; and in front stands a table upon which lies a Bible. The principal officers of the union are clothed in surplices. The proceedings open with a prayer, then the workmen who are about to be made members are admitted with their eyes bandaged. After various preliminaries the bandages are removed from the eyes of the strangers, and they are placed opposite the skeleton. An oath is taken upon the Bible, in which they bind themselves never to 'act in opposition to the brotherhood in any of their attempts to support wages,' nor to disclose the proceedings of the lodge. The oath ends with an imprecation on the violator: 'May what is now before me plunge my soul into the everlasting pit of misery.'

The commonest charge levelled against the trade unions was their alleged tyranny. They were believed in some cases to have instigated the murder of recalcitrant employers and workmen. Apart from violence and outrage the unions were accused of adopting a dictatorial manner towards the employers. One example is the Builders' Union. A contemporary writer says: 'The lofty and imperious tone assumed in their communications with the masters brings to mind the grandiloquent edicts of Chinese dignitaries. "We consider," says one of these dispatches, " that as you have not treated our rules with that deference you ought to have done, we consider you highly culpable and deserve to be highly chastised." ' They required one master in a strike to pay the sum of four shillings per day to each of his men for every day the strike lasted. A Yorkshire union is said to have ordered the woollen manufacturers to pay time rates instead of piece rates. One of the manufacturers complained that his men did less work when paid on a time basis, whereupon he was instructed to keep no books.

Yet another criticism of the unions was that they did no good even to their own members. It was argued that high wages attracted new hands, whom the union must support to prevent the beating down of wages; and the contributions for such a purpose must come out of the pockets of those in work. The members must also bear the cost of officials and meeting-rooms, and suffer curtailment of employment due to a rise in prices and a consequent fall in demand. Again those who arrogated to themselves, not always with justice, the right to speak in the name of political economy declared the impossibility of a general increase in wages as a result of trade union pressure. The theory of the 'wages-fund' was at this period the orthodox explanation of wages. It was believed that at any given moment a fixed portion of the wealth of the country was set apart to pay wages, so that if any section of the workers raised their wages by compulsion they did so at the expense of their fellow workers. And lastly trade unions were condemned on the ground that it was disastrous to put any restrictions on capital. A rise in wages, ran the contention, meant a rise in prices which would endanger the whole fabric of foreign trade, and workmen would be the first to suffer for their misguided efforts to improve their position. 'Were we asked,' said a writer on trade unionism, 'to give a definition of a trade union we should say that it was a society whose constitution is the worst of democracies, whose power is based on outrage, whose practice is tyranny, and whose end is self-destruction.'

It is a testimony to the solidity of the trade union movement that, in the face of powerful hostile criticism and an antagonistic public opinion, it was able to win for itself a great place among the constructive forces of the nineteenth century. In the thirties barely tolerated by the law of the land and bearing the stigma of a social ban, trade unionism within half a century had achieved full legal recognition and even a distinct measure of social prestige. Trade union officials were no longer contemned as paid agitators but were accorded seats in the legislature and on royal commissions, and the altered attitude of employers was reflected in a growing willingness to meet union representatives around a common board. The causes and consequences of the transformation must now be examined.

After the failure of the Grand National Union the fever of militancy burned itself out. The glowing projects of 'Owenism' were discarded, and trade unionism entered on an era of fruitful activity and sober practical administration. One reason for the change was the prosperity of the country during the fifties and sixties: another was the growth of a new spirit among trade unionists. The desire for knowledge, the anxiety to comprehend the realities of the industrial situation, became more general. The new spirit manifested itself in the institution of classes for the discussion of economic problems, and in the publication of trade journals dealing with the interests of particular industries. In one of these trade journals remarkable stress was laid on the value of education. 'If you do not wish to stand as you are and suffer more oppression, we say to you get knowledge and in getting knowledge you get power. Let us earnestly advise you to educate: get intelligence instead of alcohol—it is sweeter and more lasting.' Moreover trade unionism in itself exercised a sobering influence over the workers, for it gave them a training in self-government. Ludlow, chief registrar of friendly societies, thought this result 'the most important produced by the trade society, and one which no other form of government as yet evolved among the working class can develop on so large a scale. No greater mistake,' he added, 'can be made than, as journalists and politicians are apt to do, to treat the mass of members of a trade society as dupes, idlers, drunkards or incapables, their leaders as knaves, strikes for higher wages as their common object. They represent almost invariably the bulk of the able, industrious and provident workmen in each trade: they are habitually well governed by men fairly elected by the members as the most trustworthy, respectable and intelligent amongst them.' The effect of trade unionism upon the character of the worker was warmly disputed. Hostile critics asserted that the better elements were losing their qualities of self-reliance and independence—their desire to excel and rise in the world being damped by the thraldom in which they were held by the rules of their union. Yet the trade unions maintained that the real tendency was to raise the character of the worker by making him feel that he was not the helpless victim of an industrial machine but the member of a strong united body, capable of defending his rights and ensuring him a resource in case of temporary need.

The spread of education, coupled with the experience gained in trade union administration, evoked a great reaction against the militant ideas of the thirties which showed itself in a strenuous denunciation of strikes. One union warned its members against what it called the dangerous practice of striking. 'Keep from it,' they were urged, 'as you would from a ferocious animal that you know would destroy you. We implore you brethren, as you value your own existence, to avoid in every way possible those useless strikes.' The Smiths' Union prided itself on being the original 'anti-strike' society. The preface to the rules states that at first it had indulged freely in strikes, but in 1845 a meeting of delegates decided that strikes were an unmitigated evil; they were 'battles between the employers and the employed, too often unwisely got up by one or both parties and continued more for the purpose of trying which shall gain the mastery over the other than otherwise.' In many cases the local branches were deprived of the power of calling a strike, for it was recognized that the authority of a branch committee was more liable to be overborne by the clamours of the rank and file. As a result the spokesmen of trade unionism were able to claim that the effect of the movement was to diminish the frequency as it certainly lessened the disorder of strikes.

The growing moderation of trade unionism, alike in its aims and methods, did not imply that the leaders were prepared to acquiesce in economic oppression; but they believed that their ends could be best attained by other means. Accepting the view which was then almost universally prevalent—that wages depend upon supply and demand, and that when the demand for labour exceeds the supply wages rise—they drew the conclusion that the best line of policy was to limit the supply of labour in any given trade and to restrict the amount of work which any individual might do. One device for executing this policy was to reduce the number of apprentices; another was to get rid of surplus labour by emigration; a third was to discourage piece-work and overtime in order to make the work last longer or go round a larger number of men.

It was during the forties and fifties and sixties that the structure of trade unionism in its modern form was built up on sound lines. The keynote of the period was organization, which was marked by three features—first, the creation of a body of trade union officials; second, continuity of membership; and third, increased financial strength as a result of combining industrial with friendly benefit activities. When the unions began to expand in membership it became necessary to have whole-time secretaries; and so there arose a class of trained officials expressly chosen for their business capacity, and uniting a sense of responsibility with a more intimate knowledge of the economic situation. There can be no question that the growth of such a class was a fundamental factor in laying the foundations of modern trade unionism. Another vital development was the evolution of a 'new model' of trade unionism, as it was then called. Instead of the trade union being purely a 'trade' society, concerned mainly with protecting the professional interests of its members, a type of union emerged which in addition to its industrial functions was a benefit society serving the purpose of an insurance society. It had the two-fold result of securing for the unions additional members and bigger funds. It also re-inforced the hold of a union over its members, since any member who was expelled for disobedience might forfeit the superannuation and other benefits. The outstanding example of the 'new model' was the Amalgamated Society of Engineers established in 1851 out of a number of independent societies. In process of time the defects of the 'new model' were revealed in the unwillingness of the officials to hazard the funds of their union by aggressive action. The aim, in fact, appears to have been to create uniformity of wages and hours throughout the country rather than to engage in constant endeavours to better them. It was the combination of financial solidity and moderation of purpose which effected a revolution in the public attitude towards trade unions, and thus made it possible for them in the seventies to win a much improved legal status.

The movement must now be studied in another light. It is a mistake to consider trade unionism exclusively from one angle: as an industrial society for regulating wages and hours, and as a friendly society for providing benefits. It has played an important role in raising the whole level of working class life, and takes rank as one of the great social forces of the nineteenth century. This aspect has not received the attention which it deserves. The history of the miners' union, in particular, furnishes a striking record of achievements. Macdonald, the president of the Miners' National Association, claimed before the royal commission of 1867 that the act of 1842 prohibiting the employment of women and children in the mines was due solely to the representations of the workers. Among other reforms the union pressed for more stringent laws to ensure the safety of the miners, more efficient inspection of the mines, uniform methods of weighing the coal and the right to have a check-weigher at every pit, the prohibition of truck,[1] the punctual payment of wages and the education of the children. Fifty thousand miners signed a petition in 1854 for a compulsory assessment on their wages to raise money for educational purposes. In short the miners' union placed foremost among its objects 'legislation for the better management of mines to protect the miners' lives, promote their health, and to increase among them a higher moral status in society.' Critics of trade unionism, who fastened exclusively upon its agitation for higher wages, ignored its other activities in pressing for legislative changes which otherwise might have been indefinitely retarded.

Side by side with the growing moderation and enlarged vision of organized labour proceeded another change. Ludlow in his book *The Progress of the Working Class* published in 1867 observed that 'the offensive spirit of mastership, which sought to carry everything with a high hand and settle all matters without considering the wishes or interests of the workers, has also greatly softened within the last few years. The capitalist is beginning to acknowledge the propriety of considering the welfare of the workers whose help he needs. He has almost ceased to insist upon his right to do all things in his own way simply because the capital is his.' The more tolerant mood of employers bore fruit in two directions. One was a greater willingness to meet their men around a common board; the other was a readiness (in some instances) to foster community of interests between capital

[1] Truck wages were paid in commodities instead of money.

and labour by admitting the latter to a share in the profits of the business.

Notwithstanding, the old type of employer who declined to recognize the trade union movement—or to concede the principle of collective bargaining—yielded ground slowly. He was represented at the royal commission of 1867 by Nasmyth, a distinguished engineer and a relentless opponent of trade unionism, who refused to deal with men except 'one at a time.' Yet Nasmyth's own career furnished an instructive commentary upon the results which his attitude towards organized labour provoked. 'I was so annoyed with walking on the surface of this continually threatening trade union volcano that was likely to burst out at every moment, that I was glad to give it up and retire from the business at a period of life at least ten years before the age at which I otherwise would have retired. And I am the envy of some engineers. They say: "You are a lucky fellow, Nasmyth; you took down your sign-board at the right time." ' The new type of employer sought to solve the labour problem in other ways than by taking down his sign-board. Mundella, an example of the enlightened leader of industry who had moved with the times, rejected the 'old feudal notion' of dealing with men singly, which made it possible to 'weed out the men that have any independence and screw down the rest to any terms.' He endeavoured to encourage more friendly relations between capital and labour on the lines of arbitration and conciliation. 'This system has been a complete educational process for our men; they know as well as we do whether we can afford an advance or not; they know whether the demand is good or bad; and they are accustomed to consider the effect of a fall or rise [in prices].' In other quarters the principle of profit-sharing was attracting attention in the sixties as a means of attaining industrial harmony. Thus the pressure of trade unionism was gradually winning for the worker a new status as an equal partner to the industrial contract; and, in the face of so momentous a development, employers were constrained to recognize that their business was no longer their business alone. It was the starting-point of a new order of things.

We come to the decade of the seventies when trade unionism registered a fresh advance in the clarification of its legal position.

The legal insecurity of the trade unions was brought home to them by an event which occurred in 1867. The unions had begun to accumulate large funds, and the amount then exceeded a quarter of a million pounds. It was suddenly discovered that these funds had no legal sanction. The Boilermakers' Society summoned the treasurer of a Bradford branch for embezzlement. The magistrates ruled that, as unions did not come under the Friendly Societies Act, their funds could not be protected. The decision was confirmed upon appeal, when the judges also declared that the union was illegal on the ground that its objects were 'in restraint of trade.' To understand the judicial pronouncement it must be remembered that the act of 1825 had legalized trade unions expressly for two purposes, and two purposes only— the regulation of wages and hours. Now nearly all trade unions had rules relating to piece-work, overtime, the number of apprentices, etc.—rules which, according to the law of the land, were 'in restraint of trade.' Hence trade unions were unlawful associations and their funds therefore were unprotected. The year that witnessed this legal bombshell saw the political emancipation of the working class when the Reform Act of 1867 extended the franchise in towns, and the unions were not slow to use the influence they had acquired. The liberal government in 1871 recognized their power by bringing in a bill under which no trade union was to be considered illegal on the ground that it was 'in restraint of trade;' every union could be registered as a friendly society and so receive protection for its funds; and no trade union could be sued in a court of law. It seemed as though trade unionism had secured everything which it desired, but the bill was found to contain a serious flaw. Although the unions obtained full legal sanction, their action was restrained by the prohibition of peaceful picketing. Four years later a conservative government in its turn recognized their power by legalizing a limited degree of peaceful picketing.

The seventies also witnessed an attempt, started by Joseph Arch, to spread trade unionism among farm labourers where the movement had always been extremely backward. In all other industries the advent of the 'Industrial Revolution' did away with the isolation of the worker. The factory system served to concentrate great masses of men under one roof, and the result was not only to render possible concerted action among them but to imbue them with a consciousness of economic strength. The agricultural changes during the same period produced the opposite effect. The open field method of cultivation vanished from the face of England, and with it went the intermixed holdings and joint husbandry. The inhabitants of a village no longer toiled side by side in the fields, associated together in a general partnership and carrying on in common all the chief operations. The English countryside was now covered with hawthorn hedges and ring-fenced farms, and the labourer stood alone like the tiller of the soil in Millet's famous picture. The scattered condition of the rural population appeared to offer an invincible obstacle to the development of a vigorous trade union. The individual farm worker lacked the sense of security which is instilled into a crowd by the confidence born of numbers. Moreover his exiguous resources did not easily stand the strain of a weekly contribution to the trade union funds. The difficulty of conducting propaganda in the teeth of these discouragements was almost insuperable.

Many thousands of farm labourers had joined Robert Owen's movement (in the thirties), but the latter soon collapsed. After an interval of forty years a new campaign started in Warwickshire under the inspiration of Joseph Arch. It attracted the attention of the press and public sympathy was aroused. The National Agricultural Labourers' Union was formed and soon counted nearly a hundred thousand members. Other trade unions came to its support, realizing that underpaid labour in agriculture was a menace to organized labour in towns. The farmers retorted with a lock-out. They were unwilling to concede the right to combine or the right to strike. The struggle which had commenced auspiciously was not maintained. Agriculture began to enter upon a period of acute depression owing to the influx of American wheat. In the altered circumstances it became useless to struggle for higher wages, since arable land was everywhere being laid down to grass with a consequent reduction in the number of men employed. The membership of the National Union fell off rapidly and ultimately it barely exceeded a thousand.

In the most recent period of modern trade union history the first outstanding event was the emergence of unskilled labourers. The great mass of workmen were outside the trade unions. It is true that, as in the case of Owen's union, they were sometimes brought within the movement yet it was a temporary phenomenon. The reasons for their exclusion were the high weekly contributions and (in some unions) the fact that admission was only through apprenticeship. 'The great bulk of our labourers,' wrote a prominent leader, 'are ignored by the skilled workers. It is this selfish snobbish desertion by the higher grades of the lower that makes success in many disputes impossible.' There was thus a real danger that the trade unions would be confined to superior workers, the aristocracy of labour, and isolated from the unskilled section—with a consequent cleavage in the world of labour.

The situation was transformed by the great dock strike in 1889, one of the landmarks in the history of trade unionism because victory was achieved in spite of weakness. The success of a strike by the women employed in making lucifer matches, although they lacked funds and organization, followed by the success of the gas workers who won a reduction of hours from twelve to eight, stimulated the efforts to raise the status of the dock labourers. The dockers too were devoid of funds and organization, but public opinion rallied to their support and they gained their demand of sixpence an hour. Unions came into existence among dockers, railway servants and others, which at first were intended to be fighting unions unencumbered with sick or accident funds. They sought to bring about an improvement in the working conditions, and the funds were to be used solely for purposes of strike pay. In other words they were purely trade societies. This was known as the new trade unionism—the 'new model' of the eighties—yet actually there were always unions with only trade objects, just as there were always unions which combined trade objects with friendly benefits. The reasons why the unskilled workers favoured the trade society were partly that a union which was not burdened with friendly benefits was believed to be a better fighting instrument, less cautious and more aggressive; and partly that it was necessary to have a low contribution in order to attract the poorly paid. The refusal to combine insurance benefits with trade functions was short-lived, but the permanent effect of these years remained in the increased solidarity of the wage-earners. The older unions modified their exclusiveness, and greater sympathy was henceforth shown with the unskilled labourers.

Early in the twentieth century trade unionism found its legal position once more assailed. In 1900 a strike, at first unauthorized, occurred among the employees of the Taff Vale railway company in South Wales. The strikers committed certain unlawful acts, and the railway company against the advice of its own lawyers sued for damages not the workmen but their union—the Amalgamated Society of Railway Servants. The case was taken to the House of Lords, where it was decided that a trade union could be sued for any injury or damage done by any person deemed to be acting as an agent of the union. The decision implied that a union was responsible for unlawful acts even when committed by an agent contrary to its express instructions. The Amalgamated Society had not authorized the strike nor the unlawful acts, yet it was compelled to pay a substantial penalty. In 1906 the Trade Disputes Act gave a trade union immunity from civil action on account of any unlawful act 'committed by or on behalf of the union.'

Shortly afterwards followed the Osborne judgment. In 1908 a member of the Amalgamated Society took legal proceedings to prevent the union using its funds for political purposes, and the House of Lords returned a verdict in his favour. The law lords determined, first, that trade unions were to be deemed corporate bodies; second, that as such they existed for certain defined purposes; third, that the latter were laid down in acts of parliament; and fourth that since political action was not expressly referred to in those acts it must be considered outside the scope of trade unions. The result of the judgment was to stultify all their activities not specifically mentioned, for example, even educational work. In 1913 the Trade Union Act allowed a trade union 'to include in its constitution any lawful purpose,' so long as its chief objects were those of a trade union as defined in law, but in the case of political objects expenses were to be met out of a political fund, from which any member was at liberty to claim exemption by 'contracting out.' After the general strike of 1926 which lasted nine days,[1] the act of 1927 substituted the system of 'contracting in' for 'contracting out,' that is, a member did not pay the levy unless he entered into a contract to do so. This act was repealed in 1946 by the labour government which restored the former practice.

In other directions the movement made notable advances since the early years of the present century. There has been a great expansion of membership and the number of trade

[1] The general strike involved about 1½ million workpeople. In the strikes of this year (1926) the aggregate duration of working days of all disputes amounted to 162 millions, as compared with an annual average of 3¼ millions in the years 1927–38.

unionists runs into several millions,[1] while the financial
strength of the unions is shown by their accumulated funds.
The unskilled workers, organized at the end of the eighties,
now account for a large percentage of the total membership.
The organization of women workers was stimulated in particular by the first world war. The majority are members of
trade unions admitting both men and women, though some
belong to unions which are confined to women. In the case
of agricultural labourers the earlier trend has revived.
Another noteworthy feature has been the extension of the
movement to what is sometimes termed the black-coated
proletariat—shop assistants, clerks, teachers, civil servants,
actors, journalists, bank officers and law court officials. One
important development is the National Union of Railwaymen, which affords a striking example of a 'new model' of
trade unionism (this is the third use of the term we have
noticed): what is commonly called to-day 'industrial unionism.' The structure of a trade union may assume various
forms. A craft union embraces men engaged on the same
kind of work, for instance, cutlers or bricklayers. Occupa-
tional unionism comprises people working on processes
which are kindred, such as engineers. Industrial unionism
exists when the union brings together under one comprehensive umbrella everybody connected with the employer:
the National Union of Railwaymen endeavoured to include
employees at railway hotels, railway printing works, and so
forth. In short, instead of the workers being grouped on the
basis of their occupation, they are grouped on the basis of
the industry to which they belong.

In these latter years organized labour not only won a
unique legal status but it also came to enjoy an official status
in all affairs which implicated manual workers. This measures
the remarkable advance made by trade unionism since
the days when the movement was proscribed by law.
Even before the first world war the trade unions had been

[1] In 1938 there were 1,021 trade unions in Great Britain and Northern
Ireland, with a membership of six millions.

made agents of the state in the administration of the Insurance Act. During the war organized labour secured the greatest influence in all matters which affected labour. Trade unions have now gained the right to be consulted by the government; their position is fortified by state recognition; their dignity, prestige and strength are proportionately enhanced. Two other developments may be briefly recorded. The first is the constitution of trade unionism as a definite political movement. The second is the claim of organized labour to participate in the control of industry. Its activities are no longer confined to problems such as hours and wages: its horizon has widened and it seeks a share in the management of industry.

The future of trade unionism must depend in a considerable measure upon the discretion evinced by the leaders, and upon the discipline displayed by the rank and file, in using the extensive powers conferred on them by a privileged legal status. Yet so far as its past history is concerned, it can fairly claim the credit of notable achievements in ameliorating the condition of the wage-earners. Firstly: it has been an important factor in raising the standard of life of the workers because it has enabled them to reap fuller benefit from improvements in the economic situation. Secondly: it is almost universally recognized that collective bargaining is necessary to place employers and employees on a footing of equality—otherwise it is more difficult for the wage-earners to make their voices effectively heard. Thirdly: trade unionism protects a good employer against those competitors who seek to capture the market not by superior efficiency but by scaling down the wages bill. Fourthly: trade unionism leads on the whole to stability in industry. It discourages 'lightning' strikes—not indeed invariably but as a general rule—for where the workers are organized they tend to have a deeper sense of responsibility, and they feel more secure in the knowledge that their interests are safeguarded by their own expert officials. Most employers, in fact, prefer to deal with representatives of organized labour since it serves to diminish friction in running the industrial machine. In this connexion it may be noticed that the loss of working hours due to strikes is relatively negligible: over a period of years it does not average more than one-half of one per cent. of total working time, and is much less than the loss caused by sickness or unemployment. The evil of such stoppages lies elsewhere—in the embitterment of the relations between employers and employed. The moral effects of trade unionism in inducing a feeling of confidence, and increasing the self-respect and dignity of the workers, must also be taken into account. Finally trade unionism, wherever the members of the union are alive to their obligations, affords a training in democracy. These moral and political consequences of trade unionism have an economic reaction, because they promote greater competence and so help to create the type of artisan that modern conditions necessitate: for machinery demands of the worker intelligence, high character and regularity of conduct.

Chapter Fifteen

THE REVIVAL OF
ECONOMIC NATIONALISM
(1914–1939)

For a century after the fall of Napoleon the growth of
English society was undisturbed by any serious menace
to national security. Shielded in its impregnable
island home by the navy and by continental alliances, it
pursued the arts of peace and gave full reins to the untrammelled development of the economic system. Then in
the brief space of twenty-five years it was twice exposed to
titanic convulsions, which shook the foundations of national
life and necessitated the mobilization of all its resources in a
stupendous effort to wrest victory from the very jaws of
defeat. The two world wars produced epoch-making changes
in England's economic policy, involving a momentous
departure from the orthodox principles that held sway in the
nineteenth century. After the first world war she was confronted with the broad issue whether she should adhere to
her existing economy, which was exposed to the vicissitudes
of international trade and combined prosperity with
instability; or whether she should return to the notions
of an older economy based on self-sufficiency. The choice
which she made repudiated the concept of economic
internationalism based on specialization and reverted to
economic nationalism which had appeared extinct. After
the second world war whose effects are being worked out
before our eyes, she embarked upon the task of circumscribing the sphere of private enterprise—another deeply
cherished concept of the pre-war era. The principles of
laissez-faire, qualified only by the restraints arising out of
social legislation, had seemed practicable in an age when
this country was relieved from the fear of invasion and sea-
power gave it an unchallenged pre-eminence. Once these

419

conditions ceased to prevail, a situation parallel to that which existed before the nineteenth century restored the state to its former position of authority and control in the economic order; and the prospect opened up a vista of far-reaching possibilities. In the present chapter we shall review the outstanding feature of the troubled decades which bridge the two world wars—the resurgence of economic nationalism when the English people discarded the historic tenets of free trade and substituted a commercial system bristling with a plethora of restrictions—tariffs, imperial preferences, 'quotas,' and bilateral treaties. In the reversion to a mercantilist viewpoint long discredited the wheel had come full circle, and the clock of history appeared to have been put back a hundred years.

When the inter-war period (1919–39) is compared with the opening years of the present century one unmistakable element in the national economy clearly emerges—namely, the contraction in the oversea trade with its sharp repercussions upon the prosperity of a vital group of export industries and upon the volume of unemployment. The true meaning of the contraction can best be appreciated if it is set against the general position in international trade, by which is meant the total of exports and imports of all countries. International trade rapidly recovered from the effects of the first world war. Already in 1924 it approximated to its level in 1913, and on the eve of the great depression (1929–33) it was one-third higher. It then decreased but the set-back was only temporary. While international trade expanded, our share of it declined. Before the first world war the United Kingdom (including Ireland) accounted for one-sixth of the world's imports and one-seventh of the world's exports; yet in the two succeeding decades the percentage of imports fell frequently below its former level, while that of exports was always considerably below it. As a result the percentage of our national production which was exported began to shrink: it was 30.5 in 1907, 27 in 1924,

22 in 1930, and after the depression the fall continued. This meant that instead of shipping abroad a third of our national output we sent eventually only about a fifth.[1] The principal reason was a change in world economy which caused our older industries to lose their former markets. The nineteenth-century equilibrium based on the international division of labour was bound to be disturbed when countries emerging from a purely agricultural stage turned to a less homogeneous structure. With the aid of protective tariffs they sought to develop their own manufactures, and this limited their dependence upon English staple commodities—especially cotton products which formed a substantial part of our exports. Now a reduction in the total volume of exports is not necessarily an indication of national decline: it may imply that less capital is being invested abroad or that the terms of trade have moved in our favour (that is, imports can be purchased more cheaply). But inasmuch as the industries engaged in the export trade cannot adjust themselves overnight to the altered situation, there ensues a serious maladjustment in the economic balance of the exporting country which is reflected in a considerable increase of unemployment.

The plight of the staple export industries was one of the crucial phenomena of the inter-war years. The statistics of coal, cotton, shipbuilding, iron and steel bear eloquent testimony to their depressed condition in the years 1919–39. In the coal industry the number of workers diminished by one-third (namely, four hundred thousand), and the export of coal was reduced to about three-fifths. It has been surmised that the oversea demand for English coal was affected by substitute products, electricity and oil. In reality the loss of our external markets was due to the development of coal-mining abroad (the result of a world shortage of coal during the war) and to foreign competition in neutral spheres. A similar explanation covers the decay of the cotton

[1] It was a smaller percentage of a larger total, since the volume of national production had increased.

industry, which formerly had been *par excellence* an export industry since the home market absorbed only one-fourth of its production of cloth. Here also the number of workers diminished by one-third (namely, two hundred thousand), and the export of cotton piece goods was reduced to about one-quarter. The growth of the Indian cotton industry under the protection of a tariff ($3\frac{1}{2}$ per cent. *ad valorem* 1914 and 25 per cent. 1933) deprived Lancashire of its largest oversea customer; and the severity of Japan's competition may be gauged from the fact that eventually her exports exceeded our own by nearly 50 per cent. The consequent redundancy of spindles and looms raised an acute problem of surplus productive capacity. The protracted delay in securing agreement to schemes of reorganization was mainly the sequel of financial inflation during the boom of 1920, which left a legacy of over-capitalization (in many concerns the nominal value of the share capital was trebled) and heavy debt charges.

The difficulties of the shipbuilding industry were created by the transition from a war to a peace economy. Its yards had been enlarged to meet war-time needs; while other powers too, especially the United States, built ships. After the war the rise in freights led to an increase of one-third in total world tonnage: the subsequent drop in freights lessened the demand for new merchant vessels. Both the number of workers in the shipbuilding industry, and the tonnage of merchant vessels built in its yards, diminished ultimately by almost one-half. As a result the United Kingdom owned only one-fourth of world shipping instead of two-fifths; it built for foreign owners only one twenty-fifth of its total output instead of one-fifth; it launched only one-third of the world mercantile marine instead of three-fifths. In addition disarmament meant fewer warships, and these had been responsible for a considerable proportion of our pre-war tonnage. Thus the productive capacity of the shipbuilding industry was in excess of peace-time requirements. The situation was worsened in the thirties by economic nationalism to which even this country succumbed, for it contracted the carrying trade. A report on tramp shipping (1933) declared that in consequence 'British tramp shipping has been brought to the edge of bankruptcy.' The iron and steel industry, whose production was greatly extended during the war of 1914–18, was confronted with a similar problem of redundant capacity. Other nations had pursued a policy of expansion and our exports were adversely affected. In the group of export industries here surveyed not only was the total number of workers reduced, but unemployment among those who were retained was much above the normal percentage.

Public attention came to be focussed primarily upon the most distressing symptom of the economic malaise— unemployment, which was generally regarded as 'comparatively speaking a new phenomenon.'[1] Actually the problem has persisted for hundreds of years. Before the 'Industrial Revolution' it is probable that at least 5 per cent. of the working population was unemployed owing to normal factors such as variations in consumers' demands, seasonal fluctuations, dependence on intermittent water-power. Trade depressions (for instance in the reign of James I) increased the percentage. In addition unemployment was due to 'technology,' that is, improvements in industrial technique: during the nineteenth century it may be safely assumed that operatives were displaced when machinery worked by women and children was introduced. Unfortunately we have no precise statistics of unemployment before 1920. The trade union returns cover alone the organized and skilled workers among whom the rate of unemployment was probably below the general rate; and the early figures are based on very few records. The average was 5 per cent. in good years and 10 per cent. in bad years. The severity of the depression at the end of the seventies and in the eighties—when prices, interest and profits fell—produced figures comparable with those which impressed themselves upon the public

[1] So it is described in official reports on unemployment.

mind as 'a new phenomenon' after the first world war. Ironfounders, iron shipbuilders and boilermakers reached 22 per cent. and engineers 13 per cent. Although this depression excited much concern, other decades in the nineteenth century had also registered a high percentage of unemployment.[1]

If unemployment is not new, neither is the public awareness of it though the degree of sensitiveness has become more acute. It was a frequent complaint in earlier centuries that the local authorities neglected to discharge the duty laid upon them of finding work for the unemployed. Even those who conducted a campaign against 'the dangerous tendency' to extend the functions of government were constrained to admit (as an influential journal did in 1857) that 'this is a case where an economic law should yield to a social law to avert as far as possible the terrible strain on one class of the community.' During the American Civil War when the cotton famine brought distress to Lancashire, Parliament authorized government loans to the local authorities for putting the unemployed on relief work. This created a precedent for the 'Circular' issued in 1886 recommending municipal employment for the 'respectable unemployed' instead of leaving them to the poor law unions; and the principle was embodied in the Unemployed Workmen Act (1905), which contemplated farm colonies where men could be trained in husbandry. Next came the institution of labour exchanges in 1909—followed two years later by compulsory unemployment insurance on a contributory basis and administered by the state, which afforded a guarantee of minimum subsistence for those thrown out of service through no fault of their own. The Unemployment Insurance Act of 1911, however, was restricted to a very few industries; it was extended in 1920 to over eleven million wage-earners and

[1] The highest percentages in any decade recorded in *The Statistical Tables and Reports on Trade Unions* (1888), were as follows: *Engineers*—9·8 (1858), 8·3 (1868), 13·3 (1879), 7·4 (1886). *Ironfounders*—16·0 (1858), 18·0 (1868), 22·3 (1879), 13·9 (1886). *Iron Shipbuilders and Boilermakers*—20·4 (1879), 22·3 (1885), *Blacksmiths* reached 15·9 (1885).

subsequently its scope was widened still further. The policy of financing public works was continued by making special grants to local authorities in aid of improvements such as roads.

Although neither unemployment nor the effort to alleviate it is novel, the English people have grown more deeply conscious of the gravity of the problem. One reason is that exact figures are now available owing to the system of insurance instituted after the war of 1914-18. Another reason is that the war markedly expanded the volume of unemployment. The normal economic equilibrium was disturbed by the substitution of a war economy for a peace economy. To meet the insatiable demands of the war such industries as coal-mining, shipbuilding, iron and steel were inflated by an increase in the number of workers, and once these demands ceased the process of adjustment to peace-time requirements proved slow and intractable. The inevitable changes in oversea markets due to industrial developments in other countries also had profound repercussions on those branches of the national economy which catered for the export trade. The third reason is that this unemployment was not evenly spread over the whole country but was largely concentrated in the 'depressed' areas, so that it assumed a more sombre aspect than when it was expressed simply as a percentage of the insured workers. The fourth reason is that the community has grown more sensitive to the economic wastage and social misery caused by unemployment—the loss in production, the deterioration in skill, the decay of apprenticeship, the privations of poverty, and the lowering of morale. The fifth reason is that the workers are more articulate and the organs of public opinion pay greater attention to the problem.

The number of unemployed varied. At the end of 1921, when the slump in trade which followed a fleeting post-war boom was at its worst, it was nearly two millions or 16 per cent. of the insured workers. Then down to the thirties it averaged 11 per cent.—that is, roughly one and a quarter million people (one in nine) were unemployed prior to the great depression of 1929–33. This does not mean that the same persons were in continuous unemployment the whole time. The personnel of the unemployed kept changing. There was a 'hard core' comprising those out of work for long periods, especially in the coal-mining industry, but the main portion was unemployed for short periods. How far was the first world war responsible for the situation? To answer the question we must look at the statistics of unemployment during the preceding decade, when trade union returns show an average of 5 per cent. Allowing for their incompleteness and a different basis of calculation, the broad conclusion emerges that one of the economic consequences of the war of 1914–18 was to double the normal percentage of unemployment. Another illuminating fact is that nearly one-half of the unemployed was concentrated in the 'depressed' (or 'special') areas—south Wales, Lancashire, the north-east coast and south-west Scotland—which contained only about a quarter of the total population. In these areas were situated the staple export industries of coal, cotton and shipbuilding. The problem of unemployment was thus in a large measure a problem of the export or 'unsheltered' industries; and their plight is shown further in the fact that though the insured workers increased by three millions between 1920 and 1939, the numbers engaged in the export industries diminished. The benefit of the increase went to the 'sheltered' industries which catered for the home market. Coal, cotton, shipbuilding, iron and steel not only registered a marked decline in the numbers of their workers, but their percentage of unemployment was higher than the average for all industries: in shipbuilding it sometimes exceeded one-third, in iron and steel one-quarter.[1]

We must also inquire why the disparity between pre-war

[1] The percentages of unemployment in leading industries were as follows— *Coal* 15 (1925), 41 (1932), 22 (1938). *Pig iron* 25 (1925), 44 (1932), 16 (1938). *Steel* 26 (1925), 48 (1932), 24 (1938). *Shipbuilding* 35 (1925), 63 (1932), 21 (1938). *Cotton* 11 (1925), 44 (1930), 28 (1938). *Woollen and Worsted* 21 (1925), 36 (1931), 22 (1938).

and post-war unemployment persisted ten years after the war was ended.[1] The answer is partly to be found in another consequence of the war—the decline in emigration. Formerly there existed an outlet for the surplus elements in the labour market, and we exported men as well as goods and services. In 1913 the excess of British emigrants over immigrants was a quarter of a million;[2] in the next decade it averaged roughly one-third of the figure. On this basis of comparison the net decrease of emigration during the twenties approached two millions, of whom male adults were approximately one-third. It is reasonable to infer that, if the pre-war rate of emigration had been maintained, the disparity between pre-war and post-war unemployment would have diminished year by year, and perhaps it might have been almost completely eliminated. Either the unemployed in the 'depressed' areas would have been numbered among the emigrants, or they would have been recruited by prosperous industries which were expanding in size. In the thirties there were even more British immigrants returning to the homeland than there were emigrants leaving these shores. The checks on migration in the inter-war period (1919–39) were of two kinds—voluntary and involuntary. The voluntary check was the social services which mitigated the worst effects of destitution, and so tended to immobilize labour and weaken the incentive to face the hazards of a new life abroad. It is difficult to assess the extent to which this check operated, since the arrest of emigration was not confined to England but was general throughout Europe. The involuntary check lay in the legislative restraints imposed on immigration by other countries, especially the United States. It was part of a universal restrictive system which after the first world war hindered the free movement of persons, commodities and capital. Efforts were made under the Empire Settlement

[1] The explanation is commonly found in the rigidity of the price structure, which in turn was ascribed to an inflexible wage structure. This overlooks the prime causes of the decline of the export industries noticed above. Another alleged factor, the return to the gold standard, is considered below.

[2] See Chapter Thirteen.

Act of 1922 to stimulate emigration but they were unsuccessful. One reason may have been the requirements laid down
by the countries of immigration; another reason was doubtless that settlement on the land had lost much of its
appeal.

In the first decade following the war of 1914–18 there was
a prospect that England would weather the storm and
gradually recover from the dislocation of her oversea markets
without any departure from the traditional lines of her
currency and fiscal policies. In the course of the twenties
her exports steadily rose: in 1920 they were 30 per cent.
below the pre-war (1913) level but in 1929 only 13 per cent.
Then with startling suddenness the position of the export
industries gravely deteriorated under the influence of an
economic blizzard, which swept over the world with the force
of a tornado and created a widely different international
framework. The great depression (1929–33), the most
dramatic episode that occurred between the two world wars,
cannot be ascribed to a single cause. In its broad aspect it
takes its place in the normal sequence of booms and slumps
which follow each other in our productive processes with
unfailing regularity. The volume of economic activity is not
uniform but expands and contracts in a sort of rhythm. This
alternation which has always characterized progressive
communities (the trade cycle is over three hundred years
old[1]) appears to obey a natural law whereby an outburst
of violent energy is succeeded by lassitude and recuperation.
The unprecedented severity of the great depression was
aggravated by the fact that a cyclical fluctuation in industry
was combined both with a structural change in agriculture
due to mechanization—which came later to farming than to
manufactures and increased the output of primary commodities in excess of effective demand—and with a virtual
cessation of foreign loans which provoked a financial crisis
abroad. Apart from the main causes, there were all kinds of

[1] See Chapter Six.

contributory influences in operation—the legacy bequeathed by the war of 1914–18 in the shape of inflated industries, violent changes in the price level, fluctuating currencies and high taxation; rationalization designed to eliminate duplication of plant, together with 'technology' designed to replace men by machines; the rigidity of the domestic price structure which delayed the adjustments needed to bring the national economy into harmony with the downward trend of world prices; misdirected international lending which encouraged debtor countries to live beyond their means; the political situation exacerbated by acrimonious controversy over reparations and war debts and disarmament.

The catastrophic effects of the great depression are writ large over the whole decade preceding the second world war, for whose advent it was partially responsible. The economic and financial chaos that it brought in its train was reflected in a score of staple commodities of which world prices were halved,[1] while the gold value of international trade dwindled to one-third. The sequel to these sweeping reductions was shown in the volume of unemployment for the sixteen principal industrial nations: in 1932 it was three times as great as in 1929. A more permanent consequence was the immense impetus given to an unbridled economic nationalism by the frantic efforts of each country to protect itself from a flood of cheap imports. One and all they took steps to insulate the domestic price level against the collapse of world prices, and to insulate domestic employment against the erratic course of international trade. Nevertheless the resurgence of economic nationalism was not due solely to economic factors. There was behind it also a political driving force, whose objective was to buttress national security with the pillars of a strategic economy (especially the building up of heavy industries which could provide armaments). The widespread revulsion against a world economy based on

[1] The price of cotton in 1938 was one-third of its price in 1924; the price of wool was halved.

429

specialization dominated the situation at a critical time when war clouds were gathering on the horizon. We have now to see how England in her turn was drawn into the maelstrom.

The great depression produced upon this country a reaction which was out of proportion to the cause. It is true that for a space the volume of unemployment was more than doubled,[1] yet the percentage was lower than in other leading countries. Nor was the great depression due to maladjustments in our own economic structure but to influences which were world-wide. We suffered from a temporary decline in the purchasing power of our customers overseas, the result of a slump in the prices of their products, and it was responsible for an adverse balance of trade; yet we had enjoyed a long succession of credit surpluses and could well afford occasional deficits. The determining element in the situation was really psychological. A wave of pessimism passed over the nation and induced the belief that its economic interests were no longer bound up with those of the world at large. The opinion became general that international trade and finance were a source of danger to our general well-being, and that it was necessary to insulate ourselves against forces which were beyond our own control and threatened at any moment to bring disaster. From a short-sighted view of a grave emergency proceeded events of the first magnitude, for England's abrupt abandonment of the two main pillars of her economy—the integrity of the pound sterling and the open door in commerce—was due to an atmosphere of 'defeatism' emanating from the great depression, in which the nation blinded by panic hastily and without thought of the ulterior consequences discarded its historic policy. This startling development was aided by the fact that for a decade the existence of over a million unemployed had weighed heavily upon the national spirits, and created an attitude of mind favourable to far-reaching changes—although, as we have shown, the excess of

[1] In 1932 it was nearly 3 millions or 2¼ times the amount in 1929.

unemployed over the pre-war figure was only about half a million, and it was owing to the aftermath of war, the slow adjustment to altered conditions, and the decline in emigration. The prevailing pessimism reached its climax during the great depression, and the conviction was then almost universal that England's race was run, that her industry had been stricken with a mortal disease, and that on the national scroll of her economic achievements must be inscribed the word 'Ichabod.'

The new direction given to the economic statecraft of England in the reversal of her traditional currency and fiscal policies had massive consequences. The one ushered in an international repudiation of the gold standard and unmoored the currencies of the world from their safe anchorage: the other widened the circle of the protectionist countries by eliminating the chief bulwark of the free trade movement. The dissociation of the national currency from gold and the abandonment of free trade marked England's capitulation to a system of economic nationalism.

The term 'gold standard' means that a national currency is converted into foreign currencies at fixed rates of exchange in gold. When a country is 'on' the gold standard it accepts the obligation to conform to an international basis of exchange rates. When it goes 'off' the gold standard it substitutes monetary nationalism for monetary internationalism and determines exchange rates by its own arbitrary action. Thus the issue involved is whether a country prefers monetary autonomy or monetary collaboration. The former enables it to regulate the domestic price level and support the volume of purchasing power at home, but is liable to wide fluctuations in the value of the currency abroad. The latter ensures that the value of the currency remains steady abroad, but requires the domestic price level to keep in step with the world price level even at the cost of a serious dislocation of industry. England had suspended the gold standard during the war of 1914–18 and restored it in 1925 at the pre-war parity, that is, she exchanged the pound for exactly the same number of dollars as before 1914. It is often asserted that the pound sterling was given an external value higher than was warranted by its internal value as expressed in purchasing power. The deterioration in the position of the export industries was attributed to the alleged overvaluation of the pound, yet actually the total volume of our exports increased: in 1929 it was over 8 per cent. greater than in 1924.

Six years after the return to the gold standard England again suspended it owing to a situation which was not of her making. One of the phenomena of international finance during the decades 1919–39 was the accumulation of immense liquid assets known as 'nervous' or 'hot' money. These floating balances, which at the beginning of 1931 were estimated at two thousand million pounds distributed between the different money centres, flitted from country to country in the form of short-term credits in lieu of long-term investments—accordingly as they were attracted by the high rates of interest or repelled by apprehension of political or financial insecurity. They became a menace to the normal operation of the gold standard, because they involved the abrupt transfer of large amounts of gold, whereas in earlier days only small amounts were moved to balance trade transactions. The London market, instead of discouraging the influx of precarious and fugitive deposits of foreign money, utilized them to make advances to German banks. Early in 1931 it found its resources seriously strained by the locking-up of substantial funds abroad under a 'stand-still' agreement, whereby its claims upon Germany were held in abeyance—that is, its assets became 'frozen.' At the same time there was foreshadowed a deficit on the budget, which raised fears of monetary inflation. Misgivings were enhanced by the adverse balance on our international payments. The credit balance, which we had hitherto possessed year by year, was converted in 1931 into a debit balance.

These various factors combined to impair confidence

abroad in the soundness of England's financial situation. In a race for security foreign creditors hastened to transfer their deposits in London to other money centres. After unavailing efforts to check the flight from the pound, the government suspended the export of gold (September 1931) in order to put an end to the drain on its depleted gold reserves. The involuntary repudiation of the gold standard was an event of more than national significance, for it gave a profound shock to the international monetary system and threw all currencies into disorder. Within a year over forty states had followed England's example; the United States did so in 1933; France, Netherlands and Switzerland not until 1936. Our position in the world economy almost necessarily involved the alignment of other powers in their currency policy. Altogether the pound depreciated 40 per cent. This meant that it was worth only three-fifths of its former value in gold, but its value in terms of other currencies was much less affected since they too suffered depreciation. The confusion which ensued from the break-down of the gold standard had the most demoralizing impact on the structure of world prices which suffered a fresh collapse; and the results were seen in the constriction of world trade, in the chaos of exchange rates, in the raising of tariffs, in the institution of 'quotas,' and in the impulse given to economic nationalism. These grave international repercussions particularly concerned a country like England, who was vitally dependent upon oversea commerce and upon the income which she drew from shipping freights, investments and other financial services abroad.

One of the main reasons advanced in favour of the suspension of the gold standard was the adverse balance of trade. There is a widespread misconception about the balance of international payments. It is popularly supposed that a surplus of exports over imports is an indication of prosperity, and a surplus of imports over exports is a premonition of disaster. Yet a debtor country may have an export surplus owing to the discharge of its liabilities, and a creditor country may have an import surplus owing to the receipt of interest on its investments abroad. To avoid misunderstanding, we must bear in mind that exports are both visible (commodities) and invisible (services). The latter include the income from oversea investments, shipping freights, insurance premiums, bankers' commissions and charges, brokerages, tourist expenditure, emigrants' remittances home, authors' royalties and other items. England had an adverse balance of trade in respect of visible exports, but she had a favourable balance in respect of invisible exports which cancelled out the adverse balance on merchandise and also gave her a net surplus. The surplus was considerable.[1] It was due principally to the interest on investments abroad coupled with shipping freights; and it enabled the English people to maintain a higher standard of life than would otherwise have been possible. The value of our oversea investments on the eve of the first world war is estimated at £4,000 millions. During the war over £600 millions were requisitioned and sold by the government, and it is believed that £150 millions were lost in the belligerent countries. However, owing to the growing yields from old investments combined with new investments, there was an increase in money income.[2] The value of the investments on the eve of the second world war is estimated at £3,750 millions. The receipts from shipping were also very large, because about three-fourths of our imports and exports were carried in British ships.[3] The net surplus on international revenue transactions was one of the sources of capital for new investments. Another source was the sinking

[1] In the three pre-war years 1907, 1910 and 1913, the credit balance amounted to £138, £153 and £181 millions respectively. After the war the amounts (in millions of pounds) were as follows: 154 (1922), 153 (1923), 86 (1924), 54 (1925), 9 (1926—the year of the coal strike), 114 (1927), 137 (1928), 103 (1929). Incidentally these figures do not lend support to the statement that, owing to the return to the gold standard at the pre-war ratio in 1925, 'the British balance of payments was labouring in difficulties.'

[2] It was £210 millions in 1913, and averaged £240 millions between 1922 and 1929.

[3] They amounted to £94 millions in 1913 and averaged £130 millions between 1922 and 1929.

funds on and maturity repayments of oversea loans; and a third was the money derived from foreign purchases of home securities. Altogether a considerable sum was rendered available year by year for making fresh investments in territories abroad.

Let us see what happened in consequence of the great depression. The credit balance of our international payments was converted (1931) into a debit balance.[1] Hence England now had an adverse balance not only on merchandise but on her total current account, and in five out of the next seven years she continued to have deficits although they were much smaller. These debit balances were usually offset by the proceeds which became available from the sinking funds on and maturity repayments of oversea loans. As a result the value of our capital assets abroad was impaired, yet this did not mean (as a chancellor of the Exchequer deplored) that we were 'living upon our capital.' We might be making at the same time substantial additions to our capital assets at home, for instance, the erection of new factories and plant. On the eve of the second world war, when the debit balance of our external payments was £55 millions,[2] internal investment in capital equipment was expanded by £376 millions so that the net investment at home and abroad in this year (1938) was £321 millions. In any event the disappearance or reduction of our former credit balance was mainly due to the decline in the yields from oversea investments and from shipping and financial services, caused by the slump in world prices and the contraction in international trade.

The suspension of the gold standard was immediately followed in England by the abandonment of free trade.

---

[1] In 1930 the credit balance was £28 millions: in 1931 the debit balance was £104 millions.

[2] In 1938 the estimated net income from (1) oversea investments =£200 m. (2) shipping =£100 m. (3) short interest and commissions=£35 m. Total = £335 m. The excess of imports of merchandise and of government payments made overseas =£390 m. Debit balance =£55 m.

As early as 1921 a Safeguarding of Industries Act afforded protection to certain 'key' industries, officially described as 'articles of a pivotal character which were regarded as vital to the national safety or of outstanding importance to industry.' Thereby a breach was made in the ramparts of the fortress, however justifiable may have been the occasion, and it facilitated the subsequent capitulation to the besieging forces. The nation became accustomed to a marked modification of its traditional fiscal practices, and grew disposed to accept without demur the more drastic changes for which the ground was being prepared. Moreover a campaign conducted before the first world war had won over one of the political parties to the cause of imperial preference. Nevertheless the conservative government which appealed to the electorate in 1923 in favour of protection suffered a reverse, showing that at heart the country still remained wedded to free trade. When protection was eventually adopted, it came in by the side door: it was a hasty improvisation born of panic. Just as free trade itself owed its final victory over the last defences of mercantilism to 'the rain that rained away the corn laws,' so the nation was stampeded into protection by the collapse of the great bulwark of British credit, the pound sterling. In the face of a dire calamity, their minds filled with dark forebodings that the currency might follow the way of the German mark (although the circumstances were completely different), the people accorded to the 'national government' the blank cheque, the free hand which was demanded. After the general election in 1931 the 'national government' proceeded to fill in the blank cheque with the word 'protection.' It was explained that protective duties were necessary to reduce the volume of imports, and 'redress the highly adverse trade balance which was one of the main factors in the flight from the pound in 1931.' A doubtful proposition: but in any case the argument was invalidated by the depreciation of the currency which at the time furnished substantial protection. The Import Duties Act (1932) provided that each industry should present an application for its own requirements to a body known as the Import Duties Advisory Committee. By entrusting the responsibility into the hands of a technical commission, it was hoped to eliminate the discreditable practices prevalent in other countries of exerting political pressure upon the administration with the object of manipulating the tariff schedules.

The extent and character of the protective system may be indicated in general terms as follows. Whereas only one-seventh of our imports had formerly been taxed (for purposes of revenue) the proportion was now increased to nearly three-fifths, and those remaining on the free list were mainly Empire products. The average duty on manufactured goods approximated to one-fifth of their value. In the case of agriculture conflicting needs made themselves felt. The aim of protecting the farmer was at variance with the desire to encourage imports from the dominions; and the interests of countries like Denmark, whose economy had become dependent upon the English market, could not be entirely ignored. A variety of devices was adopted. The best method of assisting an 'infant' industry, or any other industry whose maintenance is considered necessary for national reasons, is the payment of a subsidy—raised from general taxation since the burden ought to fall on the community as a whole and not on the section which consumes a particular product: this method was adopted in the sugar beet industry. More open to criticism was the Wheat Act: it imposed a levy on flour to establish a fund out of which native wheat-growers received a subsidy to make up the difference between the guaranteed price and the market price. The levy was a tax upon bread of which the poor are the largest consumers— 'It is a tolerable safe prophecy [Morley the biographer of Cobden had written half a century earlier] that no English statesman will ever revive a tax upon bread.' Still the subsidy was preferable to an import duty, for it was only paid on the quantity produced at home which was one-fifth of the total supply. Subsequent measures extended the system

437

of guaranteed prices to barley, oats and milk. Other food-stuffs, meat, dairy produce, vegetables and fruit, were made subject to tariffs. Lastly the quantitative restriction of imports was introduced. Some foreign commodities were assigned 'quotas' which limited the amount admitted into England: they included bacon, meat, potatoes and seafish. Subsidies, tariffs and 'quotas'—supplemented by the concession of immunity from local rates and by favoured treatment in the payment of income tax—failed to arrest the decline in the number of agricultural workers: cultivated land continued to shrink although the acreage under wheat and sugar beet was expanded. The description of England in the late seventies, as a country which was becoming less and less of a farm and more and more of a meadow, a garden and a playground, seemed truer than ever before. One very useful though belated development may be mentioned here, namely, afforestation. 'Aye be sticking in a tree,' was the counsel of an old Scottish laird to his son, 'it will be growing when you're sleeping.'

Nothing evinces so clearly the decay of the traditional maxims of commercial relationships as the trend towards bilateral trade, which balances commodity exports and imports with each nation. Here also England returned to an older standpoint, the doctrine of 'the particular balance' which was held by some of the early mercantilists but was eventually discarded in favour of 'the general balance.' Bilateralism is destructive of the multilateral system where commodities are bought in one market and sold in another—thus enabling all parties to choose the markets best suited for their requirements—and where a state strikes the balance on the whole of its international transactions. In an expressive seventeenth-century phrase bilateralism breaks 'the links and chains by which all traffics hang together.' For one thing, when the stream of commerce is diverted into artificial channels, the total volume of exports is likely to suffer contraction. For another, the encroachment of bilateralism can only be viewed as a retrograde step. It sets up false criteria which measure the benefits of a world economy not by the advance in the standard of living but by 'the particular balance' of trade with each territory; and it poisons the atmosphere of international economic co-operation. No country was more deeply concerned in the maintenance of multilateral trade than our own. By offering a market to the products of every land we provided each with the means to buy foodstuffs, raw materials and manufactures from our customers, our debtors and our colonies. All this was to our direct advantage, but in addition we received back a considerable share of our payments for imports in the form of shipping freights, while we drew a large income through financing the movement of commodities by commercial credits. The substitution of a bilateral trade policy was part of the short-sighted opportunism which jeopardized the durable factors of national prosperity in order to snatch at a temporary benefit. The claim that the use of a bargaining weapon—namely, the threat to restrict imports from a state which resisted pressure to buy English goods—would enable us to increase our exports, by forcing them upon reluctant markets, is refuted by the fact that our exports failed signally to recover. In another direction the nation which had once led the world in economic thought, and (more important still) in enlightened economic practices, displayed during the inter-war period (1919–39) a remarkable avidity for absorbing the most fashionable economic nostrums. We adopted the system of 'quotas' by which limitations were placed on the quantity of imports which a government was willing to accept. Quantitative control of trade was another rediscovery of the twentieth century, for it re-introduced in a modified form the mercantilist device of prohibition since it involved a stoppage of imports once the 'quota' was exhausted.

The ultimate consequences of the revolutionary change in English fiscal policy—unless it is reversed—may not work themselves out in one generation. Perhaps for several decades they will continue, as hitherto, to be masked by counteracting

439

influences. None the less, as economic conditions throughout the world return in the fulfilment of the years to the normal, the renunciation of free trade must exert on England its cumulative and far-reaching effects. An immediate result was to alter the proportions of Empire and foreign trade. The proportion of our imports from the Empire increased by one-third (they rose from 30 per cent. to 40 per cent.); that of our exports to the Empire increased by one-ninth (they rose from 45 per cent. to 50 per cent.). This diversion was the outcome of the Ottawa Agreements concluded between the mother country and the dominions in 1932. The former undertook not to levy duties on Empire products already on the free list; to strengthen the duties on certain foreign imports; and to adopt the 'quota' system for meat. Six years later the Anglo-American Trade Agreement secured concessions for farmers in the United States, which modified the preferential position accorded to the dominions. The real criterion which should be applied to the new commercial policy is how it will eventually re-act upon the total volume of commerce, the extent of the carrying trade, the vitality of the banking and insurance services, and the maintenance of a relatively high standard of living. The shape of things to come lies hidden in the future. The historian can only place on record that during the first decade of protectionism our visible and invisible exports remained on a lower level, and imports (as well as unemployment) on a higher level, than they were before the institution of tariffs. It would be wrong to isolate a single factor, however important, and to overlook other elements in a complex situation; but at any rate protective duties and bilateral trade agreements did not succeed in solving our economic problems.

Already it is possible to measure the reaction produced upon other states by our renunciation of free trade. To begin with, it had a restrictive influence on their commerce and so contributed to the resurgence of economic nationalism. Moreover it had a marked psychological effect, inasmuch as it profoundly discouraged the forces beyond our frontiers which were inspired by our example to work for the breaking down of the barriers to international intercourse. So long as England adhered to her century-old policy, she was the outstanding argument in favour of a universal reduction or abolition of tariffs: her failure to maintain this policy in a grave emergency seemed to her former admirers almost in the light of a betrayal. Again the reversal of her trade practices focussed attention upon the vexed problem of raw materials. While she offered an open door to imports, all countries were enabled to purchase their requirements in any part of the Empire by the sale of their products to the motherland; hence there was less disposition to challenge her monopoly of a vast sector of the globe with its wealth of raw materials and foodstuffs, when the trade of other nations suffered from no handicaps. And lastly her oversea investments amounted to several thousand million pounds, and both interest and repayment were made in goods. In a long view of the situation England's fiscal policy needed to be shaped by the broadest conception of her fundamental interests—and these concerned her commanding position in international trade, her mercantile marine, her oversea investments, her banking and insurance services abroad, and the obligations of her world status.

England emerged eventually from the trough of depression. Primarily the recovery was due to the natural forces of recuperation. After all neither booms nor slumps are permanent, and there is bound to be a swing of the pendulum. As stocks became exhausted, the demand for foodstuffs and raw materials and manufactured products revived; and the wheels of economic activity were once again set in motion. The movement was world-wide, and of all countries England was the least likely to be unaffected by world forces. Nevertheless recovery was only partial. The staple export industries manifested a melancholy decline; our income from invisible exports (investments, shipping, banking) contracted; and the balance of our international payments ceased to be in our favour.[1] The percentage of unemployment did not return to its pre-depression level—whereas formerly one in nine was unemployed, in 1938 one in eight was out of work. There is however another side to the picture, namely, a growing improvement in the standard of living of the wage-earners. During the post-war boom which reached its peak in 1920, when the cost-of-living index was 176 per cent. higher than in 1914, wages soared. Labourers earned between three and four times as much as they did in 1914; the average rise for all grades of workers was 170–180 per cent.; and the length of the working week was reduced to 44–48 hours (as compared with 48–60 hours before the war). Then in 1921 wage rates slumped rapidly and at the end of the next year they were stabilized at about 70–75 per cent. above the pre-war level. The actual increases varied from industry to industry. Thus labourers in the building industry received double; railway porters and dock labourers more than double; cotton workers, coal-miners and skilled engineers about half as much again.[2] The cost-of-living

[1] The statistics of oversea trade in 1938 were as follows. Exports of British produce and manufactures amounted to £471 millions. Nearly four-fifths were articles wholly or mainly manufactured. In order of magnitude they were machinery, cotton manufactures (now displaced from the premier position), vehicles (locomotives, motor cars and cycles, ships, aeroplanes), iron and steel, coal, woollen manufactures, etc. Textile yarns and fabrics accounted for 18 per cent of the total exports. South Africa received the largest share of our exports, followed by Australia, India, Canada and the United States (who now took only 4 per cent.), etc. Imports amounted to £920 millions (of which £62 millions were re-exported). One-half was food, drink and tobacco, one-quarter raw materials, and one-quarter articles wholly or mainly manufactured. In order of magnitude they were meat, grain and flour, butter, wool, petroleum, tea, etc. The United States sent us one-eighth of the imports. She was followed by Australia, Canada, India, New Zealand, etc. Our exports went half to the Empire and half to foreign countries. Our retained imports came roughly equally from the Empire and foreign countries as to food and raw materials, but foreign countries sent much more manufactured articles.

The invisible exports and the balance of international payments in 1938 are noticed above.

[2] The following are weekly wages in certain occupations in 1924 (and in brackets in 1938). *Agricultural labourers* 28s. (34s. 7d.). *Engineers, skilled* about 60s. (70s.). *Engineers, labourers* 40s. (50s. 4d.). *Bricklayers* 73s. 5d. (73s.). *Building labourers* 55s. 6d. (55s.). *Railway labourers* 49s. (47s.). *Railway porters* 45s. (43s.). *Boot and shoe operatives* 57s. (58s.).

index was 74 per cent. higher in 1923 than in 1914: this implies that wages in general had barely kept pace with the cost of living, but in the next half-dozen years the index fell ten points while nominal (that is, money) wages kept steady. Hence in these years real earnings rose, and the recipients of wages and salaries enjoyed a larger share of the national income for fewer hours of labour (about 63 per cent. as compared with about 55 per cent. in 1911).[1] The remuneration of employees was enhanced by the value of the social services—unemployment and health insurance, old age pensions, education, working class housing.

The great depression, though it augmented the amount of unemployment, had in compensation a beneficial influence on the standard of living of those who remained in work. In spite of the depreciation of sterling the fall in world prices of primary products was so sharp that imports of foodstuffs and raw materials were decidedly cheaper. Accordingly real wages improved,[2] and so the wage-earners had a wider margin for extra expenditure. The average diet in the worst year of the depression was actually better than in the relatively prosperous years preceding it. Between 1929 and 1938 the quantity of imported butter even increased 50 per cent.—at a reduced cost it provided seven ounces a week per head of the population in 1938—and the consumption of other commodities (including tobacco) registered a substantial advance.[3] Altogether if the condition of the working community on the eve of the two world wars is compared

[1] The net national income in 1938 is estimated at £4,595 millions. (Rent of land and buildings =£373 m. Profits and interest =£1,351 m. Salaries =£1,081 m. Wages =£1,790 m.) Personal expenditure on consumption =£3,467 m. Expenditure by public authorities (excluding the post office, etc.) =£807 m. Private net investment (additions to capital assets) =£321 m. For the sources of income assessed for income tax, see Chapter Thirteen.

[2] The cost-of-living index fell to 140 in 1933 (1914 = 100). It rose to 156 by 1938, but this was still below 1929 (when it was 164).

[3] The quantities of imports (in lb.) retained for home consumption per head of the population in 1913 (and in brackets in 1938) were—*butter* 9·88 (approximately 23); *cheese* 5·47 (approximately 7); *wheat and flour* 298·24 (347·45); *sugar* 95·13 (100·53); *tea* 6·68 (10·18); *tobacco* 2·10 (4); *meat* 55·80 (approximately 76); *eggs* number 56·17 (approximately 70). Home production should be added for all these commodities (except tea and tobacco).

443

the rise in real income is impressive,[1] while there is a marked extension in the size of the working community since the total number of persons in employment was much higher. It is noteworthy that a considerable decline occurred in the proportion of families living below the 'poverty line,' that is, the minimum subsistence level as defined by social investigators. What promoted a rise in real income was a conspicuous growth in the volume of industrial production in the inter-war decades.[2] Technical progress not only enlarged the output of the older industries but also made possible the newer industries mentioned below.

An important result of the redistribution of the national income was the expansion of the home market into which native capital and energy, diverted from the export industries, were now flowing. The increased purchasing power of the great mass of the nation stimulated the demand for better staple commodities (houses,[3] clothing, etc.), for the services which accompany a higher standard of living (hotels, entertainments, etc.), and for the products of the nascent industries—in particular automobiles and rayon. The origin of the automobile is linked with the invention of the internal combustion engine, the discovery of oil fields which supplied the fuel, and the removal of legal restrictions—an act of 1865, enjoining horseless vehicles not to exceed four miles an hour and to be preceded by a man with a red flag, was repealed in 1896 when the maximum speed was fixed at fourteen miles. The first decade of the twentieth century witnessed the rapid adoption of motor vehicles both for

[1] Progress between 1924 and 1938 is shown by the rise in wages (6 points); by the fall in the cost of living (19 points); by the increase in deposits in post office savings banks in the United Kingdom (from £280 millions to £509 m.) and in trustee savings banks (from £107 m. to £239 m.).

[2] In 1929 industrial production was nearly one-eighth—and in 1937 one-third—higher than in 1924.

[3] The annual average number of houses built in 1925–29 was about 203,000, and in 1934–39 it was 348,000. The building boom was stimulated by the low rates of interest—the bank rate stood at 2 per cent. from June 1932 to August 1939. Membership of building societies in Great Britain was doubled between 1924 (one million) and 1938 (two millions); and the share capital was five times as large.

444

private and commercial uses. On the eve of the first world war they counted three hundred thousand: on the eve of the second nearly ten times as many,[1] for the experience of mechanized warfare made the English people automobile-minded, and the technical training then given to large numbers of men and women provided a reservoir of labour for mechanized occupations. Rayon illustrates the importance of research and experiment in starting new industries or developing old ones. It is produced mainly from wood pulp to which chemical processes have been applied. The manufacture dated from the closing years of the nineteenth century; it was French in origin but England wrested the lead. Another synthetic industry was dye-making. Its scientific basis had been laid in the seventies by British chemists, though others reaped the profit since nine-tenths of the synthetic dyes used here were 'made in Germany.' War, which ruthlessly lays bare the weak spots in a nation's defences, disclosed the degree to which England was dependent upon imports of vital products—synthetic dyes needed for uniforms, drugs for health, optical instruments required for a variety of purposes together with optical glass to make them. These 'key' industries now received protection; and the growing of sugar beet was also encouraged with the aid of a subsidy. The measures taken to free this country from its reliance on foreign sources for certain 'pivotal' articles recall the efforts made in the spacious days of Queen Elizabeth to foster new branches of economy in which England was behind the Continent.

One natural consequence of these structural changes—that is, the rise of new industries focussed primarily upon the home market in preference to the export market—is reflected in the expansion of employment which catered for domestic consumption. Between the two world wars

[1] In Great Britain. The increase has been accompanied by a slaughter of human life on the roads. The number of fatal accidents caused by vehicles was approximately 10 a day in 1924 and 18 in 1938. Non-fatal accidents numbered 260 a day in 1924 and 520 in 1938. The number of horse-drawn vehicles fell from 181,416 (1924) to 9,274 (1938).

the distributive trades absorbed a million more insured workers; services of all kinds (national and local government, professional, hotels, laundry, entertainments, sports) three-quarters of a million more; the building industry a third of a million more; motor vehicles, cycles and aircraft a quarter of a million more; the electrical industry a quarter of a million more; food, drink, tobacco and transport a fifth of a million more.[1] A second development has reversed a historic trend. For a century and a half the major manufactures (textiles, iron and steel) had shown a tendency to migrate northwards. The new manufactures of a semi-luxurious character began to move to the south and the midlands, especially in order to be nearer the greatest centre of the home market—the metropolitan area. The redistribution of industry has been affected by a third factor. When industry was dependent on steam as its motive force, it tended to congregate in close proximity to the coal-fields. Now electric power, which can be transmitted from a generating station over great distances, may promote the decentralization of industry. This will mean the reversal of yet another historic trend. The sharp lines of demarcation between town and country will become increasingly blurred with the return to an older system under which industry was widely dispersed. The need for decentralization is shown by the fact that four-fifths of the population dwell in urban areas, and over one-half is concentrated in five industrial districts[2] which embrace only one-tenth of the realm.

[1] The number of workers insured in Great Britain in 1938 amounted to nearly 15 millions. Among other industries and services they were classified (in round figures: thousands) as follows—*distributive* 2,100; *building* 1,380; *textiles* 1,130; *transport* 900; *engineering* 860; *coal* 860; *metal trades* 740; *agriculture* (*farming, forestry, gardening*) 720; *national and local government* 630; *clothing* 625; *food, drink and tobacco* 590; *hotels, restaurants, clubs, etc.* 500; *vehicles* 460; *paper and printing* 445; *iron, steel and other metals* 335; *commerce, banking and insurance* 280; *woodworking* 250; *chemicals* 245; *gas, water and electricity* 225; *professional services* 215; *laundry* 180; *shipbuilding* 175; *entertainments and sports* 150; *bricks and tiles* 110; *pottery* 75; *leather* 70; *glass* 50; a variety of other industries and services about 500.

[2] Greater London, round Birmingham, Lancashire and the West Riding of Yorkshire, Glamorgan, round Glasgow and Edinburgh.

The aftermath of the second world war discloses a coherent pattern which makes it possible to attempt a comparison with the aftermath of the first world war. On the face of it the general background seems widely dissimilar, though before the tale of the years is told it may well be that a situation will emerge not unlike that which existed in pre-war days.

The most marked contrast lies in the sphere of unemployment. In the twenties the percentage of unemployed[1] averaged 11; in the fifties it was barely 2. Even when allowance is made for the expansion of the armed forces and the increase in public administration and clerical occupations, the disparity is impressive. The second contrast is that the terms of trade (that is, the terms on which exports are exchanged for imports) were formerly in our favour, because the supply of raw materials and foodstuffs exceeded the demand. Subsequently the position was reversed owing to the devastation of the war, the redistribution of incomes and military stock-piling. (At one period, 1951, the price of wool was fifteen times its pre-war figure; cotton, jute, tin, rubber, etc., also reached unprecedented heights.) The terms of trade accordingly turned in favour of the primary producers; and this meant that we had to export more goods to pay for our imports. In addition England carried a heavy load of indebtedness contracted during the war; and her creditors liquidated their sterling balances by buying English products for which she received no return. The consequent strain on her balance of international payments resulted in a fresh devaluation of the currency (1949), which has thus been devalued four times in the space of a generation. The third contrast is that producers have experienced since the second world war a 'sellers market.' As a result employers were willing to concede repeated claims for higher wages, owing partly to the shortage of labour and partly to the ease of passing on the cost in higher

---

[1] *i.e.* insured workers, of which the number is now nearly double.

446a

prices.[1] This creeping inflation, which has inflicted serious hardships on those with small fixed incomes, has created an atmosphere of fictitious prosperity.

During the war England was forced to sell some of her investments abroad, but she has now resumed on a substantial scale her traditional practice of making long-term investments overseas. In addition capital investments at home have taken a larger share of the national product than before the war. The high rate is due to technological progress—the requirements of industries built on the new techniques. Besides investments for productive purposes there have been considerable social investments, especially in the sphere of housing.

England's achievements in the field of technology are outstanding, and leave no doubt as to her capacity for leadership in the 'brave new world' of inventions and discoveries. They comprise nuclear power stations, 'Zeta' (the thermonuclear apparatus for developing atomic fusion as a source of power), radar equipment, jet propulsion in aircraft, the spectacular increase in the production of the chemicals industry (new plastics, drugs, pharmaceutical products—especially penicillin and other anti-biotics now so prominent in medical treatment—paints and detergents), and the electronics industry.

[1] The price indices are as follows (1900 is the base year, *i.e.* 100) 1910—110, 1920—285, 1939—184, 1957—492. It will be noticed that the price index in 1920 was $2\frac{3}{5}$ the pre-war figure of 1910; and in 1957 it was $2\frac{2}{3}$ the pre-war figure of 1939.

EPILOGUE

A hundred years ago an eminent French author, Taine, wrote: 'Germans make intolerable hypotheses, Frenchmen make none, Englishmen do not even suspect that one could make any.' In the foregoing pages I have endeavoured to demonstrate the hypothesis that the tide of human affairs is governed by the law of flow and ebb; and that the swing of the pendulum constitutes the agency whereby all extremes are eventually brought under control. In the middle ages English society assumed a corporate character, in which economic conduct was required to conform to an ethical pattern. The dissolving forces of individualism burst the cramping bonds imposed by communal discipline, and substituted the standard of enlightened self-interest. Now the wheel is beginning to come full circle. In a world economy with its baffling complexities and international repercussions, and under the pressure of an awakened social conscience, the driving-force of the individual needs to be supplemented by the collective forethought of the community and the dictates of social justice. This modern trend involves a return to many of the older concepts of economic organization and policy.

*   *   *

Accordingly it behoves us to profit by the experience of the past. The study of English economic development affords valuable lessons which have a profound application at the present day. They are best conveyed in three striking quotations from seventeenth-century writers.

> 'England never throve by trade but while she was an universal merchant.'
>
> 'The merchants of England are an industrious people and lovers of trade. They do not upon small—no, not upon great—discouragements give it over.'
>
> 'No people ever yet grew rich by policies; but it is

peace, industry and freedom that brings trade and wealth, and nothing else.'

Upon a free commercial system, and upon the maintenance of the spirit of initiative and enterprise, it must depend whether England will continue to play in the future a part commensurate with her role in former centuries.

* * *

Napoleon described the English people as 'a nation of shopkeepers.'[1] The reply to the taunt was foreshadowed by one of England's great prime ministers at the end of the eighteenth century: 'It has been the theme of historians that as nations became mercantile they lost in martial spirit, that it is of the essence of trade to be sordid, and that high notions of honour are incompatible with the prosecution of traffic.' Pitt claimed that England's record exposed the falsity of this view; and the imperishable achievements which are woven into the tapestry of the last hundred and fifty years do not belie the essential truth of his contention.

[1] Napoleon—with whom the phrase 'nation of shopkeepers' is traditionally associated—did not originate it. It appears in Adam Smith, *The Wealth of Nations.*

INDEX

449